International Criminal Justice Series

Volume 38

The *International Criminal Justice Series* aims to create a platform for publications covering the entire field of international criminal justice. It, therefore, deals with issues relating, among others, to:

— the work of international criminal courts and tribunals;
— transitional justice approaches in different countries;
— international anti-corruption and anti-money laundering initiatives;
— the history of international criminal law.

It is peer-reviewed and seeks to publish high-quality works emanating from excellent scholars.

Editorial Office

Prof. Dr. Moritz Vormbaum
University of Münster
Faculty of Law
Bispinghof 24-25
48143 Münster, Germany
vormbaum@uni-muenster.de

Laura Burgers · Merle Kooijman ·
Stavros Evdokimos Pantazopoulos ·
Christophe Paulussen
Editors

Ecocide: Criminalising Serious Harm against the Environment

ASSER PRESS

Springer

Editors
Laura Burgers
Amsterdam Centre for Transformative Private Law
University of Amsterdam
Amsterdam, The Netherlands

Stavros Evdokimos Pantazopoulos
School of Law
National and Kapodistrian University of Athens
Athens, Greece

Merle Kooijman
Amsterdam Center for Criminal Justice
University of Amsterdam
Amsterdam, The Netherlands

Christophe Paulussen
Research Department
T.M.C. Asser Instituut
The Hague, The Netherlands

ISSN 2352-6718 ISSN 2352-6726 (electronic)
International Criminal Justice Series
ISBN 978-94-6265-714-4 ISBN 978-94-6265-715-1 (eBook)
https://doi.org/10.1007/978-94-6265-715-1

Published by T.M.C. ASSER PRESS, The Hague, The Netherlands www.asserpress.nl
Produced and distributed T.M.C. ASSER PRESS by Springer-Verlag Berlin Heidelberg

This T.M.C. ASSER PRESS imprint is published by the registered company Springer-Verlag GmbH, DE, part of Springer Nature.
The registered company address is: Heidelberger Platz 3, 14197 Berlin, Germany

Foreword

Science is clear about the destructive human impact on the environment.[1] Nature loss, pollution and destruction of ecosystems, the emission of greenhouse gases—and much more—already have and will continue to have catastrophic effects on the environment, and on humans therein.

Law, including international law, is addressing these challenges, but remains largely limited to procedural and managerial approaches. Criminalisation of environmentally destructive behaviour, however, is a rather recent phenomenon, and one that is hoped to have significant impact on human behaviour and consciousness.

Ecocide and other environmental criminal law classify certain harmful actions against the environment as crimes and prescribe criminal penalties for those actions. Rather than implying a mere cost for environmentally destructive actions, they penalise as criminal the conduct that seriously harms the environment and apply sanctions—such as fines or imprisonment—for actions that violate environmental regulations or cause significant environmental damage.

In recent years, the discussions around a potential international crime of ecocide have gathered renewed attention: the criminalisation as a most serious crime of international concern. While this is not a new idea, the recent interest was arguably sparked by the proposed definition of ecocide by the international expert panel, convened by the Stop Ecocide Foundation in 2021.

In recognition of the severe impact of human actions on the environment, the expert panel proposed a new preambular paragraph to the Rome Statute of the ICC, which would express the concern "that the environment is daily threatened by

[1] See for the latest global reports: IPCC (2023): *Climate Change 2023: Synthesis Report. Contribution of Working Groups I, II and III to the Sixth Assessment Report of the Intergovernmental Panel on Climate Change,* Core Writing Team, H. Lee and J. Romero (eds.), Geneva, Switzerland; and IPBES (2019): *Global assessment report on biodiversity and ecosystem services of the Intergovernmental Science-Policy Platform on Biodiversity and Ecosystem Services*, E. S. Brondizio, J. Settele, S. Díaz, and H. T. Ngo (editors), IPBES secretariat, Bonn, Germany.

severe destruction and deterioration, gravely endangering natural and human systems worldwide".[2]

Moreover, the panel proposed a comprehensive definition of ecocide as meaning "unlawful or wanton acts committed with knowledge that there is a substantial likelihood of severe and either widespread or long-term damage to the environment being caused by those acts" —and suggested definitions of the terms "wanton", "severe", "widespread", "long-term" and "environment".[3]

This most timely book *Ecocide: Criminalising Serious Harm against the Environment*, wonderfully edited by Laura Burgers, Merle Kooijman, Stavros Evdokimos Pantazopoulos and Christophe Paulussen, is the first comprehensive publication that engages with this definition of ecocide and the wider debate around how criminalisation of serious harm against the environment fits within international criminal law.

Its structure around the "What", "How", "Where", and "Who" allows for the de- and re-construction of the crime and in-depth discussions. The line-up of excellent contributors guarantees the necessary quality and academic diligence and rigour of the legal assessments.

My hope is that this book will not only widen and deepen the academic discourse on ecocide but also support policy-makers in the effort to include it as a fifth international crime in the Rome Statute, and to criminalise environmentally destructive actions and omissions, including as ecocide, also at the national level.

July 2025

Prof. Christina Voigt[4]
Department of Public and International Law
University of Oslo
Oslo, Norway

---

[2] See *Independent Expert Panel for the Legal Definition of Ecocide* COMMENTARY AND CORE TEXT, June 2021, available at: https://www.stopecocide.earth/legal-definition Accessed 13 June 2025.

[3] Ibid. See also C. Voigt, «Ecocide» as an international crime: Personal reflections on options and choices, EJIL: Talk! 3 July 2021.

[4] Professor of Law at the University of Oslo, Chair of the IUCN World Commission on Environmental Law, and Member of the Independent Expert Panel for the Definition of "Ecocide".

Contents

Contributors

Judith Alkema Utrecht University, Utrecht, The Netherlands;
Stop Ecocide NL & EcoJustice, Amsterdam, The Netherlands

Borys Babin Association of Reintegration of Crimea, Kyiv, Ukraine

Laura Burgers Amsterdam Centre for Transformative Private Law, University of Amsterdam, Amsterdam, The Netherlands

Clémentine Dècle-Classen Université Paris 1 Panthéon-Sorbonne, Paris, France

Ana Stella Ebbersmeyer Faculty of Law, University of Copenhagen, Copenhagen, Denmark

Giovanna Maria Frisso University of Lincoln, Lincoln, UK

Tomas Hamilton Guernica 37 Chambers, London, UK

Merle Kooijman Amsterdam Center for Criminal Justice, University of Amsterdam, Amsterdam, The Netherlands

Kate Mackintosh Promise Institute Europe, UCLA School of Law, The Hague, The Netherlands

Lisa Oldring Faculty of Law, University of Amsterdam, Amsterdam, The Netherlands;
Promise Institute Europe, UCLA School of Law, The Hague, The Netherlands

Stavros Evdokimos Pantazopoulos School of Law, National and Kapodistrian University of Athens, Athens, Greece

Christophe Paulussen Department of Research, T.M.C. Asser Institute, The Hague, The Netherlands

Oleksii Plotnikov The Tenth of April, Odesa, Ukraine

Ava Schuster University of Amsterdam, Amsterdam, The Netherlands

Göran Sluiter University of Amsterdam, Amsterdam, The Netherlands; Open University, Heerlen, The Netherlands

Marc Tiernan Faculty of Law, University of Amsterdam, Amsterdam, The Netherlands

Harmen van der Wilt University of Amsterdam, Amsterdam, The Netherlands

Barbara van Straaten Prakken d'Oliveira Human Rights Lawyers Coöperatief U.A., Amsterdam, The Netherlands

Abbreviations

2SLGBTQQIA	Two-Spirit, Lesbian, Gay, Bisexual, Transgender, Queer, Questioning, Intersex and Asexual People
AP	Additional Protocol
BUE	Big Ukrainian Encyclopaedia
CAH	Crime(s) Against Humanity
CBD	Convention on Biological Diversity
CBDR	Common But Differentiated Responsibilities
CCU	Criminal Code of Ukraine
CITES	Convention on International Trade in Endangered Species of Wild Fauna and Flora
ECCC	Extraordinary Chambers in the Courts of Cambodia
ECD	Environmental Crime Directive
EESC	European Economic and Social Committee
ENMOD	Convention on the Prohibition of Military or Any Other Hostile Use of Environmental Modification Techniques
EOA	Economic Offences Act
EU	European Union
GHG	Greenhouse Gas
IAC(s)	International Armed Conflict(s)
ICA	International Crimes Act
ICC	International Criminal Court
ICL	International Criminal Law
ICTR	International Criminal Tribunal for Rwanda
ICTY	International Criminal Tribunal for the former Yugoslavia
IEP	Independent Expert Panel for the Legal Definition of Ecocide
IHL	International Humanitarian Law
ILC	International Law Commission
INPE	National Space Research Institute
IPCC	Intergovernmental Panel on Climate Change
NGO	Non-Governmental Organisation
NIAC(s)	Non-International Armed Conflict(s)

OHCHR	Office of the United Nations High Commissioner for Human Rights
OPG	Office of the Prosecutor General
OSCE	Organization for Security and Co-operation in Europe
OTP	Office of the Prosecutor
PFOA	Perfluorooctanoic Acid
RDS	Royal Dutch Shell
RPE	Rules of Procedure and Evidence
SCSL	Special Court for Sierra Leone
SEPO	Specialized Environmental Prosecutor's Office
SGBV	Sexual and Gender-Based Violence
SIDS	Small Island Developing States
STL	Special Tribunal for Lebanon
TIC	Team International Crimes
UNDP	United Nations Development Programme
UNEP	United Nations Environment Programme
UNFCCC	United Nations Framework Convention on Climate Change
UNGA	United Nations General Assembly
US	United States
VAVA	Vietnam Association for Victims of Agent Orange/Dioxin
WWII	World War II

Part I
What?

Chapter 1
Ecocide: Analysing the Compatibility of the Crime of Seriously Harming the Environment with International Criminal Law

Laura Burgers, Merle Kooijman, Stavros Evdokimos Pantazopoulos and Christophe Paulussen

Contents

Abstract Apart from sketching the background to the book *Ecocide: Criminalising Serious Harm against the Environment* and providing an overview of its chapters, this introductory chapter by the editors briefly reflects on the difficult and at times tautological question of what ecocide is. It does so by analysing the compatibility of this 'novel' legal concept with international criminal law (hereinafter: ICL), the

---

L. Burgers (✉)
Amsterdam Centre for Transformative Private Law, University of Amsterdam, Amsterdam, The Netherlands
e-mail: l.e.burgers@uva.nl

M. Kooijman
Amsterdam Center for Criminal Justice, University of Amsterdam, Amsterdam, The Netherlands
e-mail: m.kooijman@uva.nl

S. E. Pantazopoulos
School of Law, National and Kapodistrian University of Athens, Athens, Greece
e-mail: s.pantazopoulos@asser.nl

C. Paulussen
Department of Research, T.M.C. Asser Institute, The Hague, The Netherlands
e-mail: c.paulussen@asser.nl

L. Burgers et al. (eds.), *Ecocide: Criminalising Serious Harm against the Environment*, International Criminal Justice Series 38, https://doi.org/10.1007/978-94-6265-715-1_1

subfield of public international law dealing with (including regulating accountability processes for individuals responsible for violations of) international crimes, namely war crimes, crimes against humanity, genocide, and the crime of aggression. Indeed, how does the criminalisation of serious harm against the environment fit within ICL broadly construed, including the Rome Statute, the founding document of ICL's most prominent actor, the International Criminal Court (ICC)? To this end, the book's chapters address key questions: *what* constitutes ecocide, *how* can it be prosecuted, *where* should it be prosecuted, and *who* are its perpetrators and victims? In this critical-theoretical introduction, which is informed by the chapters in this book, we submit that the crime of ecocide can be compatible with ICL. However, paradoxically, we should be vigilant to not both expect too much of a crime of ecocide due to the inherent limitations of ICL as a discipline and to not expect too little either, since the crime could potentially capture a wide range of behaviour that could be considered part and parcel of everyday life, such as corporate activity.

Keywords Ecocide · International Expert Panel · Criminalisation · International criminal law

1.1 Introduction: The Only Crime Is Stubbornness

In Sophocles' tragedy *Antigone,* the blind prophet Tiresias tells King Creon: "All men are liable to err; but when an error hath been made, that man is no longer witless or unblest who heals the ill into which he hath fallen, and remains not stubborn. Self-will, we know, incurs the charge of folly."[1] Creon's initial reaction is to ridicule the prophet for this warning. A little later, however, he does follow up on the advice. However, by then it is too late.

How similar Creon seems to how industrialised societies collectively behave—wilfully blind to the crises the environment as well as the climate is facing, as species go extinct at an alarming rate and the effects of climate change increasingly affect life on this planet,[2] coming very close to unwarranted stubbornness. Soon, it could be too late to stop climate change and rapid environmental degradation altogether, and it is already too late for the many species that went extinct in the meantime. Is this indeed the crime called 'ecocide'? And, if so, how would it work, where should it be prosecuted, and who would be its perpetrators and victims?

This book explores the many intricacies of a potential crime of ecocide that come up in the Anthropocene, "our current moment in time: when human beings are having profound impacts on the living and physical world".[3] As for the legal concept of ecocide, its first known use was by bioethicist Arthur W. Galston in 1970 to condemn environmental atrocities taking place in the Vietnam War, proposing the adoption of

---

[1] Sophocles 1904, p. 161, lines 1023–1027.

[2] Hunt 2023.

[3] Fisher 2024.

a new international agreement to ban ecocide.[4] More than 50 years later, a lot more is expected of a crime of ecocide than to denote environmental warfare that results particularly in environmental harm as far as it impacts human beings. Ecocide is now meant to also cover destructive behaviour affecting the environment *per se*, also in peacetime.[5]

In June 2021, an Independent Expert Panel (IEP or Panel), convened by the Stop Ecocide Foundation, drafted a definition of ecocide. The idea was to insert it, as a new (the fifth) core international crime, next to war crimes, crimes against humanity, genocide, and the crime of aggression, into the Rome Statute—the treaty establishing the International Criminal Court (ICC), international criminal law (ICL)'s most prominent actor—as its Article 8*ter.* This definition reads as follows: "For the purpose of this Statute, "ecocide" means unlawful or wanton acts committed with knowledge that there is a substantial likelihood of severe and either widespread or long-term damage to the environment being caused by those acts".[6]

The Panel agreed that an international crime of ecocide "could contribute to a change of consciousness, in support of a new direction, one that enhances the protection of the environment and supports a more collaborative and effective legal framework for our common future on a shared planet."[7] Therefore, the expectations of ecocide as a new core international crime can be considered very high, despite the political difficulties of including it as the fifth core crime in the Rome Statute.

Against the background of the adoption of the ecocide definition by the IEP, the University of Amsterdam as well as the Asser Institute each issued a call for papers to further analyse the topic of ecocide. It was soon decided to join forces and to follow-up with a book publication: the one you are reading right now.

We organised the chapters as a roadmap in four parts, each addressing, in turn, a key question: *What* is a crime of ecocide? *How* can it be prosecuted? *Where* should it be prosecuted? And *who* are the perpetrators and victims of such a crime? These questions are viewed through the prism of ICL broadly conceived, the subfield of public international law dealing with (including regulating accountability processes for individuals responsible for violations of) international crimes. Naturally, the answers to these questions inform each other. Indeed, those reading this edited book closely will discover some overlap in the various chapters. We purposively allowed this to cater for all kinds of possible commentaries on the IEP's definition, united by the overarching theme of the compatibility of ecocide with ICL broadly conceived. After all, the ongoing planetary crisis is urgently demanding us to act, but a tricky question is looming large: is the path of international criminalisation the appropriate way forward? This recurring theme of compatibility provides the focus point of this introductory chapter, which generally follows the quadripartite division of the present book but does not strictly adhere to the chapter sequence, due precisely to the overlaps noted above.

---

[4] See The New York Times 1970.

[5] See e.g. Bustami and Hecken 2021. Mwanza 2018.

[6] Stop Ecocide Foundation 2021.

[7] Stop Ecocide International, https://www.stopecocide.earth/scientists. Accessed 15 January 2025.

1.2 *What* Is Ecocide? Key Aspects of the IEP Definition

As explained above, the IEP took up the challenge to come up with a detailed, legal definition that could be included as the fifth core international crime in the Rome Statute of the ICC. Below, we set out three central pillars of the definition that warrant specific attention as highlighted by the authors in this book: firstly, knowledge about the substantial likelihood of the threshold of prohibited damage to the environment; secondly, wanton acts as balancing acts; and lastly, the alleged anthropocentric nature of ICL.

1.2.1 Acts Committed with Knowledge That There Is a Substantial Likelihood of Severe and Either Widespread or Long-Term Damage

The crime of ecocide as defined by the Panel is characterised by a relative open-endedness regarding the relevant 'acts'. Following this definition, it will therefore not always be easy to say which conduct can be considered 'ecocidal' (and who is capable of committing ecocide, a question that will be further discussed below). In their chapter, 'Ecocide as an International Crime? Perspectives on Prosecution at the ICC and in the Netherlands',[8] Göran Sluiter, Barbara van Straaten and Ava Schuster emphasise in that regard how the ecocide definition differs from all the other core international crimes in the Rome Statute, as it lacks a list of punishable acts.

In a way, the 'severe and either widespread or long-term' criteria are no strangers to international law. After all, it could be argued that they have their basis in the existing body of international law, as illustrated by the Panel. The terms are borrowed from Articles 35 (3) and 55 (1) of the 1977 First Additional Protocol to the Geneva Conventions ('Additional Protocol I'); Article 8 (2) (b) (iv) of the Rome Statute, which establishes an environment-specific war crime committed in the context of an international armed conflict; the 1976 Convention on the Prohibition of Military or any other Hostile Use of Environmental Modification Techniques (ENMOD Convention)[9] and the 1991 International Law Commission draft of an international crime

[8] Chapter 6 of this volume.

[9] To be precise, the ENMOD Convention employs the term long-lasting instead of long-term in its Article 1(1). Interestingly, the Understanding relating to article I of the ENMOD Convention provides: "It is the understanding of the Committee that, for the purposes of this Convention, the terms 'widespread', 'long-lasting' and 'severe' shall be interpreted as follows: a) 'widespread': encompassing an area on the scale of several hundred square kilometres; b) 'long-lasting': lasting for a period of months, or approximately a season; c) 'severe': involving serious or significant disruption or harm to human life, natural and economic resources or other assets. It is further understood that the interpretation set forth above is intended exclusively for this Convention and is not intended to prejudice the interpretation of the same or similar terms if used in connexion with any other international agreement." See Convention on the Prohibition of Military or Any Other

of wilful and severe damage to the environment.[10] However, the Panel attempted to provide a middle ground between the disjunctive used in ENMOD (widespread, long-lasting or severe) and the conjunctive Rome Statute formulation (widespread, long-term and severe): it opted for 'severe and either widespread or long-term'.

Furthermore, Sluiter, Van Straaten and Schuster argue that the interpretation of the elements differs from the interpretation of the same or similar terms under Additional Protocol I and the ENMOD Convention, which ultimately complicates the possible application and interpretation of ecocide. In her chapter 'Protecting the Environment through International Criminal Law—A Legal Analysis of Available Options',[11] Ana Stella Ebbersmeyer moreover argues that the three criteria are vague, also considering that their interpretation does not follow from Additional Protocol I. Hence, the seamless alignment of the proposed Article 8*ter* with existing international law should not be overestimated, notwithstanding the various terminological affinities and continuities with relevant international legal instruments.

In a similar vein, the use of the *mens rea* threshold appears not to be fully consistent with existing ICL standards. Sluiter, Van Straaten and Schuster explicate in their chapter how 'knowledge' is indeed the default *mens rea* standard in the Rome Statute. There, 'knowledge' entails relative certainty of the results of one's acts. In the Panel's definition, 'knowledge', however, establishes a much lower threshold considering that it includes 'recklessness' and '*dolus eventualis*' (willingness to accept likely risks). Accordingly, further consideration and refinement are needed to ensure the smooth alignment of the *mens rea* elements in the IEP definition with the established mental thresholds under the Rome Statute.

1.2.2 Wanton Acts Are Balancing Acts

As clarified by Kevin Jon Heller, the definition of the IEP introduces a cost–benefit analysis or proportionality test with regard to the *actus reus* of a crime of ecocide.[12] Acts deemed lawful under national jurisdictions may nonetheless attract criminal liability when they are wanton, i.e. "with reckless disregard for damage which would be clearly excessive in relation to the social and economic benefits anticipated". Therefore, the requirement, as drawn from the environmental law principle of sustainable development, involves a balancing act between, on the one hand, expected environmental damage, and on the other, anticipated social and economic benefits.

Hostile Use of Environmental Modification Techniques, adopted 10 December 1976, 1108 UNTS 151, entered into force 5 October 1978 (ENMOD), Article 1(1).

[10] ILC 1991, p. 107.

[11] Chapter 3 of this volume.

[12] See Heller 2021.

Sluiter, Van Straaten and Schuster argue that the requirement of wantonness prevents ecocide from being a truly 'ecocentric' crime. A crime grounded in ecocentrism should consider nature to be worthy of protection because of its inherent value.[13] However, the authors posit that differentiating between human profit and environmental harm is unnecessary considering that ecocide affects both people and their environment equally.

In a similar vein, Ebbersmeyer argues in her chapter that acts of environmental harm are often lawful, and this only serves to foreground the practical and applicability challenges that the 'wanton' requirement entails. On a similar note, Ebbersmeyer posits that the latter requirement is anthropocentric in nature, and this is contrary to the ultimate goal of environmental protection. As the distinction between anthropocentrism and ecocentrism has preoccupied most of the authors of this volume, we move to address it separately in the following subsection.

1.2.3 ICL and Anthropocentrism and Ecocentrism

The issue of anthropocentrism and ecocentrism is furthermore explored in-depth by Clémentine Dècle-Classen in her chapter 'Crime Against Who or What? A Historical and Ontological Inquiry into Ecocide Discourse',[14] She critically inquires how the conceptual binary of anthropocentrism and ecocentrism has entered the discourse in international law concerning environmental protection. She then goes on to demonstrate how this logic of the binary is perpetuated in discussions on the potential criminalisation of ecocide in the Rome Statute. This discourse bifurcates *anthropos* ('humanity') from *oikos* ('the natural environment'), although such bifurcation was, as Dècle-Classen demonstrates, not intended by initial proponents of ecocide as a core crime. She argues that in order for ecocide to become a crime under the Rome Statute, the discussion on 'ecocidal violence' needs to be salvaged from its imbued and mistaken boundaries. Hence, ecocide ought to be explored in its full, materially and historically situated 'sublimity'.[15] The Proposed International Convention on the Crime of Ecocide by Professor Richard Falk could thereby function as a touchstone to navigate such a re-oriented and grounded discussion of ecocide as an international crime.

[13] Kooijman 2023, pp. 101–131.

[14] Chapter 2 of this volume.

[15] In Kantian aesthetics the notion of the sublime refers to an overwhelming (possible negative) feeling of greatness. Kant 2004.

1.3 *How* Can Ecocide Be Prosecuted? Conceptual Consistency in the Rome Statute

Part II of the book addresses the *how* question. In her chapter, Ebbersmeyer investigates how existing ICL can account for large-scale environmental damage and what the added value of ecocide would be in this regard. She concludes that an additional crime of ecocide should be welcomed, because existing ICL can only prosecute environmental damage to a limited extent. After all, she points out, the substantive law of the Rome Statute is targeted at human beings (and their property) and is, therefore ill-equipped to properly deal with environmental damage *per se*. As a mostly ecocentric standalone crime, ecocide would stand out in a legal framework that is human-focused.

Lisa Oldring and Kate Mackintosh take a different approach and draw on existing human rights law to show how ecocide can be an instrument in the fight for climate justice in their chapter: 'The Crime of Ecocide Through Human Rights: Towards Environmental Protection and Justice'.[16] Hence, rather than focusing on the 'ecocentric' side of ecocide, they explore how various marginalised groups are already entitled to a healthy environment and thus may bundle forces to protect it, which can in turn inform the normative content of a crime of ecocide. They show that a crime of ecocide can be conceptually consistent with the existing core crimes in the Rome Statute, considering that all these crimes are (implicitly) centred around the core notion that human rights ought to be respected.

Another relevant point of conceptual consistency is illustrated by Tomas Hamilton and Marc Tiernan in their chapter 'Who Could be Responsible for Ecocide under the Rome Statute?'.[17] They argue that ecocide is conceptually aligned with the Rome Statute to the extent that the most serious environmental harm that constitutes ecocide, such as climate change, ocean pollution and marine debris, and the destruction of the Amazon rainforest, forms a collective act, similar to crimes such as genocide, war crimes, and crimes against humanity. Conceptual consistency is, however, missing when it comes to the usual perpetrator(s) of ecocide. Unlike the other core international crimes in the Rome Statute, much of the severe, and either widespread or long-term environmental damage, such as in the context of climate change through greenhouse gas emissions, is caused in the daily, normalised interaction of supply and demand in a capitalist society, as shown by Harmen van der Wilt in his chapter 'Climate Change as the Ultimate Form of Ecocide: Are Producers and Consumers 'Partners in Crime'?'.[18] Nevertheless, as Hamilton and Tiernan argue, this is mitigated by the fact that although we share the common responsibility to prevent environmental harm, some contributions are inevitably much greater than others.

[16] Chapter 5 of this volume.

[17] Chapter 9 of this volume.

[18] Chapter 8 of this volume.

Moreover, Sluiter, Van Straaten and Schuster demonstrate how an international crime of ecocide is conceptually ill-suited, considering that genocide, war crimes, crimes against humanity and the crime of aggression are all considered crimes in which the State, or at least an organised political entity, is always in some way involved. In the case of the crime of aggression, only the leaders of a State could qualify as the perpetrators, and in the case of war crimes, the perpetrators are members of national armed forces or of non-State armed groups, while in the context of crimes against humanity and genocide, such crimes must be part of State(-like) policy. The primary target of the Rome Statute is therefore organs of States or State-like entities, whereas serious environmental damage is in most cases caused by the accumulation of normal, ordinary corporate activities (in conjunction with those of States). This ties in with the desire of many proponents of the crime of ecocide to target corporations. Against this background, Sluiter, Van Straaten and Schuster move on to emphasise how the extension of criminal liability to private legal entities under the Rome Statute would amount to conceptual inconsistency within the Rome Statute.

In their chapter entitled 'Ecocide: Toward Autonomous Environmental Crimes',[19] Judith Alkema and Michael Faure argue that, despite this being unusual, the assessment of whether certain behaviour amounts to the crime of ecocide should be done independently of the question of whether that behaviour is administratively permitted under national law in order to protect the environment directly. In other words, they claim that for environmental criminal law to be effective, large-scale environmental damage should be a crime that is autonomous from administrative law. Accordingly, a crime of ecocide is required to be of a different nature than the other core crimes, given that the former can also be committed in situations that are deemed lawful. In this respect, it could be plausibly argued that the 'wanton' requirement in the Panel definition could encompass conduct that is detrimental to the environment, even when it is permitted under national law, in line with the authors' argument on criminalising serious environmental harm irrespective of its legality under national law. To this end, Alkema and Faure argue that the recently adopted revised Environmental Crime Directive of the European Union seems to be heading in the right direction, even though, on closer inspection, the said Directive does not establish an autonomous environmental crime *proper*, as envisioned by these authors.

1.4 *Where* Should Ecocide Be Prosecuted?

In discussing the necessity of a crime of ecocide, it is often believed that it should be a core crime first and foremost, to be prosecuted at the international level. This line of thinking brings into sharp relief the ubiquitous question of the *locus* of the crime and where it should be prosecuted. Arguably, large-scale environmental damage often crosses borders and transgresses moral boundaries to such an extent that it affects the international community, necessitating an international approach. Conversely, one

[19] Chapter 4 of this volume.

could assert that domestic jurisdictions are actually best placed to organise prosecutions. Ecocide is notably already adopted in numerous domestic jurisdictions,[20] including Ukraine and Russia.

Part III of this book looks at *where* to prosecute the crime of ecocide—this can happen not only at the international but also at the national level. At this juncture, it is important to note that the Office of the Prosecutor of the ICC has expressed its intention to issue a Policy Paper on Environmental Crimes, which "sets out how the Office will use its mandate and powers to investigate and prosecute environmental crimes within the Court's jurisdiction" in its attempt to "support national efforts to prosecute illegal conduct that has an environmental dimension".[21] Against this backdrop, Borys Babin and Oleksii Plotnikov analyse how Ukraine uses this legal basis to defend itself against the attacks by Russia since 2014 in their chapter entitled 'Lawfare against Ecocide: How Ukraine Prosecutes Environmental Crimes Committed During Armed Conflict'.[22] The Ukrainian experience provides useful insights for the ongoing talks on recognising ecocide at the international level. In their comprehensive account of Ukrainian investigations of ecocide in the context of the armed conflict in Ukraine, the authors outline in detail the prospects and challenges of prosecuting the crime of ecocide, based on a domestic law definition, with the further objective of projecting how this experience could impact upon the international efforts to criminalise ecocide.

Subsequently, the chapter by Sluiter, Van Straaten and Schuster, carves out what should be the role of the Dutch national public prosecutor in fighting ecocide under existing ICL. Considering that the Netherlands prides itself on taking the lead in the advancement of ICL, they plead for the Dutch Public Prosecution Service to take an active role, making use of the (limited) options under existing ICL and national criminal law. Considering that Article 51 of the Dutch Penal Code would allow for the prosecution of corporations, this would furthermore make the Netherlands an attractive jurisdiction for prosecuting incidents of ecocide. The authors suggest that ecocide is most likely to be charged under "other inhumane acts" as a crime against humanity, but they emphasise the necessity for the Public Prosecution Service to establish alternative charges in order to prevent impunity for grave harms against the environment. Building on the principle of complementarity and the fact that the Netherlands is the host country of the ICC, Sluiter, Van Straaten and Schuster highlight the pivotal role that the Netherlands could assume in prosecuting environmental harm as an independent international crime or in connection with another international crime.

[20] For the list of existing and proposed domestic laws on ecocide, see https://ecocidelaw.com/existing-ecocide-laws. Accessed 15 January 2025.

[21] ICC Office of the Prosecutor 2024, p. 3. At the time of writing (January 2025), the draft policy is under public consultation and is expected to be finalised and officially issued later in 2025.

[22] Chapter 7 of this volume.

1.5 *Who* Should Be Prosecuted for Ecocide and *Who* Are Its Victims?

Part IV of the book circles around the question of *who* the perpetrators and victims are of a crime of ecocide. This begs the questions of whose behaviour the international community deems so morally reprehensible as to constitute "unimaginable atrocities that deeply shock the conscience of humanity",[23] and who we can consider to be its victims. Severe environmental damage is omnipresent, as acutely evinced by the geological period humanity finds itself in—the Anthropocene.[24] It is therefore not always easy to establish the perpetrator or to even pinpoint exact liability. Living in a capitalist society entails that large-scale environmental damage is often produced in the interaction between producers and consumers, and thus constitutes an outcome of supply and demand. Consequently, could the commission of ecocide in all related incidents be attributed to specific individuals, and is that actually fair?

In his chapter, Van der Wilt starts with the observation that, at face value, climate change could amount to ecocide because the damage it entails is of the requisite large scale. On the other hand, climate change is caused not only by a few big corporate players but also by the aggregate actions of many consumers. Are those to be held accountable for ecocide as well? Comparing the relations between fossil fuel companies and their consumers to those engaged in illicit drug trafficking and money laundering, Van der Wilt concludes that the liability of consumers for climate change cannot be excluded if ecocide were to become a crime. Considering that individual liability for international crimes forms part and parcel of ICL as a discipline, it would be unfair, according to Van der Wilt, to only hold the producers criminally liable while leaving 'us' -namely the consumers contributing to climate change- off the hook.

The question of (individual) criminal liability for ecocide is also addressed by Hamilton and Tiernan in their chapter. Rigorously analysing the doctrines of (1) perpetration; (2) aiding and abetting; (3) failing to prevent and punish; and (4) attempting, they explore how individuals can be held accountable for ecocide, a crime that will usually be of a collective nature. Their analysis is centred on the principles of legality and legal certainty, considering that criminal liability could potentially be overstretched if all existing modes of criminal liability under the Rome Statute were applied.

Through an elaborate case study of the establishment and the operation of a coal mine, Hamilton and Tiernan demonstrate that, for example, applying the mode of 'aiding and abetting' liability (Article 25 (3) (c) of the Rome Statute) could, under the present, relatively vague, definition, extend the scope of ecocide-liability to an extremely large group of arguably relatively insignificant enablers and facilitators within a corporation. Based on their findings, they posit that the definition by the IEP is currently too broad and vague, and thus would lead to overcriminalisation, if adopted.

---

[23] Rome Statute of the International Criminal Court, opened for signature 17 July 1998, 2187 UNTS 3, entered into force 1 July 2002, Preamble, para 2.

[24] Keys et al. 2019.

In the last chapter of the book, entitled 'Ecocide: The Environment as a Victim at the International Criminal Court',[25] Giovanna Maria Frisso delves into the question of who or what can be protected by a crime of ecocide. She posits that under existing ICL, it is not only possible to classify 'non-humans' as victims, but that it is also desirable in light of the paradigmatic shift recognising the materiality that both humans and non-humans have in common. For Frisso, the inclusion of a crime of ecocide would amount to the recognition of the environment as a victim, therefore correcting and enriching the notion that international crime only harms (individual) humans. The environment constitutes a natural person, which can suffer harm, similar to humans, according to Frisso. On this account, Frisso explores in depth to what extent the environment could qualify as a victim as defined in Article 85 of the ICC Rules of Procedure and Evidence, cautioning that such an interpretative exercise could prove to be a double-edged sword; the failure to recognise non-humans as victims could be construed as denying that a specific act constitutes ecocide if it does not harm humans, thus undermining the paradigmatic shift that underpins efforts to criminalise ecocide.

1.6 Concluding Remarks

In light of the preceding reflections, a crucial question lurking in the background should be foregrounded: is the stubbornness and intransigence of the profit-driven industrialised societies something that can be redeemed by the criminalisation of ecocide? The foregoing discussion provides a basis for (tentative) reflections concerning the prospect of ecocide as a legal concept in ICL, but mostly it invites the reader to read the chapters of our book to demonstrate the intricacies of integrating environmental damage (in peacetime) into ICL's discipline. Paradoxically, we should be wary of not expecting too much of a crime of ecocide. As has been pointed out before, ecocide is not a panacea due to the inherent limitations of ICL. Similarly, we should not expect too little of a crime of ecocide either because, if it were to become an actual crime, it could cover 'normal' corporate behaviour in the Anthropocene.

Coming full circle—though Sophocles might have deemed it a crime—'stubbornness' proved excusable, if not necessary, when we encountered a few challenges within the group of authors and editors that affected the publication timeline of this book. That said, during the same period we also saw the joyful arrival of new world citizens within both groups. We are therefore not only relieved by the delivery of our common baby but also excited to see how it will be received by students, teachers, scholars, practitioners, policymakers, and legislators. We hope it will help flesh out crucial parameters in the lead-up to the potential inclusion of the fifth core international crime in the Rome Statute of the ICC, as well as in relation to efforts to criminalise ecocide at the national level—both of which have gained unprecedented momentum in recent times.

---

[25] Chapter 10 of this volume.

Acknowledgements Finally, a word of thanks. We are extremely grateful to everyone who has patiently contributed to making this book a reality. We are indebted to Nashab Parvez, for his idea to issue a call on ecocide for the Asser Institute's International Crimes Database, to the Sustainable Global Economic Law (SGEL) research project and the T.M.C. Asser Institute for allowing us to organise workshops in Amsterdam and The Hague, to all the authors for having travelled on this long journey with us, and to Frank Bakker and Kiki van Gurp from Asser Press for their understanding and professionalism. We would also like to thank Konstantina Karagkouni and Eylül Kabakci for their diligent work in creating the list of abbreviations, as well as for putting the final versions of the chapters in the correct format.

References

Articles, Books and Other Documents

Bustami A, Hecken MC (2021) Perspectives for a New International Crime Against the Environment: International Criminal Responsibility for Environmental Degradation Under the Rome Statute. Goettingen Journal of International Law 11:145–189

Fisher R (2024) Why it's proving difficult to define the official dawn of the Anthropocene. https://www.bbc.com/future/article/20240306-why-its-proving-difficult-to-define-the-official-dawn-of-the-anthropocene. Accessed 15 January 2025

Heller KJ (2021) Ecocide and Anthropocentric Cost-Benefit Analysis. https://opiniojuris.org/2021/06/26/ecocide-and-anthropocentric-cost-benefit-analysis. Accessed 15 January 2025

Hunt K (2023) What is a mass extinction, and why do scientists think we're in the middle of one? https://edition.cnn.com/2023/12/23/world/mass-extinctions-explained-scn-climate/index.html. Accessed 15 January 2025

ICC Office of the Prosecutor (2024) Draft Policy on Environmental Crimes Under the Rome Statute. https://www.icc-cpi.int/sites/default/files/2024-12/2024-12-18-OTP-Policy-Environmental-Crime.pdf Accessed 15 January 2025

International Law Commission (ILC) (1991) Summary Records of the meetings of the 43rd Session (1991) 2 Yearbook International Law Commission, UN Doc. A/CN.4/SER.A/1991/Add.l (Part 2)

Kant I (2004) Observations on the Feeling of the Beautiful and the Sublime. In: Goldthwait JT (ed) University of California Press, Berkeley, CA

Keys PW, Galaz V, Dyer M, Matthews N, Folke C, Nyström M, Cornell SE (2019) Anthropocene risk. Nature Sustainability 2:667–673

Kooijman M (2023) From Anthropos to Oikos in International Criminal Law: A Critical-Theoretical Exploration of Ecocide as an 'Ecocentric' Amendment to the Rome Statute. In: Dam-de Jong D, Amtenbrink F (eds) Netherlands Yearbook of International Law 2021: A Greener International Law - International Legal Responses to the Global Environmental Crisis. T.M.C. Asser Press, The Hague, pp. 101–131

Mwanza R (2018) Enhancing Accountability for Environmental Damage Under International Law: Ecocide as a Legal Fulfillment of Ecological Integrity. Melbourne Journal of International Law 19(2):586–613

Sophocles (1904) Antigone. In: Jebb R (ed) The Tragedies of Sophocles, translated into English prose. Cambridge University Press, Cambridge.

Stop Ecocide Foundation (2021) Independent Expert Panel for the Legal Definition of Ecocide: Commentary and Core Text. https://www.stopecocide.earth/s/SEFoundationCommentaryandcoretext2025-kbee.pdf. Accessed 15 January 2025

The New York Times (1970) ...and a Plea to Ban 'Ecocide'. https://www.nytimes.com/1970/02/26/archives/and-a-plea-to-ban-ecocide.html. Accessed 15 January 2025

Dr. Laura Burgers works as an assistant professor at the Amsterdam Centre for Transformative private law (ACT) at the University of Amsterdam. She wrote a dissertation about the role of the judge in climate change litigation and has published on the rights of nature and rights of future generations. She is one of the national experts in the UN Network Harmony with Nature. She frequently collaborates with the artistic collective Embassy of the North Sea.

Merle Kooijman MA is a philosopher and criminal law scholar. She works as a researcher and lecturer at the University of Amsterdam, Amsterdam Center for Criminal Justice. Her research is on the philosophical foundations of a crime of ecocide. Merle was a visiting research fellow at the Faculty of Law of the Hebrew University in 2023.

Dr. Stavros Evdokimos Pantazopoulos is a Teaching Fellow at the School of Law, National and Kapodistrian University of Athens, and a visiting researcher at the Erik Castrén Institute, University of Helsinki. He is also a Senior Research Fellow at the Hellenic Foundation for European and Foreign Policy (ELIAMEP) and a Fellow at the Athens Public International Law Center. Stavros is a founding member of the Environmental Peacebuilding Association and a member of the World Commission on Environmental Law. Previously, he was a postdoctoral researcher with the Toxic Crimes Project at the University of Helsinki and a researcher at the T.M.C. Asser Institute. His research focuses on the legal dimensions of environmental protection during and after armed conflict. He has published in the fields of international humanitarian law, international environmental law, international cultural heritage law, and the regulation of autonomous weapons systems.

Dr. Christophe Paulussen is a senior researcher at the T.M.C. Asser Institute and coordinator of the institute's research strand 'In the public interest: accountability of the state and the prosecution of crimes'. From 1 December 2023 to 15 March 2025 he was acting chair of the executive board and academic director of the Asser Institute. Christophe is a member of several boards, including editor-in-chief of the journal 'Security and Human Rights' (since June 2018). Christophe's areas of interest are international humanitarian law, international criminal law and counter-terrorism & human rights. He has written extensively in all the above-mentioned areas. Moreover, Christophe has been involved as project leader in the development and implementation of numerous lectures, expert meetings, summer programmes, conferences, databases, trainings, and needs assessment & capacity building missions in public international law-related projects.

Chapter 2
Crime Against Who or What? A Historical and Ontological Inquiry into Ecocide Discourse

Clémentine Dècle-Classen

Contents

Abstract The campaign to recognise 'ecocide' as an atrocity crime under the Rome Statute of the International Criminal Court (ICC) has gained traction since the 2010s, driven by the inadequacy of existing legal instruments to confront large-scale 'environmental destruction' amid intensifying ecological discontinuities. Informed by existing international humanitarian and criminal norms against 'environmental destruction' during international armed conflicts, a likely definition of 'ecocide' as an ICC crime would revolve around "damage to the (natural) environment". However, this normative basis betrays the original political and epistemic force of what the term 'ecocide' initially sought to condemn. Coined during the Second Indochina War (the Vietnam War), early articulations of 'ecocide' did not target an abstract offence against the 'natural environment', but the material and epistemic violence underlying 'ecocidal warfare' aimed at severing people from land, life-systems, and collective self-determination. However, a strand of contemporary legal discourse

C. Dècle-Classen (✉)
Université Paris 1 Panthéon-Sorbonne, Paris, France
e-mail: clementine.decle@etu.univ-paris1.fr

L. Burgers et al. (eds.), *Ecocide: Criminalising Serious Harm against the Environment*, International Criminal Justice Series 38, https://doi.org/10.1007/978-94-6265-715-1_2

constrains the conceptual stakes underlying an international crime of 'ecocide' by staging 'anthropocentrism' and 'ecocentrism' as conceptual binaries, reinforcing a worldview inherited from international law's normative groundings: one that for centuries has reduced earthly materialities and relationalities to a prophetical duel between *anthropos* as 'humanity' against an externalised *oikos* as 'nature'. This chapter problematises such bifurcation by revisiting the ontological and doctrinal assumptions underlying contemporary discourse on 'ecocide'. It situates the erasure of earlier 'ecocide' discourse within a historical trajectory shaped by strategic interpretive practices by the United States regarding the legality of environmental warfare in Indochina—arguably enabled by ontological assumptions that naturalise the divide between 'humanity' and 'nature'. Rather than a rushed amendment to the Rome Statute, the chapter calls for slowing down to articulate the phenomena and structures that have normalised 'ecocidal violence' under the guise of legality and 'human nature'. In this regard, Richard Falk's proposed *International Convention on the Crime of Ecocide* stands as a solid benchmark that requires far more sustained consideration than it has been afforded thus far.

Keywords Ecocide · Anthropocentrism · Ecocentrism · Vietnam War · Richard Falk · Ontology

2.1 Introduction

As nearly absolute scientific consensus on 'human-induced' or 'anthropogenic' climate change[1] gained traction, public concerns soared transnationally regarding 'environmental destruction' resulting from ostensibly 'normal' activities by human societies (*e.g.*, burning fossil fuels).[2] The proliferation of technical target-oriented and (alleged) non-binding institutional responses to address this multidimensional planetary crisis, allegorised by the sustainable development goals,[3] is increasingly perceived as insufficient. This perceived inadequacy has notably sparked a campaign to recognise 'ecocide' as a standalone international crime under the Rome Statute of the International Criminal Court (ICC).[4] Currently, the only prohibition of 'environmental destruction' under the Rome Statute—framed as "widespread, long-term, and severe damage to the natural environment"—is limited to international armed

[1] Allen et al. 2018; Lynas et al. 2021. On quotation marks: when this chapter uses single 'quotation marks', it hints at the ambiguity of a certain term. Double quotation marks indicate a direct quote, including for single terms, as to insist on the use of these terms specifically in the doctrine under review.

[2] Tomuschat 1996, para 45.

[3] UN General Assembly 2015, Preamble. See also UN General Assembly 2012, 2016.

[4] Higgins 2010; Higgins 2012; Higgins et al. 2013; Stop Ecocide Foundation 2021; Stop Ecocide International 2023; Rome Statute of the International Criminal Court, opened for signature 17 July 1998, 2187 UNTS 3, entered into force 1 July 2002 (Rome Statute).

conflicts (IACs) under Article 8(2)(b)(iv).[5] The campaign to include 'ecocide' as its own offense alongside other ICC core crimes therefore seeks to expand international criminal accountability for 'environmental destruction' by extending the ICC's jurisdiction over similar acts committed in peacetime.

The questions of whether and to what extent 'environmental destruction' should be criminalised under international criminal law (ICL) and prohibited under international humanitarian law (IHL) trace back to the 1970s.[6] However, earlier considerations to make "wilful and severe damage to the environment" an atrocity crime alongside the crime of genocide, crimes against humanity, and war crimes were ultimately omitted.[7] Moreover, despite growing normative traction of 'ecocide' within legal and activist circles, no international criminal norm currently codifies a crime of 'ecocide'.

At time of writing, the official procedure to negotiate an amendment of the Rome Statute to include a crime of 'ecocide' was launched in September 2024.[8] These negotiations may be informed by the most recently proposed definition of a crime of 'ecocide' by the Independent Expert Panel for the Legal Definition of Ecocide (IEP/Panel), convened by the Stop Ecocide Foundation—a non-governmental organisation founded by Scottish lawyer Polly Higgins, whose work propelled the post-2010s campaign.[9]

As this chapter further explores, the IEP's proposed definition of 'ecocide' is predominantly inspired by existing international humanitarian and criminal prohibitions of "damage to the natural environment", which, altogether, betray the original conceptualisations of 'ecocide' as both a phenomenon and its incipient doctrinal articulation in the 1970s by law Professor Richard Falk.[10] Indeed, an epistemological account of existing yet limited prohibitions of "damage to the natural environment" under ICL and IHL, substantiated with the geopolitical circumstances surrounding their drafting history, suggests that these do not amount, doctrinally and conceptually, to condemning 'ecocide'.

---

[5] An international armed conflict (IAC) corresponds to a declared war, a military occupation, or any other armed conflict occurring between two or more States. See International Criminal Court (ICC), Elements of Crimes, reproduced in the Official Records of the Assembly of the States Parties to the Rome Statute of the International Criminal Court, First Session, New York, 3–10 September 2002, ICC-ASP/1/3 and Corr.1, part II.B, Article 8(2)(b)(iv). Geneva Convention I for the Amelioration of the Condition of the Wounded and Sick in Armed Forces in the Field, opened for signature 12 August 1949, 75 UNTS 31, entered into force 21 October 1950, Article 2; In comparison, a non-international armed conflict amounts to an armed conflict that is not of an international character, but occurs within the territory of a State between governmental authorities and organised groups or between groups, excluding situations of internal disturbances and tensions. See Rome Statute, above n 4, Article 8(2)(f).

[6] Bertram 2024; Tomuschat 1996, para 19.

[7] ILC 1991; ILC 1996. Also see Sect. 2.2.2.1.

[8] Bertram 2024.

[9] Higgins 2010; Higgins 2012; Higgins et al. 2013; Stop Ecocide Foundation 2021; Stop Ecocide International 2023. Also see Sect. 2.2.2.

[10] See Sect. 2.3. Also see Falk 1973.

However, as the post-2010 campaign for an ICC crime and accompanying doctrinal definitions gained traction, a deeper conceptual and epistemic dimension has unsettled doctrinal inquiry. Indeed, several scholars and advocates deplore the "clearly *anthropocentric* (...) nature of the crimes currently covered by the Rome Statute", which, they argue, reflect "a concern only with atrocities and actions committed by humans with human implications and impacts."[11] Against this backdrop, some envision criminalising 'ecocide' as a normative vehicle to extend the ICC's jurisdiction over crimes that are "ecocentric in nature and that affect the ecosystem of the planet", which would thereby be expected to facilitate an 'ecocentric' shift to ICL.[12]

An ICC crime of 'ecocide' is therefore hoped to offer an *oikos*-centred response to a purported *anthropos*-centred epistemological issue.[13] Specifically the 'Anthropocene' terminology, popularised in 2002 by meteorologist and atmospheric chemist Paul Crutzen, denotes "the present, in many ways human-dominated, geological epoch," said to supplement the Holocene.[14] This hypothetical geological shift—often traced back to the Industrial Revolution (18th century)—is associated with an accelerated increase in global concentrations of 'anthropogenic' greenhouse gases (*e.g.*, carbon dioxide, methane),[15] major drivers of climate change,[16] directly assigned to 'humanity' as a species. While not formally recognised as a new geological epoch,[17] historian and geographer Jason W. Moore conceives of the Anthropocene as a groundbreaking discourse that has sparked "a wider conversation around humanity's place in the web of life."[18] This chapter hopes to nurture this conversation through an ontological and historical inquiry into discourses pertaining to the international criminalisation of 'ecocide'.

Indeed, by envisioning an *oikos*-centred shift as a remedy to an alleged *anthropos*-centred planetary crisis—in both cause and consequences—some contemporary 'ecocide' discourses may have spiralled into what Moore terms Green Arithmetic: the conceptual separation of "humanity" on one hand and "environmental consequences" on another, sustaining the "tale of humans 'overwhelming the great forces of nature'."[19] Against this 'logic', a flourishing strand of scholarship has interrogated the inadequacy of an *anthropos*-centred framing of the problem, underlying both the

---

[11] Emphasis added. Crook et al. 2018, p. 304, cited in Lindgren 2023, p. 311. The critiques of 'anthropocentrism' expand beyond ICL. Other areas of international law and other disciplines have equally been criticised for their 'anthropocentrism'. More in Sect. 2.2.

[12] Also see the norms and proposals analysed in Kooijman 2023.

[13] Also see Grear 2015.

[14] Crutzen 2002; Crutzen and Steffen 2003.

[15] Crutzen's observations have been inferred from air trapped in polar ice; Crutzen 2002.

[16] Crutzen equally identifies a Great Acceleration period from the 1950s onwards with intensive fossil fuel burning and agriculture: Crutzen 2002; Crutzen and Steffen 2003. For alternative findings on when the Anthropocene began: Zohari 1986; Ruddiman 2003; Steffen et al. 2011; Waters et al. 2016; Moore 2017.

[17] International Commission on Stratigraphy 2024.

[18] Moore 2017, p. 595.

[19] Moore 2017, pp. 595–598.

'Anthropocene' discourse and doctrinal criticisms of 'anthropocentrism'. Indeed, these narratives generally portray *anthropos* as the epistemological and biophysical root-cause of planetary socio-ecological troubles. This in turn not only naturalises an imaginary in which a unified, singular, "human enterprise" behaves tyrannically against a singular, externalised 'nature', but also obscures the historically unequal and uneven contributions of different human collectives and individuals as drivers of these very issues.[20]

Under the assumption that ICL's 'anthropocentrism' stands as the epistemological root of 'ecocide' as a phenomenon, several scholars envision an ICC crime of 'ecocide' as an 'ecocentric' solution to the planetary destruction of home. Seen in this light, a 'non-ecocentric' crime of 'ecocide' amounts to a conceptual betrayal of what the term epistemologically and doctrinally signifies, whereas existing proposals and other scholars promote an 'anthropocentric' articulation of the crime as the only alternative for a provision that stands realistic prospects to be adopted by ICC State Parties as an amendment of the Rome Statute.[21] This brings us to the conceptually and doctrinally boiling question: can 'we' conceptualise an 'ecocentric' crime of 'ecocide'? Guided by this interrogation, this chapter exemplifies the relevance of not too hastily reducing the epistemic and doctrinal scope of 'ecocide' to a binary opposition between an 'ecocentric' or 'anthropocentric' ICC crime.

The analysis is informed by the necessity to resituate core notions (*i.e.*, *oikos*, *anthropos*, subjectivity) in their ontological and epistemic boundaries. Indeed, terms relevant to 'ecocide' discourses may be derived from these notions, which include 'ecocentrism' or 'ecocide' and 'anthropocentrism', the 'Anthropocene', or 'humanity'. This theoretical backbone helps engage with contemporary 'ecocide' discourses on two levels.

First, debates tied to contemporary calls for an international crime of 'ecocide' have been informed and pervaded by the idea of 'anthropocentrism' and 'ecocentrism' as conceptual binaries. This fallacy may be explained by surface-level articulations of 'ecocentrism' and 'anthropocentrism' in doctrinal inquiry, where both are premissed on 'nature' as an undifferentiated whole, external to 'humanity' as a singular enterprise. Yet, in doing so, a strand of contemporary 'ecocide' discourse reinforces an ontologically constructed distinction between 'humanity' and 'nature'—cornerstone to international law's normative groundings—as if such a divide accurately translated earthly materialities and relationalities. This ontological split has long underpinned representations of whatever realm signified by ontologies

[20] Ibid. Also see Lindgren 2018; Parrique 2019, p. 2. It is worth noting, though that the United Nations Framework Convention on Climate Change (UNFCCC) recognises the notion of "common but differentiated responsibility", because 'anthropogenic' greenhouse gas emissions key drivers of climate change historically and overwhelmingly originate from "developed economies" in opposition to less economically 'developed' countries (e.g., Small Island Developing States who reportedly contributed the least to the climate crisis yet suffer some of its worst impact). Note that the use of "developed" or "developing" here refers to the language found in the United Nations Framework Convention on Climate Change, opened for signature 9 May 1992, 1771 UNTS 107, entered into force 21 March 1994 (UNFCCC), Preamble Article 3.

[21] Heller 2021; Ambos 2021; Voigt 2021.

associated with 'nature' as passive matter or property—thus a background stage upon which (a restricted set of) legal subjects assigned to the realm of 'humanity' act.

Foremost among this historical trajectory was a series of strategic moves by the United States, which invoked the legality of techniques and tools of environmental warfare in Indochina under international law, claiming there were no positive norms nor customary rules prohibiting "damage to the natural environment". That interpretive vacuum arguably facilitated an erasure of earlier conceptualisations of 'ecocide' as a phenomenon during the Second Indochina War (or the Vietnam War) and its incipient doctrinal articulation as an international crime by Richard Falk. Specifically, the latter situated a crime of 'ecocide' in its structural and epistemic dimension. As explored throughout this chapter, the origins of a crime of 'ecocide' had nothing to do with—and more potential than—contemporary approaches restricted to a singular, all-encompassing prohibition of "damage to the (natural) environment."

2.2 Ecocide, *Anthropos*-Centrism and *Oikos*-Centrism

Would it make sense for 'ecocide' to be anything other than an 'ecocentric' international crime? In order to be consistent with its etymological roots, *oikos*-cide, which translates from Greek and Latin into the 'destruction of home', some argue that a non-'ecocentric' or an 'anthropocentric' articulation of a crime of 'ecocide' would be inadequate.[22] Likewise, the plausible incorporation of a crime of 'ecocide' into the Rome Statute has been hoped to strengthen accountability against 'environmental destruction' and to tackle the 'anthropocentrism' of international law by inducing an 'ecocentric' shift to ICL.[23] Similarly to the Anthropocene's account of 'humanity' as a driving geological force over the planet,[24] critiques of 'anthropocentrism' attribute the epistemological root cause of collapsing earthly ecological equilibria to centring international law—and all other disciplines and areas of society—around *anthropos* as subject-at-the-centre, predominantly associated with 'humanity' as a species.[25] Until recently,[26] a significant strand of legal scholarship has envisioned 'anthropocentrism' as a unitary concept, a "thinking disorder"[27] urging for an 'ecocentric' shift in international law.

Conventionally, 'anthropocentrism' denotes an exceptionalist or supremacist view of *Homo sapiens*' superiority over the planet.[28] The critique of 'anthropocentrism' thus denounces a utilitarian worldview that reduces 'nature' to its *instrumental* value

[22] Heller 2021; Ambos 2021. Also see Dècle-Classen 2022.

[23] Crook et al. 2018, p. 304, cited in Lindgren 2023, p. 311.

[24] Crutzen 2002.

[25] Moore 2017; Lindgren 2023; Grear 2015.

[26] For brilliant contributions to this discussion, see Chapaux et al. 2023.

[27] See various sources cited in Burdon and Alexander 2023, p. 216.

[28] See Lawrence and Heller 2007, pp. 64–65; Kooijman 2023, pp. 107–108.

to 'humanity'—as a "giant gasoline station, an energy source for modern technology and industry,"[29] an object of profitable value, or as an exploitable resource for 'humanity'—as *anthropos*.[30] Conversely, scholarship of interest to this chapter associates *oikos*, which etymologically means 'home', with 'nature' or the 'natural environment' understood as everything other than 'humans' and their 'creation'.[31]

In international law, 'anthropocentrism' more precisely translates into the "idea that only humans have value in their own rights and therefore (…) worthy of ethical considerations."[32] The 'anthropocentric' critique of law thus deplores rules claimed in the name of 'environmental protection' to the utility such rules afford to 'humanity'.[33] In its orthodox doctrinal understanding, an 'anthropocentric' strain of thought is deemed inextricable from an epistemological disregard of 'nature's' inherent right to exist, independently of "human desires and interests."[34] In response, some argue the limits of 'anthropocentrism' could be addressed through an 'ecocentric' shift to international law that recognises the *intrinsic* value of 'nature' or the 'natural environment' independently of its utility for 'humanity'.[35] This indicates that legal scholarship stages 'ecocentrism' and 'anthropocentrism' as mirrors, hinting at a reversal 'logic': if 'anthropocentrism' is the issue, its self-evident solution could only be 'ecocentrism'. Swap *anthropos*- with *oikos*- and 'humanity's' relational framework over 'nature' from *instrumental* to *intrinsic* in order to heal law's 'anthropocentric' plague and *voilà!*: the long-awaited happily-ever-after where 'humanity' thrives in harmony with 'nature' emerges.[36]

What is missing from existing doctrinal analysis is an inquiry that acknowledges how such accounts of 'ecocentrism' and 'anthropocentrism' embody the way earthly materialities and relationalities have been ontologically abstracted by associating *anthropos* to 'humanity' as a species (*Homo sapiens*) as one that is quintessentially distinct from 'nature' (or the 'natural environment') as signifiers of *oikos*.[37] The fact that 'ecocentrism' and 'anthropocentrism' have been staged as conceptual antagonists might then be explained by an epistemological account of *anthropos* (= *Homo sapiens*) and *oikos* (= 'nature') as materially dissociated ontologies. However, environmental philosophy provides more nuanced articulations on 'ecocentrism'

---

[29] Burdon and Alexander 2023, p. 216. Also see Prost 2023.

[30] Loft et al. 2015, p. 151; Kooijman 2023, pp. 106–109; Lawrence and Heller 2007, pp. 64–67.

[31] Rülke et al. 2020, p. 2; Kortenkamp and Moore 2001.

[32] Kooijman 2023, pp. 106–107, citing *inter alia* Kopnina et al. 2018, p. 115.

[33] Kooijman 2023, p. 106; Loft et al. 2015, p. 151.

[34] Loft et al. 2015, p. 151. It is worth noting that, as Loft et al. specify, in the field of conservation biology and in the governance of biodiversity and ecosystems, intrinsic value and inherent value are two different value-systems—which are sometimes confused and used interchangeably. Indeed, the latter amounts to the value that an entity possesses in and of itself, by virtue not of its utility, but of its mere existence, whereas intrinsic value amounts to the value an entity possesses on its own and for itself (so, while subtle, this difference essentially involves that an entity's intrinsic value does not depend on such recognition by another, as opposed to inherent value).

[35] Lawrence and Heller 2007; Kooijman 2023.

[36] See, e.g., UN General Assembly 2023. Also see Moore 2017 for a similar criticism.

[37] Lawrence and Heller 2007; Kooijman 2023.

and 'anthropocentrism', untangled in the following subsection. Moreover, insofar as 'anthropocentrism' and 'ecocentrism' etymologically differ on whether *oikos* or *anthropos* is subject-at-the-centre (*-centrism*), what follows also clarifies what subjectivity means in international law—a crucial aspect to this chapter's analysis.

2.2.1 Untangling the Subject-at-the-Centre from Environmental Philosophy to International Law

In environmental philosophy, Ben Mylius articulates three forms of 'anthropocentrism' to characterise certain *paradigms*[38]—a level of theory which "represent[s] and encompass[es] the large narratives that build and drive societies and cultures, including science."[39] Without delving into the specifics, Mylius' contribution challenges the orthodox reduction of 'anthropocentrism' as a singular concept, which shall instead be envisioned and articulated in plural forms. Namely, Mylius articulates three understandings of 'anthropocentrism'. Firstly, normative anthropocentrism refers to inquiry that privileges, actively asserts, or passively assumes the superiority of *Homo sapiens* as a species. Secondly, descriptive anthropocentrism refers to premising or centring inquiry around *Homo sapiens* without claiming or assuming its superiority. Lastly, Mylius identifies perceptual anthropocentrism as paradigms shaped by data collected from human sensory organs and experience,[40] which is inherent to all human beings since it is situated in human embodiment rather than merely ontologically constructed.

Similarly, Adrien Estève delineates three foundational *frameworks*[41] for 'ecocentric' inquiry in environmental philosophy, namely: *(1)* Land Ethic, *(2)* Deep Ecology, and *(3)* the Gaia hypothesis.[42] While this chapter's analysis does not demand delving into detailed nuances of such frameworks, what matters is understanding that 'ecocentrism' is not a unitary concept, nor an exact mirror of 'anthropocentrism'. Instead, 'ecocentrism' encompasses diverse *frameworks* to guide scientific inquiry towards a paradigm shift in relation to *oikos*—which *can* encompass multiple ontologies and signifiers such as land, biotic and abiotic communities—of which *anthropos*, which *can* also encompass and signify multiple ontologies, is a part of rather than (subject-)at-the-centre.[43]

---

[38] Burdon and Alexander 2023, pp. 216–217; Mylius 2018, pp. 159–194.

[39] Partelow 2023, p. 1. For a meticulous yet digestible articulation of 'paradigm', I strongly recommend reading Ben Mylius' work in the original: Mylius 2018.

[40] Chapaux 2023, p. 295; Burdon and Alexander 2023, p. 215; Mylius 2018, p. 159.

[41] Partelow 2023, p. 1.

[42] Estève 2020. Also see Higgins 2020; Chapaux et al. 2023; Mégret 2023, p. 51; Rolston 1997; Leopold 2018; Næss and Sessions 1986.

[43] Also see Sect. 2.3.3.

Notwithstanding, environmental philosophy's account of various forms of 'anthropocentrism' as a tool to characterise paradigms and 'ecocentrism' as frameworks to instigate a paradigm shift has become garbled in its doctrinal transposition regarding (the concept of) a crime of 'ecocide'. This garbling may be explained by international law's distinction from other disciplines, where 'subject' or 'subjectivity' can have different meanings. Indeed, not only does 'subject' pertain to a *paradigm* in (legal) science, but it also pertains to *legal subjectivity* (or legal personality).[44] Thus, subject-at-the-centre in international law can be understood as *(1)* the subject around which a paradigm revolves and that guides doctrinal inquiry, or a discipline's normative focal point, as well as *(2)* the legal subject(-at-the-centre) of a norm or body of rules, meaning "the capacity of an actor to bear rights or duties in a legal order (here, the international legal order)."[45] In the following pages, whenever I use 'subject' or 'subjectivity' in relation to international law specifically, I refer to both meanings or I intentionally hint at some ambiguity.[46] Otherwise, I will specifically indicate whether this concerns 'subjectivity' in terms of legal personhood or normatively speaking.

2.2.2 Reviewing the Debate: What Is (Not) an Ecocentric Crime?

Lack of explicit recognition of the polysemic scope of 'subject' in international law—as a notion either denoting a normative focal point or a legal person—may have generated doctrinal confusion. Specifically, critiques labelling existing 'ecocide' proposals and existing IHL and ICL norms prohibiting "damage to the (natural) environment" as 'anthropocentric' operate in a reversal and binary logic: what is not considered 'ecocentric' is deemed necessarily 'anthropocentric'. What follows suggests examined literature overwhelmingly assumes a norm prohibiting "damage to the natural environment" is 'ecocentric' if it is not 'anthropocentric', where 'anthropocentrism' is understood as conditioning liability either to 'human' victims in the *actus reus* or to 'human interests' in the *mens rea*.[47] Whether the norms or proposals under examination are, *in fine*, 'ecocentric' or 'anthropocentric' is not what I am particularly interested in nor what I am trying to argue in this chapter. Rather, through the following subsections, I retrace the assumptions underlying the doctrinal identification of norms and proposals concerning a crime of 'ecocide' as either 'ecocentric' or 'anthropocentric'. This approach informs the order of the norms and proposals

---

[44] Peters and Sparks 2024a, p. 12. Also see Peters 2016.

[45] Ibid.

[46] Reminder: the use of single 'quotation marks' in this chapter hints at the ambiguity of a specific term.

[47] Shy attempts to escape this binary have provided a continuum, ranging from "broadly ecocentric" to the "height of ecocentrism" in cases of ambiguity. Jenkin 2022, p. 230. Also see Sects. 2.2.2.3 and 2.2.2.4.

under review as follows, and therefore, does not necessarily follow a chronological order.

2.2.2.1 Early Articulations of the Tension: The International Law Commission's Draft Code of Crimes Against the Peace and Security of Mankind

The first indication of a tension associated with an 'anthropocentric' norm in the doctrine under study appears during the drafting of the International Law Commission (ILC)'s Draft Code of Crimes against the Peace and Security of Mankind (Draft Code).[48] Discussing draft Article 26, which sought to prohibit "widespread, long-term and severe damage to the natural environment" as a standalone crime in wartime and peacetime, some members expressed concerns the draft Article would be "unduly restrictive" and "too anthropocentric" insofar as it eventually conditioned liability on whether "health or survival of a population would be gravely prejudiced".[49] Yet, this criticism itself may be regarded as 'anthropocentrically' motivated in its situated context: it reflected concerns that an excessively 'anthropocentric' norm would weaken deterrence and limit prosecutions of serious "damage to the natural environment", thereby undermining the Draft Code's objective of safeguarding the peace and security of *anthropos* as 'humankind'. Ultimately, the final Draft Code rejected the explicit criminalisation of "damage to the natural environment" as its own offence or as an element of genocide and crimes against humanity (CAH),[50] which informed the drafting of the Rome Statute.

2.2.2.2 Article 8(2)(b)(iv) of the Rome Statute: An 'Ecocentric' Compromise?

Despite considerations to make "wilful and severe damage to the environment" an atrocity crime alongside the crime of genocide, crimes against humanity, and war crimes,[51] the Rome Statute's sole explicit criminalisation "damage to the natural

---

[48] ILC 1996, para 14, p. 8; Tomuschat 1996, p. 24.

[49] Ibid.

[50] Prior to the adoption, Chairman Mahiou rejected "wilful and severe damage to the environment" as its own offence in peacetime and wartime without a vote, relegating such considerations to crimes against humanity (CAH) and war crimes. In the end, Members only voted favourably for the inclusion of "damage to the natural environment as a war crime". Ibid., pp. 8–14. Also see Rome Statute, above n 4, Articles 5, 6, 7.

[51] ILC 1991, 1996.

environment" appears under Article 8(2)(b)(iv), which specifically makes it a war crime[52] during IACs[53] to:

> Intentionally launch an attack in the knowledge that such attack will cause incidental loss of life or injury to civilians or damage to civilian objects or *widespread, long-term and severe damage to the natural environment* which would be *clearly excessive* in relation to the *concrete and direct overall military advantage* anticipated.[54]

Because "damage to the natural environment" is not conditioned to 'human' victims in the *actus reus*, scholars wondered whether this provision could be considered an 'ecocentric' crime. For Mark A. Drumbl, the provision represents a compromise from an "environmental perspective"[55] because it does not require 'human' harm or victims to trigger liability for "damage to the natural environment."[56] Yet, the requirement of "severe" damage along with the provision's restricted scope to IACs hints at an "anthropocentric" provision, Drumbl argues, insofar as liability is conditioned to "humanity's need to make use of [the natural environment]", which indicates a rationale where liability is conditioned to damage that "affects human life and human consumption of natural resources."[57]

Jessica C. Lawrence and Kevin Jon Heller observe that the absence of a conditional element of 'human harm' in the *actus reus* does not offset the provision's nearly impossible-to-establish liability standards. For example, the cumulative "widespread, long-term, and severe" requirement for damage is built upon undefined thresholds in the Rome Statute and Elements of Crimes,[58] which undermines legal certainty.[59] The

[52] Rome Statute, above n 4, Article 8(2)(b)(iv). Indeed, Chairman Ahmed Mahiou decided to leave aside considerations for criminalising "wilful and severe damage to the environment" as its own offense under Article 26 without putting it to vote, instead requesting members whether it would be more appropriate as a CAH. See ILC 1996, pp. 13–14.

[53] See above n 5.

[54] Rome Statute, above n 4, Article 8(2)(b)(iv). Emphasis added.

[55] Drumbl 1998, p. 126.

[56] Note that the ICC only recognises natural human persons as victims or, in certain cases, legal persons who suffered damage on their property. See International Criminal Court (ICC), Rules of Procedure and Evidence, reproduced in the Official Records of the Assembly of States Parties to the Rome Statute of the International Criminal Court, First Session, New York, 3–10 September 2002, ICC-ASP/1/3 and Corr.1, part. II.A, Rule 85.

[57] Drumbl 1998, p. 129.

[58] The Assembly of State Parties could also amend such terms, but it would require a two-third majority which makes it unlikely that they would agree on those. See Rome Statute, above n 4, Article 121. For a detailed analysis of the implications of such a threshold, see Drumbl 1998. Also see Lawrence and Heller 2007.

[59] Drumbl 1998; Lawrence and Heller 2007, p. 77; ICC, Elements of Crimes, above n 5. Moreover, even external instruments do not consistently define the terms "widespread", "long-term", and "severe". Under Article 21 of the Rome Statute on applicable law, the Court may interpret these terms by reference to treaties such as the Protocol Additional to the Geneva Conventions of 12 August 1949, and relating to the Protection of Victims of International Armed Conflicts, opened for signature 8 June 1977, 1125 UNTS 3, entered into force 7 December 1978 (AP I) and Convention on the Prohibition of Military or Any Other Hostile Use of Environmental Modification Techniques, opened for signature 10 December 1976, 1108 UNTS 151, entered into force 5 October 1978

lack of precise definitions for this provision combined with the principle of *nullum crimen sine lege* further complicates the imposition of liability because, in such instances, the Court is bound to interpret any ambiguity in favour of the person under investigation, prosecution, or conviction.[60] Compared to ILC members' concerns regarding the "unduly restrictive" scope of draft Article 26, had it been adopted and conditioned to 'human harm', Heller and Lawrence's contribution indicates that the absence of 'human harm' in the *actus reus* does not necessarily translate into a more realistic test to establish liability.

The standard of liability is all the more complicated by Article 8(2)(b)(iv)'s *mens rea* test. It requires that the perpetrator knew that intentionally launching an attack *would*, not that it may,[61] result in "widespread, long-term, and severe" damage *and* be *clearly* excessive in relation to the "overall military advantage anticipated."[62] The

(ENMOD). While both instruments influenced the framing of Article 8(2)(b)(iv), Protocol I is more appropriate for interpretation, as it concerns the protection of the *natural environment*, whereas ENMOD protects its State Parties. However, the ICRC 1987 Commentary on Protocol I defines only *long-term*—as lasting several decades—while leaving *widespread* and *severe* undefined. See ICRC 1987, paras 1451–1455. The Commentary provides a joint interpretation of the three terms, both considering ENMOD and AP I, depending on the nature of the action: deliberate modification of natural phenomena (*e.g.* weather) affecting any State, party or not, must have effects lasting more than three months; by contrast, warfare methods resulting in "damage to the natural environment" by collateral effect must result in damage that is simultaneously *widespread*, *long-term* (decades), and *severe*. ENMOD, on the other hand, defines *widespread* as "several hundred square kilometres", *long-term* as "months or approximately a season", and *severe* as "serious or significant disruption or harm to human life, natural and economic resources or other assets". See ENMOD, Annex p. 91. These terms may be interpreted either through treaty provisions or their *travaux préparatoires*, including Protocol I's Commentary (1987) and ENMOD's Annex. The ILC's Draft Code of Crimes Against the Peace and Security of Mankind also provides a complementary interpretative source: it frames the three terms as cumulative indicators of seriousness, referring respectively to geographical extent, duration, and intensity. The Commission clarified that *long-term* refers to the durability of the effect, not its delayed onset, and acknowledged debate over whether this would delay prosecutions or could be assessed early on. See ILC 1991, pp. 106–107. While the ICC's Assembly of States Parties could theoretically amend the terms under Article 121 of the Rome Statute, doing so would require a two-thirds majority, making any revision unlikely. See Lawrence and Heller 2007, p. 72; Drumbl 1998, p. 122. More on ENMOD and AP I in Sect. 2.3.3. Also see UNODA 1976.

60 See Rome Statute, above n 4, Article 22.

61 The term 'knowledge' in the Rome Statute requires proving a natural person knew the crime will occur, not that it may occur. Minkova's interpretation is based on the Rome Statute Article 30 and its interpretation by the ICC's Pre-Trial Chamber. See Minkova 2021, p. 21.

62 Rome Statute, above n 4, Article 8(2)(b)(iv). Also see Lawrence and Heller 2007, p. 77.

conditioning of intent to subjective knowledge[63] renders the test extremely subjective.[64] Indeed, the *mens rea* test for intent becomes conditioned to the attacker's, judges', and potential victims' appreciation of "damage"—based on vague thresholds—as well as morals, values, interests, or methods regarding what the "natural environment" signifies to them—which inevitably varies across settings and legal subjects involved (including both legal and natural persons).[65] Interestingly, despite these limitations, Lawrence and Heller still categorise Article 8(2)(b)(iv) as 'ecocentric',[66] while Merle Kooijman regards it as 'anthropocentric', given that military advantage remains the axis against which damage is balanced (which is assumed here as 'human' interests).[67]

---

[63] The last version of Article 8(2)(b)(iv) looks like a middle ground between ILC draft Article 22 (war crime) which sought to prohibit "employing methods or means of warfare which are intended or may be expected to cause widespread, long-term and severe damage to the natural environment" and draft Article 26 (autonomous offense) that required "wilfully" causing damage. Article 8(2)(b)(iv) seems to have mingled intent and expectation that conduct would result in damage, by conditioning intent to subjective knowledge that a given attack would result in such damage. For critiques of the distinction between draft Article 22 and draft Article 26, see e.g. UN 1993. The final outcome of Article 8(2)(b)(iv) seemingly accounted for Tomuschat's critique on draft Article 26, suggesting "wilfully" to be replaced with "knowingly". A person, he argues, may act "wilfully" without knowing the consequences of their conduct, which may be partly contingent on scientific knowledge at a given time. Conversely, a person may act knowing their conduct will, but without intending to, harm the 'environment'. He illustrates the issue of knowledge when States like France did atmospheric testing of nuclear bombs or grenades, whose 'environmental' and health consequences were not, some argue, as certain as nowadays. See Tomuschat 1996, pp. 25–26, paras 37–42, 49.

[64] Indeed, liability first depends on the perpetrator's appreciation of this balancing element prior to launching a military attack; the ICC judges would then have to assess whether the author engaged in an unreasonable judgement or failure to make such judgement in good faith based on IHL requirements. If the ICC finds the author failed to satisfy such pre-emptive requirements, it would have to determine such damage was excessive based on the available information to the author at the time. See ICC, Elements of Crimes, above n 5, Article 8(2)(b)(iv), fn 37: "As opposed to the general rule set forth in paragraph 4 of the General Introduction, this knowledge element requires that the perpetrator make the value judgement as described therein. An evaluation of that value judgement must be based on the requisite information available to the perpetrator at the time." Also see Dörmann 2003. Also see Minkova 2024, p. 95.

[65] On the issue of methodological choices by the Court to assess the extent of 'environmental damage', the case before the International Court of Justice between Costa-Rica against Nicaragua can be of interest. Indeed, both parties presented different methods to assess the amount of reparations owed by Nicaragua to Costa-Rica as a result of "the material damages caused by Nicaragua's unlawful activities in the border area", which induced "damage to the environment" based on methodologies developed by different UN organs whose results varied considerably based on the methods, data points, and the expertise relied on by different parties, submitted to the Court. However, the Court, in the end, evaluated the amount of reparation *in concreto*, without privileging any method presented by the parties or relying on a particular method provided for by an external organ or actor. See for the memorials International Court of Justice (ICJ) 2017a, 2017b, 2017c, 2017d. See for the judgment on compensation International Court of Justice (ICJ), *Certain Activities Carried Out by Nicaragua in the Border Area* (*Costa Rica v. Nicaragua*), Compensation, Judgment, 2 February 2018, ICJ Reports 2018.

[66] Lawrence and Heller 2007, p. 94.

[67] Kooijman 2023, p. 116.

Thus, the underlying assumption seems to be that if the *mens rea* is not exclusively aligned with the interests of what is deemed the "natural environment"—also considered the "nonhuman environment"[68]—the norm remains 'anthropocentric'. Conversely, another assumption is that a norm prohibiting "damage to the (natural) environment" while excluding 'human' victims from its *actus reus* could indicate that the "natural environment" counts as the provision's victim (hypothetically as 'subject' in the sense of legal personality). This is why it would be considered (partially) 'ecocentric'. However, this idea of the "natural environment" as a 'victim' can only be symbolic, irrespective of a norm's articulation. Indeed, the ICC's Rules of Procedure and Evidence restrict the definition of 'victims' to natural persons (human individuals) or to organisations or institutions that have suffered damage to their property or any other places or objects for humanitarian purposes.[69] This already hints at a procedural limit against hopes for an 'ecocentric' crime of 'ecocide', that would supposedly set the "natural environment" as subject-at-the-centre (at least in the sense of legal personality).

2.2.2.3 The Independent Expert Panel on the Legal Definition of Ecocide: A Broad Ecocentric Proposal?

In June 2021, the Independent Expert Panel (IEP) proposed amending the Rome Statute to criminalise 'ecocide', defined as: "*Unlawful* or *wanton acts* committed with *knowledge* that there is a substantial likelihood of *severe and either widespread or long-term damage to the environment* being caused by those acts."[70] Similarly to Article 8(2)(b)(iv), this definition technically enables liability for "damage to the environment" irrespective of human victims in its *actus reus*. The Panel allegedly intended "to make the protection of the environment an end in itself,"[71] through so-called 'ecocentric' *actus reus* requirements where the 'environment' appears as the (symbolic) victim of the crime,[72] against 'anthropocentric' *mens rea* requirements.[73] However, the Panel introduced a proportionality test with wantonness, defined as "reckless disregard for damage that would be clearly excessive in relation to the social and economic benefits anticipated".[74] This balancing test conditions "environmental

[68] See Lawrence and Heller 2007, p. 64.

[69] ICC, Rules of Procedure and Evidence, above n 56, Rule 85. See also Chap. 10 of this volume.

[70] Stop Ecocide Foundation 2021, p. 5. Emphasis added.

[71] Kooijman 2023, p. 119 citing Philippe Sands (citation omitted).

[72] Ibid. On the quintessentially 'symbolic' scope of introducing the "natural environment" as the 'victim' of a crime, resituate the idea of victim to the way it is defined in the ICC, Rules of Procedure and Evidence, above n 56, Rule 85.

[73] Heller 2021.

[74] Stop Ecocide Foundation 2021, p. 5. Note that the IEP's definition of 'knowledge' amounts to recklessness or *dolus eventualis* (and thus, is not 'knowledge'). See Heller 2021.

harms against social and economic benefits, which is expressed in the principle of sustainable development".[75]

Consequently, some consider the IEP's definition as "broadly ecocentric"[76] because it seemingly preserves an 'ecocentric' *actus reus* while accommodating an 'anthropocentric' *mens rea*, as the Panel intended. However, Heller rejects labelling the Panel's definition as 'ecocentric' altogether, arguing that the proportionality element legitimises "damage to the environment" when, he argues, "humans benefit enough from the destruction".[77] Similarly, Liana G. Minkova criticises the Panel's balancing approach, noting that it wrongfully suggests "the problems of the environment and [that] of human communities can be separated" and that "the costs and benefits of environmentally harmful acts could be assessed with respect to human beings in the abstract, without taking into consideration global inequality."[78] Aligned with this chapter's critique, Minkova's inquiry rejects strictly mapping existing norms and discourses across the assumed ecocentric/anthropocentric binary in this doctrinal strand.

2.2.2.4 Polly Higgins' Proposal: The Height of Ecocentrism?

Polly Higgins' early 2010s proposal to criminalise 'ecocide' stands apart from both Article 8(2)(b)(iv) and the IEP's definition. Advocating for the criminalisation of 'ecocide' in wartime and peacetime through an amendment of the Rome Statute, Higgins defines 'ecocide' as:[79] "the extensive destruction, damage to or loss of *ecosystem(s) of a given territory*, whether by *human agency or by other causes*, to such an extent that peaceful enjoyment by the *inhabitants of that territory* has been severely diminished."[80] Unlike the IEP's proposal and relevant IHL and ICL provisions, Higgins does not rely upon the "damage to the (natural) environment" framing, and instead uses broader all-encompassing categories—"inhabitants," "ecosystems," of a given "territory"—aimed at encompassing both human and more-than-human realms.[81]

---

[75] Stop Ecocide Foundation 2021, p. 10.

[76] Voigt 2021; Jenkin 2022.

[77] Heller 2021. This critique was also raised by Minkova 2021.

[78] Ibid. On global inequalities' relationship to 'ecocide', see below n 196.

[79] Higgins 2010, p. 257; Higgins 2020, p. 180.

[80] Higgins 2010, p. 257. Emphasis added.

[81] However, it is important to note that Higgins draws on Article 73 of the UN Charter to legitimise her 'ecocentric' proposal, interpreting it as recognising a duty of care owed to all human and more-than-human "inhabitants" and their "territories" that deviates from staging 'humanity' against 'nature'. However, this reading warrants the provision's original context. Indeed, Article 73, also known as the "doctrine of trusteeship", was intended to regulate colonial powers' responsibilities toward non-self-governing peoples and territories. Hence it codified a hierarchical legal order in which colonised populations were denied full legal personality and sovereignty as legitimate representatives of their oikos, their land. Thus, Higgins' interpretation and reliance on Article 73 to sustain her point disregards the colonial legacy and structural asymmetries embedded in the

In this spirit, Anna Jenkin describes Higgins' proposal as the "height of ecocentrism."[82] First, Higgins herself envisioned 'ecocide' as a crime against all life, (including but) not just human life.[83] Moreover, Jenkin interprets "human agency or by other causes"[84] as extending to "natural causes" for 'ecocide'.[85] The moral rationale underpinning Higgins' proposal aligns with this interpretation. For Jenkins, the strict liability approach embedded in Higgins' definition reflects the view that the transgression of Earth's inherent value constitutes the "morally abhorrent action justifying criminal liability".[86] Thus, the absence of a *mens rea* requirement for establishing liability for the *actus reus* strikes as a deliberate choice to recognise 'ecocide' as a crime irrespective of intent or knowledge.

This choice sets Higgins' proposal apart from both existing legal norms and the IEP's definition, because it rejects a framework that positions the "natural environment" as ontologically or interest-wise antagonistic to "humanity", or in which only humans are recognised as agents, victims, and bearers of rights or responsibilities—thus, as subjects. Indeed, Jenkins' reading of Higgins indicates that recognising more-than-human agency entails an extension of legal subjectivity beyond the human, not limited to a condition of victimhood. Yet because agency could also hint at the capacity to bear duties, extending legal responsibility to more-than-human entities would be both inappropriate and absurd—*i.e.* imagine criminally prosecuting a tornado for meeting the material thresholds underlying Higgins' definition. Albeit its doctrinal limits, Higgins' aim does not seem to extend accountability on more-than-human entities, but to foreground socio-ecological harm as the outcome of complex, entangled processes that an abstract construct of 'humanity' as boundless master of the planet cannot account for.

---

article, which is a serious omission that warrants deeper engagement. Unfortunately, such inquiry lies beyond the scope of this chapter for reasons of space and time. See Higgins 2020, pp. 117–119. Charter of the United Nations, opened for signature 26 June 1945, 1 UNTS XVI, entered into force 24 October 1945 (UN Charter), Article 73.

[82] Jenkin 2022, p. 230.

[83] Higgins 2010, p. 257.

[84] Jenkin 2022, p. 230, citing Higgins et al. 2013, p. 257. Another possible reading of "other causes" may suggest structural or systemic agency—potentially involving legal persons such as corporations—rather than actions attributable to individual human beings, which fall within the Rome Statute's limited personal jurisdiction over natural persons. See Rome Statute, above n 4, Article 25. On the ICC's restricted *ratione personae* jurisdiction to natural persons in relation to proposed definitions for a crime of 'ecocide', see Aparac 2021; Gonzalez 2024, p. 512.

[85] Jenkin 2022, p. 230.

[86] Ibid.

2.2.3 *From* Anthropos *to* Oikos*? Engaging with Ecocide Discourse Beyond Humanity and Nature*

2.2.3.1 Ecocide and the Fiction of a Conceptual Binary: Ecocentrism vs. Anthropocentrism

Our analysis in Sect. 2.2.2 indicates that, with the exception of Higgins' proposal, a significant strand of doctrinal analyses, norms, and proposals under review overwhelmingly assumes that the *oikos* of 'ecocentrism' and 'ecocide' corresponds to the "(natural) environment", considered as a realm distinct and external from "humanity"—as *Homo sapiens* or the human species. In sum, the prevailing doctrinal view at hand seemingly suggests that a norm is 'ecocentric' if it: *(1)* criminalises 'ecocide' or "damage to the (natural) environment" independently of human harm (*actus reus*); *(2)* recognises the "(natural) environment" in the *actus reus* as a 'victim' (although such recognition can only be symbolic);[87] and *(3)* excludes an 'anthropocentric' *mens rea*. Accordingly, the doctrinal articulation of an international crime of 'ecocide' is deemed 'ecocentric' only if both its material and mental elements are fully independent of 'human' interests or victims, insofar as those are viewed as antithetical to 'ecocentrism'. By extension, this premise implies 'non-human' 'victims' or 'interests', abstracted as 'nature' or the 'natural environment', are antithetical to considerations for 'human interests' or victims.

All considered, 'anthropocentrism' and 'ecocentrism' have been staged as conceptual binaries, premised on a singularised 'humanity' instrumentalising a singularised 'nature' versus a vision of 'nature' as intrinsically valuable. However, this 'logic' anchors discussions on criminalising 'ecocide' in conceptual contradictions: it posits inherently antagonistic interests between 'humanity' and 'nature', while claiming 'environmental' protection is necessary for humanity's broader wellbeing and, to some extent, the peace and security of humankind,[88] yet precluding instrumental motives when brought into (international) law. Altogether, this presupposes the interests of 'humanity' versus the '(non-human) environment', 'nature', or the '(natural) environment', can be singularised and universalised *per* each ontological category—for example, treating military advantage as universally serving humanity, somehow as if an attack was conducted from 'humanity' as a singular enterprise against the 'natural environment' as an undifferentiated whole.[89]

Such tensions indicate that merely designating the environment as a symbolic 'victim'[90] is insufficient to generate a shift from *anthropos* to *oikos* as the normative

---

[87] *Per* the ICC Rules of Procedure and Evidence, above n 56, Rule 85. See also Chap. 10 of this volume.

[88] The idea of criminalising "damage to the natural environment" as legitimate politically and morally insofar as the peace and security of humankind is at stake was evoked e.g., in Tomuschat 1996, p. 22.

[89] Also see Sect. 2.3.2. on 'ecocidal warfare'.

[90] ICC, Rules of Procedure and Evidence, above n 56, Rule 85.

focal point of an international crime of 'ecocide', nor does treating both ontologies as mutually exclusive. These underlying assumptions cast the legal subject as either *anthropos* (as 'humanity') or *oikos*—either with the 'natural environment' as a distinct ontology, or an all-encompassing *oikos* incorporating both human and more-than-human entities as agents and 'victims' of ecocide (*e.g.*, Higgins' proposal's "inhabitants" and "ecosystems" of a given territory).[91]

Thus, the set of assumptions underlying the literature examined thus far can be summarised as follows:

1. International law—ICL in particular—is considered structurally 'anthropocentric', revolving around *anthropos*, equated with 'humanity' as a species, as its subject-at-the-centre, staged against 'ecocentrism';
2. Assuming 'anthropocentrism' as the epistemological driver of planetary discontinuities, including 'ecocide', the literature invites for an ontological shift that would either require reconceiving the legal subject by including humans within an expanded *oikos* or maintaining the 'humanity'/'nature' dualism while setting the latter as subject-at-the-centre;
3. Altogether, the literature assumes that law, which it considers 'anthropocentric', is anchored in the intrinsic value of all members of the human species as 'humanity'—but not that of 'nature', thereby reducing it to its instrumental value.

Section 2.3 explores how such assumptions obscure ICL's ontological and relational architecture, as well as the historical circumstances that have informed the contemporary 'ecocide' discourse and the articulation of proposed legal definitions.

2.2.3.2 From Concept to Context: Resituating the Historical and Ontological Boundaries of *Anthropos* and *Oikos*

Prior to challenging this set of assumptions in Sect. 2.3, it is important to flag certain dimensions that will be implied all along but cannot warrant an extensive examination in this chapter. Chief among these is the political instrumentalisation of the idea of 'humanity'—historically moulded as an ontological benchmark to doctrinally and politically discriminate what or who falls under the realm of subjectivity. Indeed, whether one embraces the 'Anthropocene' discourse or goes on a rant against 'anthropocentrism', both standpoints generally attribute planetary socio-ecological discontinuities to *anthropos*—therein signified as the 'human species' and thus framed in a neutral biological sense. This veil of neutrality however obscures how certain ideas of 'humanity' have long been constructed and instrumentalised to justify the exclusion of vast segments of the human population from legal subjectivity, rights, and political representation. As Frédéric Mégret notes, many human beings, now included into the equation of 'humanity' as *Homo sapiens*, have been historically excluded from 'humanity' normatively when associated with pejorative

[91] This all-encompassing approach inscribed itself in the metaphysical strive for totality and towards universal knowledge. See Lindgren 2023, p. 313, citing Matthews 2019, p. 667.

traits (*e.g.*, 'savage', 'primitive') drawn from what was deemed 'nature'—including 'non-human' animals, plants, and other 'non-human' life forms.[92]

This exclusion operated through a deeper ontological division: 'humanity' has been normatively constructed around one's propensity to engage with the capacity for reason detached from corporeality—that is, disembodied rationality—which in turn shaped the doctrinal and political recognition of 'subjectivity' to members of the human species, both individually and collectively. This hierarchy arguably draws from naturalism's construction of *Homo sapiens* as uniquely endowed with the privilege of interiority.[93] Hence, disembodied rationality came to be regarded as the highest expression of this species uniqueness—when such a capacity is scarcely attainable by any corporeally thick human being, and thus effectively relegated to the corporate legal form.[94] Conversely, 'nature' came to signify all that is deemed external to this political construction of 'humanity', reduced to matter and devoid of interiority. All relegated to the realm of 'nature' thus came to be reduced as something that could be possessed among recognised subjects. Grounded in naturalism, anthropologist Philippe Descola considers such division as the epistemological driver of Western modern thought,[95] one that stages a representation of earthly materialities and relationalities as a strict division between an abstract, disembodied ideal of 'humanity' on the one hand and everything else relegated to 'nature' on the other.[96]

More specifically, prior to the mid-20th century, international law's conception of 'humanity'—as a situated signifier of *anthropos*—was deeply exclusionary: it legitimised colonialism, slavery, and property regimes by elevating an abstract ideal of the human person—white, Christian, detached from corporeality, rational, male, property-owning—whose alleged duty was to uncover 'nature's' secret so as to master and shape the planet accordingly.[97] Those who failed to embody this ideal, particularly feminised, racialised, and colonised bodies,[98] were relegated to the less-than-human; (more-than-human) bodies and entities categorised as non-human, were relegated to and treated as inert 'nature' to be possessed, dominated, extracted, exploited, or exterminated.[99] Pointing at the historical construction of 'humanity' through an equally constructed idea of 'nature' does not mean law should at all abandon the idea of 'humanity', and even less all human beings on Earth it tangibly encompasses nowadays. Instead, engaging with the idea of 'humanity'—*i.e.* 'humanity' as an ontological or normative category—requires engaging with it as a value-laden political object that has been historically naturalised in legal and scientific discourse, oftentimes for instrumental purposes which did not in fact serve all human beings

[92] Mégret 2023, p. 36.

[93] Descola 2006.

[94] Descola 2006; Grear 2015.

[95] While delving into the details of this observation is beyond the scope of this chapter, note that 'naturalism' here is not intended as the same as *jus naturalis*—although there are some overlaps.

[96] Descola 2006; Moore 2017; Sciences Po 2024. Also see Grear 2015; Lindgren 2023.

[97] Grear 2015; Prost 2023.

[98] Grear 2015; Mégret 2023.

[99] Grear 2015; Lindgren 2023.

on Earth. Seen in this light, *anthropos* and *oikos* cannot be regarded as signifiers of a universal or neutral representation of earthly materialities and relationalities. Rather, *anthropos* and *oikos* carry specific ontological and historical assumptions that have shaped and informed the development and interpretation of international law.

Section 2.3 thus explores how disregarding the historical roots of what the term 'ecocide' initially sought to signify—as a phenomenon and proposed international crime—and the way naturalism's legacy of an ontologically constructed 'humanity'/ 'nature' divide have shaped existing IHL and ICL norms condemning "damage to the (natural) environment". These norms, which continue to influence contemporary legal discourse on 'ecocide', prove deeply inadequate when reconsidering what the invention of 'ecocide' initially condemned. Altogether, Sect. 2.3 challenges assumptions of a perceived conceptual binary between 'ecocentrism' and 'anthropocentrism' in this strand of doctrinal scholarship, which ultimately reinforces conventional representations of *oikos* and *anthropos* through an ontologically constructed divide between 'humanity' and 'nature'. Crucially, the following Section informs the conclusion that revolving around such assumptions doctrinally and epistemologically betrays the stakes underlying the invention of 'ecocide', which correspondingly impairs our collective ability to conceptualise and address 'ecocidal violence'.

2.3 Returning to the Invention of 'Ecocide' to Understand Ecocidal Warfare

From its inception in an expert-led campaign against the weapons and tactics of environmental warfare in Indochina, 'ecocide' as a concept was coined to expose the entanglement of the American chemical industry with the military-industrial complex, as herbicides like Agent Orange were deployed both in domestic agriculture and as weapons of war.[100] Articulating 'ecocide' conceptually and doctrinally thus requires recognising that 'ecocidal warfare' as a phenomenon was not driven by malice toward 'nature' or the 'natural environment' itself—whatever this means—but rather was employed as a strategic tool to secure military, epistemic, and socio-economic global hegemony.[101] By 'ecocidal warfare', I mean forms of warfare designed "for comprehensive and systematic destruction"[102] or disruption

[100] The rate of application of herbicides, including Agent Orange, as weapons of war reportedly amounts to thirteen times the dose recommended for domestic use. Falk 1973, p. 292. Estimates may vary depending on sources. The general idea would be that rates of the use of herbicides as weapons of war astronomically exceeded the rate recommended for domestic use, supported by varying sources. On this, and for a more specific inquiry into the tensions induced by varying results and scientific evidence specifically with respect to Agent Orange, see Martini 2012.

[101] Chomsky 1970.

[102] Falk 1973, p. 287.

of the socio-ecological fabric of a given milieu to gain direct or indirect control over the means of livelihoods of a single or multiple areas.[103]

Revisiting the doctrinal and historical grounds that have shaped international humanitarian and criminal legal approaches to 'environmental destruction', Sect. 2.3.1 argues 'ecocidal warfare' is not restricted to materially salient tactics and weapons—which I denote as weapons and tactics of 'environmental' warfare—but instead encompasses significant epistemological and normative dimensions that have been (strategically) swept under the rug. Namely, the belief that IHL contained no provisions for protecting the 'natural environment' (as external from 'humanity') in itself pertains to a rhetorical strategy mobilised by the U.S. and its mandated chemical corporations to deny any sort of (legal) liability for the production and use of herbicides as weapons of war in Indochina. Arguably, this idea of a legal void has significantly influenced the systematic reliance on articulating a distinct prohibition against "damage to the (natural) environment" across different IHL and ICL instruments, leading up to contemporary discourse and proposals over an international crime of 'ecocide', as though 'environmental destruction' or 'protection' could only be meaningfully addressed through a norm revolving around this clause.

Section 2.3.2 contrasts the influence of this rhetorical distraction on contemporary approaches to 'ecocide' with the significant yet overlooked proposed *International Convention on the Crime of Ecocide* (Ecocide Convention) by Richard Falk. Indeed, instead of a single all-encompassing provision as a part of a more general instrument, normatively anchored in an absolute distinction between 'human' and the 'natural environment' as to prohibit a certain degree of "damage" to the "natural environment," Falk's Ecocide Convention was initially conceived differently. Specifically, the Ecocide Convention reveals an international crime of 'ecocide' was initially envisioned to target specific acts through a multilateral treaty, in order to identify, prevent and punish, certain courses of conduct that could still pose a threat to international peace and security, even if not targeted or "intentionally" aimed at disrupting or destroying human beings or a human population directly.

2.3.1 The Influence of the United States' Position on Weapons and Tactics of Environmental Warfare in Indochina on the Foundations of Contemporary 'Ecocide' Proposals

While the invention of 'ecocide' initially fostered legal and epistemological consciousness of environmental interrelatedness,[104] IHL and ICL norms that have

---

[103] The literature may refer to environmental, ecological, biophysical, geochemical, or geophysical warfare, terms that mostly differ in scope—*e.g.*, whether land was destroyed and rendered uninhabitable by directly targeting the land, or if disruption or destruction of given milieu was enabled by knowingly and intentionally interfering on *e.g.*, atmospheric or weather conditions for this purpose.

[104] For instance, see Weisberg 1970a.

informed contemporary 'ecocide' proposals have abstracted the notion from its conceptual and doctrinal origins. Indeed, the term 'ecocide' originated three decades prior to the Anthropocene discourse and four decades prior to the post-2010s campaign for an ICC crime of 'ecocide'. Specifically, the invention of 'ecocide' emerged from an expert-led campaign that sought to condemn 'ecological warfare'[105]—*i.e.* the total destruction of the "living landscape by war as well as the effects of such a war upon the people and culture",[106] through *inter alia*, crop destruction, defoliation, or chemical warfare[107]—carried out by the U.S. in Indochina.[108]

In 1970, at the Conference on War and National Responsibility, plant-biologist Arthur W. Galston proposed a new international agreement to ban 'ecocide', which he defined as the "wilful destruction of the environment".[109] The term, popularised by Swedish Prime Minister Olof Palme at the 1972 United Nations Conference on the Human Environment,[110] inspired Professor Richard Falk who introduced, the same year, his proposal for an International Convention on the Crime of Ecocide.[111] Although Falk's Ecocide Convention was never formally negotiated nor adopted by States, the campaign against such unprecedented atrocities soared international concerns about 'ecocide' as a weapon of total destruction. As Barry Weisberg warns in *Ecocide in Indochina: The Ecology of War* (1970):

> Ecocide may be less dramatic, less immediately apparent than atomic war — but it is every bit as conclusive. (...) The forces at work now in Indochina are at work around the world, in the towns of America as well as the jungles of Asia. The chemical poisoning of Indochina by the Military parallels the poisoning of America by our Chemical industry. To believe for an instant that one will stop without the other would be a grave miscalculation (...) It is tragic that many of America's environmental crusaders have not fully reali[s]ed the interconnection between the destruction of Indochina and the destruction of our total environment. The power of this destruction cannot be circumvented by consumer boycott or draft resistance alone. The power of the Military, the power of excess production, as well as imperial consumption, must be broken at the source.[112]

---

[105] Weisberg 1970c, p. v.

[106] Ibid.

[107] Falk 1973. Note that this definition of "ecological warfare" differs from that of the International Committee of the Red Cross Commentary on Protocol Additional to the Geneva Conventions of 12 August 1949, and relating to the Protection of Victims of International Armed Conflicts (Protocol I). See ICRC 1987, para 1462. Whereas Falk refers to "environmental warfare", Weisberg referred to "ecological warfare". Scholarship and doctrinal sources are often inconsistent in the use of these terms. These can be used interchangeably or to signify slightly different things. In this chapter, unless we refer to 'ecocidal warfare' or 'tools and techniques of environmental warfare', I use both interchangeably. Further inquiry relating to the various meanings and uses of these terms would be doctrinally and conceptually valuable. Also see above n 103.

[108] Zierler 2011; Weisberg 1970c.

[109] Weisberg 1970b; The New York Times 1970.

[110] Palme 1972.

[111] Falk 1972, pp. 94–97. Also see Falk 1973, Appendix I.

[112] Weisberg 1970c, p. vi.

"The source" in Weisberg's words, is "America's preeminent role in the chemical poisoning of [Earth's] life support systems."[113] Accordingly, consciousness of 'ecocide' as a phenomenon that required a legal and institutional response attacked the military-industrial complex and the power of America's chemical industry over the "ecological peril that faces the entire Earth."[114]

Shortly after the Vietnam War, the 1970s unfolded with the normative development regarding IHL and ICL's relevance to address 'environmental destruction' and 'environmental protection', characterised by the adoption of a series of positive legal instruments, including the multilateral and binding Convention on the Prohibition of Military or Any Other Hostile Use of Environmental Modification Techniques (ENMOD) in 1976,[115] followed by the prohibition of severe, widespread, and long-term "damage to the natural environment" under the 1977 Protocol Additional to the Geneva Conventions of 12 August 1949, and relating to the Protection of Victims of International Armed Conflicts (Protocol I).[116] Both ENMOD and Protocol I inspired the ILC's work on the Draft Code,[117] which conversely influenced the articulation of the Rome Statute's Article 8(2)(b)(iv) and the rejection of "damage to the (natural) environment" as a standalone ICC crime.[118]

Nowadays, ENMOD and Protocol I's influence—both directly and through their legacy in the ILC's Draft Code proceedings and the Rome Statute's Article 8(2)(b)(iv)—extends to contemporary proposals and campaigns to establish an international crime of 'ecocide', particularly illustrated by the IEP's proposed definition for a crime of ecocide.[119] However, this Section argues that relying on these instruments' prohibitions against "damage to the natural environment" to inform the doctrinal articulation of an international crime of 'ecocide' betrays its historical origins and is both normatively and epistemologically inappropriate. To sustain this claim, this Section first traces back how the implied assertion that any criminal or humanitarian norm to prevent or condemn 'environmental destruction' or adopted in favour of 'environmental protection' should be framed around "damage to the natural environment" has been facilitated—though not admittedly—by the U.S. strategic response to accusations that its use of the 'environment' as a 'military' target in Indochina violated applicable international rules.[120] Specifically, by instrumentalising scientific uncertainty and leveraging the naturalist ontological divide between 'humanity' and 'nature', the U.S. was able to instigate a sense of legal ambiguity and deny liability while simultaneously entrenching its global hegemony. It is within this

[113] Ibid.

[114] Ibid.

[115] ENMOD, above n 59.

[116] AP I, above n 59.

[117] The ILC was tasked to draft the Formulation of the principles of recognized in the Charter of the Nuremberg Tribunal and in the Judgement of the Tribunal. See. UN General Assembly 1947b. Also see UN General Assembly 1947a. See ILC 1991, 1996.

[118] Rome Statute, above n 4. Also see Sect. 2.2.2.

[119] More on this in Sect. 2.3.1.2.

[120] Falk 1973.

context that the epistemological and normative architecture of 'ecocidal' warfare can be more fully understood, as explored in Sect. 2.3.2 with Falk's Ecocide Convention.

2.3.1.1 The United States Position and the Politics of Uncertainty

Among weapons and tactics of 'environmental' warfare used in Indochina, the use of herbicides such as Agent Orange to defoliate millions of acres of crops and forest vegetation not only marked collective memory of the war, but significantly informed the U.S. position on the legality of this kind of conduct.[121] In 1971, Wil D. Verwey observed that the U.S. government's position entails that none of the applicable rules prohibited its military use of chemicals in Indochina, which it alleged not "toxic" or "lethal" in the sense of the 1925 Protocol for the Prohibition of the Use of Asphyxiating, Poisonous, or Other Gases, and of Bacteriological Methods of Warfare.[122] The U.S. even argued that the use of herbicides was "not aimed at harming people but, on the contrary, at saving lives"[123] and "used to kill plants", not to kill or inflict suffering on 'humans'.[124]

A good-faith interpretation of applicable rules during the Vietnam War does not, *in extremis*, align with an alleged legal vacuum by the U.S. and some of its allies.[125] As Falk observes, "not all international law is reduced to treaty form."[126] Customary international rules, for instance, already forbade "reliance on tactics and weaponry that are indiscriminate in impact".[127] In addition to the prohibition of the use of poisonous gases,[128] applicable positive rules proscribe the infliction of unnecessary

---

[121] Falk 1973, p. 292.

[122] Protocol for the Prohibition of the Use of Asphyxiating, Poisonous or Other Gases, and of Bacteriological Methods of Warfare, opened for signature 17 June 1925, 94 LNTS 65, entered into force 8 February 1928 (1925 Protocol).

[123] Verwey 1971, p. 218.

[124] United States District Court Eastern District of New York, *Re-Amended Memorandum, Order and Judgment "Agent Orange" product liability litigation*, MDL no. 381, the Vietnam Association for Victims of Agent Orange 04-cv-400, 10 March 2005 (Eastern District Court of New York, VAVA, 2005), p. 176.

[125] Falk specifically builds a strong case based on customary principles of international law. Falk 1972, pp. 94–97. Also see UN General Assembly 1969; Verwey 1977; Falk 1973; Verwey 1971, p. 225.

[126] Falk 1972, p. 94.

[127] Ibid., p. 95.

[128] 1925 Protocol, above n 122.

suffering[129]—despite claims that herbicide-use was intended to save lives[130]—as well as the "extensive destruction and appropriation of property, not justified by military necessity and carried out unlawfully and wantonly".[131] Such rules arguably suffice to establish the unlawfulness of, *inter alia*, the U.S. use of Agent Orange and other herbicides as a weapon of war. Yet, insofar as positive rules did not *literally* prohibit harm or damage to the "natural environment" (as external to 'humanity') in itself, but rather implied protection of the 'non-human'[132] according to their function for a given 'human' group or entity (*e.g.*, property or objects indispensable for survival, which could include crops, foodstuffs, or agricultural areas),[133] the U.S. gradually construed the idea of a legal void in this respect through the "politics of uncertainty".[134]

A representative example of the U.S. position and its use of the politics of uncertainty can be inferred from its judiciary's reasoning when faced with a collective tort action brought by Vietnamese plaintiffs who alleged serious damages, including death, as a result of being exposed to the military use of Agent Orange as a weapon of war.[135] The plaintiffs sought to establish the unlawful nature of such herbicide use

[129] The plaintiff, the *Vietnam Association for Victims of Agent Orange v. Dow Chemical Co.*, namely referred to the 1907 Hague Regulations Respecting the Laws and Customs of War on Land, Annex to the 1907 Hague Convention (IV) Respecting the Laws and Customs of War on Land, opened for signature 18 October 1907, 36 Stat. 2277 TS No. 539, entered into force 26 January 1910, Article 23(e), which prohibits "to employ arms, projectiles, or material calculated to cause unnecessary suffering" and Geneva Convention IV relative to the Protection of Civilian Persons in Time of War, opened for signature 12 August 1949, 75 UNTS 287, entered into force 21 October 1950 (Geneva Convention IV), Article 147: "Grave breaches to which the preceding Article relates shall be those involving any of the following acts, if committed against persons or property protected by the present Convention: wilful killing, torture or inhuman treatment, including biological experiments, *wilfully causing great suffering or serious injury to body or health*, unlawful deportation or transfer or unlawful confinement of a protected person, compelling a protected person to serve in the forces of a hostile Power, or wilfully depriving a protected person of the rights of fair and regular trial prescribed in the present Convention, taking of hostages and extensive destruction and appropriation of property, *not justified by military necessity and carried out unlawfully and wantonly*." Emphasis added.

[130] Verwey 1971, p. 218.

[131] Geneva Convention IV, above n 129, Article 147.

[132] The notion of 'protection of the non-human' here excludes norms protecting certain objects indispensable to survival (or elements of 'nature' as 'property') along with cultural property and heritage—the latter can be considered as an extension of the 'human' based on an idea that 'humanity' as a notion extends beyond the 'human'. See The Hague Conventions protection of cultural property in times of armed conflicts, *e.g.*, Convention for the Protection of Cultural Property in the Event of Armed Conflict and its First Protocol, opened for signature 14 May 1954, 249 UNTS 215, entered into force 7 August 1956.

[133] Also see Kooijman 2023, p. 116 about the Rome Statute.

[134] Martini 2012.

[135] Agent Orange was produced by private agrochemical corporations at the request of the U.S. government under the Defense Production Act of 1950. While a full analysis of this movement and its full doctrinal implications exceeds the scope of this chapter, it is notable that transnational activism and tort claims were brought against manufacturers—agrochemical companies—such as Dow Chemical before U.S., French, and Korean courts, seeking recognition and reparations for harm to Vietnamese victims. No court has formally recognised the plaintiffs' claims or awarded

and thereby hold its manufacturers liable.[136] Yet, the Eastern District Court of New York held in 2005 that such use of herbicides did not violate the principles of proportionality or military necessity, core international norms that govern the conduct of war.[137] Moreover, in 2008, the U.S. District Court of Appeals further narrowed the application of the proportionality principle by requiring proof of a demonstrable intent from the defendant to "injure human populations".[138] The Court's introduction of this intentionality requirement arguably diverted judicial analysis away from the standard of foreseeable harm, which typically governs tort claims, particularly in product liability cases.[139]

By framing liability around intent rather than foreseeability of harm in its interpretation of the principle of proportionality, the Appeals Court effectively marginalised the plaintiffs' argument that accountability should be established based on whether defendants knew or should have known of the risks of human exposure to Agent Orange.[140] The Court's interpretation arguably (though controversially) strengthened the idea that liability could not be established unless there was clear, deliberate intent to harm human beings.[141] Yet, the Court's reading seemingly conflates "intent"

---

reparations. Cour d'Appel de Paris, *TRAN To Nga c. Dow Chemical & co.*, Pôle 4, Chambre 10, Arrêt du 22 Août 2024, N° RG 21/106/06 - N° Portalis 35L7-V-B7F-CD2CC, Décision déférée à la Cour : Jugement du 10 Mai 2021 - Tribunal Judiciaire d'Evry, RG n°14/04980, more specifically at p. 15. Eastern District Court of New York, VAVA, 2005. United States Court of Appeals for the Second Circuit, United States, *Vietnam Association for Victims of Agent Orange v. Dow Chemical Co.* 05-1953-cv, 22 February 2008 (United States Court of Appeals for the Second Circuit, VAVA, 2008). A key defence rested on the invocation of the Defense Production Act and the contested extension of jurisdictional immunity for acts *de jure imperii* to private corporations (before U.S. Courts and French Courts on the basis of customs). For a contrary view, see *Nevsun Resources Ltd. v. Araya*, 2020 Supreme Court of Canada 5, para 121, where the Canadian Supreme Court held that state immunity does not necessarily extend to corporations.

[136] The case involved Vietnamese victims, represented by the Vietnam Association for Victims of Agent Orange (VAVA), bringing a claim against Dow Chemical Co. under the Alien Tort Statute (28 U.S.C. § 1350), which grants U.S. district courts jurisdiction over civil actions by foreign plaintiffs for torts committed in violation of international law or U.S. treaties. See United States Court of Appeals for the Second Circuit, VAVA, 2008, p. 5. The plaintiffs argued that the use of Agent Orange constituted a breach of international norms derived from both treaty law and customary international law. However, the court held that determining corporate liability under the Alien Tort Statute required first establishing that the U.S. military's use of Agent Orange itself violated international law. Both decisions held that the U.S. did not infringe applicable rules.

[137] Also see Eastern District Court of New York, VAVA, 2005, p. 218.

[138] See United States District Court of Appeals, VAVA, 2008, p. 32.

[139] For more, see Schuck 1987.

[140] Eastern District Court of New York, VAVA, 2005, p. 54. Martini 2012, pp. 231, 246. The Court specifically relied on the 'intent' argument to engage with allegations that the use of herbicides in Vietnam constituted a genocide. The Court concluded "The United States did not use herbicides in Vietnam with the specific intent to destroy any group. Nor were those herbicides designed to harm individuals or to starve a whole population into submission or death. The herbicides were primarily applied to plants in order to protect troops against ambush, not to destroy a people." Eastern District Court of New York, VAVA, 2005, p. 181.

[141] Eastern District Court of New York, VAVA, 2005, p. 176.

with other legal terms like "wanton" and "wilful",[142] which in both domestic tort law, IHL, and ICL are more accurately associated with recklessness or disregard rather than purposive intent.[143]

Altogether, this manoeuvre facilitated a selective interpretation of rules that, *prima facie*, were only aimed at protecting 'human beings', framed by the U.S. as distinct from protection of the 'natural environment' as some kind of undifferentiated external entity to 'human beings'. On this understanding, responsibility hinged on proving that herbicides used as weapons of war had been manufactured and deployed with a reasonable or high degree of certainty that their effects on human health were known, thus intentional *per* the Court's reasoning, in order to fall under existing prohibitions (*e.g.*, destruction and appropriation of property, inflicting unnecessary suffering). In addition, the deliberate cultivation of scientific uncertainty regarding a direct causal link between exposure to Agent Orange and the plaintiffs' alleged harm made this threshold virtually impossible to meet. Not only did it require empirical proof of causation on a scientific basis, but it also demanded that the harm be shown to have been intended by the defendants.[144] Importantly, this whole interpretation was rendered possible by a naturalist premise embedded in the U.S. rhetoric: the claim that damage was intended toward the 'natural environment' (allegedly permitted or not explicitly prohibited by applicable rules), rather than toward human beings, was enabled precisely because it was implicitly admitted—ontologically and epistemologically—that the 'natural environment' materially exists as an undifferentiated realm external to 'humanity'.

2.3.1.2 "Damage to the Natural Environment": A Half-Century Old Doctrinal Blind Spot

As controversy soared over the U.S. reliance on 'ecological warfare' during the Vietnam War, various lawyers, academics, and a majority of the United Nations General Assembly (UNGA) declared the use of chemical agents of warfare in IACs

---

[142] See United States District Court of Appeals, VAVA, 2008, p. 32. The Court cites the 1907 Hague Regulations, Article 23(e) to justify that "[t]he principle of proportionality implicates the element of intent, e.g., "calculated to cause unnecessary suffering," "wanton destruction," "willfully causing great suffering," and "carried out unlawfully and wantonly." Because Plaintiffs do not allege, nor could they on this record prove, the required *mens rea*, they fail to make out a cognizable basis for their ATS claim. The purpose behind spraying Agent Orange was only to destroy crops and "to [s]ave the lives of Americans and those of our allies," and not to injure human populations."

[143] Also see Heller 2021.

[144] Ibid.

to be contrary to generally recognised rules of international law[145]—an interpretation that arguably extends to herbicides used by the U.S.[146] While clarification by the UNGA was perhaps deemed adequate to address minority claims that this kind of conduct did not violate existing international rules, it may have inadvertently reinforced the assumption of legal ambiguity of the applicable legal framework. This, in turn, may have contributed to the entrenchment of a narrow interpretive framework—one in which the regulation of 'environmental destruction' or 'environmental protection' under IHL and ICL is conceived almost exclusively through the lens of "damage to the (natural) environment". Consider the following assertion by the Eastern District Court of New York in *Vietnam Association for Victims of Agent Orange v. Dow Chemical Co.*:

> [A]fter the conclusion of the Vietnam War, the 1977 Additional Protocol I (...) articulated *for the first time* an obligation to take care in warfare "*to protect the natural environment* against widespread, long-term and severe damages." (…) The explicit recognition *in the late 1970s* that *this was a new obligation* (one which the U.S. has yet to ratify) confirms that military use of herbicides did not violate customary international law during the Vietnam War.[147]

As the Court duly indicates, Protocol I embodies the first positive international humanitarian rules around the notion of the "natural environment".[148] It is also true that the drafters of Protocol I sought to enhance protection of the "natural environment" as such—thus, as external to 'humanity'—beyond humanitarian norms aimed at protecting civilians, 'natural resources' implied under objects indispensable for survival, and other infrastructures.[149]

Hence, Protocol I deliberately introduced specific prohibitions around "the natural environment", protected from "severe, long-term, and widespread damage".[150]

---

[145] See UN General Assembly 1969. Namely, the UNGA, "[d]eclares as contrary to the generally recognised rules of international law, as embodied in the Protocol for the Prohibition of the Use in War of Asphyxiating, Poisonous or Other Gases and of Bacteriological Methods of Warfare, signed at Geneva on 17 June 1925, the use in international armed conflicts of: (a) Any chemical agents of warfare—chemical substances, whether gaseous, liquid or solid—which might be employed because of their direct toxic effects on man, animals, or plants;" adopted with 80 votes in favour, 3 against, and 36 abstentions. For the sake of this chapter, we do not have the time to elaborate as to whether the UNGA had—or has—the competence to give authoritative interpretations of treaties. Also see Verwey 1977; Falk 1972, 1973; Verwey 1971, pp. 225.

[146] Ibid.

[147] Emphasis added. Eastern District Court of New York, VAVA, 2005, pp. 40–41, citing "Protocol Additional to the Geneva Conventions of 12 Aug. 1949, and Relating to the Protection of Victims of International Armed Conflicts, June 8, 1977, art. 55, 1125 U.N.T.S. 3, 16 I.L.M. 1391, 1415." N.B.: The Court situated this specifically as a counter-argument to Wil D. Verwey's contestation of the U.S. position. Also see Verwey 1971, 1977.

[148] Protocol I's Article 35(3) prohibits Parties from employing direct or indirect "methods or means of warfare which are intended, or may be expected, to cause widespread, long-term *and* severe damage to the natural environment." Emphasis added. Furthermore, Protocol I's Article 55(1) requires from State Parties that "[c]are shall be taken in warfare to protect the *natural environment* against widespread, long-term *and* severe damage." Article 55(2) prohibits "attacks against the natural environment by way of reprisals." Emphasis added. See AP I, above n 59.

[149] ICRC 1987, paras 2129–2130, pp. 662–663.

[150] Ibid.

However, interpretation in good faith of applicable rules did not require explicit norms around the 'natural environment' to establish the unlawfulness of the U.S. military's use of herbicides in Indochina, as argued. More importantly, although Protocol I drafters sought to strengthen legal safeguards for the "natural environment" independently of direct 'human' harm or interest,[151] it may have induced the opposite of its intended effects in the long-term.

First, the introduction of a distinct prohibition on "damage to the natural environment" under Protocol I anchored IHL and ICL into wider imaginaries of 'humanity' over an externalised 'nature'. Except for Higgins' definition of 'ecocide', formal proceedings and attempts to address 'environmental destruction' or 'environmental protection' through IHL and ICL have revolved around finding appropriate balancing elements to restrict the scope of "damage to the (natural) environment".[152] Specifically, Protocol I's cumulative "widespread, long-term, and severe" formula, inspired by the ENMOD's Convention disjunctive "widespread, long-lasting, *or* severe" formula,[153] has been *systematically* transposed into all subsequent (attempted) articulations of "damage to the (natural) environment" as a war crime or standalone offense in wartime and peacetime, named 'ecocide' or differently, be it cumulative, disjunctive, or a middle-ground (as suggested by the IEP's "severe *and* either widespread *or* long-term").[154]

On the one hand, setting a threshold for "damage to the natural environment" and conditioning liability to *vital* 'human' interests sounds logical to distinguish damage caused by "normal activities by human societies"[155] from punishable acts warranting recognition as international crimes for threatening the peace and security of (hu)mankind.[156] For instance, critical of distancing 'environmental protection' from 'anthropocentrism', ILC member Christian Tomuschat argued that prohibiting severe "damage to the natural environment" as a standalone crime in wartime and peacetime[157] under the Draft Code was politically and morally justified insofar as

---

[151] Note that Article 55(1) reads entirely as: "[C]are shall be taken in warfare to protect the *natural environment* against widespread, long-term *and* severe damage. This protection includes a prohibition of the use of methods or means of warfare which are intended or may be expected to cause such damage to the natural environment and thereby to prejudice the health or survival of the population." Emphasis added. Hence, the first part of the prohibition requires States to prevent widespread, long-term, and severe damage against the "natural environment" independently of 'human' harm. But the second part of the article specifies a scenario in which such damage was intended or expected to cause damage to a (human) population—therefore, the prohibition can apply independently of harm to 'human beings', but it also includes a scenario in which 'human beings' could be harmed. See AP I, above n 59, Article 55(1).

[152] AP I, above n 59. ILC 1991, ILC 1996. Rome Statute, above n 4, Article 8(2)(b)(iv).

[153] ENMOD, above n 59, Article I. More on the ENMOD Convention follows in Sect. 2.3.3.

[154] Stop Ecocide Foundation 2021, p. 5.

[155] Tomuschat 1996, p. 26, para 45.

[156] Also see ILC 1995, para 120, p. 30.

[157] Until 1996, the ILC's draft versions of the Draft Code included one draft article prohibiting "damage to the natural environment" as a standalone crime (draft Article 26), and another as a war crime (draft Article 22). See ILC 1991. Also see ILC 1995.

it addresses cases where "vital human interests are adversely affected",[158] rather than "protect[ing] ecosystems as such."[159] Hence, Tomuschat endorsed criminalising individuals who "wilfully cause or order" such damage to the "natural environment", provided it satisfied the "widespread, long-term, and severe" cumulative threshold and gravely prejudiced "the health or survival of a population," as proposed by draft Article 26.[160]

On the other hand, articulating the right thresholds and conditioning liability to 'human interests' in the *mens rea* or 'human harm' in the *actus reus* only makes sense as long as "damage to the (natural) environment" remains an undisputed starting point. Once this baseline is challenged, limiting doctrinal debates to the right articulation of thresholds or balancing elements around "damage to the (natural) environment" becomes somewhat futile and speaks to the binary character of doctrinal discussions over whether existing norms or proposed definitions of 'ecocide' are framed in 'ecocentric' or 'anthropocentric' terms. Such debates would not exist if IHL and ICL tried to engage with such concerns independently from this baseline. Had the U.S. not insidiously introduced an idea of a legal void concerning the protection of the "natural environment" under applicable humanitarian rules, perhaps Falk's incipient articulation of an international crime of 'ecocide' in 1972 would have received more careful consideration.

2.3.2 Understanding Ecocidal Warfare with Richard Falk's Proposed International Convention on the Crime of Ecocide

2.3.2.1 Richard Falk's Proposed International Convention on the Crime of Ecocide

In 1972, Falk proposed an International Convention on the Crime of Ecocide.[161] Never negotiated nor adopted, the Ecocide Convention was intended as a binding multilateral treaty to prevent and punish 'ecocide',[162] offering accountability avenues against "constitutionally responsible rulers, public officials, military commanders, or private individuals"[163] through its State parties' own jurisdiction.[164] Differing from succeeding IHL and ICL approaches, Falk's proposal does not revolve around

[158] Tomuschat 1996, p. 24 para 29.

[159] Ibid.

[160] See ILC 1996, pp. 7–10. Also see above n 48.

[161] Falk 1972, 1973.

[162] Ibid.

[163] Ibid.

[164] Falk 1973, Appendix I, p. 300, Article VI, Article VII, on the specific implications that a transposition of the Convention into the Parties' respective jurisdictions and measures against persons charged with 'ecocide' would have entailed.

prohibiting "damage to the natural environment." Instead, the Convention qualifies as 'ecocide' specific acts[165] committed in wartime or peacetime with *intent* to "disrupt or destroy, in whole or in part, a human ecosystem".[166] For instance, this includes an absolute prohibition on the use of weapons of mass destruction.[167] Conversely, deforestation does not qualify as 'ecocide' in absolute but does *if* committed with the intent to disrupt or destroy a "human ecosystem" through the use of herbicides for military purposes.[168] These examples suggest the Ecocide Convention excludes various forms of destruction or disruption of a "human ecosystem" or 'environmental destruction' from its scope. Thus, an international crime of 'ecocide' was not initially envisioned through an absolute distinction between 'humanity' and the 'natural environment' nor was it limited to an all-encompassing prohibition of a certain level of "damage" to the "natural environment". Rather, it was about identifying the most threatening behaviours of the time—actions that, even if not 'intentionally' aimed at disrupting or destroying a human population or human beings—individually or collectively, could still pose a threat to international peace and security.

By articulating an international crime of 'ecocide' through a multilateral treaty criminalising specific conducts substantiated with an overarching definition of 'ecocide', Falk's Ecocide Convention could not possibly include all possible or foreseeable forms of 'environmental destruction'. This does not mean Falk rejected prohibiting other forms of 'environmental destruction' within the scope of the Ecocide Convention and beyond. In fact, the Convention includes a revision procedure[169] allowing for the list of acts prohibited as 'ecocide' to be amended over time. Moreover, the Ecocide Convention shares a similar structure to that of the Genocide Convention and Rome Statute's crimes, namely: a general definition of a crime substantiated with a list of acts, situated in context, circumstances, objectives, purposes, and intentionality if applicable. Hence, the Ecocide Convention's structure reflects the way international crimes are usually articulated. What is unusual is the

[165] Falk 1973, Appendix I, p. 300, Article II. "In the present Convention, ecocide means any of the following acts committed with intent to disrupt or destroy, in whole or in part, a human ecosystem: (a) The use of weapons of mass destruction, whether nuclear, bacteriological, chemical, or other; (b) The use of chemical herbicides to defoliate and deforest natural forests for military purposes; (c) The use of bombs and artillery in such quantity, density, or size as to impair the quality of the soil or to enhance the prospect of diseases dangerous to human beings, animals, or crops; (d) The use of bulldozing equipment to destroy large tracts of forest or cropland for military purposes; (e) The use of techniques designed to increase or decrease rainfall or otherwise modify weather as a weapon of war; (f) The forcible removal of human beings or animals from their habitual places of habitation to expedite the pursuit of military or industrial objectives."

[166] Falk's articulation of 'ecocide' around the intentional disruption or destruction "in whole or in part, of a human ecosystem" arguably draws from the 1948 Genocide Convention, more specifically the provision on inflicting conditions of life calculated to bring about a group's destruction. See Convention on the Prevention and Punishment of the Crime of Genocide, opened for signature 9 December 1948, 78 UNTS 277, entered into force 12 January 1951, Article 2(c).

[167] Falk 1973, Appendix I, p. 300, Article II(a).

[168] Ibid., p. 300, Article II.

[169] Ibid., p. 301, Article XVII.

way IHL and ICL approaches to 'environmental destruction' have been systematically restricted around articulating a single, all-encompassing prohibition around "damage" to the "natural environment".[170]

At its core, Falk's Ecocide Convention reflects concerns particularly salient in the 1970s over conducts posing 'planetary'-scale threats. As Hannah Arendt warned in 1951, 'humanity' had come to "master [nature] to such an extent that the destruction of all organic life on earth with man-made instruments" had "become conceivable and technically possible."[171] Yet, not all of 'humanity' contributed to the arms race that made it possible for weapons of mass destruction to see the light of day.[172] Only a minority of subjects—namely, few States and their constitutionally responsible rulers or military commanders—wield direct decision-making power to develop and command the use of weapons that could annihilate a significant part, if not all, human beings and more-than-human bodies in the process.[173]

2.3.2.2 The Epistemic Turn of 'Ecocidal Warfare'

Compared to the normative basis of contemporary 'ecocide' proposals and discourse, Falk did not conceptualise an international crime of 'ecocide' as an abstract attack onto 'nature' (as external) but as a wider military and political process designed to separate "the people from their land and its life-support characteristics".[174] What this means is that an adequate articulation of an international crime of 'ecocide' pre-emptively requires understanding:

> the extent to which environmental warfare is linked to the overall tactics of high-technology counterinsurgency warfare, and extends the indiscriminateness of warfare carried out against people to the land itself. Just as counterinsurgency warfare tends towards genocide with respect to the people, so it tends toward ecocide with respect to the environment.[175]

Put differently, weapons and tactics of 'environmental warfare' in Indochina pertained to a wider military process—one that is not restricted to weaponry, but extends to policies systematically designed to render the countryside unfit for civilian habitation. With respect to the Vietnam War, Noam Chomsky considered the massive

---

170 Section 2.3.3 specifically delves into the 'problem' with the 'natural environment'.

171 Full quote: "But it is not only the, as it were, human aspect of nature that has become questionable to us. *Ever since man learned to master it to such an extent that the destruction of all organic life on earth with man-made instruments has become conceivable and technically possible, he has been alienated from nature.* Ever since a deeper knowledge of natural processes instilled serious doubts about the existence of natural laws at all, nature itself has assumed a sinister aspect. How should one be able to deduce laws and rights from a universe which apparently knows neither the one nor the other category?" Emphasis added. Arendt 1958, p. 298.

172 Also see International Court of Justice (ICJ), Dissenting Opinion of Judge Weeramantry, *Legality of the Threat or Use of Nuclear Weapons*, Advisory Opinion, 8 July 1996, ICJ Reports 1996, p. 226.

173 Also see Rome Statute, above n 4, Article 28 on command and superior responsibility.

174 Falk 1973, p. 288.

175 Ibid.

destruction of rural ecosystems was no incidental byproduct but a calculated military strategy designed to displace populations and restructure the region's political economy to sustain post-war dependency on U.S.-dominated markets.[176]

What this process reveals, is what I refer to as 'ecocidal warfare'—a formative condition that not only gave rise to the invention of 'ecocide', but also indicates where and how that concept ought to be grounded. Where 'ecocidal warfare' takes an epistemic turn, it becomes clear how doctrinal narratives on 'environmental destruction' and 'ecocide' under IHL and ICL have increasingly deviated from the structure and historical context of Falk's original proposal. Although the Ecocide Convention has not been entirely ignored, references to it are typically relegated to footnotes or cursory summaries, while legal and doctrinal developments have instead privileged the language of Protocol I and the ENMOD Convention.[177] Yet both instruments arguably miss the core of Falk's incipient doctrinal articulation of an international crime of 'ecocide' and, in some ways, actively undermine it.

Indeed, Falk's proposed Ecocide Convention was initially introduced before the U.S. Senate, which held a series of hearings to inform the drafting of a new international treaty coveted by the U.S.—one that would eventually unfold into the ENMOD Convention.[178] Although Falk did not explicitly accuse the U.S. of manipulating scientific and legal ambiguities, he clearly warned of the dangers posed by the absence of "explicit rules and principles of prohibition",[179] particularly as governments expanded "technological frontiers for weather and terrestrial manipulation far beyond the horizons of present anticipation."[180] These dangers included the risk of covert military environmental modifications disguised as peaceful, or conversely, the misinterpretation of natural phenomena as deliberate attacks.[181] To address this, Falk proposed the Ecocide Convention and a Draft Protocol on Environmental Warfare, grounded in an understanding of systemic behaviours and epistemic infrastructures behind 'ecocidal warfare'.[182] Protocol I and ENMOD, by contrast, largely set an opposing direction. Rather than politicise these practices or target the strategic use of ambiguity in 'environmental' modification techniques, the U.S. and Soviet Union pursued ENMOD, while Protocol I was negotiated and adopted under the assumption that a legal void in IHL existed, justifying distinct prohibitions of damage to the "natural environment" in IACs.

Seen in this light, the international community may have missed a crucial opportunity. Aiming for a multilateral treaty listing specific *acts*, akin to Falk's Ecocide

[176] Chomsky 1970.

[177] Ibid.

[178] Falk 1972.

[179] Ibid., p. 96.

[180] Ibid., p. 97.

[181] Original quote: Falk warned on geophysical warfare, including the danger that "the target society or region may not even know that it is being intentionally victimized by its adversary or it may suspect that it is a target when adverse natural phenomena are indeed accidents of nature." Ibid., p. 100.

[182] Falk 1973, Appendix II.

Convention, could have provided a clearer foundation to identify behaviours, as well as structural and epistemological dynamics, worthy of international concern and cooperation in accordance with "with the spirit and aims of the United Nations".[183] Negotiating a binding multilateral treaty analogous to the Ecocide Convention could have helped conceptualise 'ecocide' as a phenomenon and enact adequate legal responses accordingly—including, but not exclusively, through identifying and recognising certain 'environmentally destructive or disruptive' conducts that could warrant recognition as international crimes. Instead, tethered to the language and logic of Protocol I and ENMOD, legal doctrine has contorted itself around a single, vague provision that attempts to capture various forms of "damage to the natural environment" while exempting those caused by "normal activities of human societies".[184] In doing so, it not only bypasses Falk's account of ecocidal warfare but also overlooks a deeper conceptual flaw: the problematic category of the "natural environment" itself.

2.3.3 'Ecocide': The Problem with the 'Natural Environment'

As explored in Sect. 2.2, the doctrinal approaches under review tend to classify as 'anthropocentric' those provisions that condition criminal liability for "damage to the (natural) environment" on demonstrable harm to 'human interests' in the *actus reus* or *mens rea*, rather than recognising harm to the 'environment'—as external to 'humanity'—in and of itself. This doctrinal fallacy reinforces the premise that earthly materialities and relationalities factually operate across the 'humanity' and 'nature' divide, as dissociated ontologies with irreconcilable interests.[185] That ontological divide is compounded by the way the "natural environment" is construed in the examined doctrine. While positive law offers no formal definition of the term—perhaps due to concerns over its contestability—formal proceedings leading to relevant norms under study (including the preparatory work and commentaries to Protocol I, the ILC's Draft Code, and Article 8(2)(b)(iv)) nonetheless attempt to conceptualise what the "(natural) environment" is. Yet, these efforts often rest on questionable premises that are arguably incompatible with the substantive basis of 'ecocentrism' and, more generally, limit the prospects of any coherent articulation of an 'ecocentric' crime of 'ecocide'.

[183] Falk 1973, Appendix I, Preamble, p. 300: "The Contracting Parties acting on the belief that ecocide is a crime under international law, contrary to the spirit and aims of the United Nations, and condemned by peoples and governments of good will throughout the world (…)". Also see the UN Charter, above n 81.

[184] Tomuschat 1996, p. 26 para 45.

[185] Also see Lindgren 2023, p. 313. Also see Descola 2006; Sciences Po 2024; Viveiros de Castro 1998.

2.3.3.1 ENMOD's Legacy and the Epistemology of Mastery

The ENMOD Convention prohibits "destruction, damage, or injury to *any other State Party*" with "widespread, long-lasting, *or* severe effects" resulting from military or any other hostile use of "environmental modification techniques".[186] These techniques are defined as the manipulation of natural (planetary) processes, namely: "the dynamics, composition, or structure of the *Earth*, including its *biota*, *lithosphere*, *hydrosphere*, and *atmosphere*, or of *outer space*."[187] Originally aimed at regulating warfare and hostile conduct, the epistemic technoscientific architecture underlying the Cold War arms race from which ENMOD emerged have informed on IHL and ICL responses to 'environmental destruction' and 'environmental protection', leading up to contemporary 'ecocide' discourse. However, the underlying epistemology of mastery and hostile context that gave rise to ENMOD is reflected in its language. Indeed, its implied account of "natural processes" essentially demands that expert knowledge intervenes to demonstrate one party's conduct has contributed to the modification of such planetary scale processes, with a hostile or military motive against one of its State parties. Thus, the ENMOD Convention's framing leaves little room to acknowledge the lived, physical experience of 'ecocidal' warfare.

Notwithstanding, ENMOD's implied understanding of "natural processes" has been consistently referred to for conceptualising the "(natural) environment"—from Protocol I's 1987 Commentary to the IEP's proposed definition for an ICC crime of 'ecocide'—when it was never intended as a reference point.[188] The IEP even includes a positive definition of the "environment" to its 'ecocide' proposal, namely as "the *Earth*, its *biosphere*, *cryosphere*, *lithosphere*, *hydrosphere*, and *atmosphere*, as well as *outer space*."[189] This definition strongly resembles ENMOD's formulation, although the IEP does not refer to it explicitly.[190] Yet, considering how ENMOD's epistemic framework centres expertise and planetary mastery—thereby sidelining embodied,

[186] ENMOD, above n 59, Article I.

[187] Emphasis added. ENMOD, above n 59, Article II.

[188] ICRC 1987, paras 1448, 1451, 2127. ILC 1991, p. 107, paras 1–4. Also see ILC 1996, p. 111, para 29. NB: In the Draft Code's debates, the ILC chose to use "environment" and "natural environment" interchangeably rather than "human environment". See ILC 1995. If not referred to as a direct reference to inform a conceptualisation of the 'natural environment', it was relied on as a precedent to articulate thresholds of damage (widespread, severe, long-term—although long-term comes from Protocol I, not ENMOD, which uses long-lasting) with Higgins 2010. Stop Ecocide Foundation 2021, p. 8.

[189] Stop Ecocide Foundation 2021, pp. 5, 11. Emphasis added.

[190] Note that the IEP did not refer to ENMOD in its definition of the "environment". On the basis that criminal law requires clarity and specificity, the IEP's proposed this definition of the 'environment' in its definition of 'ecocide', arguing "the definition draws upon scientific recognition of the interactions that make up the 'environment'" inferred from a well-cited paper in Earth System Science. See Stop Ecocide Foundation 2021, p. 11. The cited paper does indeed focus "largely on the surface Earth System, that is, the interacting physical, chemical and biological processes among the atmosphere, cryosphere, land, ocean and lithosphere". See Steffen et al. 2020, cited in Stop Ecocide Foundation 2021, p. 11, fn 12. Yet, I find it surprising that the IEP does not expressly admit that its definition of the 'environment' was visibly informed by the one embedded in ENMOD's definition of "the dynamics, composition, or structure of the earth" as "including its

lived experience of 'ecocidal warfare'—reliance on its implied definition of "natural processes" is inadequate to inform an articulation of a crime of 'ecocide' insofar as it is ingrained in a vision where such processes, implied as *oikos*, represent an object of epistemic and planetary domination.

2.3.3.2 The 'Natural Environment' as Property

Other doctrinal sources, such as the 1987 Commentary on Protocol I and the ILC's Draft Code negotiations similarly describe the "natural environment" as a "permanent or transient equilibrium (...) always relatively fragile",[191] to be preserved as "common property" for "everyone's use'.[192] Yet any entity reduced to the status of another's "property", even when framed as a common, cannot hold or exercise rights or responsibilities, thus claiming subjectivity. Indeed, as brilliantly articulated by Tim Lindgren, "from sovereignty and property to development and progress, the normative groundings of international law are (...) situated in a view of the world" where earthly materialities and relationalities only come alive through extraction and domination.[193]

Thus, when reduced to one's—or everyone's—'property', whatever realm is abstracted under the 'natural environment' can only be represented through the legal and political perspective of a subject, or a collectivity of subjects.[194] Any protection it receives remains limited to subjects' 'totalitarian' enjoyment of and exercise of property rights—that is, it may be acquired, exchanged, destroyed, manipulated, modified, or exterminated, so long as such actions are not prohibited by law.[195] Consequently, signifying *oikos* through the 'natural environment' effectively reduces it to 'property' in international law, thereby foreclosing any possibility of recognising the subjectivity of more-than-human earthly materialities and relationalities it encompasses.

Conceptually, this means that 'ecocentrism' cannot be grounded in a conception of *oikos* that is discursively confined to the "(natural) environment" as it is implied in the doctrine under review—where it is explicitly or implicitly relegated to the realm

---

biota, lithosphere, hydrosphere and atmosphere, or of outer space" embedded in its definition of environmental modification techniques—e.g., "outer space" appears under ENMOD, but not in the paper the IEP refers to. Also see ENMOD, above n 59.

191 ICRC 1987, para 1451.

192 Ibid., para 1462. This understanding specifically aligns with that underlying the ILC's Draft Code Commentary on Article 26, namely that the "safeguarding and preservation of the human environment" is of fundamental interest to the international community, which is why the Draft Code should view "some particularly serious attacks against this fundamental interest of mankind" as important in order to incur international criminal responsibility for its perpetrators. See ILC 1991, p. 107, para 1.

193 Lindgren 2023, pp. 314–315.

194 For an alternative perspective, see Mattei and Monterossi 2023 for their analysis on the eco-legal subject of law as part of a post-anthropocentric legal system.

195 Lorite Escorihuela 2023.

of 'property', even if symbolically held in common by all of 'humanity'. This is not to say that a meaningful articulation of the idea of "common property" or "commons" is fundamentally incompatible with addressing 'ecocidal warfare' and planetary discontinuities, or even 'ecocentrism'.[196] In fact, mounting evidence suggests endless wealth accumulation and concentration, thus (severe) wealth inequalities, stand as a more specific and accurate correlate of planetary discontinuities, including climate change, than one that is assigned to generalised 'human' activity and blamed over 'humanity' as a species (*e.g.*, through the Anthropocene discourse).[197] However, the relational foundation of 'ecocentrism' depends on extending the recognition of intrinsic value to *oikos*, positioning it as a subject-at-the-centre. This requires signifiers of *oikos* that are intelligible as legal and normative subjects—a condition irreconcilable with being reduced to the status of another's 'property' as it is currently ontologically embedded in international law. Thus, the 'problem' is that reducing *oikos* to the "natural environment", as implied and understood in the doctrine under review—positioned as external to 'humanity' and governed by the logic of property regimes—cannot qualify as an 'ecocentric' signifier of *oikos*.

2.3.3.3 (Mis-)Understanding 'Ecocidal Warfare': The Influence of the 'Natural Environment' over the 'Ecocentrism'/'Anthropocentrism' Debate

Since the "natural environment" as conceptualised in the doctrine under study currently stands as an inadequate signifier of *oikos* considering 'ecocentrism's' underlying rationale, what if 'ecocentrism' was premised on *oikos* that held a different significance? Considering ENMOD's influence over the normative background that informs contemporary 'ecocide' proposals and scholarly discussions, acknowledging this conceptual tension becomes particularly instructive. In this spirit, what follows illustrates how one's ontological assumption about *oikos* or *anthropos* can influence the classification of a norm as either 'ecocentric' or 'anthropocentric'.

---

[196] This includes indications that "a small fraction of the global population in emerging and high-income countries is responsible for a disproportionate share of greenhouse gas emissions". See Chancel et al. 2024. This phenomenon could be, e.g., addressed through international cooperation towards globally binding mechanisms for a minimum tax on ultra-high-net-worth individual billionaires (e.g., billionaires roughly represent ±3000 out of over 8 billion individual human beings) equal to 2% of their wealth, which "would raise \$200–\$250 billion per year globally from about 3,000 taxpayers" while "extending the tax to centimillionaires would add \$100–\$140 billion". See Zucman 2024, p. 2. Adding to this more adequate cooperation to address corporate tax avoidance and setting a global minimum tax on "multinational companies, free of loopholes, would raise an additional \$250 billion per year". See EU Tax Observatory 2023, p. 7. To give a sense of the magnitude, estimates indicate that developing countries require approximately \$500 billion in additional annual public funding to effectively address climate change. See ibid. In short, trying to conceptualise and criminalise 'ecocide' without accounting for wealth inequalities' contribution to 'ecocidal' violence is a serious strategic mistake.

[197] Ibid.

First, if *oikos* signifies plural and situated ontologies of embodied earthly materialities and relationalities—instead of being relegated to the "natural environment" as a singular, all-encompassing ontology, *in fine* reduced to "property"—then ENMOD is clearly not 'ecocentric'. ENMOD's core prohibition is narrowly limited to the military or hostile use of "environmental modification techniques" causing "destruction, damage or injury" to its States Parties, with such effects needing to be "widespread, long-lasting or severe".[198] This indicates destruction, damage, or injury needs to impact a State party, not embodied earthly materialities and relationalities in and of themselves. Quite the contrary, ENMOD even promotes inter-party cooperation for the 'peaceful' use of "environmental modification techniques". Put differently, ENMOD encourages intervention over, as well as disruption or destruction of so-called "natural processes", whose hostile or military use is otherwise prohibited, without any significant oversight or control mechanisms.[199]

However, even if ENMOD cannot qualify as 'ecocentric', this does not mean that ENMOD is necessarily 'anthropocentric'. Indeed, if 'anthropocentrism' is premised on a signifier of *anthropos* as 'humanity', itself defined primarily as a species by its shared distinction from an externalised 'nature',[200] and if norms that omit to recognise the intrinsic value of 'nature' are systematically categorised as 'anthropocentric', then ENMOD may be considered 'anthropocentric', insofar as it is not grounded in any acknowledgment of such intrinsic value in 'nature' or the "natural environment". However, if we shift that premise, where *anthropos* is no longer quintessentially envisioned as 'humanity' through a shared distinction from whatever 'nature' signifies, but is rather signified by an understanding of 'humanity' as all human beings on Earth owing each other mutual respect, in their collective and individual embodiments,[201] then the conclusion radically changes. Indeed, from this perspective, ENMOD cannot meaningfully qualify as anthropocentric, since its protection is limited to its State

---

[198] ENMOD, above n 59, Article I.

[199] Although not explicitly, ENMOD does not reject environmental modification techniques for peaceful purposes because it conventionally recognises the possibility to rely on such techniques, without much procedural specifications except that exchanges on scientific and technological information must take place to the fullest possible extent. Still, it remains vague in terms of commitment and ambiguous. Some argue it would have been better to not codify anything on peaceful purposes or, rather, be much more specific, such as imposing the publication of all research and peaceful activities on this, guarantee that activities for peaceful purposes are not pursued for hostile purposes, etc. Also see Fischer 1977, p. 834. See as well ENMOD according to which Parties "undertake to *facilitate*, and have the *right* to participate in, *the fullest possible exchange of scientific and technological information on the use of environmental modification techniques for peaceful purposes* (…)" Emphasis added. In this sense, ENMOD encourages scientific and technological exchange of information on the use of environmental modification techniques—otherwise prohibited—for peaceful purposes, while it invites States in a position to do so to engage in international cooperation in the "*preservation, improvement, and peaceful utili[s]ation of the environment* with due considerations for the needs of the developing areas of the world." Emphasis added. ENMOD, above n 59, Article III (2).

[200] Mégret 2023, pp. 38–39. This rationale is also referred to as 'distinctive equality'. See Lorite Escorihuela 2023, p. 249.

[201] Peters and Sparks 2024a, p. 4.

Parties. Moreover, it arguably aims to facilitate cooperation on 'environmental modification techniques' for ostensibly peaceful purposes between its State parties, but without procedural oversight nor with the interest of all human beings on Earth in mind—a serious limitation that warrants closer scrutiny given Falk's safeguards.[202]

2.4 Conclusion

Asking whether 'we' can conceptualise an 'ecocentric' crime of 'ecocide' is a complex question that has hitherto been answered in an arguably misleading way. Considering how 'environmental destruction' is shaped by "structural violence of economic coercion, resource extraction, global wealth distribution, and enforced impoverishment",[203] and the epistemic groundings of 'ecocidal warfare', answering this question requires resituating 'we', '*oikos*', '*anthropos*', 'subjectivity', and, perhaps, the idea of 'international crime' itself, as historically contingent, epistemically determined, and materially situated ontologies, which cannot unfold into an absolute answer. Conversely, doctrinal quests as to whether an international crime of 'ecocide' should be 'ecocentric' or 'anthropocentric' obscure more than they reveal. A careful examination of these doctrinal developments demonstrates that a lack of historical and ontological depth has drained much of the original spirit that initially sparked the concept of 'ecocide'.

To conceptualise a crime of 'ecocide' capable of addressing the structural and epistemic violence at hand, one must first resist reducing the stakes underlying its recognition as an international crime to an illusory conceptual binary between 'anthropocentrism' and 'ecocentrism'. This dichotomy entrenches a naturalist legacy that reifies an ontological representation of earthly materialities and relationalities as strictly divided between 'humanity' against the 'natural environment'—the former agentive, subjective, and sovereign, positioned as the sole producer of knowledge and steward of earthly materialities; the latter encompassing all realms relegated to passive, inert matter, legally relegated to the status of 'property' for epistemic and extractive purposes.

In this naturalist 'logic', 'humanity' is not understood as all human beings on Earth—members of the 'human species'—in their individual and collective embodiments as inadvertently presupposed in doctrinal critiques and articulations of 'anthropocentrism' under review, but rather as a juridically constructed category: abstracted, disembodied, and historically aligned with endeavours of planetary mastery. Embedded in such a framework, even well-intended legal endeavours to introduce 'ecocide' as a standalone ICC crime—shaped by existing prohibitions revolving around "damage to the (natural) environment" and conceptually informed by an assumption of 'anthropocentrism' and 'ecocentrism' as conceptual binaries—risk reinforcing this ontological division that naturalises and thereby

[202] Also see Falk 1972.

[203] Gonzalez 2024, p. 512.

legitimises 'ecocidal' violence as collateral to 'human nature'—as implied by the Anthropocene discourse and critiques of 'anthropocentrism'. Such premises reduce 'ecocidal violence' to a prophetical battle between a homogenised 'humanity' as a species against an undifferentiated externalised 'nature', thereby encompassing all more-than-human realms and universalising historically contingent ontologies. This obscures the fact that terms such as 'humanity' and 'nature'—as signifiers of *anthropos* and *oikos* respectively—are themselves historically and ontologically situated—and not immediately accurate, let alone neutral, depictions of pre-existing earthly materialities and relationalities. In turn, this naturalises the idea that *anthropos* can only be signified by a fallacious naturalist representation of the 'human' species as one doomed to drive planetary destruction due to an innate thirst for planetary domination.

As Richard Falk already conveyed in 1973, 'ecocide' is not an abstract attack against 'nature' (as external to 'humanity') but a wider military and political process designed to separate "the people from their land and its life-support characteristics."[204] Yet, as the contemporary campaign to criminalise 'ecocide' has evolved—narrowly revolving around "damage to the natural environment"—much of the concept's early political and conceptual vitality has been diluted. Its original focus on the epistemic and material violence of 'ecological warfare' in Indochina has been depoliticised and dehistoricised, absorbed into the very ontological assumptions that enabled such violence in the first place—one that persists through judicial denial of victims' claims for recognition and reparation of the transgenerational harm caused by 'ecocidal warfare' against their body, people, and land. This metaphysical strive for "*global* or even *planetary* scales"[205] domination clashes with what Lindgren identifies as "the ecological uncertainties of the present" that "quite physically, demand that we attend to the irreducibility of the earthly web of life and soil beneath our feet."[206]

Thus, finding adequate *responses*—extra-emphasis on the plural—to the scope and complexities of 'ecocidal violence' demands more grounded and specific considerations: of what it entails, of its root causes, and of specific courses of conducts and actors that most significantly contribute to planetary socio-ecological ruptures. This may first require slowing down to adequately identify phenomena—*e.g.*, from warfare to extreme wealth inequalities[207]—that underpin 'ecocidal violence' historically, and how such violence unfolds in the 21st century and for the foreseeable future. This includes identifying conducts as well as epistemes and structures schemes that drive conducts warranting criminalisation, as international crimes and beyond. One thing is surer: informing a definition of an international crime of 'ecocide' that uncritically blames *anthropos* in the sense of 'humanity' as all 'human beings' on Earth, extending the doctrine of human rights, for 'ecocidal violence' is a strategic

[204] Falk 1973, p. 288.

[205] Matthews 2019, p. 670, cited in Lindgren 2023, p. 313. Emphasis in the original.

[206] Lindgren 2023, p. 313.

[207] See above n 196.

mistake.[208] Should an international crime of 'ecocide' remain on the table of considered solutions—and it should—to address the sum of aforementioned considerations that hint at 'ecocidal violence', it would be preferable for States to negotiate a Convention on an International Crime of Ecocide, as a binding, multilateral treaty, prior to any precipitated amendment to the Rome Statute on the basis of definitions that in fact betray the conceptual and doctrinal origins of 'ecocide'. Falk's proposed Ecocide Convention in this regard stands out as a solid benchmark and, in any event, requires far more sustained and careful consideration than it has been afforded thus far.

Acknowledgements Many thanks to Dr. Christophe Paulussen, Dr. Laura Burger, Dr. Stavros Pantazopoulos, and Merle Kooijman, for trusting me and valuing my contribution to this œuvre, as well as for their insightful feedback and relentless support. I would like to thank Mrs. Nwamaka Okany and Dr. Carola Westermeier for supervising my BSc thesis, which embodies my first academic piece on the issue of 'ecocide'. I would also like to express my gratitude to Professor Evelyne Lagrange for her supervision, guidance, and solicitude during my studies at Université Paris 1 Panthéon-Sorbonne, which I pursued in parallel to finalising this chapter. My gratitude extends to my high-school history teacher, Mr. Aurélien Chapolard who, in addition to being a strong source of support, introduced me to key conceptual, geopolitical, and historical insights upon which this chapter is grounded. I address my most sincere regards and gratefulness to Professor Kevin Jon Heller for his precious mentorship and lessons on intergenerational friendship. Thanks to the many scholars and artistic figures whose work have inspired this chapter, with a special acknowledgement to Dr. Tim Lindgren, Professor Richard A. Falk, Professor Anna Grear, Professor Frédéric Mégret, Professor Jason W. Moore, Professor Philippe Descola and Professor Anne Peters. Last but not least, none of this work would have been possible without fiscal policies that sustain public commons, including academic institutions and access to higher education. Special thanks to my friends and to my grandmother, Michelle, for everything.

References

Articles, Books and Other Documents

Allen MR et al. (2018) Framing and Context. In: Mason-Delmotte V et al. (eds) Global Warming of 1.5°C: An IPCC Special Report on the impacts of global warming of 1.5°C above pre-industrial levels and related global greenhouse gas emission pathways, in the context of strengthening the global response to the threat of climate change, sustainable development, and efforts to eradicate poverty. https://www.ipcc.ch/site/assets/uploads/sites/2/2022/06/SR15_Full_Report_HR.pdf. Accessed 23 June 2025

Ambos K (2021) Protecting the Environment through International Criminal Law. https://www.ejiltalk.org/protecting-the-environment-through-international-criminal-law/. Accessed 23 June 2025

Aparac J (2021) A Missed Opportunity for Accountability? Corporate Responsibility and the Draft Definition of Ecocide. https://voelkerrechtsblog.org/a-missed-opportunity-for-accountability/. Accessed 23 June 2025

Arendt H (1958) The Origins of Totalitarianism. The World Publishing Company, Cleveland/New York

[208] Also see Mégret 2023. Peters and Sparks 2024b.

Bertram D (2024) Should Ecocide be an International Crime? It's Time for States to Decide. https://www.ejiltalk.org/should-ecocide-be-an-international-crime-its-time-for-states-to-decide/. Accessed 23 June 2025

Burdon P, Alexander S (2023) Anthropocentrism and Neoliberal Rationality. In: Chapaux V, Mégret F, Natarajan U (eds) The Routledge Handbook of International Law and Anthropocentrism. Routledge, New York, pp 215–230

Chancel L, Bothe P, Voituriez T (2024) The potential of wealth taxation to address the triple climate inequality crisis. Nature Climate Change. https://doi.org/10.1038/S41558-023-01891-2

Chapaux V (2023) Non-Human Animals as Epistemic Subjects of International. In: Chapaux V, Mégret F, Natarajan U (eds) The Routledge Handbook of International Law and Anthropocentrism. Routledge, New York, pp 295–307

Chapaux V, Mégret F, Natarajan U (2023) The Routledge Handbook of Anthropocentrism and International Law. Routledge, New York

Chomsky N (1970) From After Pinkville. In: Weisberg B (ed) Ecocide in Indochina: Ecology Of War. Canfield Press, San Francisco, pp 126–140

Crook M, Short D, South N (2018) Ecocide, Genocide, Capitalism and Colonialism: Consequences for Indigenous Peoples and Glocal Ecosystems Environments. Theoretical Criminology 22(3):298–317

Crutzen PJ (2002) Geology of Mankind. Nature. https://doi.org/10.1038/415023a

Crutzen PJ, Steffen W (2003) How Long Have We Been in the Anthropocene Era? Climatic Change https://doi.org/10.1023/B:CLIM.0000004708.74871.62

De Castro EV (1998) Cosmological Deixis and Amerindian Perspectivism. Journal of the Royal Anthropological Institute 4(3):469–488.

Dècle-Classen (2022) Ecocide and the End of the Anthropocene: An Ecocentric Critique of the (Failed) Developments of an International Crime of Ecocide. https://www.internationalcrimesdatabase.org/upload/documents/20220831T115656-Ecocide%20and%20the%20End%20of%20the%20Anthropocene.pdf. Accessed 23 June 2025

Descola P (2006) Beyond Nature and Culture. Radcliffe-Brown Lecture in Social Anthropology. In: Proceedings of the British Academy: 2005 Lectures. Oxford University Press, Oxford, pp 137–155

Dörmann K (2003) War crimes under the Rome Statute of the International Criminal Court, with a special focus on the negotiations on the elements of crimes. Max Planck Yearbook of United Nations Law Online 7(1):341–407

Drumbl MA (1998) Waging War Against the World: The Need to Move from War Crimes to Environmental Crimes. Fordham International Law Journal 22(1), Article 3. https://ir.lawnet.fordham.edu/cgi/viewcontent.cgi?article=1587&context=ilj

Escorihuela AL (2023) Global Animal Law, Pain, and Death: An International Law for the Dominion. In: Chapaux V, Mégret F, Natarajan U (eds) The Routledge Handbook of International Law and Anthropocentrism. Routledge, New York, pp 231–260

Estève A (2020) Introduction à la théorie politique environnementale. Hachette, Paris

EU Tax Observatory (2023) Global Tax Evasion Report 2024. https://www.taxobservatory.eu//www-site/uploads/2023/10/global_tax_evasion_report_24.pdf. Accessed 10 November 2025

Falk RA (1972) Statement of Professor Richard A. Falk, Professor of International Law at Princeton University, before the Committee on Oceans and International Environment of the Committee on Foreign Relations. https://www.govinfo.gov/content/pkg/CHRG-92shrg82892/pdf/CHRG-92shrg82892.pdf. Accessed 23 June 2025

Falk RA (1973) Environmental Warfare and Ecocide—Facts, Appraisal, and Proposals. Bulletin of Peace Proposals 4(1):80–96

Fischer G (1977) La Convention sur l'interdiction d'utiliser des techniques de modification de L'environnement à des fins hostiles. Annuaire français de droit international 23:820–836

Gonzalez CG (2024) Racial Capitalism, Climate Change, and Ecocide. Wisconsin International Law Journal 41:479–517

Grear A (2015) Deconstructing Anthropos: A Critical Legal Reflection on 'Anthropocentric' Law and Anthropocene 'Humanity'. Law and critique 26:225–249

Heller KJ (2021) Skeptical Thoughts on the Proposed Crime of "Ecocide" (That Isn't). https://opiniojuris.org/2021/06/23/skeptical-thoughts-on-the-proposed-crime-of-ecocide-that-isnt/ Accessed 23 June 2025

Higgins P (2010) Eradicating ecocide: laws and governance to prevent the destruction of our planet. Shepheard-Walwyn, London

Higgins P (2012) Earth is our Business: Changing the Rules of the Game. Shepheard-Walwyn, London

Higgins P (2020) Dare to be Great: Unlock Your Power to Create a Better World. Flint, Gloucestershire

Higgins P, Short D, South N (2013) Protecting the planet: a proposal for a law of ecocide. Crime, Law and Social Change 59:251–266

Jenkin A (2022) The Case for an International Crime of Ecocide. New Zealand Journal of Environmental Law 26:221–243

Kooijman M (2023) From Anthropos to Oikos in International Criminal Law: A Critical Theoretical Exploration of Ecocide as an 'Ecocentric' Amendment to the Rome Statute. In: Jong DD, van der Wilt H (eds) Netherlands Yearbook of International Law. T.M.C Asser Press, The Hague, pp 101–131

Kopnina H, Washington H, Bron T, Piccolo JJ (2018) Anthropocentrism: More than Just a Misunderstood Problem. Journal of Agricultural and Environmental Ethics 31:109–127

Kortenkamp KV, Moore C (2001) Ecocentrism and anthropocentrism: Moral reasoning about ecological commons dilemmas. Journal of Environmental Psychology. https://doi.org/10.1006/jevp.2001.0205

Lawrence JC, Heller KJ (2007) The First Ecocentric Environmental War Crime: The Limits of Article 8(2)(b)(iv) of the Rome Statute. Georgetown International Environmental Law Review 20:61–96

Leopold A (2018) The Land Ethic Aldo Leopold. In: Gunn AS, Veslind PA (eds) Environmental Ethics For Engineers. CRC Press, Florida, pp 43–53

Lindgren T (2018) Ecocide, Genocide and the Disregard of Alternative Life-Systems. The International Journal of Human Rights 22(4):525–549.

Lindgren T (2023) Grounding Ecocide, Humanity, and International Law. In: Chapaux V, Mégret F, Natarajan U (eds) The Routledge Handbook of International Law and Anthropocentrism. Routledge, New York, pp 307–322

Loft L, Mann C, Hansjürgens B (2015) Challenges in ecosystem services governance: Multi-levels, multi-actors, multi-rationalities. Ecosystem Services 16:150–157

Lorite Escorihuela A (2023) Global Animal Law, Pain, and Death: An International Law for the Dominion. In: Chapeaux V, Mégret F, Natarajan U (eds) The Routledge Handbook of International Law and Anthropocentrism. Routledge, New York, pp 231–260

Lynas M, Houlton B, Perry S (2021) Greater than 99% Consensus on Human Caused Climate Change in the Peer-Reviewed Scientific Literature. Environmental Research Letters. https://doi.org/10.1088/1748-9326/ac2966

Martini EA (2012) Agent Orange: History, science, and the politics of uncertainty. University of Massachusetts Press, Massachusetts

Mattei U, Monterossi MW (2023) What Would a Post-Anthropocentric Legal System Look Like? In: Chapeaux V, Mégret F, Natarajan U (eds) The Routledge Handbook of International Law and Anthropocentrism. Routledge, New York, pp 263–278

Matthews D (2019) From Global to Anthropocenic Assemblages: Re-Thinking Territory, Authority and Rights in the New Climatic Regime. The Modern Law Review 82(4):665–691

Mégret F (2023) The Anthropocentrism of Human Rights. In: Chapaux V, Mégret F, Natarajan U (eds) The Routledge Handbook of International Law and Anthropocentrism. Routledge, New York, pp 35–60

Minkova LG (2021) The Fifth International Crime: Reflections on the Definition of "Ecocide". Journal of Genocide Research 1–22. https://doi.org/10.1080/14623528.2021.1964688

Minkova LG (2024) Ecocide, sustainable development and critical environmental law insights. Journal of International Criminal Justice 22(1):81–97

Moore JW (2017) The Capitalocene, Part I: on the nature and origins of our ecological crisis. The Journal of Peasant Studies 44:594–630

Mylius B (2018) Three types of anthropocentrism. Environmental Philosophy 15:159–194

Næss A, Sessions G (1986) The Basic Principles of Deep Ecology. https://trumpeter.athabascau.ca/index.php/trumpet/article/view/579. Accessed 23 June 2025

Palme O (1972) Statement by Prime Minister Olof Palme in the Plenary Meeting. https://olofpalme.arbark.se/wp-content/dokument/720606a_fn_miljo.pdf. Accessed 23 June 2025

Parrique T (2019) The Political Economy of Degrowth. Clermont-Ferrand: Doctoral dissertation, Université Clermont, Auvergne

Partelow S (2023) What is a framework? Understanding their purpose, value, development and use. Journal of Environmental Studies and Sciences 13(3):510–519

Peters A (2016) Beyond Human Rights, The Legal Status of the Individual in International Law. Cambridge University Press, Cambridge

Peters A, Sparks T (2024a) Introduction: The History and Theory of the Individual in International Law. In: Sparks T, Peters A (eds) The Individual in International Law: History and Theory. Oxford University Press, Oxford, pp 1–30

Peters A, Sparks T (2024b) Conclusions: Reconsidering the Individual in International Law. In: Sparks T, Peters A (eds) The Individual in International Law: History and Theory. Oxford University Press, Oxford, pp 387–418

Prost M (2023) 'One Vast Gasoline Station for Human Exploitation': Sovereignty as Anthropocentric Extraction. In: Chapaux V, Mégret F, Natarajan U (eds) The Routledge Handbook of International Law and Anthropocentrism. Routledge, New York, pp 13–34

Rolston H (1997) Nature for real: Is nature a social construct? In: Chappell TDJ (ed) The philosophy of the environment. Edinburgh University Press, Edinburgh, pp 38–64

Ruddiman WF (2003) The anthropogenic greenhouse era began thousands of years ago. Climatic Change 6(3):261–293

Rülke RJ, Nzau JM, Teucher M (2020) How ecocentrism and anthropocentrism influence human–environment relationships in a Kenyan biodiversity hotspot. Sustainability. https://doi.org/10.3390/su12198213

Schuck PH (1987) Agent Orange on trial: Mass toxic disasters in the courts. Harvard University Press, Cambridge, Massachusetts

Sciences Po (2024) Bruno Latour ou l'art d'assembler, 5 December 2024. https://www.youtube.com/watch?v=9I3vHM7NQmw

Steffen W, Grinevald J, Crutzen P, McNeill J (2011) The Anthropocene: conceptual and historical perspectives. Philosophical Transactions of the Royal Society A: Mathematical, Physical and Engineering Sciences. https://doi.org/10.1098/rsta.2010.0327

Steffen W, Richardson K, Rockström J. et al (2020) The emergence and evolution of Earth System Science. Nature Reviews Earth and Environment 1:54–63

Stop Ecocide Foundation (2021) Independent Expert Panel for the Legal Definition of Ecocide: Commentary and Core Text. https://www.stopecocide.earth/legal-definition. Accessed 23 June 2025

Stop Ecocide International (2023) Agreement reached! EU to criminalise severe environmental harms "comparable to ecocide". https://www.stopecocide.earth/breaking-news-2023/agreement-reached-eu-to-criminalise-severe-environmental-harms-comparable-to-ecocide. Accessed 23 June 2025

The New York Times (1970) … and a Plea to Ban 'Ecocide'. https://www.nytimes.com/sitemap/1970/02/26/#:~:text=...%20and%20a%20Plea%20to%20Ban%20%E2%80%98Ecocide%E2%80%99 Accessed 23 June 2025

Tomuschat C (1996) International Law Commission (ILC) Document on crimes against the environment. https://www.legal-tools.org/doc/17db65/pdf. Accessed 23 June 2025
Verwey WD (1971) Chemical Warfare in Vietnam: Legal or Illegal? Nederlands Tijdschrift voor Internationaal Recht 18(2):217–244
Verwey WD (1977) Riot Control Agents and Herbicides in War: Their humanitarian, toxicological, ecological, military, polemological, and legal aspects. Brill, Leiden
Voigt C (2021) "Ecocide" as an international crime: Personal reflections on options and choices. https://www.ejiltalk.org/ecocide-as-an-international-crime-personal-reflections-on-options-and-choices/. Accessed 23 June 2025
Waters CN et al. (2016) The Anthropocene is functionally and stratigraphically distinct from the Holocene. Science. https://doi.org/10.1126/science.aad2622
Weisberg B (1970a) Ecocide in Indochina: Ecology of War. Canfield Press, San Francisco
Weisberg B (1970b) Introduction: On Ecocide. In: Weisberg B (ed) Ecocide in Indochina: Ecology Of War. Canfield Press, San Francisco, pp 1–16
Weisberg B (1970c) Preface. In: Weisberg B (ed) Ecocide in Indochina: Ecology Of War. Canfield Press, San Francisco, pp v–vii
Zierler D (2011) The invention of ecocide: Agent Orange, Vietnam, and the scientists who changed the way we think about the environment. The University of Georgia Press, Georgia
Zohari D (1986) The origin and early spread of agriculture in the Old World. Developments in Agricultural and Managed Forest Ecology 16:3–20
Zucman G (2024) A blueprint for a coordinated minimum effective taxation standard for ultrahigh-net-worth individuals. https://www.taxobservatory.eu//www-site/uploads/2024/06/report-g20.pdf Accessed 23 June 2025

Treaties, Cases and Other Legal Sources

Alien Tort Statute, 28 USC § 1350 (1789)
Charter of the United Nations, opened for signature 26 June 1945, 1 UNTS XVI, entered into force 24 October 1945
Convention for the Protection of Cultural Property in the Event of Armed Conflict and its First Protocol, opened for signature 14 May 1954, 249 UNTS 215, entered into force 7 August 1956
Convention on the Prevention and Punishment of the Crime of Genocide, opened for signature 9 December 1948, 78 UNTS 277, entered into force 12 January 1951
Convention on the Prohibition of Military or Any Other Hostile Use of Environmental Modification Techniques, opened for signature 10 December 1976, 1108 UNTS 151, entered into force 5 October 1978
Cour d'Appel de Paris, *TRAN To Nga c. Dow Chemical & co.*, Pôle 4, Chambre 10, Arrêt du 22 Août 2024, N° RG 21/106/06 - N° Portalis 35L7-V-B7F-CD2CC, Décision déférée à la Cour : Jugement du 10 Mai 2021 - Tribunal Judiciaire d'Evry, RG n°14/04980
First Protocol to The Hague Convention for the Protection of Cultural Property in the Event of Armed Conflict (The Hague, 14 May 1954, entered into force 7 August 1956) 249 UNTS 358
Geneva Convention (IV) relative to the Protection of Civilian Persons in Time of War, opened for signature 12 August 1949, 75 UNTS 287, entered into force 21 October 1950
Geneva Convention I for the Amelioration of the Condition of the Wounded and Sick in Armed Forces in the Field (Geneva, 12 August 1949) 75 UNTS 31
ICRC (1987) Commentary on the Protocol Additional to the Geneva Conventions of 12 August 1949, and relating to the Protection of Victims of International Armed Conflicts (Protocol I), 8 June 1977 https://ihl-databases.icrc.org/en/ihl-treaties/api-19770. Accessed 23 June 2025
ILC (1991) Report of the Commission to the General Assembly on the work of its forty-third session, UN Doc. A/CN.4/SER.A/1991/Add.1(Part 2)

ILC (1995) Report of the Commission to the General Assembly on the work of its forty-seventh session, UN Doc. A/CN.4/SER.A/1995/Add.1(Part 1)
ILC (1996) Summary Record of the Meetings of the 48th Session, UN Doc. A/C.6/51/SR.48
International Commission on Stratigraphy (2024) Joint statement by the IUGS and ICS on the vote by the ICS Subcommission on Quaternary Stratigraphy. https://stratigraphy.org/news/152. Accessed 23 June 2025
International Court of Justice (2017a) Certain Activities Carried Out by Nicaragua in the Border Area (Costa Rica v. Nicaragua) Memorial of Costa Rica on Compensation on 3 April 2017. https://www.icj-cij.org/sites/default/files/case-related/150/150-20170403-WRI-01-00-EN.pdf. Accessed 24 June 2025
International Court of Justice (2017b) Certain Activities Carried Out by Nicaragua in the Border Area (Costa Rica v. Nicaragua) Counter-Memorial of Nicaragua on Compensation on 2 June 2017. https://www.icj-cij.org/sites/default/files/case-related/150/150-20170602-wri-01-00-en.pdf. Accessed 24 June 2025
International Court of Justice (2017c) Certain Activities Carried Out by Nicaragua in the Border Area (Costa Rica v. Nicaragua) Reply of Costa Rica on Compensation on 8 August 2017. https://www.icj-cij.org/sites/default/files/case-related/150/150-20170808-wri-01-00-en.pdf. Accessed 24 June 2025
International Court of Justice (2017d) Certain Activities Carried Out by Nicaragua in the Border Area (Costa Rica v. Nicaragua) Rejoinder of Nicaragua on Compensation on 29 August 2017. https://www.icj-cij.org/sites/default/files/case-related/150/150-20170829-wri-01-00-en.pdf. Accessed 24 June 2025
International Court of Justice, *Certain Activities Carried Out by Nicaragua in the Border Area* (*Costa Rica v. Nicaragua*), Compensation, Judgment, 2 February 2018, ICJ Reports 2018
International Court of Justice, *Legality of the Threat or Use of Nuclear Weapons*, Advisory Opinion, Dissenting Opinion of Judge Weeramantry, 8 July 1996, ICJ Reports 1966
International Criminal Court, Elements of Crimes, reproduced in the Official Records of the Assembly of the States Parties to the Rome Statute of the International Criminal Court, First Session, New York, 3–10 September 2002, ICC-ASP/1/3 and Corr.1, part II.B
International Criminal Court, Rules of Procedure and Evidence, reproduced in the Official Records of the Assembly of States Parties to the Rome Statute of the International Criminal Court, First Session, New York, 3–10 September 2002, ICC-ASP/1/3 and Corr.1, part. II.A
Protocol Additional to the Geneva Conventions of 12 August 1949, and relating to the Protection of Victims of International Armed Conflicts, opened for signature 8 June 1977, 1125 UNTS 3, entered into force 7 December 1978
Protocol for the Prohibition of the Use of Asphyxiating, Poisonous or Other Gases, and of Bacteriological Methods of Warfare, opened for signature 17 June 1925, 94 LNTS 65, entered into force 8 February 1928
Rome Statute of the International Criminal Court, opened for signature 17 July 1998, 2187 UNTS 3, entered into force 1 July 2002
Supreme Court of Canada, *Nevsun Resources Ltd v Araya*, Judgment, 28 February 2020, 2020 SCC 5
UN (1993) Yearbook of the International Law Commission 1993, Volume II, Part One: Documents of the forty-fifth session, UN Doc. A/CN.4/SER.A/1993/Add.1 (Part 1)
UN General Assembly (1947a) Establishment of an International Law Commission, UN Doc. A/RES/174(II)
UN General Assembly (1947b) Formulation of the principles recognised in the Charter of the Nuremberg Tribunal and in the Judgment of the Tribunal, UN Doc. A/RES/177(II)
UN General Assembly (1969) Question of chemical and bacteriological (biological) weapons, UN Doc. A/RES/2603(XXIV)[A]
UN General Assembly (2012) The Future We Want, UN Doc. A/RES/66/288
UN General Assembly (2015) Transforming our world: 2030 Agenda for Sustainable Development, UN Doc. A/RES/70/1

UN General Assembly (2016) Follow-up and Review of the 2030 Agenda for Sustainable Development at the Global Level, UN Doc. A/RES/70/299

UN General Assembly (2022) The human right to a clean, healthy and sustainable environment, UN Doc. A/RES/76/300

UN General Assembly (2023) Twelfth Interactive Dialogue of the General Assembly on Harmony with Nature. http://files.harmonywithnatureun.org/uploads/upload1438.pdf. Accessed 23 June 2025

UNODA (1976) Report of the Working Group on the Prohibition of Military or Any Other Hostile Use of Environmental Modification Techniques to the plenary of the Conference of the Committee on Disarmament, UN Doc. A/31/27/CCD/518

United Nations Framework Convention on Climate Change, opened for signature 9 May 1992, 1771 UNTS 107, entered into force 21 March 1994

United States Court of Appeals for the Second District, United States, *Vietnam Association for Victims of Agent Orange v. Dow Chemical Co.* 22 February 2008, 05-1953-cv https://www.refworld.org/jurisprudence/caselaw/usaca2/2008/en/55023 Accessed 23 June 2025

United States District Court Eastern District of New York, *Re-Amended Memorandum, Order and Judgment "Agent Orange" product liability litigation,* MDL no. 381, the Vietnam Association for Victims of Agent Orange, 10 March 2005, 04-cv-400 https://www.asser.nl/upload/documents/DomCLIC/Docs/NLP/US/AgentOrange_DistrictJudgement_10-3-2005.pdf Accessed 23 June 2025

Clémentine Dècle-Classen is an aspiring legal scholar, finalising her graduate studies in International Law and International Organisations at Université Paris 1 Panthéon-Sorbonne. Her Master's thesis focuses on the representations of future generations in international law. She holds an interdisciplinary BSc (Honours) in Politics, Psychology, Law, and Economics (PPLE) from the University of Amsterdam.

Part II
How?

Chapter 3
Protecting the Environment through International Criminal Law—A Legal Analysis of Available Options

Ana Stella Ebbersmeyer

Contents

Abstract This chapter provides a comprehensive and systematic account of the different ways in which international criminal law (ICL) can be operationalised to protect the environment. To do so, the existing legal framework is examined, resulting in the finding that ICL does not protect the environment sufficiently. The chapter divides the different possibilities of protecting the environment through ICL into an 'anthropocentric' (human-focused) and 'ecocentric' (environment-focused) approach. On the one hand, it finds that the anthropocentric approach, namely protecting the environment under the already existing provisions of the Rome Statute, does not offer suitable environmental protection. On the other hand, the ecocentric approach stands better chances in this regard, especially in the context of a possible crime of ecocide and its inclusion into the Rome Statute.

Keywords International criminal law · Environment · Ecocide · Anthropocentrism · Ecocentrism · Rome Statute

A. S. Ebbersmeyer (✉)
Faculty of Law, University of Copenhagen, Copenhagen, Denmark
e-mail: stella.ebbersmeyer@jur.ku.dk

L. Burgers et al. (eds.), *Ecocide: Criminalising Serious Harm against the Environment*, International Criminal Justice Series 38, https://doi.org/10.1007/978-94-6265-715-1_3

3.1 Introduction

The past decades have shown environmental destruction happening at rapid speed with no end in sight.[1] Anthropogenic environmental destruction has, *inter alia*, led to a decrease in biodiversity, a high increase in deforestation and greenhouse gas (GHG) emissions, and contributed to climate change.[2] Moreover, examining the occurring environmental destruction shows that it is not solely states who are responsible for it; in fact, also individuals and corporations are contributing largely to environmental destruction.[3] Some of the damage is inflicted during times of armed conflict, with environmental destruction occurring either as a by-product of warfare or as a distinct means of warfare.[4] In addition, humans are also harming the environment during peacetime.[5] Cases of this are manifold and are happening worldwide, with some examples including oil spills, deforestation and fracking.[6]

One such example is the case of the destruction of the Amazon rainforest in Brazil. The Amazon is the biggest rainforest in the world and around 60% of it is located in Brazil.[7] It is a crucial element in combatting environmental problems such as global warming and is therefore sometimes being referred to as the 'lungs of the world'.[8] Nonetheless, in the past years, anthropogenic environmental destruction has harmed the Amazon to an unprecedented extent: in the first eight months of 2019 alone, 125,000 hectares of the Amazon had been cleared and then burned, destroying ecosystems, communities' livelihoods, and contributing to land degradation and climate change.[9]

Brazil's former president, Jair Bolsonaro, has been one of the individuals contributing to the Amazon's destruction, *inter alia*, by rolling back the environmental policies that protect the rainforest: since the start of his presidency, he has reduced approximately 30% of the environmental agency's budget to prevent fires,[10] has called on people to initiate mining in a natural reserve,[11] and has fired the director of the National Space Research Institute (INPE) after it had published data that revealed how much rainforest had been cleared.[12] Moreover, other actors such as state officials, logging companies and military and security forces might also carry

---

[1] United Nations Environment Programme (UNEP) 2020; Intergovernmental Panel on Climate Change (IPCC) 2019; UN Sustainable Development Blog 2016.

[2] United Nations Statistics Division 2016, https://unstats.un.org/unsd/environment/interlinks.htm. Accessed 20 Oct 2020.

[3] Mehta and Merz 2015, p. 7.

[4] Gillett 2010.

[5] Killean 2020, p. 324.

[6] Mehta and Merz 2015, pp. 5–6.

[7] Fonseca and Spring 2019.

[8] Ibid.

[9] Mendes 2019.

[10] Jordan and Sandler Clarke 2019.

[11] Fonseca and Spring 2019.

[12] Walker 2019.

some of the responsibility. However, no one has been held responsible for these actions.

This chapter deals with situations such as this one, namely with the most serious offenses against the environment. These offenses presuppose a high level of harm, which is often transboundary in nature and therefore of international concern.[13] Due to the pressing nature of this topic and the immediate threat that accompanies environmental destruction such as this one, several steps have been taken by the international community to protect the environment. In this regard, next to domestic legislative and jurisprudential efforts,[14] at the international level, states have adopted multiple international environmental agreements.[15] Nonetheless, despite this attempt to adequately regulate environmental destruction at the global level, the environment is being further damaged and cases, such as the destruction of the Amazon rainforest, are not infrequent.[16] In this context, the potential of international criminal law (ICL) arises since this legal discipline can help bring to justice the individuals behind such serious cases of environmental destruction.[17]

Indeed, there seems to be a general consensus in the literature that the environment should be protected through ICL.[18] However, there is some divergence of opinions when it comes to how best to protect the environment through ICL. In general, the literature can be divided into two strands: first, those authors that believe that in order to protect the environment, no additional legislation needs to be introduced, such as a new provision in the Rome Statute.[19] It is their opinion that the environment can and should best be protected by making use of the already existing provisions in the Rome Statute and the infrastructure of the International Criminal Court (ICC).[20] This strand of literature takes a more anthropocentric view, meaning that the crime of environmental destruction is focused on humans and human harm, instead of

---

[13] Crasson 2017, p. 45.

[14] An example of domestic environmental efforts can be seen in the case: Irish Supreme Court, *Friends of the Irish Environment CLG v the Government of Ireland, Ireland and the Attorney General*, Appeal No: 205/2019, 31 July 2020, in which the national law Irish Climate Action and Low Carbon Development Act (2015) No 46 was invoked.

[15] Some examples include the Paris Agreement, opened for signature 12 December 2015, 55 ILM 740, entered into force 4 November 2016 (Paris Agreement). Convention on International Trade in Endangered Species of Wild Fauna and Flora, opened for signature 3 March 1976, 993 UNTS 243, entered into force 1 July 1975 (CITES). Convention on Biological Diversity, opened for signature 5 June 1992, 1760 UNTS 70, entered into force 29 December 1993 (CBD). Vienna Convention for the Protection of the Ozone Layer, opened for signature 22 March 1985, 1513 UNTS 293, entered into force 22 September 1988 (Ozone Convention).

[16] UN Sustainable Development Blog 2016.

[17] Gillett 2010; Pereira 2015; Crasson 2017.

[18] Mégret 2011, 2013; Pereira 2015; Crasson 2017; Gillett 2010; Greene 2019; Peterson 2009.

[19] Rome Statute of the International Criminal Court, opened for signature 17 July 1998, 2187 UNTS 3, entered into force 1 July 2002 (Rome Statute).

[20] In this context, Durney and Prosperi and Terrosi can be mentioned who argue that environmental crimes could fall under the Rome Statute provision of crimes against humanity, see Durney 2018; Prosperi and Terrosi 2017. Moreover, Weinstein can be cited, who holds that environmental attacks could be prosecuted as acts of genocide or as crimes against humanity, see Weinstein 2005.

on environmental harm *per se*. The second strand that can be observed is rather ecocentric in nature, meaning that its proponents focus more on environmental harm *per se*, which is not necessarily connected to humans. The authors of this strand either argue that to properly protect the environment through ICL, a separate route from the Rome Statute and the ICC should be chosen due to the limitations that this forum entails,[21] or that the existing infrastructure of the ICC should be utilised, but only under the circumstances that the Rome Statute is amended to include a specific environmental crime.[22]

Zooming further into this latter aspect: one way of protecting the environment through ICL has received special attention in the literature over the past decade, namely the crime of ecocide. While the definition of this crime warrants a discussion on its own (see Sect. 3.3.2.2), generally speaking, ecocide describes the destruction of the environment. Scholars argue that a crime of ecocide should be included into the Rome Statute as the fifth international crime.[23] While agreeing with the importance of having a crime of ecocide, other authors, however, believe that the Rome Statute is not the right avenue for such a crime and that it be dealt with by a separate tribunal.[24] Besides this, other scholars again hold a rather reserved view regarding the crime of ecocide,[25] believing that making ecocide an international crime is a utopian endeavour,[26] "hopeless and unrealistic",[27] or at least that "the time is not yet ripe for such a change to occur".[28]

Although the literature has established that the environment should be protected through ICL and that the current regime does not do so to an appropriate extent, there is no agreement on how this protection should be achieved exactly. This chapter will provide an analysis of the different possibilities for the protection of the environment through ICL, assessing which approach is most suited for protecting the environment. To make this determination, this chapter relies on the concept of ecocentrism, which emphasises the intrinsic value of the environment. As noted above, ecocentrism essentially shifts the focus from anthropocentric, i.e. human-centred, approaches to ones that prioritise the protection of the environment *per se*.[29] By employing the concept of ecocentrism, this chapter will evaluate current ICL and will critically analyse how an ecocentric perspective can be integrated therein to create a legal framework that not only punishes environmental crimes but also fosters a legal culture of environmental protection and respect for nature's intrinsic value. Hence,

---

[21] Patel 2016.

[22] Kemp 2013; Rauxloh 2011; Lindgren 2017; McLaughlin 2000.

[23] Mehta and Merz 2015; Mwanza 2018; Higgins 2012a; Gauger et al. 2012; Higgins et al. 2013. The report by Gauger and others does not provide any page numbers; I have therefore numbered them according to the pdf-file numbering.

[24] Greene 2019.

[25] Mistura 2018; Greene 2019; Pereira 2020, p. 223; Mégret 2011.

[26] Mégret 2011, p. 254.

[27] Greene 2019, p. 48.

[28] Mistura 2018, p. 226.

[29] De Lucia 2015, p. 95; Kooijman 2023.

for the purposes of this chapter, a legal approach is seen as most suited to protect the environment if it is ecocentric in nature.

3.2 Legal Framework

3.2.1 History and Failed Attempts

Taking a closer look at the history of environmental crimes, it becomes clear that utilising the international criminal legal system in order to protect the environment is not a new idea, but in fact a subject of constant legal and academic debate from the 1970s onwards until today.

Already in the 1970s, the protection of the environment through ICL was a subject of debate in the international community. In response to the enormous environmental damage which had occurred in South-Vietnam due to the use of the chemical defoliant Agent Orange by the United States during the Vietnam War, Arthur W. Galston firstly introduced the term 'ecocide' in 1970.[30] Following this, Richard Falk drafted the International Convention on the Crime of Ecocide, which, however, never entered into force.[31] Moreover, in the 1980s, the International Law Commission (ILC) considered including a crime of "[w]illful and severe damage to the environment" in the Draft Code of Crimes against the Peace and Security of Mankind, but eventually dropped this version and instead included a narrower prohibition of environmental damage during wartime, which can now be found in Article 8 Rome Statute.[32]

Efforts to protect the environment through I(C)L were also considered throughout the 1990s, as for example in 1995, when the UN urged states to "consider acknowledging the most serious forms of environmental crimes in an international convention",[33] or in 1996, when at the 5th Session of the UN Commission on Crime Prevention and Criminal Justice, the importance of agreeing on international conventions in the area of environmental criminal justice was stressed.[34] Moreover, in 1970, the ILC proposed to include "a serious breach of an international obligation of essential importance for the safeguarding and preservation of the human environment such as those prohibiting massive pollution of the atmosphere or of the seas" as an international crime in the Draft Articles on State Responsibility.[35] Other initiatives by scholars and international organisations were taken throughout the 2000s and until today. In this regard, Polly Higgins' 'Stop Ecocide' campaign can be pointed out,[36]

[30] Crasson 2017, p. 39.

[31] Kemp 2013, p. 186.

[32] Crasson 2017, p. 39. This provision will be dealt with in more detail below.

[33] United Nations Economic and Social Council (ECOSOC) 1994, Annex, Recommendations Concerning the Role of Criminal Law in Protecting the Environment, para k. Mégret 2013, p. 50.

[34] Loibl and Reiterer 1996, p. 192.

[35] International Law Commission (ILC) 2001, p. 113, n 651; Rauxloh 2011, p. 446.

[36] Stop Ecocide Campaign, https://www.stopecocide.earth/. Accessed 24 June 2025.

as well as the initiatives taken by INTERPOL and the UN Environment Programme (UNEP) to stop environmental crimes.[37] However, as the following overview of ICL shows, these efforts are currently not reflected in this legal system.

3.2.2 *International Criminal Law*

3.2.2.1 Background

Contrary to other international regimes which have states as their main subject, the overarching function of ICL is to hold individuals criminally responsible who committed the most serious crimes of international concern.[38] Due to this nature, ICL mainly developed as a response to mass atrocities. This system thus interferes with the traditional concept of state sovereignty, including by holding individuals criminally liable who are usually protected by their domestic legal systems, such as heads of states, governments or high-ranking military officials.[39]

After its first steps following WWII in Nuremberg and Tokyo, the ICL regime took shape with the *ad hoc* international criminal tribunals for the former Yugoslavia (ICTY) and Rwanda (ICTR) in the 1990s, and further developed with the establishment of the Special Court for Sierra Leone (SCSL), the Extraordinary Chambers in the Courts of Cambodia (ECCC) and the Special Tribunal for Lebanon (STL). The establishment of the ICC marked a significant milestone in this evolution.[40] Since the ICC is the sole permanent international criminal court with potentially global jurisdiction, it has been heralded as "one of the most important developments in international criminal law"[41] and will constitute the basis for this chapter's analysis. The following section will provide information on the Court itself, as well as on the Rome Statute and its core crimes, to understand the framework within which environmental offenses could potentially be addressed.

3.2.2.2 Core Crimes

The ICC only has jurisdiction over "the most serious crimes of international concern",[42] the so-called 'core crimes'.

The first crime that can be found in the Rome Statute is genocide (Article 6). This crime "is a denial of the right of existence of entire human groups, as homicide is

[37] Mistura 2018, p. 198. United Nations Environment Programme (UNEP), https://www.unep.org/. Accessed 25 June 2025. INTERPOL 2020.

[38] Cryer et al. 2019, p. 3.

[39] Ibid.

[40] For an overview of the different courts and tribunals, see ibid., pp. 113–201.

[41] Ibid., p. 144.

[42] Rome Statute, above n 19, Article 1.

the denial of the right to live of individual human beings".[43] It has at its core the special intent requirement of "destroy[ing], in whole or in part, a national, ethnical, racial or religious group, as such",[44] which distinguishes it from other international crimes and underlines its seriousness.[45] An exhaustive list of underlying genocidal acts can be found in Article 6(2) Rome Statute. It has been argued that its prohibition has become a *jus cogens* norm, meaning a peremptory norm of general international law that holds the highest hierarchical position in international law,[46] and an *erga omnes* obligation.[47] Additionally, it is important to clarify that genocide does not necessarily have to be connected to an armed conflict, but, on the contrary, can occur during peacetime as well.

The second core crime under the Rome Statute is that of crimes against humanity (CAH) (Article 7). As stated by David Luban, "[c]rimes against humanity are universally odious because they injure something fundamental to being human in a way that municipal legal systems fail to address".[48] The Rome Statute lists several underlying acts, including e.g., murder (Article 7(1)(a)), extermination (Article 7(1)(b)) and persecution (Article 7(1)(h)). These crimes qualify as CAH when they are "committed as part of a widespread or systematic attack directed against any civilian population, with knowledge of the attack".[49] It is required that the conduct is part of a state or organisational policy and that there is a nexus between the acts of the accused and the attack.[50] Like genocide, CAH can occur both in times of war and peace. However, in contrast to the crime of genocide, CAH do not require specific intent.

The third crime that the ICC has jurisdiction over is that of war crimes (Article 8). Under the Rome Statute, a war crime is either a "[g]rave breach[] of the Geneva Conventions of 12 August 1949" (Article 8(2)(a)), or another serious violation of the laws and customs of armed conflict, "within the established framework of international law" (Article 8(2)(b)).[51] War crimes under the Rome Statute are thus connected to the field of international humanitarian law (IHL) (the laws and customs of armed conflict), in the sense that they criminalise a certain subset of IHL violations and through the Rome Statute give rise to individual criminal responsibility.[52] Contrary

[43] Ibid., p. 205.

[44] Rome Statute, above n 19, Article 6.

[45] Examples that can be cited include the 1994 genocide in Rwanda in which members of the Hutu ethnic majority murdered nearly 800,000 people, mostly of the Tutsi minority, and more recently the alleged genocide of the Rohingya in Myanmar. See International Court of Justice (ICJ) *Application of the Convention on the Prevention and Punishment of the Crime of Genocide (The Gambia v Myanmar)*, Request for the Indication of Provisional Measures, 23 January 2020, ICJ Rep 2020.

[46] Cassese 2004.

[47] ICJ, *Reservations to the Convention on the Prevention and Punishment of the Crime of Genocide*, Advisory Opinion, 28 May 1951, ICJ Rep 15, paras 15, 23. Cryer et al. 2019, p. 205.

[48] Luban 2004, p. 90.

[49] Rome Statute, above n 19, Article 7.

[50] Ibid, Article 7(2)(a).

[51] Ibid. Article 8.

[52] Cryer et al. 2019, p. 259.

to CAH, there is no requirement of "widespread or systematic",[53] meaning that, under specific circumstances, a single isolated act could constitute a war crime.[54] Nonetheless, certain requirements do need to be fulfilled to fall under this definition, such as the existence of an armed conflict, either of an international or non-international character, a nexus between the conduct and the armed conflict, and the specific roles of the perpetrator and victim.[55]

This provision describes the only core crime which makes reference to environmental protection, namely in Article 8(2)(b)(iv) Rome Statute, which prohibits:

> [i]ntentionally launching an attack in the knowledge that such attack will cause incidental loss of life or injury to civilians or damage to civilian objects or widespread, long-term and severe damage to the natural environment which would be clearly excessive in relation to the concrete and direct overall military advantage anticipated.[56]

From an anthropocentric viewpoint, the advantage of having such an environmental protection provision in the Rome Statute is, of course, the fact that it entails individual criminal responsibility.[57] Moreover, the fact that actual damage is not required for a violation, but that the likelihood of possible environmental damage suffices can be seen as another advantage of Article 8(2)(b)(iv).[58] However, there are also multiple drawbacks of this provision. Firstly, this provision allows for a defence arguing that the damage was not excessive in relation to the military advantage. Secondly, the provision presupposes a high *mens rea* threshold, meaning that criminal intent is required and that e.g. recklessness or knowledge would not suffice.[59] Thirdly, problems arise as to the three conditions of widespread, long-term and severe damage.[60] These conditions are cumulative and thus all have to be fulfilled to fall within the scope of this provision. This sets a high threshold of harm and can lead to confusion and inconsistencies since there is no guidance as to their interpretation.[61] Lastly, this provision only deals with international armed conflicts (IACs) and thus also does not address either environmental damage arising from non-international armed conflicts (NIACs) or during peacetime.[62] This highlights the shortcomings of this provision

[53] Although it should be noted that the Rome Statute states in Article 8(1) that "[t]he Court shall have jurisdiction in respect of war crimes in particular when committed as part of a plan or policy or as part of a large-scale commission of such crimes." See Rome Statute, above n 19, Article 8(1).

[54] Ibid.

[55] Ibid.

[56] Ibid., Article 8(2)(b)(iv).

[57] Gillett 2010, p. 333.

[58] Peterson 2009, p. 327.

[59] Ibid.

[60] For a more detailed discussion on these terms, see Sect. 3.2.3 of this chapter.

[61] Mistura 2018, p. 211. Although there is a general consensus in the literature that "widespread" refers to the geographical scope of the damage, "long-term", to its temporal dimension and "severe" to its intensity, there are no clear guidelines as to how many square kilometres need to be affected, how many months/years need to have passed and how severe the damage needs to be for these requirements to be fulfilled. The provision thus remains rather vague and unclear.

[62] For a discussion on the possible application of this provision to NIACS, see Gillett 2022, pp. 95–96.

in protecting the environment's intrinsic value. Not only is there hardly a situation which would fulfil all the requirements of Article 8(2)(b)(iv), but even if there was, the blind spot of environmental damage in NIACs and during peacetime would still not be covered. Since it can be argued that environmental damage during peacetime occurs more frequently and is often more severe than that arising during wartime,[63] this situation should arguably be included in the Rome Statute.

Lastly, the Rome Statute includes the crime of aggression (Article 8 *bis*). This crime diverges from the other crimes in the Rome Statute since it is connected to an 'act of aggression', meaning the unlawful use of force by one state against another.[64] It is committed by a political or military leader or a policymaker of a state, who participates, through planning, preparation, initiation or execution, in an act of aggression, which constitutes a manifest violation of the UN Charter.[65] Contrary to the other crimes of the Rome Statute, the crime of aggression is a leadership crime and hence can only be committed by persons in policy-making positions.[66] Controversies arose as to the definition of the crime, which led to a delay in the ICC's jurisdiction over it. Nonetheless, after the decision of a two-thirds majority of state parties to activate the ICC's jurisdiction in 2017, the Court, as of 17 July 2018, has jurisdiction over the crime.[67]

It is thus clear that while the establishment of the Rome Statute and the ICC has provided the international community with tools to prosecute individuals for the "most serious of crimes", namely genocide, CAH, war crimes and the crime of aggression, having examined these four crimes, they are not focused on environmental protection as such.[68] However, the drafting history of the Rome Statute and the crime of aggression has shown that there seem to be both tools and room for amendment to include situations which fall in the intersection between environmental and international crimes. The first steps towards such an approach have been taken by the former ICC Prosecutor Fatou Bensouda who published a Policy Paper in 2016.[69]

3.2.2.3 Office of the Prosecutor (OTP) Policy Paper

When the OTP published its Policy Paper on case selection and prioritisation in 2016, it firstly seemed like a victory for the efforts of protecting the environment through the ICC.[70] The paper stated that when selecting cases, the Prosecutor will prioritise

---

[63] Mégret 2013, p. 57.

[64] Ibid., p. 297.

[65] Rome Statute, above n 19, Article 8.

[66] Cryer et al. 2019, p. 303.

[67] Ibid., p. 312.

[68] Article 8(2)(b)(iv) is the only provision of the Rome Statute which refers to environmental protection. The benefits and drawbacks of this provision have been discussed above.

[69] Office of the Prosecutor of the International Criminal Court 2016.

[70] Anton 2016, p. 1.

those crimes which are "committed by means of, or result[] in, the destruction of the environment".[71] Consequently, many believed that the focus of the ICC had shifted, and that 'environmental crimes' could and would now be prosecuted at the Court.[72] This was intensified by the fact that a previous Policy Paper (from 2013) had brought 'environmental damage' into the realm of the ICC.[73] Many believed that this was a turning point in the history of the ICC and that previously untouchable individuals could now be held accountable for environmental crimes.[74]

Nonetheless, a closer look reveals that the Policy Paper does not, in fact, entail these implications. Although the Policy Paper refers to prioritising crimes that entail environmental destruction, it does not extend the jurisdiction of the Court.[75] And this jurisdiction, as shown above, is rather limited. Thus, in order for the Prosecutor to prioritise a crime that entails environmental destruction, this crime must firstly fall within the established core crimes of the Rome Statute. Hence, the Policy Paper does not focus on environmental protection as such, and will most likely, due to the difficulty of environmental crimes falling within the jurisdiction of the ICC, not find much applicability in upcoming cases.

As this section has shown, although the international community has regarded this topic as highly important for over 50 years and efforts have been made to adequately address the problem, real legislative solutions have still not been introduced in ICL. Moreover, no official legislative effort has to date been made to either expand the scope of the ICC's jurisdiction on environmental crimes or to prosecute an individual under the existing, albeit limited, provision of Article 8(2)(b)(iv) that exists currently in the Rome Statute.

3.2.3 International Humanitarian Law

As has been mentioned above, ICL is connected to the field of IHL. This connection arises from the fact that the Rome Statute criminalises a subset of IHL violations which can be seen in the provision on war crimes (Article 8 Rome Statute). Due to this connection, the following section analyses IHL in the context of the environment. In particular, it examines the Hague Conventions II[76] and IV,[77] Geneva Convention

[71] Office of the Prosecutor of the International Criminal Court 2016, para 40.

[72] Mistura 2018, p. 182.

[73] Office of the Prosecutor of the International Criminal Court 2013; Anton 2016, p. 1; Prosperi and Terrosi 2017, p. 516.

[74] Durney 2018, p. 414.

[75] Patel 2016, p. 181; Mistura 2018, p. 183.

[76] Hague Convention (II) with Respect to the Laws and Customs of War on Land and its Annex: Regulations concerning the Laws and Customs of War on Land, opened for signature 29 July 1899, 187 CTS 429, entered into force 5 September 1900 (Hague Convention II).

[77] Hague Convention (IV) respecting the Laws and Customs of War on Land and its annex: Regulations concerning the Laws and Customs of War on Land, opened for signature 18 October 1907, 205 CTS 277, entered into force 26 January 1910 (Hague Convention IV).

IV,[78] Additional Protocols (AP) I[79] and II[80] to the Geneva Conventions and the Convention on the Prohibition of Military or Any Other Hostile Use of Environmental Modification Techniques (ENMOD).[81]

Hague Convention II contains two articles which, indirectly, address the environment.[82] Firstly, Article 55 can be mentioned, which holds that the occupying state shall protect the "real property, forests and agricultural works belonging to the hostile State, and situated in the occupied country".[83] Secondly, Article 23(g) of the Convention can be considered, which ensures that the enemy's property shall be protected.[84] However, it is not clear to what extent the term 'property' in this regard can be interpreted as encompassing natural resources and the environment.[85] Additionally, even if this term is interpreted broadly, the protection is restricted by the defence of 'military necessity' in the same article, thus weakening the chances of a successful application of this provision to punish environmental offenders.[86] Disregarding the military necessity defence, this avenue for environmental protection seems fruitful at first glance since violations of the Hague Conventions entail compensations (Article 3 Hague Convention IV).[87] However, taking a closer look, it is clear that the Hague Conventions are not equipped with enforcement mechanisms of any kind and, moreover, do not entail criminal responsibility. Lastly, since the nature of the Convention is to deal with armed conflict, it is clear that any environmental protection it might contain is only applicable during armed conflict. This avenue is thus not beneficial for catching and prosecuting high-scale environmental polluters, especially during peacetime.

Next are the Geneva Conventions.[88] Relevant articles in this context stem from the Fourth Geneva Convention, namely Article 33, which prohibits pillaging;[89] Article

[78] Geneva Convention (IV) relative to the Protection of Civilian Persons in Time of War, opened for signature 12 August 1949, 75 UNTS 287, entered into force 21 October 1950 (Geneva Convention IV).

[79] Protocol Additional to the Geneva Conventions of 12 August 1949, and relating to the Protection of Victims of International Armed Conflicts (Protocol I), opened for signature 8 June 1977, 1125 UNTS 3, entered into force 7 December 1978 (AP I).

[80] Protocol Additional to the Geneva Conventions of 12 August 1949, and relating to the Protection of Victims of Non-International Armed Conflicts (Protocol II), opened for signature 8 June 1977, 1125 UNTS 609, entered into force 7 December 1978 (AP II).

[81] Convention on the Prohibition of Military or Any Other Hostile Use of Environmental Modification Techniques, opened for signature 10 December 1976, 1108 UNTS 151, entered into force 5 October 1978 (ENMOD).

[82] Rauxloh 2011, p. 428.

[83] Hague Convention II, above n 76, Article 55.

[84] Ibid., Article 23(g).

[85] See Erdem 2017, pp. 444–445 for a discussion on the protection of property in an environmental context.

[86] Ibid. Rauxloh 2011, p. 428.

[87] Hague Convention IV, above n 77, Article 3.

[88] Geneva Convention IV, above n 78.

[89] Ibid., Article 33.

53, which ensures the protection of property;[90] and Article 147, which includes "extensive destruction and appropriation of property, not justified by military necessity and carried out unlawfully and wantonly" as a 'grave breach' of the Convention.[91] Although the Convention prescribes criminal responsibility to 'grave breaches', due to definitional uncertainties it is difficult to ascertain whether environmental protection falls within the scope of the above-mentioned articles. Another difficulty arises as to the fact that this Convention also contains the military necessity defence. Moreover, the scope of the Convention limits any possible environmental protection to times of armed conflict. In sum, the Geneva Conventions provide neither clear nor suitable international environmental protection.

Apart from these Conventions, there are other instruments of IHL that were introduced as a result of the atrocities that occurred during the Vietnam War, namely AP I, II and the ENMOD.[92]

Contrary to the Hague and Geneva Conventions, AP I, which deals with IACs, explicitly mentions the natural environment by prohibiting the employment of "methods or means of warfare which are intended, or may be expected, to cause widespread, long-term and severe damage to the natural environment".[93] AP I also contains a separate article on the "[p]rotection of the natural environment" (Article 55),[94] which prohibits "widespread, long-term and severe damage" to the environment. However, it should be mentioned (1) that the three conditions of widespread, long-term and severe are rather vague and it is not clear from the Protocol how they should be interpreted,[95] (2) that they are cumulative and thus prescribe a high threshold of damage,[96] and (3) that although this provision does not entail the 'military necessity' defence, the lack thereof resulted in a low ratification rate, which also means that it is unclear whether the Protocol, and in particular its provisions related to the environment, can be regarded as part of customary international law.[97]

AP II, which deals with NIACs, does not mention the environment as such. It could be argued that the environment is indirectly protected[98] under certain circumstances under Article 14 ('Protection of objects indispensable to the survival of the civilian population'),[99] Article 15 ('Protection of works and installations containing dangerous forces'),[100] Article 16 ('Protection of cultural objects and of places of

---

[90] Ibid., Article 53.

[91] Ibid., Article 147. Rauxloh 2011, p. 429.

[92] Rauxloh 2011, p. 430.

[93] AP I, above n 79, Article 35.

[94] Ibid., Article 55.

[95] Rauxloh 2011, p. 430.

[96] Ibid.

[97] Ibid.

[98] Ibid.

[99] AP II, above n 80, Article 14.

[100] Ibid., Article 15.

worship'),[101] and Article 17 ('Prohibition of forced movement of civilians').[102] However, it is clear that environmental protection is rather weak in AP II, since there is no specific mention of the environment and it lacks the 'grave breach' provisions.[103]

Finally, there is ENMOD, which is the first international treaty covering environmental damage in the context of an armed conflict.[104] It entails several advantages such as (1) being applicable to both IACs and NIACs, (2) not including the military necessity defence,[105] and (3) using a disjunctive 'or' for the three conditions of widespread, long-term and severe.[106] Nonetheless, despite this lower threshold, it is important to note that this Convention deals specifically with 'environmental modification techniques' and therefore has a rather limited scope of application.[107] Thus, while environmental protection is a cornerstone of this treaty, it might not find much applicability in practice since it does not cover the environmental damage which might occur through conventional combat means.

The analysis of the legal framework examined above has shown that the current laws do not limit activities that damage the environment and thus fail to uphold the intrinsic value of nature as emphasised by ecocentrism. This shortcoming can be said to be partly due to the ICC's limited jurisdiction, which does not extend to environmental crimes. To address this issue, in addition to other options that will be discussed below, there is a possibility to extend the core crimes in the Rome Statute to include environmental protection. This avenue will be examined in the following section.

3.3 Protecting the Environment through ICL: Available Options

3.3.1 Anthropocentric Approach

In general, it can be said that there are at least two ways of approaching an environmental crime, the anthropocentric approach and the ecocentric approach. Utilising an anthropocentric approach means protecting the environment primarily for the sake of humans and human life, and not for its own protection as such.[108] In the context of environmental protection in the Rome Statute, this means that prosecutions of environmental crimes would occur in the context of the core crimes that concern the

[101] Ibid., Article 16.

[102] Ibid., Article 17.

[103] Rauxloh 2011, p. 431.

[104] Ibid.

[105] Ibid.

[106] ENMOD, above n 81; Ahmed 2017, p. 142; Greene 2019, p. 5.

[107] Rauxloh 2011, p. 431.

[108] Pereira 2015, p. 51.

protection of humans. Proponents of the anthropocentric view, such as Weinstein, argue that this approach entails many advantages,[109] such as being more effective, since it can be pursued immediately, without the time, effort and perhaps infeasibility of amending the Rome Statute to include a new environmental provision.[110] Moreover, proponents also hold that much environmental destruction occurs in the context of other international crimes and that perpetrators could thus be brought to justice for this destruction through this avenue.[111] The following section will explain in more detail how such an anthropocentric approach would be utilised under the Rome Statute.

3.3.1.1 Genocide

The first anthropocentric provision that could, in theory, be utilised to protect the environment is that of genocide. Genocide is inherently human-focused and utilising it to protect the environment would only come subsidiary to protecting humans.[112] Nonetheless, there are certain underlying acts of genocide which could result from environmental destruction, such as Article 6(b).[113]

Article 6(b) covers the situations of "[c]ausing serious bodily or mental harm to members of the group", which could, in fact, occur as a result of environmental damage.[114] As stated in the ICC Elements of Crimes, the conduct causing this harm "may include, but is not necessarily restricted to, acts of torture, rape, sexual violence or inhuman or degrading treatment",[115] indicating that this is not an exhaustive list and that other means of conduct, such as environmental destruction could be included.[116] It is not difficult to imagine acts of environmental destruction that cause serious bodily or mental harm. Regarding bodily harm, the dumping of toxic waste or oil spills and their accompanying health problems can be advanced.[117] Moreover, environmental destruction can in many instances also cause mental harm, such as in the context

---

[109] Weinstein 2005, p. 715; Gillett 2010, p. 334.

[110] Gillett 2010, p. 334.

[111] Ibid.

[112] Ibid., p. 226.

[113] Rome Statute, above n 19, Article 6(b); Mistura 2018, pp. 204–205. Another article that could be of interest is Article 6(c) Rome Statute: "[d]eliberately inflicting on the group conditions of life calculated to bring about its physical destruction in whole or in part". An example that can be cited here is the *Al Bashir* case, in which the ICC found that the contamination of wells and water pumps can constitute a pursuance of genocidal policy, see ICC, Pre-Trial Chamber I, *The Prosecutor v Omar Hassan Ahmad Al Bashir*, Second Decision on the Prosecution's Application for a Warrant of Arrest, ICC-02/05-01/09, 12 July 2010, para 37 ff.

[114] Rome Statute, above n 19, Article 6(b); Mistura 2018, pp. 204–205.

[115] International Criminal Court, Elements of Crimes, reproduced in the Official Records of the Assembly of the States Parties to the Rome Statute of the International Criminal Court, First Session, New York, 3–10 September 2002, ICC-ASP/1/3 and Corr.1, part II.B, p. 2, footnote 3.

[116] Mistura 2018, p. 205.

[117] Ibid., p. 206.

of indigenous communities whose mental wellbeing is intricately connected to their natural environment.[118]

However, although this approach looks promising on a theoretical level, utilising genocide to protect the environment seems almost impossible in practical terms, due to its high *mens rea* threshold.[119] As described above, to fall within the definition of genocide under the Rome Statute, a specific (genocidal) intent is required. It is not sufficient to demonstrate that the individual responsible acted knowingly in an environmentally damaging conduct that seriously harmed a certain group of persons, but there must also be a specific intention to destroy this group of persons.[120] To utilise this provision in practice to protect the environment, this *mens rea* threshold is arguably too high to be used in practice.[121]

3.3.1.2 Crimes Against Humanity

A second avenue that could be taken is that of utilising the provision of CAH in order to protect the environment. Unlike genocide, CAH do not require specific intent. It might therefore be easier to fulfil the *mens rea* requirements under this provision. Although again, this provision is inherently anthropocentric, it can be argued that certain acts of environmental destruction fall within the requirements of this provision since they can be characterised as an 'attack' against a civilian population under Article 7(1) Rome Statute.[122] Moreover, many instances of serious environmental damage could fulfil the requirement of 'widespread', since they are generally of a large-scale nature and include a high number of victims.[123]

One example of an underlying act of CAH that could be used is that of deportation or forcible transfer of population. This means "forced displacement of the persons concerned by expulsion or other coercive acts from the area in which they are lawfully present, without grounds permitted under international law".[124] Multiple conducts that harm the environment in this context can be brought forward here, such as deforestation that leads to the expulsion of communities dependent on the forest,[125] or the dumping of toxic waste making a population's homeland uninhabitable.[126] Additionally, land-grabbing could be argued to fall under this provision, as can be observed in Cambodia, where the government has been seizing farmland and thereby

118 Ibid., p. 205.

119 Patel 2016, p. 189; Gillett 2017, p. 226; Mistura 2018, p. 207.

120 Patel 2016, p. 189.

121 Mistura 2018, p. 207.

122 Prosperi and Terrosi 2017, p. 510.

123 ICTY, Trial Chamber II, *Prosecutor v Tadić*, I, Opinion and Judgment T-94-1-T, 7 May 1997, para 206; Cryer et al. 2019, p. 232.

124 Rome Statute, above n 19, Article 7(1)(d).

125 Prosperi and Terrosi 2017, p. 520.

126 Mistura 2018, p. 209.

forcibly displaced the civilian population.[127] Other underlying acts that could be relevant in this regard are (a) murder, (b) extermination, (h) persecution and (k) other inhumane acts.[128]

In a sense, utilising CAH in order to protect the environment would be less difficult than utilising the crime of genocide. Not only is there more flexibility regarding the different underlying acts that could be employed, but there is also a lower *mens rea* threshold. Nonetheless, there is the requirement that the harm must have occurred as part of a 'bigger picture', namely a state or organisational policy.[129] In the context of environmental protection, this could be problematic since environmental harms often occur on a one-time basis (e.g. oil spills),[130] and are oftentimes not part of a discriminatory policy,[131] but instead part of a business plan or solely an accident. This might hinder the prosecution of environmental offenders to a considerable extent.

3.3.1.3 War Crimes

A third option of protecting the environment through ICL would be to utilise the war crimes provision of Article 8 Rome Statute. Currently, this is the only provision which mentions environmental protection. However, as established above, this route is not very promising in regard to environmental protection due to its many drawbacks, such as the military advantage defence, its *mens rea* requirement, and the high harm threshold of 'widespread, long-term and severe'.[132] Further limitations arise from the fact that this provision solely deals with IACs and neither encompasses environmental damage arising from NIACs nor during peacetime. Therefore, due to the many drawbacks mentioned above, also this provision has limited potential to safeguard the environment.

3.3.1.4 Crime of Aggression

Lastly, environmental protection could be observed in light of the crime of aggression (Article 8 *bis*).[133] As established above, this crime is different from the other core crimes of the Rome Statute since it is connected to an 'act of aggression' and a leadership crime, meaning that in order to fall under this provision, the perpetrator(s) must be in control of the military or political action of the state. Although environmental destruction is not explicitly mentioned in Article 8 *bis*, it can be imagined

[127] Durney 2018, pp. 418, 425–428.

[128] See Prosperi and Terrosi 2017.

[129] Rome Statute, above n 19, Article 7(2)(a).

[130] Durney 2018, p. 416.

[131] Prosperi and Terrosi 2017, p. 523. Although it is true that in some instances they can disproportionately affect indigenous communities.

[132] Rome Statute, above n 19, Article 8.

[133] Ibid.

that certain environmentally damaging conduct that occurs in the course of an act of aggression would fall within the scope of this crime. In this sense, one can, for example, think back to the usage of the chemical defoliant Agent Orange, which was utilised during the Vietnam War and which formed a great part of the attack of the United States in Vietnam. Since an attack by the armed forces of a state qualifies as an act of aggression under paragraph 2 (a) of the article, this provision could potentially be utilised to protect the environment in this set of circumstances (provided that the acts of environmental harm were part of the initial attack).[134]

Nonetheless, it is clear that even if this provision was interpreted in an environmental manner, it would only cover a small set of acts of environmental destruction. Due to the fact that it firstly has to be established that an act of aggression has taken place and secondly that the person responsible was in a leadership position, it becomes clear that many acts of environmental destruction would not be covered by this article, such as deforestation or oil spills, cases in which perpetrators are individuals not in military or state leadership positions. Therefore, although an environmental interpretation of Article 8 *bis* could perhaps help protect the environment in the context of the commission of an act of aggression, the narrow set of circumstances that this article covers means that it is not suitable to protect the environment as such.

Having analysed the anthropocentric approach of protecting the environment through ICL as it currently stands, it has become clear that while the anthropocentric approach might solve some environmental issues, it does not cover any situations which do not directly impact humans. Therefore, this approach also covers less environmental damage than might have occurred in a particular situation, as only the damage done to humans will be falling under these provisions. Additionally, the anthropocentric approach entails a 'symbolic' drawback. Utilising the existing Rome Statute provisions for environmental protection, and thus only protecting the environment indirectly by protecting humans, sends a message to the international community signalling that environmental destruction is not condemned as such, but only as a subsidiary harm to that of humans.[135] As a consequence, the deterrent and declaratory effect of environmental crimes could become undermined[136] and, probably, no real change in behaviour is to be expected. Therefore, it is important to advance in the analysis and examine the ecocentric approach.

3.3.2 *Ecocentric Approach*

As described above, contrary to the anthropocentric approach, the ecocentric approach recognises the intrinsic value of the environment and protects it *per se*. This approach does not regard the environment as a secondary means that exists

[134] Ibid., Article 8 *bis* 2(a).
[135] Gillett 2017, p. 227.
[136] Gillett 2017, p. 227.

to protect humans, but, on the contrary, awards it inherent values which must be protected.[137] The two main options of protecting the environment through criminal law from an ecocentric perspective will now be explored.

3.3.2.1 New Convention Against Environmental Crimes

One way of approaching environmental protection through ICL utilising an ecocentric approach would be to enact a new international convention and separate court on this matter. Such an approach would entail many advantages. Firstly, a comprehensive legal framework would be established in order to protect the environment through criminal law on a global scale. Secondly, environmental protection would be ensured in all (desired) circumstances since distinctions could be drawn in the convention between peacetime and wartime environmental crimes and between the different levels of the seriousness of the harm. Thirdly, this convention could also ensure that acts of environmental destruction that are of a certain magnitude, such as ecocide, would not require proving intent. As such, environmental accidents could fall under this convention, be prosecuted and thus hopefully lead to more careful behaviour on the part of the perpetrators. Moreover, a fourth benefit of this approach that can be mentioned is the fact that this convention could introduce corporate criminal responsibility. In this way, many perpetrators of environmental crimes that are otherwise not covered by ICL, namely corporations, could be held responsible for their actions, and their *de facto* immunity would cease to exist.[138] Lastly, this convention could also create a specialised international environmental court that would solely rule on matters regarding the abovementioned convention.

Nonetheless, although such an approach does sound promising on paper, it might entail far-reaching practical difficulties. Negotiating a whole new instrument in this regard would undoubtedly be a difficult and lengthy process, with many contentious points arising, such as definitional issues, the crimes which should be included, the threshold of harm, *mens rea* requirements, corporate criminal responsibility, etc. Moreover, it is not clear how many states would agree to ratify this convention considering the fact that they would be bound by a whole new legal system and court. Due to the pressing nature of the environmental crisis and issues such as climate change, there might not be enough time for such a lengthy process. As pointedly remarked by the Republic of Maldives: "Countries at the frontline of climate change, such as the Maldives, do not have the luxury of time to negotiate for another international legal instrument to fight against environmental crimes".[139] Instead of going through this lengthy process with no guarantee of success, they propose instead "an amendment

[137] Pereira 2015, pp. 51–52.

[138] Mwanza 2018, p. 14.

[139] Republic of Maldives 2019.

to the Rome Statute that would criminalise acts that amount to Ecocide".[140] The following section will analyse this proposal for a new crime of ecocide.

3.3.2.2 Ecocide

Historical Background

The term ecocide stems from the Greek 'oikos' (meaning house or home) and the Latin 'caedere' (meaning to destroy or kill) and generally speaking describes the destruction of the environment.[141] Ecocide is not a new concept on the international agenda; in fact, it has been circulating within international law since the 1970s.[142] As explained above, it was firstly introduced by scientist Arthur W. Galston at the Conference on War and National Responsibility in 1970.[143] Galston coined the term in reference to the Vietnam War, during which the US military utilised the chemical mixture Agent Orange to defoliate around five million acres of South Vietnamese forests hoping to gain a military advantage.[144] At the conference, Prof Galston asked the international community to condemn ecocide and proposed a new law to ban it at the international level.[145] Two years later, at the 1972 United Nations Conference on the Environment in Stockholm, Olof Palme, then prime minister of Sweden, also referred to ecocide, namely in the context of the tactics utilised during the Vietnam War.[146] Moreover, parallel to the conference, a demonstration was held to recognise ecocide as a crime that drew over 7000 participants; and a working group was formed to draft a new law on ecocide.[147] This group drafted the International Convention on the Crime of Ecocide, which was published by one of its members, Richard Falk, in a journal in 1973.[148] Although this Convention was never more than a draft, it was later included in a study by the UN which examined the possibility of enacting other conventions which would criminalise acts that had previously not been included in the Genocide Convention.[149] This study, however, never came to any conclusions in this regard.[150] Nonetheless, ecocide again gained momentum in the 1980s when the ILC considered including it in the Draft Code of Crimes Against the Peace and

[140] Ibid. However, an amendment is not necessarily an easy endeavour. To do so, parties have to follow Article 121 Rome Statute, which requires approval for negotiations, a two-thirds majority for adoption and subsequent ratification.

[141] Mehta and Merz 2015, p. 4.

[142] Greene 2019, p. 8.

[143] Higgins et al. 2013, p. 256; Greene 2019, p. 8.

[144] Ahmed 2017, p. 140.

[145] Gauger et al. 2012, p. 1; Mehta and Merz 2015, p. 4; Greene 2019, p. 8; Pereira 2020, p. 185.

[146] Ahmed 2017, pp. 140–141; Malhotra 2017, p. 52; Greene 2019, p. 10.

[147] Mehta and Merz 2015, p. 4; Greene 2019, p. 11.

[148] Falk 1973.

[149] Greene 2019, p. 13.

[150] Ibid., pp. 14–15.

Security of Mankind (Draft Code).[151] Nevertheless, without any record as to the reasons for this decision, and contrary to the wishes of the working group on this matter, the ILC unilaterally removed the crime of ecocide from the Draft Code.[152] Instead, it settled on a 'crime against the environment' in Article 26. Nevertheless, disagreements arose as to whether this crime would be one of intent or not;[153] and, instead of finding a compromise on this matter, this article was also removed by the ILC in 1996,[154] without any real records as to why.[155] The result was the reduction of all these efforts into the war crime provision of Article 8 Rome Statute, whose "conditions of applicability" according to Tomuschat, "will almost never be met even after humankind would have gone through disasters of the most atrocious kind as a consequence of conscious action by persons who were completely aware of the fatal consequences their decisions would entail".[156]

The crime of ecocide has thus been on the international agenda for decades; and although no political progress has been made for years, scholars and other activists have not stopped advocating for the crime. In this regard, environmental lawyer Polly Higgins and her Stop Ecocide project can be mentioned.[157] In 2010, Higgins helped putting ecocide on the international agenda once again and co-founded the Stop Ecocide campaign, aiming to include ecocide as the fifth international crime in the Rome Statute.[158] Multiple scholars, activists and lawyers are supporting this cause and several sovereign states, such as Vanuatu,[159] the Maldives[160] and Belgium[161] have called for the inclusion of such a crime in the Rome Statute at the ICC's Assembly of State Parties.[162] The following section will explore how such a crime of ecocide would look like if it were to be included in the Rome Statute.

---

151 Higgins et al. 2013, p. 260.

152 Gauger et al. 2012, p. 11.

153 Higgins et al. 2013, p. 261; Greene 2019, p. 15.

154 Higgins et al. 2013, p. 261; Malhotra 2017, p. 53.

155 Higgins et al. 2013, p. 261. According to Christian Tomuschat, a member of the ILC from 1985 to 1996 and of the working group on the environmental provision, the existence and threat of nuclear arms might have been part of the decision, see Mehta and Merz 2015, p. 4.

156 Gauger et al. 2012, p. 12.

157 Stop Ecocide Campaign, https://www.stopecocide.earth/. Accessed 28 June 2025.

158 Ibid.; Mehta and Merz 2015, p. 5.

159 Government of the Republic of Vanuatu 2019.

160 Republic of Maldives 2019.

161 Stop Ecocide International 2020a.

162 Malhotra 2017, p. 53; Stop Ecocide International, https://www.stopecocide.earth/who-we-are-. Accessed 19 December 2020.

Material Elements of the Crime

One of the difficulties of the crime of ecocide is the fact that there are many different definitions of the crime.[163] Recently, however, as part of Polly Higgins' and co-founder Jojo Mehta's Stop Ecocide Foundation, an expert drafting panel of international lawyers and judges, the Independent Expert Panel for the Legal Definition of Ecocide (IEP), has worked on a new legal definition of ecocide. The IEP recommends including the following definition in the Rome Statute:[164]

1. For the purpose of this Statute, "ecocide" means unlawful or wanton acts committed with knowledge that there is a substantial likelihood of severe and either widespread or long-term damage to the environment being caused by those acts.[165]

Analysing the article, several factors should be pointed out. Firstly, it is important to note that, according to this definition, ecocide can occur both during times of war and peace. Acts of environmental destruction that are committed during peacetime, such as oil spills or deforestation, could thus be covered by this article. Secondly, it should be noted that the definition of the environment, which can be found in paragraph (2)(e) is rather broad, encompassing not only the earth and its spheres, but also outer space. And thirdly, this definition includes both acts and omissions as ecocide, thereby further broadening the scope of the article.[166] This would mean that situations such as e.g. failing to apply the correct filters in a coal power station could also be covered.

Taking a closer look at the *actus reus* of the crime, we see that there are several qualifiers to the damage requirement. Firstly, the damage has to be "severe and either widespread or long-term". This definition thus takes a middle-way between the Article 8(2)(b)(iv) Rome Statute definition and that of the ENMOD.[167] The IEP justified this choice by arguing that only cases that are of a severe nature should fall

[163] Different definitions of ecocide can be found in Gray 1996; Higgins 2010; Mwanza 2018; Greene 2019.

[164] Stop Ecocide Foundation 2021.

[165] Paragraph 1 introduces the crime and paragraph 2 defines several elements of the definition: Paragraph 2: a. "Wanton" means with reckless disregard for damage which would be clearly excessive in relation to the social and economic benefits anticipated; b. "Severe" means damage which involves very serious adverse changes, disruption or harm to any element of the environment, including grave impacts on human life or natural, cultural or economic resources; c. "Widespread" means damage which extends beyond a limited geographic area, crosses state boundaries, or is suffered by an entire ecosystem or species or a large number of human beings; d. "Long-term" means damage which is irreversible or which cannot be redressed through natural recovery within a reasonable period of time; e. "Environment" means the earth, its biosphere, cryosphere, lithosphere, hydrosphere and atmosphere, as well as outer space.

[166] The Panel decided that 'acts' include both acts or omissions as well as cumulative acts or omissions, see Stop Ecocide Foundation 2021.

[167] Ibid.

under ecocide and the Rome Statute, due to the seriousness of the crime.[168] Additionally, it includes 'widespread' and 'long-term' only as disjunctive criteria, thereby lowering the threshold of harm as opposed to Article 8(2)(b)(iv) Rome Statute. Paragraph 2 of the IEP definition includes definitions for these three criteria, which, while being less precise than those of the ENMOD,[169] are therefore also more multidimensional and can be argued to allow for the flexibility that comes along with real-life environmental damage.[170] In this sense, the criterion of 'widespread' not only refers to a specific physical distance, but also to damage that has been caused upon entire ecosystems or species,[171] and 'long-term' to damage which is generally "irreversible or which cannot be redressed through natural recovery within a reasonable period of time".[172]

Secondly, another threshold can be found in the definition, namely that of 'unlawful or wanton'. As described by the IEP, this requirement was added to "balance social and economic benefits with environmental harms".[173] This poses challenges of a normative nature as contrary to the nature of the crime and its ultimate goal to protect the environment, this part of the provision can be argued to be of an anthropocentric, rather than ecocentric nature. The 'wanton' element is of particular relevance here since it introduces a proportionality test, weighing environmental harm against social and economic benefits. While the IEP Commentary justifies this test with reference to the principle of sustainable development, arguments have been raised that this is not a solid justification considering that damage which would amount to ecocide would arguably not be sustainable, neither for the environment as such nor, through a more anthropocentric lens, for future generations.[174] Additionally, these qualifiers pose difficulties of a practical nature and applicability since, for example, acts of environmental damage are often lawful.[175] These two criteria thus narrow the scope of the article and introduce a more anthropocentric element to the crime. From an ecocentric perspective, this can be seen as problematic because it thereby detracts from the goal of protecting the environment itself.

As concerns the *mens rea* of ecocide, the IEP decided to lower the threshold from the usual criminal intent (Article 30 Rome Statute) to "knowledge that there is a

[168] Ibid.

[169] For the drafting committee of the ENMOD "'widespread' meant an area of about several hundred square kilometres; 'long lasting' meant a period of months, approximately a season", and "'severe' referred to serious or significant disruption or harm to human life, natural and economic or other assets". See Greene 2019, p. 5.

[170] Minkova 2021, p. 12.

[171] Ibid.

[172] IEP definition. See Stop Ecocide Foundation 2021.

[173] Stop Ecocide Foundation 2021.

[174] See ibid. for more on this issue.

[175] Minkova 2021, p. 13.

substantial likelihood" of the damage.[176] Under these circumstances, situations like accidental oil spills or nuclear accidents could thus be prosecuted.[177]

Having examined how a crime of ecocide could look like, the chapter will now delve into both challenges and benefits that such a provision would entail, were it to be included in the Rome Statute.

Arguments in Favour

Firstly, this crime would ensure that the environment is also protected under ICL during peacetime. As mentioned above, serious acts of environmental destruction, such as oil spills, deforestation or nuclear accidents, which usually occur during peace- and not wartime, could thus fall under the scope of this article, thereby also improving normative consistency under the Rome Statute.

Secondly, this crime, which mainly falls on the ecocentric side of the spectrum, would ensure that the environment is protected in the Rome Statute as such, not merely secondarily to human protection. This would send a signal to the international community that the environment is regarded as interconnected with human life and well-being, and that it therefore should receive at least the same level of protection.[178] The wantonness element that was introduced by the IEP however weakens this argument to a certain extent.

Thirdly, this signal that would be sent would not only be of symbolic value, but also of a practical one, since it can be hoped that the inclusion of this crime in the Rome Statute would ensure prevention of the conduct. Having the deterrent effect of ICL in mind, it could be assumed that including ecocide as an international crime could lead to people rethinking their behaviour before they act due to the punishment they would receive were they to engage in acts of ecocide, thus acting in a more 'preventive' way. This would also entail that several instances of the complicated and expensive ways to adapt to environmental damage would become obsolete.[179]

Another argument in favour of including a crime of ecocide into the Rome Statute is the fact that such a crime has already been included into the domestic legal systems of several states. At the time of writing, ten countries provide for a crime of ecocide in their national legal systems,[180] and others, such as France,[181] Belgium,[182] Sweden,[183]

---

[176] This is more in line with Higgins' original proposal and many other scholars, see Harvey 2012, p. 11; Higgins et al. 2013, p. 262; Greene 2019, p. 3; Pereira 2020, p. 195.

[177] Greene 2019, p. 3; Pereira 2020, p. 195.

[178] Mwanza 2018, p. 593.

[179] Higgins 2012b; Kotter 2014, p. 229.

[180] Higgins et al. 2013, p. 263; Greene 2019, pp. 19–20; Ecocide Law in National Jurisdictions, https://ecocidelaw.com/existing-ecocide-laws/. Accessed 30 October 2020.

[181] Dell'Anna 2020.

[182] Stop Ecocide International 2020b.

[183] Stop Ecocide International 2020c.

Spain[184] and the Netherlands[185] have decided on or are considering its inclusion. Vietnam, most likely due to its experiences during the war, was the first country to include this crime in its domestic criminal system in 1990.[186] Following suit, after the fall of the Soviet Union, the countries of Georgia,[187] Armenia,[188] Ukraine,[189] Belarus,[190] Kazakhstan,[191] Kyrgyzstan,[192] Moldova,[193] Russia,[194] and Tajikistan[195] included ecocide into their newly established criminal codes.[196] Interestingly, in many of these criminal codes the crime of ecocide is listed as a 'Crime Against Peace', along with the core crimes of the Rome Statute.[197] These countries are thus already putting these crimes on equal footing, and the question might be asked whether other countries would do the same, were they to establish their penal codes now. Nonetheless, in order for these criminalisations to be effective the crimes must be properly enforced and judged upon. In countries with a rather low respect for the rule of law and no independent judiciary this is unlikely.[198] Including the crime into the Rome Statute would not only allow for effective prosecution through an international court, but it would also lead to a broad applicability of the crime to all states parties to the Rome Statute. It can hence be argued that this would reflect the needs of the time and the already existing views of several states.

Lastly, including this crime into the Rome Statute has the advantage that the infrastructure already exists. No new convention would have to be negotiated and no new court would have to be established. As described below, the Rome Statute would solely have to follow its amendment procedure in order to include a new article. Following this, the already existing ICC would be able to rule on this matter.

Contentious Issues

Next to these advantages of including ecocide in the Rome Statute, there are also issues of contention, such as the fact that, according to the above definition, ecocide

---

184 Stop Ecocide International 2020d.

185 Stop Ecocide International 2023.

186 Greene 2019, p. 19; Viet Nam Penal Code (21 December 1999), No 15/1999/QH10, Article 278.

187 Criminal Code of Georgia (22 June 1999), LGH 41(8) 2287, Article 409.

188 Criminal Code of the Republic of Armenia (18 April 2003), Article 394.

189 Criminal Code Ukraine (1 September 2001), Article 441.

190 Penal Code of Belarus (9 July 1999) No 420, Article 131.

191 Criminal Code of the Republic of Kazakhstan (16 July 1997) No 167, Article 161.

192 Criminal Code of the Kyrgyz Republic (18 September 1997) No 68, Article 374.

193 Criminal Code of the Republic of Moldova (18 April 2002) No 985-XV, Article 136.

194 Criminal Code of the Russian Federation (13 June 1996) No 63-Fz, Article 358.

195 Criminal Code of the Republic of Tajikistan (21 May 1998), Article 40.

196 Ecocide Law in National Jurisdictions, https://ecocidelaw.com/existing-ecocide-laws/. Accessed 26 June 2025.

197 Ibid.

198 Ibid.

would be a crime that is not based on intent; a concept on which the criminal system of the Rome Statute is based,[199] as provided for in its Article 30.[200] The reason for this lower threshold in the IEP definition, however, is the fact that many environmental disasters that occur are not intended as such, but usually happen as an accident or collateral damage.[201] Thus, if intent was required to fall within the IEP definition of ecocide, many actual situations of environmental destruction would not be covered, with individuals using the argument that they simply did not intend to cause this environmental damage.[202] The *mens rea* approach taken by the IEP, on the other hand, would result in these scenarios leading to prosecution due to the knowledge of the substantial likelihood of the damage.[203] This approach would thus also go hand-in-hand with the aims of punishment, such as deterrence.[204]

Another issue of contention of including this crime into the Rome Statute might be the possibility of the ICC being flooded with 'frivolous litigation', due to the extension of peacetime environmental damage.[205] It has been argued that the language of the Rome Statute was carefully chosen in order to ensure that only the most serious of crimes would fall within its scope and that the Court would thus not be overwhelmed with cases of less concern. Although it is true that more cases would pass through the doors of the Court if peacetime environmental crimes were to be included in the Statute, this would finally solve the above-analysed problem that the environment is currently only protected, and merely to a limited extent, by the Rome Statute in times of war. Moreover, the ecocide provision does contain several thresholds of harm, namely that the damage must be unlawful or wanton and that its impacts must be severe and widespread or long-term. As mentioned above especially the wantonness criterion is rather high and would restrict access to the Court in certain cases.

Another concern that has been raised is that the inclusion of ecocide into the Rome Statute might diminish the seriousness of the other core crimes. In this regard, international lawyer Wesley J. Smith has noted that "[e]quating resource extraction and/or pollution with genocide trivializes true evils such as the slaughter in Rwanda".[206] However, as has been established above, serious environmental destruction, on the level of ecocide, can be just as detrimental as the other core crimes. Not only can acts of ecocide, seen through an anthropocentric view, lead to the deaths of many people, but they also lead to the death and sometimes total erasure of entire ecosystems and species. This, in turn, can lead to a vicious cycle in which the erasure and decline of ecosystems can have further negative effects on both human and non-human life.

[199] Mistura 2018, p. 224.

[200] Greene 2019, p. 33.

[201] Ibid.

[202] Ibid.

[203] White 2017; Greene 2019, p. 33.

[204] Mwanza 2018, p. 611.

[205] Ibid., p. 605.

[206] Smith 2010; Greene 2019, p. 37.

Moreover, as stated by Mark Allan Gray, the fact that acts of ecocide threaten international peace and security means that "it must be treated with the same gravity as apartheid and genocide".[207] In order to understand the seriousness of the crime of ecocide, one has to change one's values and perception from an anthropocentric view to an ecocentric one, which "treats human wellbeing as indispensable and inseparable from the wellbeing of the ecosystem".[208] When this change in focus has appeared, it becomes clear that ecocide is just as serious as the other core crimes of the Rome Statute and thus does not diminish them in the least.

Besides this, it has been argued that it might not make sense to include ecocide into the Rome Statute since the judges of the ICC lack expertise in this area.[209] It is true that the current judges on the bench have a background in criminal, human rights or humanitarian law and might thus not be too familiar with matters on environmental law.[210] It has been argued that were these judges to rule on ecocide matters, without the necessary expertise on the matter, this might be rather counterproductive to the credibility of the crime and the Court.[211] One option to remedy this issue would be to add a separate panel of judges with expertise in environmental matters that would solely deal with cases on ecocide.[212] This would ensure that the specialised knowledge that dealing with a crime of ecocide requires is provided while making use of the already existing infrastructure of the Court. Another possible solution would be to work more closely together with expert witnesses to provide the necessary expertise.

A further issue that can be mentioned is the fact that acts of ecocide are often committed by states or corporations, but that the ICC can only charge individuals. It is clearly stated in Article 25 Rome Statute (individual criminal responsibility) that the Court has jurisdiction over 'natural persons', meaning individuals, and not over 'legal persons' such as corporations.[213] As concerns the issue of states, meaning a state committing a crime, this has been remedied by the fact that individual high-ranking members of the state, such as heads of state or government can be held responsible for their actions before the Court. The legal basis for this can be found in Article 27 Rome Statute (irrelevance of official capacity), which holds that individuals such as heads of state or government are not exempt from criminal responsibility and that the immunities they might have shall not hinder the Court from exercising its jurisdiction.[214] In the context of corporations it has been argued that since corporations themselves are in many instances responsible for environmental harms, corporate criminal liability should be included in the Rome Statute to ensure proper protection of the environment. However, it is clear that this would lead to

[207] Gray 1996, p. 217.

[208] Mwanza 2018, p. 595.

[209] Greene 2019, p. 38.

[210] Ibid., p. 39.

[211] Ibid., pp. 38–39.

[212] Ibid., p. 40.

[213] Rome Statute, above n 19, Article 25.

[214] Ibid., Article 27.

the need for another major amendment of the Rome Statute and would go against the concept of individual criminal responsibility as mentioned in Article 25 Rome Statute. It is therefore unlikely that such an amendment would be adopted and might possibly be the reason as to why corporations are not included in the IEP definition of ecocide. While corporations would thus not be covered by this article, it would nevertheless be a first step in signalling that this is a serious international crime.

Lastly, concerns have been raised regarding the feasibility of adding an ecocide provision into the Rome Statute. While it is clear that the amendment to the Rome Statute would be substantial and require support from a majority of state parties[215] it should be noted that (1) there seems to be growing support for a crime of ecocide in the international community;[216] (2) a substantive amendment has already taken place in the past with the inclusion of the crime of aggression; and (3) if, as advanced by Mwanza, ecological integrity should be seen as a *Grundnorm* of international law (i.e. if we start adopting an ecocentric perspective), the crime of ecocide would only be "an appropriate legal response".[217]

In sum, there are many possibilities of protecting the environment through ICL. The discussion has shown that a more ecocentric approach is favourable to an anthropocentric one, especially due to the change in normative focus it entails. In particular, within this ecocentric approach, the inclusion of ecocide into the Rome Statute seems to be the most suited to protect the environment through ICL.

3.4 Conclusion

To conclude, this chapter has established that although environmental protection has been on the international agenda for decades, the current international legal regime is arguably not well suited to protect the environment. Cases like the destruction of the Amazon rainforest illustrate this fact. This chapter established that the ICL regime specifically, with its singular provision that addresses the environment in Article 8(2)(b)(iv) Rome Statute, does not protect the environment to a sufficient extent either. Nonetheless, as the inclusion of the crime of aggression has illustrated, the possibility of amending the Rome Statute exists. The chapter found that the anthropocentric approach, namely utilising the existing core crimes of the Rome Statute to protect the environment, would not lead to suitable protection and that the ecocentric approach is more favourable in this regard. It has been shown that the inclusion of a new crime of ecocide into the Rome Statute in particular would be the most favourable approach of protecting the environment through ICL. Such an

[215] Ibid., Article 121.

[216] In this sense, i.a. the states of Vanuatu, the Maldives and Belgium, which have been calling for the inclusion of such a crime into the Rome Statute at the ICC Assembly of State Parties, can be mentioned, as well as multiple other states that have either included such a crime already or are considering its conclusion in their domestic legal systems.

[217] Mwanza 2018, p. 589.

approach can help constrain human impacts on the environment and ensure that its intrinsic value is upheld.

References

Articles, Books and Other Documents

Ahmed N (2017) Proof of Ecocide: Towards a Forensic Practice for the Proposed International Crime Against the Environment. Forensic Archaeology, Anthropology and Ecology 1(2):139–147

Anton D (2016) Adding a green focus: The Office of the Prosecutor of the International Criminal Court highlights the "environment" in case selection and prioritisation. Australian Environment Review 31:1–13

Cassese A (2004) International Law, 2nd edn. Oxford University Press, Oxford

Crasson A (2017) The Case of Chevron in Ecuador: The Need for an International Crime against the Environment. Amsterdam Law Forum 9(3):29–48

Cryer R, Robinson D, Vasiliev S (2019) An Introduction to International Criminal Law and Procedure, 4th edn. Cambridge University Press, Cambridge

Dell'Anna A (2020) France considers introducing new "ecocide" offense in pollution crackdown. https://www.euronews.com/2020/11/22/france-considers-introducing-new-ecocide-offence-in-pollution-crackdown. Accessed 24 June 2025

De Lucia V (2015) Competing Narratives and Complex Genealogies: The Ecosystem Approach in International Environmental Law. Journal of Environmental Law 27(1):91–117

Durney J (2018) Crafting a Standard: Environmental Crimes as Crimes Against Humanity Under the International Criminal Court. Hastings Environmental Law Journal 24(2):413–430

Erdem M (2017) Enforcing conventional humanitarian law for environmental damage during internal armed conflict. Georgetown Environmental Law Review 29(3):435–477

Falk RA (1973) Environmental Warfare and Ecocide - Facts, Appraisal, and Proposals. Bulletin Peace Proposals 4(1):80–96

Fonseca P, Spring J (2019) Bolsonaro says Brazil rainforest reserve may be opened to mining, Reuters. https://www.reuters.com/article/business/environment/bolsonaro-says-brazil-rainforest-reserve-may-be-opened-to-mining-idUSKCN1RO29G/. Accessed 18 October 2020

Gauger A, Rabatel-Fernel MP, Kulbicki L, Short D, Higgins P (2012) The Ecocide Project: 'Ecocide is the missing 5th Crime Against Peace'. https://sas-space.sas.ac.uk/4830/1/Ecocide_research_report_19_July_13.pdf. Accessed 24 June 2025

Gillett M (2010) Prosecuting Environmental Damage under International Criminal Law. In: Crawford J, Nouwen S (eds) Select Proceedings of the European Society of International Law, Volume 3. Bloomsbury Publishing, London, pp 329–338

Gillett M (2017) Eco-Struggles: Using International Criminal Law to Protect the Environment During and After Non-International Armed Conflict. In: Stahn C, Iverson J, Easterday JS (eds) Environmental Protection and Transitions from Conflict to Peace: Clarifying Norms, Principles and Practices. Oxford University Press, Oxford, pp 220–254

Gillett M (2022) Prosecuting Environmental Harm before the International Criminal Court. Cambridge University Press, Cambridge

Government of the Republic of Vanuatu (2019) Statement by H.E. John H. Licht Ambassador of the Republic of Vanuatu to the European Union, General Debate of the 18th Session of the Assembly of State Parties of the Rome Statute of the International Criminal Court. https://www.legal-tools.org/doc/uqwj4qhw/. Accessed 25 June 2025

Gray MA (1996) The International Crime of Ecocide. California Western International Law Journal 26(2):215–271

Greene A (2019) The Campaign to Make Ecocide an International Crime: Quixotic Quest or Moral Imperative? Fordham Environmental Law Review 30(3):1–48

Harvey R (2012) "Ecocide" – will this be the fifth international crime against peace? The Socialist Lawyer. https://doi.org/10.13169/socialistlawyer.61.0011

Higgins P (2010) Eradicating ecocide: laws and governance to prevent the destruction of our planet. Shepheard-Walwyn, London

Higgins P (2012a) Seeding Intrinsic Values: How a Law of Ecocide will Shift our Consciousness. Cadmus Journal 1(5):9–10

Higgins P (2012b) Earth Is Our Business: Changing the Rules of the Game. Shepheard-Walwyn, London

Higgins P, Short D, South N (2013) Protecting the planet: a proposal for a law of ecocide. Crime, Law and Social Change 59(3):251–266

Intergovernmental Panel on Climate Change (IPCC) (2019) Climate Change and Land: An IPCC Special Report on climate change, desertification, land degradation, sustainable land management, food security, and greenhouse gas fluxes in terrestrial ecosystems. https://www.ipcc.ch/site/assets/uploads/2019/11/SRCCL-Full-Report-Compiled-191128.pdf. Accessed 25 June 2025

International Law Commission (ILC) (2001) Draft articles on Responsibility of States for Internationally Wrongful Acts, with commentaries, UN Doc. A/56/10

INTERPOL (2020) INTERPOL marks a decade of tackling serious organized environmental crime. https://www.interpol.int/en/News-and-Events/News/2020/INTERPOL-marks-a-decade-of-tackling-serious-organized-environmental-crime. Accessed 6 Jan 2021

Jordan L, Sandler Clarke J (2019) Jair Bolsonaro's government blocked funding for fire prevention. In: Unearthed. https://unearthed.greenpeace.org/2019/09/17/jair-bolsonaro-amazon-fires-ibama-icmbio/?_ga=2.9919222.213432829.1605344923-1195599043.1605175379. Accessed 18 October 2020

Kemp G (2013) Climate Change and the (Possible) Role of International Criminal Law. In: Spier J, Magnus U (eds) Climate Change Remedies: Injunctive Relief and Criminal Law Responses. Eleven International Publishing, The Hague, pp 165–190

Killean R (2020) From ecocide to eco-sensitivity: 'greening' reparations at the International Criminal Court. The International Journal of Human Rights 25(2):323–347

Kooijman M (2023) From Anthropos to Oikos in International Criminal Law: A Critical-Theoretical Exploration of Ecocide as an 'Ecocentric' Amendment to the Rome Statute. In: Dam-de Jong D, Amtenbrink F (eds) Netherlands Yearbook of International Law 2021 (52). T.M.C Asser Press, The Hague, pp 101–131

Kotter R (2014) Eradicating ecocide: exposing the corporate and political practices destroying the planet and proposing the laws needed to eradicate ecocide. International Journal of Environmental Studies 71(2):228–233

Lindgren T (2017) Ecocide, genocide and the disregard of alternative life-systems. The International Journal of Human Rights 22(4):525–549

Loibl G, Reiterer M (1996) International Criminal Law and the Environment. Environmental Policy and Law 26(5):192–193

Luban D (2004) A Theory of Crimes Against Humanity. Yale Journal of International Law 29:85–167

Malhotra S (2017) The International Crime That Could Have Been but Never Was: An English School Perspective on the Ecocide Law. Amsterdam Law Forum 9(3):49–70

McLaughlin R (2000) Improving Compliance: Making Non-State International Actors Responsible for Environmental Crimes. Colorado Journal of International Environmental Law and Policy 11(2):377–409

Mégret F (2011) The Problem of an International Criminal Law of the Environment. Columbia Journal of Environmental Law 36(2):195–257

Mégret F (2013) The Case for a general international crime against the environment. In: Jodoin SM, Cordonier Segger M-C (eds) Sustainable Development, International Criminal Justice, and Treaty Implementation. Cambridge University Press, Cambridge, pp 50–70

Mehta S, Merz P (2015) Ecocide – a new crime against peace? Environmental Law Review 17(1):3–7

Mendes K (2019) Brazilian Amazon fires scientifically linked to 2019 deforestation: report. https://news.mongabay.com/2019/09/brazilian-amazon-fires-scientifically-linked-to-2019-deforestation-report/. Accessed 24 June 2025

Minkova LG (2021) The fifth international crime: Reflections on the definition of 'ecocide'. Journal of Genocide Research 25(1):62–83

Mistura A (2018) Is There Space for Environmental Crimes Under International Criminal Law? The Impact of the Office of the Prosecutor Policy Paper on Case Selection and Prioritization on the Current Legal Framework. Columbia Journal Environmental Law 43(1):181–225

Mwanza R (2018) Enhancing accountability for environmental damage under international law: ecocide as a legal fulfilment of ecological integrity. Melbourne Journal of International Law 19(2):586–613

Office of the Prosecutor of the International Criminal Court (2013) Policy Paper on Preliminary Examinations. https://www.icc-cpi.int/sites/default/files/iccdocs/otp/OTP-Policy_Paper_Preliminary_Examinations_2013-ENG.pdf. Accessed 24 June 2025

Office of the Prosecutor of the International Criminal Court (2016) Policy Paper on Case Selection and Prioritisation. https://www.icc-cpi.int/sites/default/files/itemsDocuments/20160915_OTP-Policy_Case-Selection_Eng.pdf. Accessed 24 June 2025

Patel P (2016) Expanding Past Genocide, Crimes Against Humanity, and War Crimes: Can an ICC Policy Paper Expand the Court's Mandate to Prosecuting Environmental Crimes? Loyola University Chicago International Law Review 14(2):175–197

Pereira RM (2015) Environmental Criminal Liability and Enforcement in European and International Law. Brill | Nijhoff, Leiden

Pereira RM (2020) After the ICC Office of the Prosecutor's 2016 Policy Paper on Case Selection and Prioritisation: Towards an International Crime of Ecocide? Criminal Law Forum 31:179–224

Peterson I (2009) The Natural Environment in Times of Armed Conflict: A Concern for International War Crimes Law? Leiden Journal of International Law 22(2):325–343

Prosperi L, Terrosi J (2017) Embracing the 'Human Factor': Is There New Impetus at the ICC for Conceiving and Prioritizing Intentional Environmental Harms as Crimes Against Humanity? Journal of International Criminal Justice 15(3):509–525

Rauxloh R (2011) The role of international criminal law in environmental protection. In: Botchway FN (ed) Natural Resource Investment and Africa's Development. Edward Elgar Publishing, Cheltenham, pp 423–461

Republic of Maldives (2019) Written Statement of the Republic of Maldives by Mr Ahmed Saleem, Member of Parliament, Chair, Standing Committee on Climate Change and Environment, 18th Session of the Assembly of State Parties to the Rome Statute of the International Criminal Court. https://asp.icc-cpi.int/sites/asp/files/asp_docs/ASP18/GD.MDV.3.12.pdf. Accessed 24 June 2025

Smith WJ (2010) Ecocide: A Crime Against Peace? https://www.discovery.org/a/14611/. Accessed 24 June 2025

Stop Ecocide Foundation (2021) Independent Expert Panel for the Legal Definition of Ecocide: Commentary and Core Text. https://www.stopecocide.earth/legal-definition. Accessed 23 June 2025

Stop Ecocide International (2020a) Belgium, first European country to raise issue of ecocide at International criminal Court. https://www.stopecocide.earth/press-releases-summary/belgium-first-european-country-to-raise-issue-of-ecocide-at-international-criminal-court. Accessed 6 Jan 2021

Stop Ecocide International (2020b) "Criminal Law to the Rescue": Belgium pledges diplomatic action to halt ecocide crime. https://www.stopecocide.earth/press-releases-summary/belgium-pledges-diplomatic-action-to-halt-ecocide-crime. Accessed 20 Nov 2020

Stop Ecocide International (2020c) Sweden to Discuss Ecocide Law: Social Democrats, Greens and Left Party submit motions. https://www.stopecocide.earth/press-releases-summary/sweden-to-discuss-ecocide-law-social-democratsgreens-and-left-party-submit-motions. Accessed 20 Oct 2020

Stop Ecocide International (2020d) Spain's Foreign Affairs Parliamentary Committee Calls for Consideration of Criminalising Ecocide. https://www.stopecocide.earth/press-releases-summary/spains-foreign-affairs-parliamentary-committee-calls-for-consideration-of-criminalising-ecocide. Accessed 6 Jan 2021

Stop Ecocide International (2023) Ecocide Law Proposed in the Netherlands. https://www.stopecocide.earth/breaking-news-2023/ecocide-law-proposed-in-the-netherlands. Accessed 6 July 2024

United Nations Economic and Social Council (ECOSOC) (1994) The role of criminal law in the protection of the environment. UN Doc. E/RES/1994/15

United Nations Environment Programme (UNEP) (2020) Emissions Gap Report 2020. https://www.unep.org/emissions-gap-report-2020. Accessed 24 June 2025

United Nations Statistics Division (2016) Environment statistics: International and regional data sources. https://unstats.un.org/unsd/environment/interlinks.htm. Accessed 20 October 2020

UN Sustainable Development Blog (2016) Rate of Environmental Damage Increasing Across Planet but Still Time to Reverse Worst Impacts. https://www.un.org/sustainabledevelopment/blog/2016/05/rate-of-environmental-damage-increasing-across-planet-but-still-time-to-reverse-worst-impacts/. Accessed 15 June 2022

Walker G (2019) The Amazon: ecocide and an emboldened far right. https://mancunion.com/2019/09/13/the-amazon-rainforest/. Accessed 18 Oct 2020

Weinstein T (2005) Prosecuting Attacks that Destroy the Environment: Environmental Crimes or Humanitarian Atrocities? Georgetown International Environmental Law Review 17:698–721

White R (2017) Carbon criminals, ecocide and climate justice. In: Holley C, Shearing C (eds) Criminology and the Anthropocene. Routledge, London, pp 50–80

Treaties and Cases

Convention on Biological Diversity, adopted 5 June 1992, 1760 UNTS 70, entered into force 29 December 1993

Convention on International Trade in Endangered Species of Wild Fauna and Flora, adopted 3 March 1976, 993 UNTS 243, entered into force 1 July 1975

Convention on the Prohibition of Military or Any Other Hostile Use of Environmental Modification Techniques, adopted 10 December 1976, 1108 UNTS 151, entered into force 5 October 1978

Criminal Code of Georgia (22 June 1999), LGH 41(8) 2287

Criminal Code of the Kyrgyz Republic (18 September 1997) No 68

Criminal Code of the Republic of Armenia (18 April 2003)

Criminal Code of the Republic of Kazakhstan (16 July 1997) No 167

Criminal Code of the Republic of Moldova (18 April 2002) No 985-XV

Criminal Code of the Republic of Tajikistan (21 May 1998)

Criminal Code of the Russian Federation (13 June 1996) No 63-Fz

Criminal Code Ukraine (1 September 2001)

Geneva Convention (IV) relative to the Protection of Civilian Persons in Time of War, opened for signature 12 August 1949, 75 UNTS 287, entered into force 21 October 1950

Hague Convention (II) with Respect to the Laws and Customs of War on Land and its Annex: Regulations concerning the Laws and Customs of War on Land, adopted 29 July 1899 187 CTS 429, entered into force 5 September 1900

Hague Convention (IV) respecting the Laws and Customs of War on Land and its annex: Regulations concerning the Laws and Customs of War on Land, adopted 18 October 1907, 205 CTS 277, entered into force 26 January 1910

ICC, Pre-Trial Chamber I, The Prosecutor v Omar Hassan Ahmad Al Bashir, Second Decision on the Prosecution's Application for a Warrant of Arrest, ICC-02/05-01/09, 12 July 2010

ICJ, Application of the Convention on the Prevention and Punishment of the Crime of Genocide (The Gambia v Myanmar), Request for the Indication of Provisional Measures, 23 January 2020, ICJ Rep 2020

ICJ, Reservations to the Convention on the Prevention and Punishment of the Crime of Genocide, Advisory Opinion, 28 May 1951, ICJ Rep 15

ICTY, Trial Chamber II, Prosecutor v Tadić, I, Opinion and Judgment T-94-1-T, 7 May 1997

International Criminal Court, Elements of Crimes, reproduced in the Official Records of the Assembly of the States Parties to the Rome Statute of the International Criminal Court, First Session, New York, 3–10 September 2002, ICC-ASP/1/3 and Corr.1, part. II B

Irish Climate Action and Low Carbon Development Act (2015) No 46

Irish Supreme Court, Friends of the Irish Environment CLG v the Government of Ireland, Ireland and the Attorney General, Appeal No: 205/2019, 31 July 2020

Paris Agreement, adopted 12 December 2015, 55 ILM 740, entered into force 4 November 2016

Penal Code of Belarus (9 July 1999) No 420

Penal Code Viet Nam (21 December 1999), No 15/1999/QH10

Protocol Additional to the Geneva Conventions of 12 August 1949, and relating to the Protection of Victims of International Armed Conflicts (Protocol I), adopted 8 June 1977, 1125 UNTS 3, entered into force 12 July 1978

Protocol Additional to the Geneva Conventions of 12 August 1949, and relating to the Protection of Victims of Non-International Armed Conflicts (Protocol II), adopted 8 June 1977, 1125 UNTS 609, entered into force 7 December 1978

Rome Statute of the International Criminal Court adopted 17 July 1998, 2187 UNTS 3, entered into force 1 July 2002

Vienna Convention for the Protection of the Ozone Layer, adopted 22 March 1985, 1513 UNTS 293, entered into force 22 September 1988

Dr. Ana Stella Ebbersmeyer is a postdoctoral researcher at the University of Copenhagen. She is interested in international climate change, maritime and Arctic law and governance. Her PhD thesis focuses on the role of non-state actors in the regulation of black carbon emissions from Arctic shipping. Stella holds an LLB in International and European Law (Honours) from the University of Groningen and an LLM and a PhD from the University of Copenhagen.

Chapter 4
Ecocide: Toward Autonomous Environmental Crimes

Judith Alkema and Michael Faure

Contents

Abstract Alongside the introduction of a crime of ecocide in the Rome Statute, initiatives to criminalise ecocide on the domestic and European level are on the rise. The developments on ecocide crimes provide an opportunity to review the administrative dependency of current environmental criminal law systems. A problem in current (domestic) environmental criminal law is that serious cases of environmental harm (that could be qualified as ecocide) often cannot be prosecuted as long as the private operator complies with the conditions of the administrative permit. This is

J. Alkema (✉)
Utrecht University, Utrecht, The Netherlands
e-mail: judithalkema@outlook.com

Stop Ecocide NL & EcoJustice, Amsterdam, The Netherlands

M. Faure
Maastricht University, Maastricht, The Netherlands
e-mail: michael.faure@maastrichtuniversity.nl

Erasmus School of Law, Rotterdam, The Netherlands

Universitas Indonesia, Jakarta, Indonesia

L. Burgers et al. (eds.), *Ecocide: Criminalising Serious Harm against the Environment*, International Criminal Justice Series 38, https://doi.org/10.1007/978-94-6265-715-1_4

related to the unlawfulness requirement. This chapter argues that for serious cases of environmental harm (potentially amounting to ecocide) criminal liability should be possible, irrespective of compliance with a permit. Hence, they should be formulated as autonomous crimes. In this respect, an important step has been taken in the recently adopted revised Environmental Crime Directive of the European Union.

Keywords Autonomous environmental crimes · Unlawfulness · Administrative dependence · Environmental Crime Directive · Administrative permit · Environmental criminal liability

4.1 Introduction

The crime of ecocide has rapidly gained traction as a response to escalating environmental destruction. In the past years, several new ecocide laws, concept laws and proposals have been published, and discussions on those are shaping its course. In 2021, a group of international experts (Independent Expert Panel, further mentioned as IEP) drafted a legal definition for an international crime of ecocide to be added to the crimes listed in the Rome Statute.[1] This proposed definition has catalysed legislative momentum and inspired legal initiatives across different jurisdictions. In Belgium,[2] Chile[3] and the European Union[4] ecocide laws have emerged, incorporating 'severe', 'widespread' and 'long-lasting' harm to the environment as core criteria. Proposed ecocide laws in Mexico, Italy, Brazil, Scotland, the United Kingdom and

[1] See Stop Ecocide Foundation 2021.

[2] The Belgian crime constitutes the words *ernstige schade* (severe damage), *grootschalige schade* (long-lasting damage), and *langdurige schade* (long-lasting damage) to define the thresholds of damage to the environment. These thresholds are further defined in article 94 paragraphs 1a-c of book II of the Belgian Criminal Code. See Belgische Staatsblad, 29 February 2024, Wet tot invoering van Boek II van het Strafwetboek. https://www.ejustice.just.fgov.be/eli/wet/2024/02/29/2024002088/staatsblad. Accessed 26 June 2025. See for the explanatory memorandum to Book II of the Belgian Criminal Code, Belgische Kamer van Volksvertegenwoordigers 2023. The three thresholds are similar to the thresholds in the IEP definition, constituting the words 'severe', 'widespread', and 'long-term'. See Stop Ecocide Foundation 2021.

[3] In Chile, a 2023 law against "attacks on the environment" integrates elements from the IEP definition. See for an overview of existing ecocide laws, Ecocide Law, existing and proposed definitions. https://ecocidelaw.com/existing-ecocide-laws/. Accessed 20 November 2024.

[4] The revised Environmental Crime Directive (ECD), adopted in April 2024, orders Member States to criminalise actions that are "comparable to ecocide". This has been given legal teeth through Article 3 (3) of the ECD, which orders Member States to ensure that criminal offences relating to conduct listed in para 2 of the ECD constitute qualified criminal offences if such conduct causes "(...) the destruction of, or widespread and substantial damage which is either irreversible or long-lasting to, an ecosystem of considerable size or environmental value or a habitat within a protected site, or (...)". The harm-criteria in Article 3 (3) show similarity to those in the IEP-definition for an international crime of ecocide. See Directive (EU) 2024/1203 of the European Parliament and of the Council of 11 April 2024 on the protection of the environment through criminal law and replacing Directives 2008/99/EC and 2009/123/EC, adopted 11 April 2024, OJ L 202, 30 April 2024 (ECD).

the Netherlands[5] use similar harm-criteria,[6] which demonstrates the emergence of a global movement towards a unified legal framework to criminalise ecocide.[7]

The development of ecocide laws is worthy of celebration. Nonetheless, it should be understood as a response to a systemic failure of legal regimes—domestic, regional and international—to protect people and nature against extreme forms of exploitation. This failure is specifically evident with regard to the insufficient protection of indigenous peoples and local communities from exploitation and industrial activity, often driven by powerful companies and governments.[8] In our opinion, one of the main reasons why current regimes fail to protect effectively against environmental harm, is that legal regimes apply a construction where criminal law is dependent on administrative law. This creates a reality where environmental harm cannot be punished when it has been allowed under a permit or another administrative authorisation, even if this harm leads to widespread and/or lasting damage to the environment. This construction is particularly concerning in the context of ecocide.

4.1.1 A Death by a Thousand Authorised Cuts

Polly Higgins, the founder of the first global campaign to create an international crime of ecocide, called ecocide a "death by a thousand cuts", many of which are authorised by perfectly legal permits.[9] The (cumulative) effect of such "permits to pollute" can cause disastrous ecological and human health damage.[10] These problems are not hypothetical. In April 2024, one of the last remaining ancient forests in Europe was cut in the Romanian Carpathians, with a permit at hand.[11] The International Seabed

---

[5] See, Tweede Kamer der Staten-Generaal 2023.

[6] See for an overview of existing ecocide laws, Ecocide Law, existing and proposed definitions https://ecocidelaw.com/existing-ecocide-laws/. Accessed 20 November 2024.

[7] See for more information about the global movement to criminalize ecocide, www.stopecocide.earth and www.ecocidelaw.com. Accessed 20 November 2024.

[8] For example, energy companies which continue to invest in fossil fuels and their infrastructure, despite continuing to cause significant ecological harm and contribute to climate change. A calling example is the environmental harm caused by Dutch oil company Royal Dutch Shell in the Niger Delta. See for examples on what types of environmental harms could be considered 'ecocide': https://www.stopecocide.be/nl/whatisecocide. Accessed 26 June 2025.

[9] Higgins 2012; Higgins 2010.

[10] See, for example, regarding the environmental harm of the (permitted) use of the pesticide 'glyphosate': Gandhi et al. 2021; PAN Europe 2023; Geissen 2023. Other examples where significant health risks result from permitted emissions include the permitted discharge of PFOA by Chemours in the Netherlands, challenged in a civil case brought by four municipalities. See de Rechtspraak 2023. Similar controversies arose in the Netherlands around Tata Steel Ijmuiden, which for years was permitted to emit significant amounts of lead and particulate matter before permits were revised following extensive proceedings and scientific evidence. see Pointer 2021; Randstedelijke Rekenkamer 2021. Another case concerns permits allowing Chemelot to emit 14,000 kg of microplastics annually into the river Maas. See Ministerie van Infrastructuur en Waterstaat 2021.

[11] Greenpeace International 2024.

Authority is under pressure to award permits to start deep-sea mining, despite strong evidence of serious, long-lasting and widespread harm to the ocean seabed and wider ocean ecosystem. The cutting down of the Amazon rainforest in Latin America has been allowed under the protection of governmental regulations and permits, with the deforestation speed peaking under the reign of Bolsonaro.[12] Companies are granted permits to strip huge parts of rainforests in Indonesia and the Moluccan islands for soy production and lithium mining.[13] And all the while, permits are still being granted for new oil and gas explorations on top of existing environmentally harmful oil and gas exploitation projects.[14]

In this chapter, we argue that ecocide crimes should be conceptualised as an autonomous crimes—i.e. fully independent of administrative law—to effectively serve its purpose. Not all scholars and practitioners agree, which makes it relevant to explore the issue further. In its obligatory advice to the submitted ecocide law proposal, the Council of State in the Netherlands for instance advised against adopting a proposed ecocide law in its autonomous form, unless the lawmaker strongly clarifies the scope and definition of criminal conduct (the thresholds of damage). It states that the abandonment of the dependency on administrative regulations proposed in the initiative law might be undesirable, as it creates uncertainty for companies and citizens and therefore might violate the legality principle.[15]

The principle of legality broadly holds that no one can be convicted of a crime that did not constitute a criminal offence under national law or international law when it was committed.[16] It is a fundamental principle for the functioning of the democratic rule of law, as it protects citizens against arbitrary use of criminal law by governments.[17] To guarantee the principle of legality, governments have to make sure that laws are clear, and that criminal behaviour is foreseeable. In domestic contexts, the principle of legality is often strictly interpreted. This is visible in the critique by the Dutch Council of State. It sees problems in the wording of the Dutch ecocide crime proposal: "the crime of ecocide is, according to the Council, so generally described that it is insufficiently clear which behaviour is criminal. For example, the damage that is created must be serious and widespread or serious and long-term, but it is not clear what this means exactly."[18] These concerns will be addressed in

[12] Fearnside 2021.

[13] See for example IUCN 2022.

[14] For example, see the tar sands in Canada. An area stretching over 140,000 square kilometres, where the land has been stripped, boreal forest cut and water and soil contamination stretches far beyond the mining site. See Danby 2011. 11 million litres of toxic waste leaks into the Athabasca River and watershed daily. See Environmental Defense 2013. See also the ecological disaster resulting from oil exploitation in the Niger Delta, Nigeria. Milieudefensie 2024; Ratcliffe 2019.

[15] Raad van State 2024a.

[16] See for example Charter of Fundamental Rights of the European Union, opened for signature 7 December 2000, OJ C 364/01, entered into force 1 December 2009 (EU Charter of Fundamental Rights), Article 49, where the principle of legality is laid out in law. There are many variations on the exact wording on the definition of the principle of legality, as can be read in Gallant 2009.

[17] Amongst other purposes, see Gallant 2009, p. 21.

[18] Raad van State 2024b (translation by the authors from the Dutch text).

Sect. 4.3.3 and further, when we discuss how to respond to potential legal uncertainty in the conceptualisation of (domestic) autonomous crimes.

Obviously, this theme raises many questions. Could the level of seriousness of a crime of ecocide justify a less strict interpretation of the principle of legality? What role do international treaties and customary law play in this matter? What level of clarity should be required in which legal contexts and can they differ between domestic contexts and international criminal law? This discussion is relevant in each ecocide criminalisation and ecocide proposal, and is a puzzle solved differently in each variant.[19]

4.1.2 A Substantiated Plea

Although relevant, this chapter will only deal with these questions in an indirect manner. The focus of this contribution is to present a plea for removing the 'administrative dependency' in ecocide crime proposals and other similar environmental crimes. In doing so, it aims to provide guidance to lawmakers, politicians, legal scholars and policy-makers in the creation of ecocide crimes that effectively serve their purpose, and to contribute to the ongoing debates on the principle of legality.

Before continuing, we would like to explicitly mention the assumptions underlying our plea. We believe that in today's world, where species-extinction, climate change, and severe forms of pollution are human-induced realities, further environmental harm must be halted and prevented as much as possible. This is especially true for cases where the environmental harm is of such an extent that it leads to the long-term or widespread destruction of ecosystems and the killing of species (including humans). To safeguard a healthy living environment for present and future generations of people and other living beings, our environment urgently needs better legal protection mechanisms, more particularly in criminal law, where environmental values should be protected as a legal interest. After all, criminal law's objectives of retribution and deterrence fit the scope of environmental crises. It is from these assumptions that our arguments are constituted.

We will proceed as follows. In Sect. 4.2, we will explain several key problems surrounding the administrative dependency of environmental criminal law. We will argue that the administrative dependence of criminal law currently limits the scope of criminal law at the domestic level, leading to the legalisation of ecocide-type

[19] In some laws, the threshold for harm is high (in the Belgian proposal the threshold is higher than in the IEP-proposal; severe, widespread *and* long-term damage to the environment), in other proposals the scope of the crime is narrowed. In the European Crime Directive (ECD) the 'ecocide crime' is formulated as a qualified offence; it is only invokable when one of the formulated criminal offences leads to serious and widespread or serious and long-term damage to the environment. See ECD, above n 4. However, in many ecocide-proposals currently under review the discussion on legality and justifying a broad scope to have maximum protective effect is extremely relevant, both in the domestic and the international context. See for considerations to further the debate about legality in the context of ecocide law Killean and Short 2023.

events all over the world, especially in countries where permits are easy to obtain for powerful economic players. We base this argument on various elements: the function of (environmental) criminal law in protecting legal interests and values; the state-corporate nexus influencing administrative authorisations and economic insights according to which autonomous environmental crimes may provide incentives to economic operators to apply measures to abate pollution beyond compliance with the conditions of a permit. In Sect. 4.3, we will assert that there are arguments to loosen the administrative dependence of environmental crimes and therefore come to autonomous crimes in case of serious environmental harm (that could amount to ecocide), and discuss several key considerations for conceptualising such crimes. We will explore recent developments in ecocide crimes, highlighting the model of the EU Directive. Lastly, we will offer a few concluding remarks in Sect. 4.4.

4.2 Problems with the Administrative Dependency of Environmental Criminal Law

4.2.1 Administrative Dependency

In most domestic legal systems, there is a strong relationship between prior administrative decisions and criminal liability.[20] The enforcement of criminal law is often an addition to an existing system of administrative decisions pertaining to the level and quality of emissions coming from an identifiable point, such as a factory or treatment plant. Also, as far as non-point source pollution—pollution which comes from multiple, diffuse sources rather than a single identifiable point—is concerned (for example, regulating the protection of habitats or products), criminal law accepts a system of prior administrative decisions. This system is based on administrative statutes regulating the conditions under which the administrative authorities can allow pollution, or more broadly an endangerment of environmental sustainability. Central within these administrative statutes are so-called emission standards or emission limit values that fix the amount of a certain compound that can be emitted. Those standards are usually laid down in individual permits or in general regulations.[21] A traditional way of criminalisation was that criminal provisions were included in a provision at the end of an administrative statute, stating that everyone who violates the provisions of the act or the regulations enacted on the basis of the act shall be punished with a specified sanction. Such an article often stated in a rather general way that everyone who violates the provisions of the act, regulation or the licenses issued pursuant thereto will be punished.[22]

[20] Faure 2017a, pp. 327–330.

[21] Country-specific examples are inter alia provided in Faure and Heine 2000, as well as in Faure and Visser 1999.

[22] Faure 2006.

In some cases, a different legislative technique was followed: rather than proscribing the violation of administrative obligations, an unlawful emission into the environment would be criminalised. This model of criminalisation therefore requires an emission (which constitutes a concrete endangerment of the environment) as well as unlawfulness of the emission. However, also in this second model, there is a strong link with administrative law through the unlawfulness requirement. This is because unlawfulness will usually be defined as violating administrative obligations. And as long as the administrative rules are followed, usually no criminal liability will follow, since the conduct will not be considered unlawful.[23] Many examples of this type of criminalisation can be found in various statutes.[24] Due to an evolution in legal systems from criminal law provisions merely at the end of an environmental statute as a backup of administrative obligations towards including environmental criminal law provisions either in penal codes or in general environmental statutes, in various statutes it is no longer merely the administrative disobedience that is punished in criminal laws, but rather an unlawful emission.[25]

There can be differences between the various models of criminalising environmental harm, whereby in some provisions the unlawfulness requirement can be interpreted more broadly, that is, not merely as a violation of administrative regulations.[26] But the bottom-line is that, with only very few exceptions,[27] criminal liability will fail as long as the operator respects the conditions of an authorisation. There is, in other words, no autonomous environmental crime; domestic criminal law does not protect the environment independently from administrative law.

4.2.2 Rationale Behind the Administrative Dependency of Environmental Criminal Law

Even though this administrative dependence of environmental criminal law has significant disadvantages, its underlying rationale is understandable. In general, administrative authorities are (or should be) better equipped and have access to more comprehensive information than the judge when asserting conditions under which specific emissions may be harmful. Determining such conditions involves a complicated balancing exercise, an area in which administrative authorities often have greater expertise than the judge. By setting specific conditions in a permit, administrative authorities will determine the conditions under which the permit holder can operate a "classified installation"—a legal term referring to sites where industrial activities with potential environmental impacts are conducted and are subject

[23] See Faure and Visser 1995, p. 328.

[24] For example, see Faure 2006, pp. 197–198.

[25] See further on this evolution in the criminalisation of environmental harm in various jurisdictions, Mandiberg and Faure 2009.

[26] See further Heine 1990; Mandiberg and Faure 2009.

[27] For example §330a of the German Criminal Code, to be discussed below.

to specific regulations.[28] In doing so, they effectively determine the extent to which such operations *de facto* endanger the environment. Relying on the administrative law system, the administrative authorities will, for example, depend on information on the best available technologies to determine standards in a permit.

In theory, this system, whereby administrative authorities have the primacy in determining the conditions under which a permit holder may endanger the environment (by fixing standards), can be equally effective as it is backed up with administrative and criminal sanctions (in case of non-respect of those prior administrative decisions). Especially for small and medium business enterprises sanctions might be sufficiently deterring, and such a system can therefore be understood from the perspective of the goal of environmental protection.

Additionally, this system serves the above-mentioned principle of legality. By requiring an *a priori* violation of administrative obligation, there is less reason to be concerned about the arbitrary use of criminal law and processes by the competent authorities. The administrative conditions (in permits or administrative laws) are usually specific and detailed; in permits it is clearly defined which acts and omissions are permitted. Linking the criminality of an act to the violation of administrative permits or laws creates a detailed codified manifestation of permittable and non-permittable—and thus criminal—behaviour.[29]

4.2.3 Problems with the Administrative Dependency of Environmental Criminal Law

There are, however, particular problems in limiting the criminal liability to a violation of prior administrative decisions and, more particularly, to exclude criminal liability as long as the conditions of an administrative authorisation are respected, especially when it comes to cases where severe environmental harm results from authorised conduct. We sketch five such problems deriving as a consequence of the administrative dependency of environmental criminal law.

1. The first consequence worth mentioning is that a strict administrative dependence on environmental criminal law does not directly protect the environment. A judge

[28] See for example the use of the word 'installation' in the Directive (EU) 2023/959 of the European Parliament and of the Council amending Directive 2003/87/EC establishing a system for greenhouse gas emission allowance trading within the Union, Decision (EU) 2015/1814 and Regulation (EU) 2015/757, adopted 10 May 2023, OJ L 130, 16 May 2023, entered into force 5 June 2023 (EU ETS Directive). For more information, see https://www.emissions-euets.com/carbon-market-glossary/875-installation. Accessed 20 November 2024.

[29] Interestingly, the principle of legality can also be jeopardised by over-codification; the myriad of rules can become so complicated that it is hard for citizens to understand which regulations apply to them. Additionally, the fact that the same article can be interpreted differently by an administrative court and a criminal court can lead to issues regarding legal certainty and foreseeability. These are some of the critiques expressed in Hendriks 2010.

will have to look only at whether an administrative rule has been violated, independent from the question of whether that violation results in pollution or other environmentally harmful conduct. Consequently, it seems that the rule of law (abiding by administrative authorisations) is protected as a legal interest, rather than the environment.

This has problematic effects. First, because environmental values are only protected by criminal law *to the extent to* which administrative laws aim to safeguard them, criminal liability can be triggered even when no environmental harm occurs. For example, operating an industrial installation without a permit might pose a risk to the environment, but without actual emissions, the harm remains abstract. Criminal law will still apply for the lack of a permit, punishing the operator for operating in absence of a required permit, rather than actual endangerment or harm to the environment.[30] This also works the other way around. If no administrative rule has been violated, no criminal penalty will apply even if substantial environmental damage occurs. This is misleading, according to Schaffmeister, who already wrote about this issue as early as 1993: "someone who emits dangerous materials into the ground with a permit still harms the environment. Whether someone has a permit to pollute should not be a basis for the distinction between bona fide and mala fide offenders of environmental crimes".[31]

2. The second issue is that since endangerment or harm to the environment is not a requirement for criminal liability, harmful effects will not be verified by a criminal court.[32] It weakens the moral aspect of criminalisation, when legal discussions focus on whether specific administrative rules were violated (e.g. limits on nitrogen emission, fertilizer use, or harmful chemicals), rather than whether or not the environment has been damaged.[33] Consequently, this can influence the case law on what constitutes legally permissible and morally unacceptable environmental damage. Moreover, levels of punishment are typically connected with the severity of the violation of the protected interest of the law. If the protected interest is the enforcement of administrative rules, or in Koopmans words, "the effective control of an orderly society", levels of punishments may not increase with the severity of the resulting environmental harm, which affect its deterring effect for causing severe forms of environmental harm.[34] Furthermore, a criminal provision, punishing administrative violations does not reflect that environmental

[30] Mandiberg and Faure 2009, p. 453.

[31] Hendriks 2010, p. 28; Schaffmeister 1993, pp. 90–91.

[32] Faure and Visser 1995, p. 321. Obviously, this may depend upon the precise formulation of the specific provision involved.

[33] To nuance this statement: we see in practice that some cases of environmental harm do lead to public outrage. However, these cases are often connected to the harmful effects for humans (such as health effects). This is visible in (criminal) case law on the emissions of Tata Steel IJmuiden and Chemours Dordrecht in the Netherlands.

[34] See Alkema 2020, p. 40; Koopmans 1996, pp. 12–16.

crime endangers ecological values as well.[35] As a result, the effect on the environment, and the harm caused to all that lives in the environment is not always a topic of debate in a criminal court. This undermines the moral function and the signalling function of criminal law in environmental cases.

3. A third, related problem is that it is not the criminal judge that determines the scope of criminal liability, but the administrative authorities.[36] Theoretically, this can be justified, as shown in Sect. 4.2.2. However, reality shows how theory and practice can diverge greatly. Public choice literature has pointed at the danger that a permit system can be vulnerable to lobbying by special interest groups, in particular powerful (multinational) companies, as a result of which either authorisations are provided when it is not in the public interest or permit conditions are included that reflect private rather than public interests.[37] The criminological literature has also pointed to the so-called state-corporate nexus whereby ecocide could *de facto* take place as a result of a regulatory framework created by the state (for example allowing deforestation).[38] Given the state-corporate nexus it is even likely that serious environmental harm could take place under the umbrella of regulation. In this way, it can enable forms of *white-collar crime.*[39]
4. A fourth problem is that within a model of strict administrative dependence, operators are only incentivised to comply with an authorisation, rather than adopting higher environmental standards. That is problematic to the extent that, as indicated, in practice efficient pollution standards may often be higher than what is required in a permit. But without a duty to adopt higher (more demanding) pollution standards, criminal law only provides incentives to follow the conditions in an (arguably inefficient/outdated) authorisation, rather than encouraging investments in cleaner, more environmental-friendly production technologies or business models.

   We can see this in the case of Tata Steel's factory in IJmuiden, the Netherlands, where insufficiently strict pollution standards have resulted in the factory's emissions of toxic chemicals for decades. As a result, the surrounding environment is heavily polluted and nearby residents experience an increase in cancer cases.[40] In its 2023 report, The Dutch Council for Safety[41] observed that, in the case of Tata Steel, environmental permits could be granted even when there was

[35] Faure and Visser 1995, p. 320.

[36] Faure and Visser 1995, p. 321. Obviously, this may depend upon the precise formulation of the specific provision involved.

[37] According to public choice literature the product delivered by wealth is incentivising politicians to favour special interest groups. Special interest groups seek so-called "rents" (economic benefits) with legislation and politicians provide those rents in exchange for political support to guarantee their re-election. See inter alia Buchanan et al. 1980.

[38] Tombs and Whyte 2020.

[39] See for an analysis on the nexus between white collar crime and the environment: Sing 2021, p. 872.

[40] Rijksinstituut voor Volksgezondheid en Milieu 2023.

[41] In Dutch: Onderzoeksraad voor de Veiligheid (OVV).

insufficient understanding of the potential health risks for nearby residents.[42] The report further states that "the province and the environmental services realized that the permitted emissions of Tata Steel are potentially not justified."[43]

The Council report highlights another significant gap between theory and practice, revealing that years of budget cuts in environmental enforcement left authorities without the knowledge, capacity and urgency to effectively monitor pollution and ensure compliance at large factories like Tata Steel's in Ijmuiden.[44] Furthermore, the companies did not take proactive steps to limit their emissions more than was strictly necessary based on their permits.[45]

The Dutch newspaper *de Volkskrant* strikingly noted: "according to the Council both companies as well as governments are fixated on the awarded permit" and "civil servants with little capacity cannot compete with the force of polluters".[46] It was only when the media pressure and the local community pushed both the government and the polluter to take action that the government began to respond more decisively.[47] Dutch authorities have given Tata Steel an ultimatum in December 2024 to limit the pollution of their 'coke oven'—the most polluting part of the factory—within a year. If they fail to do so, their permit will be revoked.[48] This decision, however, came only after year-long severe public pressure, and clear proof of severe health damage resulting from (that part of) the factory.

5. This brings us to the fifth problem; there can be errors in the permit, even if the licensing authorities did not intend to provide benefits to interest groups.[49] Moreover, as a result of technological change, permits could also easily become outdated in cases where they are not rapidly adapted to new technological insights. Additionally, the assumption that administrative authorities are always in a good position to set environmental standards efficiently may not hold in all cases, as many companies are themselves in a far better position to map their environmental impact. Moreover, local administrative authorities (such as municipalities) sometimes simply lack the expertise to set environmental standards efficiently and are therefore vulnerable to manipulation. This is illustrated in another recent court case in the Netherlands, where four Dutch municipalities sought damages at the Dutch civil court for the cleanup and reparations of the ecological and health damages created by the discharge of perfluorooctanoic acid (PFOA) by chemical company Chemours. In their decision to allow the discharge of PFOA over the past 40 years, the municipalities relied on data

[42] Onderzoeksraad voor de Veiligheid 2023.

[43] Onderzoeksraad voor de Veiligheid 2023, p. 74.

[44] Onderzoeksraad voor de Veiligheid 2023.

[45] Onderzoeksraad voor de Veiligheid 2023, acknowledged in Van den Eerenbeemt and Waarlo 2023.

[46] Ibid.

[47] Ibid.

[48] Ibid.

[49] See Olson 1965.

provided by Chemours, which, they argued, insufficiently showed the ecologically harmful character of PFOA as a forever-chemical. Later, it became apparent that the allowed discharge is leading to long-lasting, severe environmental harm and even to health damage.

Chemours defended itself by pointing at the issued permit: the emissions were allowed by the municipalities. In response, the municipalities argued that Chemours intentionally did not provide the correct up-to-date scientific data, based on which they allowed Chemours to discharge harmful amounts of PFOA into the environment. The Dutch Court interim judgement of 27 September 2023 ruled in favour of the municipalities for the period between 1984 and 1998.[50] For the period 1998-2012 the case is still pending. Although this gives reason to believe that the polluting company will have to pay for some of the damage it has caused, the way to get there is inefficient, requiring years of resources and government money spent on court cases.

Summarising: we do not generally argue against the administrative dependence of environmental criminal law. In a 'normal'[51] case, where environmental damage is relatively small and morally justified by its societal benefits (for example land-conversion for sustainable food, timber production or sustainable housing projects) the operator can rely on the conditions of a permit as a minimum to be followed. The conditions of the permit (for example emission limit values) will provide information to an operator concerning the measures to be taken to reduce environmental harm. However, merely following the conditions of a permit does not guarantee that no serious environmental harm could occur from the activity under consideration, especially considering practical examples where companies (fraudulently) influence permits to their advantage. Indeed, problems can especially arise in the more exceptional case where substantial, long-lasting or widespread environmental harm would be caused, even though the operator follows the conditions of an authorisation. We argue that precisely in those cases the permit should no longer shield the operator, and the individuals in charge of the operation, from criminal liability (the so-called permit shield).[52]

[50] See Rechtbank Rotterdam, *Gemeente Dordrecht et al. v. Chemours Netherlands B.V.*, Judgment, 27 September 2023, ECLI:NL:RBROT:2023:8987, para 2.3.(b) and de Rechtspraak 2023.

[51] The word 'normal' is placed in quotation marks to indicate that what is perceived as normal is subject to subjective interpretation.

[52] Mandiberg and Faure 2009, pp. 480–503.

4.3 Autonomous Environmental Crimes (of Ecocide)

4.3.1 Justifications

An autonomous crime is a crime where there is no strict administrative dependency. Under such a crime, the actor responsible for the serious environmental pollution can be punished even if the conditions of the license have been complied with.[53] The *theoretical* justification for autonomous environmental crimes is straightforward: criminal law should intervene in cases of serious environmental harm—especially when this endangers human health or violates human rights—even when the operator has complied with permit conditions.[54] This is justified from several perspectives, particularly an ecocentric one.

We argue that serious forms of environmental harm should be judged by its consequences, just as we do with murder or manslaughter. In those cases, the crime is defined by the act—the (intentional) killing of another person—rather than on whether it was committed lawfully or unlawfully.[55] If murder were treated like many environmental crimes, a judge would first need to determine whether the killing was *unlawful* before even considering whether it was manslaughter or murder. This would suggest that, in the absence of a specific legal violation (of administrative decisions), taking a life could be permissible—something we see as an absurd notion. While exceptional circumstances, such as self-defence or war, can legally justify taking a life, these are strictly limited and subject to clear legal requirements. The fundamental principle and normative baseline protected by criminal law remains that killing another person is inherently wrong. Applying the same reasoning to environmental harm, we see the situation turned around. The lack of autonomous environmental crimes implies that severe ecological destruction is generally acceptable, and not acceptable only when it is committed unlawfully. This idea is morally and legally flawed. Just as we recognise that taking a life is inherently wrongful and criminalise it outright, we should do the same for severe forms of environmental destruction, especially so when it directly or indirectly harms human health and well-being.

The latter part of this argument can be extended by looking at the human right to life. If we recognise and protect the right to life in criminal law, it follows logically that we should also protect ecological life, as human survival depends on it. Scientific insights increasingly show how human health and environmental health

---

[53] Faure 2017b, p. 278.

[54] For examples, see the recent study by the Dutch Research Council for Safety, which includes three examples from the Netherlands where operators follow the conditions of their permit, but where nonetheless serious health damage is caused to the citizens living in the neighbourhood of the industrial installations concerned. See Onderzoeksraad voor de Veiligheid 2023.

[55] In the Netherlands, the crime of murder is defined as follows: "he who intentionally and with premeditated intent, robs another person of life, is, as guilty of murder, punished with a lifelong prison sentence, or a temporary prison sentence of a maximum of thirty years or a fine of the fifth category". See Dutch Penal Code, Article 289.

are interlinked.[56] Next to the already existing human right to life, the right to a healthy environment and the right to be protected against climate change are now even acknowledged as separate human rights, imposing duties on both states and corporations.[57] Case law, such as the *Milieudefensie v. Shell* ruling has reinforced this duty, even though it was decided in a civil court.[58] This strengthens the moral legitimacy of demanding effective environmental protection through criminal law.

Moreover, the absence of autonomous environmental crimes creates a significant gap: because the right to a healthy environment is not explicitly protected, there is no legal obligation to demand stronger environmental laws—even as scientific evidence increasingly links environmental degradation to human health risks. This creates a self-sustaining cycle; because the by criminal law protected right to life is not linked to the environment and because the right to a healthy environment or environmental health is not a legal interest protected by criminal law, there is no *legal* reason to demand increased criminal law protection of the environment, *despite* growing evidence that a healthy environment is needed for a healthy (and not deadly) life. This stagnant reasoning where attempts to create autonomous crimes to protect environmental health are cut short because there is no legal basis for it, undermines necessary legal evolutions. New legal frameworks must evolve to reflect our growing understanding of the deep connection between environmental integrity and human well-being.

Additionally, an administrative permit can never justify very serious forms of environmental harm, especially if this harm extends to harm to humans.[59] This notion justifies that operators would have to go beyond compliance with the permit conditions to prevent serious environmental pollution from occurring. This could also concern cases where public authorities have simply wrongly awarded the permit (whether due to manipulated data, corruption or pressure of the company to whom the permit is awarded). It may also be that factual circumstances have changed or that the permitted emissions cause more harm than could be foreseen when granting the permit. Of course, one could argue that this is an example of an administrative error, which should therefore (also) be corrected by administrative law (for example by reviewing the permit conditions and imposing harsher standards). That is undoubtedly correct. However, there are many cases which show that for a variety of reasons

[56] See for a contextualisation of such interlinkages based on developments in scientific insights, the United Nations Human Rights Office of the High Commissioner 2023.

[57] The duty of the State was very recently established by the Dutch Judge in the case Shell v. Milieudefensie, in consideration 7 (17), which states (in Dutch): "uit het vorenstaande volgt dat er geen twijfel over kan bestaan dat de bescherming tegen gevaarlijke klimaatverandering een mensenrecht is. Wereldwijd wordt erkend dat staten een verplichting hebben hun burgers te beschermen tegen de nadelige effecten van gevaarlijke klimaatverandering." See Gerechtshof Den Haag, *Shell Plc v. Stichting Milieu en Mens*, 5 March 2024, ECLI:NL:GHDHA:2024:2099.

[58] Ibid, see (in Dutch): "Het is in de eerste plaats aan wetgevers en regeringen om maatregelen te nemen om gevaarlijke klimaatverandering zoveel mogelijk te beperken. Dat neemt niet weg dat ook op ondernemingen, waaronder dus Shell, een verantwoordelijkheid kan rusten om maatregelen te nemen om gevaarlijke klimaatverandering tegen te gaan. Belangrijk daarvoor is het leerstuk van de indirecte horizontale werking van mensenrechten." Consideration 7 (17).

[59] Mandiberg and Faure 2009, p. 492.

these corrections in administrative law apparently do not take place.[60] Private parties should be incentivised to monitor the environmental harm they are causing and not to lean backwards and blindly use the permits they receive from administrative authorities.

This brings us to the *practical* justification for having an autonomous environmental crime. This was already partly given in the previous section when discussing the limits of strict administrative dependency. If criminal law were not able to intervene in cases of serious environmental harm, it would simply mean that criminal law would fail to provide its remedies when it is in fact most needed to protect life for present and future generations and do justice to those harmed, including indigenous communities and non-human beings.

Moreover, the creation of an autonomous environmental crime has an important signalling effect to the general public and to industrial operators, making clear that individual criminal liability for natural persons in a position of leadership within companies can occur, irrespective of the compliance with a permit if substantial and long-lasting or widespread damage to the environment has occurred.[61] This would lead to a level of deterrence for causing such environmental harm, which is currently absent. Often, large polluting companies calculate environmental fines and damages into their cost-benefit-analysis. This is because the fines are low compared to required investments in more sustainable production methods and there is little chance to get caught, both in production-countries where enforcement capacity is low or corrupted, but also in developed countries.[62] In very few cases is it possible to impose criminal liability on individuals within companies.[63] Even if the harm is of such a level that it catches the public eye, companies still have the possibility to hide behind the permit-shield. Individual criminal liability for people within corporations (and governments) established by autonomous environmental crimes will provide an incentive to avoid and prevent severe forms of environmental damage. Additionally, its criminalisation will force a change of financial flows, tax breaks and subsidies from environmentally harmful to environmentally sustainable investments.

Most notably, autonomous environmental crimes would put a primary responsibility on the polluter, instead of on the government exclusively. This will bypass

[60] See for example the cases discussed in the report by the Dutch Research Council for Safety, Onderzoeksraad voor de Veiligheid 2023.

[61] An important question is obviously how "serious environmental pollution" can adequately be captured in legislation in compliance with the *lex certa* principle.

[62] This is evident in the motivation for the revision of the European Crime Directive (ECD).

[63] See on the subject of the influence of corporations on state action, for example Hauser et al. 2024. See on this topic and the lack of corporate accountability mechanisms Barigbon 2023. "Although, the upper management and directors of O&G companies are studied as both driving and hampering the energy transition, in practice the literature observes little change from the upper management of O&G companies. Senior executives and managers resist change (laggards) due to the individual wealth and benefits they earn in the O&G industry", in Herzog-Hawelka and Gupta 2023, section 5.11.

previously discussed vulnerabilities of the permit-system, decrease financial pressure on governments to effectively establish, monitor and enforce permit requirements, will lead to pro-active corporate behaviour to limit environmental harm and do justice to the polluter-pays-principle (as opposed to the government (read: the taxpayer) paying to clean up environmental damage).[64]

4.3.2 Examples of Autonomous Environmental Crimes

Examples of autonomous environmental crimes are rare but do exist. A classic example is Article 330a of the German Criminal Code. That provision punishes the endangerment of human life or health through the emission of toxic substances. However, in this particular case it is the serious endangerment of the life or health of persons that is criminalised. The provision therefore takes an anthropocentric rather than an ecocentric approach.[65]

In addition, in some countries it has been advanced in the literature that in order to provide a truly autonomous protection of ecological values, serious attacks on the environment should be punishable, even if these were to be allowed under an administrative licence. Therefore, for example, in the Flemish Region, a proposal has been made by an Interuniversity Commission for the reform of the environmental law in Flanders to introduce a new article within a decree on environmental policy that would criminalise cases of serious pollution irrespective of administrative law. This proposed Article 7.3.4 punishes anyone who emits substances into the water, soil or air if he/she knew or should have known that these emissions pose a concrete danger to human health.[66] While also still taking an anthropocentric approach by focusing on danger to human health, the importance of this provision is that unlawfulness is no longer required.

Another example can be found in the Council of Europe Convention for the protection of the environment through criminal law. In the 1980s and 1990s several changes in the environmental criminal law of EU Member States took place, sharpening both the criminal provisions as well as the penalties. In addition, a debate took place on whether environmental criminal law should also be regulated at the supranational level. At that moment, originally the debate did not take place within the EU, as it was still debated whether the EU had the competence to force the Member States towards a criminalisation of environmental harm. The first attempt towards the creation of a transboundary instrument covering environmental criminal law came therefore from

---

[64] This principle states that those responsible for pollution should bear the costs associated with preventing, controlling, or remedying the damage caused by their pollution. It means that the burden of environmental harm should not fall on society or future generations, but on individuals, companies or entities which cause the pollution. It is widely accepted in international environmental agreements, such as the OECD guidelines and EU policies. OECD 1992.

[65] Faure 2017b, p. 279.

[66] See Article 7.3.4 Voorontwerp Decreet Milieubeleid. Interuniversitaire Commissie tot Herziening van het Milieurecht in het Vlaamse Gewest 1995, p. 82.

the Council of Europe, which created in 1998 a Convention on the protection of the environment through criminal law.[67] In this Convention the various signatory states agreed to adopt specific provisions to protect the environment in their criminal law. It contains minimum provisions on environmental criminal law. In addition to various concrete endangerment crimes (such as punishing unlawful emissions), the Convention also created an independent crime aimed at serious pollution in Article 2.1(a): "The discharge, emission or introduction of a quantity of substances or ionizing radiation into air, soil or water, which: (i) causes death or serious injury to any person or (ii) creates a significant risk of causing death or serious injury to any person". For this crime, there is no requirement that the discharge is unlawful. In other words: this provision applies irrespective of the violation of administrative obligations and is therefore considered an autonomous crime.[68] There are other examples of autonomous environmental crimes, either in draft legislation[69] or by using traditional crimes (such as assault, homicide or other traditional crimes) to address serious environmental pollution.[70] An interesting alternative is the recently adopted revised EU Environmental Crime Directive. We will come back to this example in the following section.

4.3.3 Conceptualising Autonomous Crimes

If one agrees that for cases of serious environmental pollution there should be a provision enabling criminal law to intervene even when the conditions of a permit are respected, the question arises how this can be formulated in a manner which is compatible with the rule of law. Here we return to the principle of legality.[71] It is not easy to respect this principle when the legislator wishes to treat very serious cases of environmental harm separately from 'regular' cases of environmental harm and has to decide what the crucial criterion is to treat some cases as very serious. Merely punishing 'substantial' pollution will be too vague and might violate the principle.[72]

A second, closely related issue is whether the administrative link will only be severed in case of an endangerment of human health (like in the Council of Europe Convention, in Article 330a of the German Criminal Code, and in the proposal from the Interuniversity Commission for the reform of the environmental law in Flanders) or whether it would be possible to formulate an autonomous crime that intervenes in cases of serious environmental pollution, also when no danger for human health is

---

[67] To be found *inter alia* in Faure and Heine 2000, pp. 407–416.

[68] Faure 2017a, p. 343.

[69] See Faure and Visser 1995, p. 340.

[70] For example, see Mandiberg and Faure 2009, pp. 485–489.

[71] See Resolution 6 of the XVth International Congress of Penal Law (1995). Consistent with the principle of legality, there should be certainty in the definition of crimes against the environment.

[72] Faure and Visser 1995, p. 341.

created. The difficulty seems to be that it may not be easy to define serious environmental pollution in such an ecocentric manner (without any reference to danger to human health) in a manner that is compatible with the legality principle. An emission endangering human health still seems to be sufficiently specified, but attempts to define an autonomous crime in a more ecocentric manner often amount to rather vague formulations, for instance criminalising 'substantial damage' or 'pollution', which may not be compatible with the legality principle.[73] However, one can argue that this has in part to do with the lack of scientific consensus and data on what constitutes 'substantial damage' or 'pollution', as opposed to a wealth of scientific consensus and data on what qualifies as harmful to human health. In this way one can see the development of a generally formulated autonomous environmental crime as a necessary step in the ecological emancipation of criminal law: it forces policy-makers, judges and scientists to research and define its exact thresholds further. Aside from this, there are some examples of autonomous environmental crimes that are clearly compatible with the legality principle, focusing on one particular environmental aspect. An example would be Article L 432-2 of the French Environmental Code which criminalises "the act of throwing, dumping or allowing to flow into the waters… directly or indirectly, any substances whose actions or reactions have destroyed the fish or harmed its nutrition, reproduction or food value".[74]

A third point is that there may be various legislative techniques to sever the administrative link. The one we have discussed so far is to eliminate the unlawfulness requirement in the context of establishing criminal liability; a second possibility (already applied in some legal systems) is to allow courts to conduct a judicial review of an operating permit or license. As a result of this judicial review, the judge might hold that the defendant relied on an unlawful permit. The problem with that technique is, however, that if the defendant did not know and could also not have known that the permit was unlawful (meaning that she/he cannot be blamed for his/her ignorance or mistake), the mistake will serve as an excuse and a criminal acquittal might follow.[75] An alternative possibility is the already mentioned option to use traditional crimes (like assault, homicide or property destruction) to punish environmental pollution. That could lead to the punishment of the polluter even though the conditions of a permit were respected.[76] Nonetheless, this option also has various disadvantages.[77] Most notably, that the causal effect between the environmental harm and the assault, homicide or property destruction has to be proven, and the burden of proof lies on the prosecutor. It is hard to prove that a death has resulted solely from a specific pollution or other environmental harm. As a result, notwithstanding this theoretical possibility, one can in fact find almost no examples where these provisions have been applied to environmental pollution. Therefore, we do prefer the creation of a truly

[73] Examples are provided by Di Landro 2022, pp. 290–297.

[74] Di Landro considers this an example of a truly autonomous environmental crime. See Di Landro 2022, p. 293.

[75] Mandiberg and Faure 2009, p. 483.

[76] For examples, see Faure and Visser 1995, pp. 346–356.

[77] Faure and Visser 1995, pp. 352–354; Mandiberg and Faure 2009, pp. 485–488.

autonomous crime, by eliminating the unlawfulness element from the crime (under strict conditions) as the preferred option.

4.3.4 Current Developments in Ecocide Legislation

We discussed problematic consequences of administrative dependency of environmental criminal law and justified the creation of autonomous environmental crimes in cases of severe forms of environmental harm. 'Ecocide' amounts to such forms of environmental harm, when those harms are severe and widespread or severe and long-term.[78] Let us now assess the various definitions of ecocide crimes in more detail.

As briefly referred to in the introduction, in recent years the development of ecocide crimes has taken off. The Mexican State of Jalisco introduced an ecocide bill in its penal code in 2022.[79] Chile adopted very recently, in August 2024, a new law that modifies the Penal Code by introducing a section on "attacks against the environment".[80] In Brazil, a law introduced in Congress in 2023 is in the process of becoming formal law. This bill seeks to criminalise "illegal or wanton acts with the knowledge that they generate a substantial probability of serious and widespread or long-term damage to the environment". In Europe we also see rapid developments to criminalise ecocide. The Belgian government adopted a crime of ecocide into domestic law in February 2024, as the first European state to create a crime of ecocide. Other countries are in the process of criminalising ecocide in their own countries: in the Netherlands, a proposal for a new crime of ecocide was submitted to Parliament in November 2023, which is currently under consideration,[81] and in Spain, the Catalan Parliament has initiated a procedure in July 2023 before the National Congress of Deputies to include a crime of ecocide in the Spanish Penal Code.[82]

In these various legislative initiatives, we see several variations pertaining to administrative dependency. Some do not contain an unlawfulness element, others do contain an unlawfulness element, and some have found a compromise between the two. The Brazilian and Belgian ecocide crimes have followed the definition of the IEP, which reads: "*unlawful or wanton acts committed with knowledge that there is a substantial likelihood of severe and either widespread or long-term damage to the environment being caused by those acts.*"[83]

In this definition, 'unlawfulness' is taken up as a criterion for criminal liability. However, for cases in which the environmental damage does meet the damage-criteria in the definition, but the conduct was done lawfully (i.e. with administrative

[78] Based on the bulk of ecocide definitions, as discussed further.

[79] See Stop Ecocide International 2022.

[80] Stop Ecocide International 2023b.

[81] Tweede Kamer der Staten-Generaal 2023.

[82] Stop Ecocide International 2023a.

[83] Stop Ecocide Foundation 2021.

authorisation), the 'wanton' option is created. The word wanton means "*with reckless disregard for damage which would be clearly excessive in relation to the social and economic benefits anticipated*".[84] It thus calls for a proportionality test between the social and economic benefits of the ecocidal act and the damage caused by the act. We do not see this as a desirable formulation of an 'autonomous' crime of ecocide. Indeed, it means that even in cases in which the damage is severe and widespread or severe and long-term, it is not punishable as a crime if the social and economic benefits outweigh the damage. The 'wanton' criterion is also contested amongst scholars, as it allows for an opt-out for criminal liability for environmentally harmful conduct.[85]

Recently published proposals for crimes of ecocide at the regional and domestic levels contain some differences regarding the unlawfulness and wanton criteria of the IEP definition. For example, the Belgian proposal describes its crime of ecocide as "deliberately committing, by action or omission, unlawful or arbitrary acts causing or likely to cause serious, widespread and long-lasting damage", using 'arbitrary' as an alternative criterion to 'unlawful' instead of 'wanton'.[86] Alternatively, the recently published legal proposal for a Dutch crime of ecocide drafted by the Party for the Animals depicts no criterion of unlawfulness whatsoever, defining a crime of ecocide as "intentionally, by acts or omissions, causing serious and wide-spread or serious and long-lasting damage to the environment, or create a danger for this damage (…)."[87] They substantiate this choice by strongly criticising the current administrative dependency of all environmental criminal laws in the Dutch legal system. In the two different definitions we see different (political) visions reflected.

As one of the most significant developments to date, the European Union has introduced 'qualified offences', which Member States have to punish more severely, in cases comparable to ecocide, in the ECD, which entered into force in May 2024. The Directive refers to twenty specifically described forms of conduct criminalised in Articles 2 and 3 of the Directive, and introduces the 'ecocide-crime' as a so-called 'qualified offence'—ordering Member States to criminalise cases comparable to ecocide when they are the result of a breach of one of the twenty articles of criminal conduct listed in the Directive, and lead to "the destruction of, or widespread and substantial damage which is either irreversible or long-lasting to, an ecosystem of considerable size or environmental value or a habitat within a protected site, or […] widespread and substantial damage which is either irreversible or long-lasting to the quality of air, soil of water".[88] In this way, the European Union orders its Member States to bring into effect crimes which criminalise cases comparable to ecocide within two years; the implementation time of the Directive.

It is interesting to have a more detailed look at the progress on the creation of autonomous environmental crimes within the development of the ECD.[89] The

[84] Ibid.

[85] See Killean and Short 2025; Heller 2021.

[86] Belgische Kamer van Volksvertegenwoordigers 2023.

[87] Tweede Kamer der Staten-Generaal 2023.

[88] See ECD, above n 4.

[89] European Commission 2021.

Explanatory Memorandum accompanying the first proposal launched by the European Commission for a new directive on environmental crime,[90] refers to the option of defining environmental crime in the Directive without the requirement of a breach of relevant EU sectoral legislation.[91] This would *de facto* amount to the inclusion of an autonomous environmental crime in the Directive. This option was nevertheless not included in the Proposal as a result of which unlawfulness is still a requirement for criminal liability under Article 2(1).

However, the newly adopted EU ECD did eventually result in the possibility to exclude the operation or a permit of administrative regulation as a justification for any of the crimes formulated in the Directive. The Directive does not contain obvious autonomous environmental crimes, as the word "unlawful" remains for all crimes a condition for criminal liability. Yet the Directive has created a category of unlawfulness which extends the meaning of unlawful conduct to conduct being carried out under an authorisation, in specific circumstances. This follows from Article 3(1) of the Directive, which states that "[s]uch conduct shall be unlawful even where it is carried out under an authorization issued by a competent authority of a Member State if such authorization was obtained fraudulently or by corruption, extortion or coercion, or if such authorization *is in manifest breach of relevant substantive legal requirements*."[92]

Relevant substantive legal requirements can refer to a variety of laws, including international (human rights) law. This would open up the possibility for the domestic legislator to decide that when environmentally harmful conduct that could amount to any of the crimes prohibited under the Directive, but is in fact allowed by an administrative authorisation, should still be criminalised by Member States when such conduct infringes upon human rights, including the right to be protected against climate change, the right to life, or the right to a healthy environment. As a result, the permit would not justify the harm caused, and the operator causing the harm could be criminally liable for creating the harm.

By mid-2026, when the implementation period for implementing the ECD is finished, EU Member States have to either adapt their criminal codes or adopt new legislation to criminalise harmful conduct as defined in the ECD, even when they are authorised under a permit, when they breach substantive legal requirements, such as human rights. The green revolution in human rights pertaining to the environment (i.e. right to a healthy environment, right to be protected against climate change), obliges Member States now to make sure that permits do not infringe upon the right to a healthy environment and the right to be protected against climate change. Additionally, with this new legislation, it is now up to the criminal judge to decide whether such rights are breached. In addition, the polluting company has a responsibility to go beyond what is required by a permit and assess whether or not its environmental impact breaches one of the crimes formulated in the ECD. Lastly, it gives administrative authorities a strong incentive to strictly align permits and other types of

[90] Ibid.

[91] Ibid., p. 12.

[92] ECD, above n 4, Article 3(1) (Our emphasis).

administrative authorisations with human rights and other relevant substantive legal requirements, to avoid any breaching of one of the crimes formulated in the ECD.

However, the limitation of the ECD for environmental protection is twofold. First of all, the ECD has only formulated 20 types of criminal conduct, and the qualified offence of ecocide is only applicable in connection to the types of criminal conduct formulated in the 20 environmental crimes. Although the Directive does allow for the criminalisation of additional offences by Member States following Article 3(5) of the ECD, this means that conduct falling out of the scope of the ECD are not criminalised, leaving a realm of environmental harm unpunishable. Additionally, it will depend on the courts to interpret the vague term 'substantial legal requirements' in detail. This could decrease the effectiveness of the ECD to prevent and stop severe forms of environmental destruction and/or degradation. To safeguard robustly that acts comparable to ecocide will be punishable, it is of vital importance that Member States adopt autonomous environmental crimes (of ecocide).

4.4 Concluding Remarks

The debate on ecocide has become very topical and has received a great amount of attention in the academic literature and at the policy level. For example, the European Parliament has encouraged the EU and its Member States to promote the recognition of ecocide as the fifth international crime under the Rome Statute of the ICC[93] and various domestic legislators plead in favour of the criminalisation of ecocide in their domestic criminal code. In our contribution we focused on another aspect of the debate, which forces the (domestic and European) policymaker to think more carefully about the formulation of environmental crime, especially in relation to administrative law. The ecocide debate, for example by focusing on the state-corporate nexus, made evident that an environmental criminal law that is characterised by administrative dependency (via the notion of unlawfulness) will not be able to provide an adequate protection against the extensive destruction, damage to or loss of ecosystems. Such conduct could very well take place under the cover of either regulation or an authorisation and would therefore fail to meet the unlawfulness requirement. One can now increasingly observe spectacular cases of environmental pollution, even causing health damage, where criminal law cannot intervene as these activities take place under the cover of an administrative authorisation. The lack of autonomous environmental crimes therefore substantially limits the effectiveness of environmental criminal law altogether.

The mere fact of having destruction or irreversible or long-lasting or widespread and substantial damage to an ecosystem—to follow the words of the ECD—as an aggravating circumstance seems meaningless as that circumstance only applies if unlawfulness is required, and unlawfulness is interpreted in such a way that as long as the conditions of an authorisation are followed, criminal law cannot intervene

[93] European Parliament 2021, para 12.

(unless in the rare cases that the prosecutor could prove that the authorisation was obtained fraudulently or by corruption, extortion or coercion). We argue that the time has come to take environmental crime seriously and thus to create autonomous crimes addressing the most serious cases of environmental harm everywhere. Only by creating the possibility for criminal law to intervene in an autonomous manner can environmental crime be fought precisely where the protection from criminal law is most needed.

References

Articles, Books and Other Documents

Alkema JG (2020) Improving protection against severe damage to the environment: the potential of ecocide law (MSc thesis Wageningen University). https://edepot.wur.nl/630170. Accessed 28 June 2025

Barigbon CB (2023) State-Corporate environmental crime and human security in the Niger Delta, Nigeria. Journal of Global Social Sciences 4(14):21–43

Belgische Kamer van Volksvertegenwoordigers (2023) Wetsontwerp tot invoering van Boek II van het Strafwetboek, Doc 55 3518/001. https://www.lachambre.be/FLWB/PDF/55/3518/55K3518001.pdf. Accessed 28 June 2025

Buchanan J, Tullock G, Tollison R (1980) Toward a Theory of the Rent-Seeking Society. Texas A&M University Press, Texas

Danby G (2011) Tar Sands. House of Commons Library (No. SN06023). https://researchbriefings.files.parliament.uk/documents/SN06023/SN06023.pdf. Accessed 11 November 2025

de Rechtspraak (2023) Chemours handelde onrechtmatig met uitstoot van PFOA. https://www.rechtspraak.nl/Organisatie-en-contact/Organisatie/Rechtbanken/Rechtbank-Rotterdam/Nieuws/Paginas/Chemours-handelde-onrechtmatig-met-uitstoot-van-PFOA.aspx. Accessed 20 November 2024

Di Landro AR (2022) Environmental Criminal Law's Dependence on Administrative Law, in the Purely Accessory and Partially Accessory Models: Pluses and Minuses. Assessing the Opportunity for a Limited Number of Offences Being Autonomous From Administrative Law. https://papers.ssrn.com/sol3/papers.cfm?abstract_id=4029962. Accessed 30 June 2025

Environmental Defense (2013) Reality Check: Water and the Tar Sands. https://environmentaldefence.ca/wp-content/uploads/2016/01/WaterandTarSandsReport_FINAL.pdf. Accessed on 20 November 2024

European Commission (2021) Proposal for a Directive of the European Parliament and of the Council on the protection of the environment through criminal law and replacing Directive 2008/99/EC, COM(2021) 851 final. https://eur-lex.europa.eu/legal-content/EN/TXT/?uri=CELEX:52021PC0851. Accessed 26 June 2025

European Parliament (2021) European Parliament resolution of 20 January 2021 on human rights and democracy in the world and the European Union's policy on the matter – annual report 2019 (2020/2208 (INI)). https://www.europarl.europa.eu/doceo/document/TA-9-2021-0014_EN.html. Accessed 26 June 2025

Faure MG (2006) Towards a new model of criminalisation of environmental pollution. The case of Indonesia. In: Faure MG, Niessen N (eds) Environmental Law in Development: Lessons from the Indonesian Experience. Edward Elgar, Cheltenham, pp 188–217

Faure MG (2017a) The revolution in environmental criminal law in Europe. Virginia Environmental Law Journal 35(2): 321–356

Faure MG (2017b) The Evolution of Environmental Criminal Law in Europe: a Comparative Analysis. In: Farmer A, Faure MG, Vagliasindi GM (eds) Environmental Crime in Europe. Hart Publishing, Oxford, pp 267–317

Faure MG, Heine G (2000) Environmental Criminal Law in the European Union: Documentation of the Main Provisions with Introductions. Max Planck Institute for Foreign and International Criminal Law, Freiburg im Breisgau

Faure MG, Visser M (1995) How to Punish Environmental Pollution – Some Reflections On Various Models Of Criminalisation Of Environmental Harm. European Journal of Crime, Criminal Law and Criminal Justice 3(4):316–368

Faure MG, Visser M (1999) De strafrechtelijke bescherming van het leefmilieu in België, Duitsland en Nederland. Modellen van strafbaarstelling en hun bewijsrechtelijke implicaties. Intersentia, Antwerp

Fearnside PM (2021) 'Zero illegal deforestation' – One more Bolsonaro distortion (commentary). https://news.mongabay.com/2021/05/zero-illegal-deforestation-one-more-bolsonaro-dis tortion-commentary/ Accessed 20 November 2024

Gallant KS (2009) The Principle of Legality in International and Comparative Criminal Law. Cambridge University Press, New York

Gandhi K, Khan S, Patrikar M, Markad A, Kumar N, Choudhari A, Sagar P, Indurkar S (2021) Exposure risk and environmental impacts of glyphosate: Highlights on the toxicity of herbicide co-formulants. Environmental Challenges. https://doi.org/10.1016/j.envc.2021.100149

Geissen V (2023) Wetenschappelijke reflectie Glyfosaat, Rondetafel Tweede Kamer 4-10-23. https://www.wur.nl/en/show/violette-geissen-wetenschappelijke-reflectie-glyfosaat.htm. Accessed 30 June 2025

Greenpeace International (2024) Ikea furniture destroys some of Europe's last remaining ancient forests. https://www.greenpeace.org/international/press-release/66349/ikea-furniture-destroys-some-of-europes-last-remaining-ancient-forests/. Accessed 20 November 2024

Hauser S, Vadénm T, Nagatsu M, Obeng-Odoom F, Eronen J (2024) Early knowledge but delays in climate action: An ecocide case against both transnational oil corporations and national governments. Environmental Science & Policy. https://doi.org/10.1016/j.envsci.2024.103880

Heine G (1990) Verwaltungsakzessorietät des Umweltstrafrechts: Rechtsvergleichende Funktionsanalysen-unbestimmte Rechtsbegriffe - Reichweite von Genehmigungen. Neue Juristische Wochenschrift 39:2425–2434

Heller KJ (2021) The Crime of Ecocide in Action. https://opiniojuris.org/2021/06/28/the-crime-of-ecocide-in-action/. Accessed 26 June 2025

Hendriks LEM (2010) Milieustrafrecht, 3rd edn. Wolters Kluwer Nederland, Alphen aan den Rijn

Herzog-Hawelka J, Gupta J (2023) The role of (multi)national oil and gas companies in leaving fossil fuels underground: A systematic literature review. Energy Research & Social Science. https://doi.org/10.1016/j.erss.2023.103194

Higgins P (2010) Eradicating Ecocide. Laws and governance to prevent the destruction of our planet. Shepheard-Walwyn, London

Higgins P (2012) Earth is Our Business: Changing the rules of the game. Shepheard-Walwyn, London

Interuniversitaire Commissie tot Herziening van het Milieurecht in het Vlaamse Gewest (1995) Voorontwerp Decreet Milieubeleid. die Keure, Brugge

IUCN (2022) Nickel Mining in Indonesia: Economic Prosperity and Ecological Disaster. https://www.iucn.nl/en/blog/nickel-mining-in-indonesia-economic-prosperity-and-ecological-dis aster/ Accessed 20 November 2024

Killean R, Short D (2023) A Critical Review of the Law of Ecocide. https://ssrn.com/abstract=460 5681 Accessed 20 November 2024

Killean R, Short D (2025) A critical defence of the crime of ecocide. Environmental Politics. https://doi.org/10.1080/09644016.2025.2492441

Koopmans IM (1996) De strafbaarstelling van milieuverontreiniging. Een rechtsvergelijkende studie naar de administratief afhankelijke structuur van het milieustrafrecht. Gouda Quint, Arnhem

Mandiberg S, Faure MG (2009) A Graduated Punishment Approach to Environmental Crimes: Beyond Vindication of Administrative Authority in the United States and Europe. Columbia Journal of Environmental Law 34(2):447–511

Milieudefensie (2024) Our lawsuit against Shell in Nigeria. https://en.milieudefensie.nl/shell-in-nigeria Accessed on 20 November 2024

Ministerie van Infrastructuur en Waterstaat (2021) Beantwoording Kamervragen over het bericht Chemelot mag 14.000 kilo microplastics per jaar in de Maas lozen, IENW/BSK-2021/223898. https://open.overheid.nl/documenten/ronl-5865c854-a7da-4d03-a81b-cf16bf76c94f/pdf. Accessed 26 June 2025

Olson M (1965) The Logic Of Collective Action: Public Goods And The Theory Of Groups. Harvard University Press, Cambridge

Onderzoeksraad Voor de Veiligheid (2023) Industrie en Omwonenden. https://onderzoeksraad.nl/onderzoek/industrie-en-omwonenden/. Accessed 26 June 2025

Organisation for Economic Co-operation and Development (OECD) (1992) The Polluter-Pays Principle: OECD Analyses and Recommendations, OCDE/GD(92)81. https://one.oecd.org/document/OCDE/GD(92)81/En/pdf. Accessed 27 June 2025

PAN Europe (2023) Expert meeting shows that glyphosate is not safe for health and environment. https://www.pan-europe.info/expert-meeting-shows-glyphosate-not-safe-health-and-environment. Accessed 20 November 2024

Pointer (2021) Vergunningen Tata Steel aangescherpt en extra controle op uitstoot. https://pointer.kro-ncrv.nl/de-tata-steel-nachtmerrie-een-overzicht-van-ons-onderzoek. Accessed 20 November 2024

Raad van State (2024a) Voorstel van wet van het lid Van Raan houdende wijziging van het Wetboek van Strafrecht en het Wetboek van Strafrecht BES in verband met het strafbaar stellen van ecocide (Wet strafbaarstelling ecocide) W16.23.00358/II, 2 April 2024. https://www.raadvanstate.nl/adviezen/@140571/w16-23-00358-ii/. Accessed 20 November 2024

Raad van State (2024b) Voorstel van wet van het lid Van Raan houdende wijziging van het Wetboek van Strafrecht en het Wetboek van Strafrecht BES in verband met het strafbaar stellen van ecocide (Wet strafbaarstelling ecocide) W16.23.00358/II, 2 April 2024, Samenvatting. https://www.raadvanstate.nl/adviezen/@140571/w16-23-00358-ii/. Accessed 28 June 2025

Randstedelijke Rekenkamer (2021) Stof tot nadenken: Onderzoek naar de kwaliteit van uitvoering van VTH-taken bij Tatat Steel en Harsco. https://www.randstedelijke-rekenkamer.nl/sites/d10p.randstedelijke-rekenkamer.nl/files/2024-12/Eindrapport-Stof-tot-nadenken.pdf. Accessed 28 June 2025

Ratcliffe R (2019) 'This place used to be green': the brutal impact of oil in the Niger Delta. https://www.theguardian.com/global-development/2019/dec/06/this-place-used-to-be-green-the-brutal-impact-of-oil-in-the-niger-delta. Accessed 20 November 2024

Rijksinstituut voor Volksgezondheid en Milieu (2023) De bijdrage van Tata Steel Nederland aan de gezondheidsrisico's van omwonenden en de kwaliteit van hun leefomgeving. https://www.rivm.nl/bibliotheek/rapporten/2023-0171.pdf. Accessed 26 June 2025

Schaffmeister D (1993) Milieustrafrecht slaat op hol. In: Franken AA, van Woensel A (eds) Een rariteitenkabinet. Ars Aequi Libri, Nijmegen, pp 90–91

Sing A (2021) White Collar Criminality Nexus with Environment. International Journal of Legal Science and Innovation 3(4):872–878

Stop Ecocide Foundation (2021) Independent Expert Panel for the Legal Definition of Ecocide, Commentary and Core Text. https://www.legal-tools.org/doc/pb375e/. Accessed 25 June 2025

Stop Ecocide International (2022) Mexico: Ecocide included as a new crime in the state Penal Code of Jalisco. https://www.stopecocide.earth/new-breaking-news-summary/mexico-ecocide-included-as-a-new-crime-in-the-state-penal-code-of-jalisco. Accessed 20 November 2024

Stop Ecocide International (2023a) Catalan Parliament initiates procedure to include ecocide in Spanish Penal Code. https://www.stopecocide.earth/breaking-news-2023/catalan-parliament-initiates-procedure-to-include-ecocide-in-spanish-penal-code Accessed 20 November 2024

Stop Ecocide International (2023b) Chile: new laws introduce elements of ecocide definition. https://www.stopecocide.earth/breaking-news-2023/chile-new-laws-introduce-elements-of-ecocide-definition. Accessed 20 November 2024

Tombs S, Whyte D (2020) The Shifting Imaginaries Of Corporate Crime. Journal of White Collar and Corporate Crime 1(1):16–23

Tweede Kamer der Staten-Generaal (2023) Vergaderjaar 2023–2024, 36475, nr. 2 en nr. 3, Voorstel van wet van het lid van Raan houdende Wijziging van het Wetboek van Strafrecht en het Wetboek van Strafrecht BES in verband met het strafbaar stellen van ecocide (Wet strafbaarstelling ecocide). https://www.tweedekamer.nl/kamerstukken/wetsvoorstellen/detail?cfg=wetsvoorsteldetails&qry=wetsvoorstel%3A36475. Accessed 28 June 2025

United Nations Human Rights Office of the High Commissioner (2023) What is the Right to a Healthy Environment? Information note. https://www.undp.org/sites/g/files/zskgke326/files/2023-01/UNDP-UNEP-UNHCHR-What-is-the-Right-to-a-Healthy-Environment.pdf. Accessed 20 November 2024

van den Eerenbeemt M, Waarlo N (2023) Toezichthouders vuile industrie opnieuw onder vuur: economie ging voor op gezondheid. https://www.volkskrant.nl/nieuws-achtergrond/toezichthouders-vuile-industrie-opnieuw-onder-vuur-economie-ging-voor-gezondheid~b672a9bd/. Accessed 20 November 2024

Judith Alkema is an expert in ecocide law and a co-author of the Ecocide Crime Act, submitted to the Dutch House of Representatives on 30 November 2023 by former Parliamentarian Member, Lammert van Raan, from the Party for the Animals [Partij voor de Dieren]. She did bachelors in Law and Liberal Arts and graduated cum laude in 2021 from her MSc Environmental Sciences having written her thesis called "Improving protection against severe damage to the environment: the potential of ecocide law". In addition to her job as a lecturer at Utrecht University, Judith is also an independent researcher, advisor on ecocide law and one of the core team members of EcoJustice (formerly Stop Ecocide NL).

Prof. Michael Faure is emeritus professor comparative and international environmental law at Maastricht University, emeritus professor comparative private law and economics at Erasmus School of Law in Rotterdam and adjunct professor at the Faculty of Law of Universitas Indonesia in Jakarta.

Chapter 5
The Crime of Ecocide Through Human Rights: Towards Environmental Protection and Justice

Lisa Oldring and Kate Mackintosh

Contents

Abstract The proposal to establish a new international crime of ecocide under the ICC Statute reflects the interconnected imperatives of human rights and environmental protection. In this contribution, we explore two ways in which a human rights approach can flesh out the content of the proposed crime in a manner that supports the ultimate goals of prevention, protection, and justice. The international human rights system has elaborated the responsibilities of States and non-State actors in relation to human rights and the environment, establishing benchmarks to assist governments and businesses in their implementation. We consider how these can be drawn upon to define the parameters of the crime of ecocide and inform its interpretation. We also argue that using a human rights lens to interpret the crime helps to reveal structural inequalities and the disparate impacts of environmental destruction on vulnerable and marginalised individuals and groups. Prosecutions that reflect

L. Oldring
Faculty of Law, University of Amsterdam, Amsterdam, The Netherlands
e-mail: l.n.oldring@uva.nl

L. Oldring · K. Mackintosh (✉)
Promise Institute Europe, UCLA School of Law, The Hague, The Netherlands
e-mail: mackintosh@law.ucla.edu

L. Burgers et al. (eds.), *Ecocide: Criminalising Serious Harm against the Environment*, International Criminal Justice Series 38, https://doi.org/10.1007/978-94-6265-715-1_5

the reality of these lived experiences, and thus encompass the full impact of the criminality, hold greater potential to contribute to environmental and climate justice.

Keywords Ecocide · International Criminal Court · International human rights law · Environment · Climate change · Environmental justice

5.1 Introduction

With the increasing urgency of the global climate, biodiversity and pollution crisis, a growing number of States, the UN Secretary-General, and other stakeholders have called for the criminalisation under international law of acts that amount to ecocide.[1] The UN High Commissioner for Human Rights has "supported the call to bring the crime of ecocide within the jurisdiction of the International Criminal Court" (ICC), as a fifth crime, alongside genocide, war crimes, crimes against humanity and the crime of aggression.[2] Legal reforms have also been initiated by States that seek to criminalise ecocide in national legislation.[3]

At present there is no internationally-agreed definition of this proposed crime. In their 2024 proposal to amend the ICC Statute to include a crime of ecocide,[4] the Pacific Island States of Vanuatu, Fiji and Samoa use the definition produced in June 2021 by the Independent Expert Panel for the Legal Definition of Ecocide ('IEP' or 'Panel').[5] According to this definition ecocide means "unlawful or wanton acts committed with knowledge that there is a substantial likelihood of severe and either widespread or long-term damage to the environment being caused by those acts".[6] The Panel suggests that "proceeding to agree a crime of ecocide could contribute to a change of consciousness, in support of a new direction, one that enhances the protection of the environment and supports a more collaborative and effective legal framework for our common future on a shared planet".[7] The proposed definition is

---

[1] UN Security Council 2024, para 45; Republic of Maldives 2019; Government of Vanuatu 2019; Government of Belgium 2020. See also Stop Ecocide International, https://www.stopecocide.earth/leading-states. Accessed 3 July 2025.

[2] UN High Commissioner for Human Rights 2024.

[3] Robinson 2023. See also Mackintosh 2023.

[4] Vanuatu deposited the proposal with the UN Secretary-General on 9 September 2024. See Stop Ecocide International 2024.

[5] Stop Ecocide Foundation 2021. The Panel comprised a diverse group of lawyers from around the world, including one author of this chapter, with expertise in international criminal, humanitarian, environmental and climate law. The Panel's definition has also inspired the new EU Environmental Crime Directive. See Directive (EU) 2024/1203 of the European Parliament and of the Council of 11 April 2024 on the protection of the environment through criminal law and replacing Directives 2008/99/EC and 2009/123/EC, adopted 11 April 2024, OJ L 202, 5 July 2024. The crime of ecocide in the Belgian criminal code, Article 94. See https://www.lachambre.be/FLWB/PDF/55/3518/55K3518011.pdf. Accessed October 2022, as well as numerous national legislative proposals.

[6] Stop Ecocide Foundation 2021.

[7] Ibid.

informed, in its form and substance, by existing international criminal law, as well as international humanitarian law provisions protecting the environment in armed conflict. It also draws on environmental law principles.

The creation of an international crime of ecocide would bring concern for the environment into a system of law primarily concerned with the protection of human life and dignity. It would introduce individual accountability on an international level for extreme environmental damage, in the same way that individual responsibility for gross human rights violations was created by earlier international criminal law. International criminal law, in the words of the Rome Statute of the ICC, deals with "unimaginable atrocities that deeply shock the conscience of humanity" and that "threaten the peace, security and well-being of the world".[8] Adding ecocide to the pantheon of international crimes would recognise that extreme environmental damage is of the same order and threatens the same interests as the existing international crimes: genocide, crimes against humanity, war crimes and the crime of aggression.

Recognition of an international crime of ecocide complements developments in international human rights law that acknowledge human rights and protection of the environment as interconnected imperatives. The declaration by the UN General Assembly of a universal human right to a clean, healthy and sustainable environment, for example, recognises environmental degradation, climate change, biodiversity loss, desertification and unsustainable development as among the most serious threats to the human rights of present and future generations.[9] The normative content of this right reflects a subjective, anthropocentric dimension, as well as an objective ecocentric one, acknowledging the intrinsic value of nature, as such.[10] The UN High Commissioner for Human Rights has emphasised that securing the right to a clean, healthy and sustainable environment "requires that we use the tools of the law—including criminal law—more expansively to address environmental harms", noting that recognition of the crime of ecocide by international, regional and domestic legal systems would strengthen accountability for environmental harms.[11]

In this chapter, we look at the connection between human rights and a crime of ecocide (as proposed by Vanuatu, Fiji and Samoa) further, exploring two areas in which a human rights approach to the framing and prosecution of the crime can improve its effectiveness in terms of prevention, protection and justice.

In the following section, Sect. 5.2, we outline developments that have helped to clarify the standards of conduct expected of States and private (corporate) actors with regard to human rights and the protection of the environment, and suggest how these standards, and related benchmarks, can help prevent and define the parameters of the crime of ecocide.

---

[8] Rome Statute of the International Criminal Court, opened for signature 17 July 1998, 2187 UNTS 3, entered into force 1 July 2002, Preamble.

[9] UN General Assembly 2022a.

[10] Human Rights for the Planet 2022. See also UN Human Rights Council 2019a; UN Human Rights Council 2018.

[11] UN High Commissioner for Human Rights 2024.

In Sect. 5.3, we theorise how interpreting the crime of ecocide through a human rights lens can increase the potential of the crime to contribute to environmental and climate justice, with reference to the precedent of the emergence of sexual and gender-based violence as a stand-alone crime in international law, and the broader international protection mechanisms that ensued.

5.2 Using International Human Rights Law to Set Benchmarks for a Crime of Ecocide

5.2.1 Introduction

Developments within the international human rights system reflect a deepening appreciation of the interlinkages between human rights and the protection of the environment, including against climate change. While international human rights law sets out obligations of States, the UN treaty bodies, the General Assembly, the Human Rights Council and its special procedures have elaborated the responsibilities of both States and non-State actors in relation to human rights and the environment, establishing benchmarks to assist both governments and businesses in their implementation.

These developments offer procedural and substantive guidance that can help to define the parameters of an ecocide crime. Failure to comply with human rights obligations on the part of a State actor, or with the standards agreed to govern business activities on the part of a corporate executive, will not automatically equate to a crime of ecocide—although it may render acts unlawful, satisfying one element of the crime. Compliance with human rights responsibilities by State and corporate actors, on the other hand, can serve as a path to prevent ecocide and contribute to certainty around criminal responsibility.

5.2.2 The Universal Right to a Clean, Healthy and Sustainable Environment

Perhaps the most notable development in this area is the landmark declaration by the UN General Assembly (UNGA) in July 2022 that access to a clean, healthy and sustainable environment is a universal human right.[12] Reflecting support across all regions of the world, the resolution was adopted with 117 State co-sponsors and a

[12] UN General Assembly Resolution 2022a. While the right to a healthy environment is enshrined, with different formulations, in domestic legislation in over 150 states, as well as in a number of regional and international treaties, the General Assembly resolution represents the first time this autonomous right has received international endorsement, significantly bolstering its normative value.

remarkable 161 countries voting in favour, 8 abstentions and no votes against. As such, the resolution reflects a now-widely accepted view that a clean, healthy and sustainable environment is both an autonomous human right, and one that is interrelated with the enjoyment of all other rights. This right is reflected in legislation in more than 150 States,[13] in some human rights treaties,[14] in the Kunming-Montreal Global Biodiversity Framework adopted in December 2022,[15] and in the 2024 Declaration of the UN Environment Assembly.[16] At the regional level, recognition of a justiciable right to a healthy environment under the American Convention on Human Rights was affirmed by the Inter-American Court of Human Rights in its landmark Advisory Opinion in 2017. In its Opinion, the Court also addressed the main contours of this autonomous right, along with corresponding State obligations.[17] At the international level, the UN Human Rights Council has since reaffirmed the right to a healthy environment and urged governments to adopt policies and an effective legal framework to implement it.[18]

In its declaration, the UNGA acknowledges the impact of climate change and environmental degradation as among the most pressing threats to humanity and stresses the negative implications of these threats for the enjoyment of human rights. The resolution bridges States' obligations under international human rights law and international environmental law by noting that promotion of the right to a healthy environment requires the full implementation of multilateral environmental agreements.[19] It

---

[13] UN Human Rights Council 2019a, p. 4.

[14] African Charter on Human and Peoples' Rights, opened for signature 27 June 1981, OAU Doc. CAB/LEG/67/3 rev.5, 21 ILM 58, entered into force 21 October 1986, Article 24. Additional Protocol to the American Convention on Human Rights in the Area of Economic, Social and Cultural Rights (Protocol of San Salvador), opened for signature 17 November 1988, OAS Treaty Series No.69, entered into force 16 November 1999, Article 11. Arab Charter on Human Rights, opened for signature 22 May 2004, reprinted in 12 IHRR 893, entered into force 15 March 2008, Article 38.

[15] Conference of the Parties to the Convention on Biological Diversity 2022.

[16] UNEP 2024.

[17] Inter-American Court of Human Rights, *The Environment and Human Rights*, Advisory Opinion OC-23/17, IACtHR Series A No 23, 15 November 2017. The eco-centric approach adopted by the Court is reflected in para 62, where it explains that the right to a healthy environment "protects the components of the environment, such as forests, rivers and seas, as legal interests in themselves, even in the absence of the certainty or evidence of a risk to individuals".

[18] UN Human Rights Council 2023.

[19] Recognition of ecocide as an international crime under the Rome Statute could also be considered as a measure to promote and protect the right to a healthy environment. See, for example, the European Parliament resolution of 17 February 2022 on human rights and democracy in the world which, in promoting "the right to a safe and healthy environment", "welcomes the UN's call for global recognition of the right to a safe, clean, healthy and sustainable environment; underlines the vital role played by environmental human rights defenders and local and indigenous populations in preserving such an environment, despite the threats of violence that they often face from those responsible for, and profiting from, environmentally harmful practices; encourages the EU and its Member States to promote the recognition of ecocide as an international crime under the Rome Statute of the ICC, and requests that the Commission study the relevance of ecocide to EU law and

also acknowledges that the exercise of human rights is vital to environmental protection. It calls on States to step up efforts to ensure access to a clean, healthy and sustainable environment for all, including through international cooperation.

The UNGA declaration does not specify the content of the right to a clean, healthy and sustainable environment in detail.[20] However, it follows the work of two successive UN Special Rapporteurs on human rights and the environment who, over the course of several years, studied obligations related to the right to a healthy environment in various constitutions, domestic legislation and treaties, as well as across State practice, to distil a series of framework principles and identify good practices.[21] Drawing on these bodies of work, the right to a healthy environment is considered to encompass procedural elements, such as public participation in environmental decision-making and climate action, access to environmental information and access to justice; as well as substantive rights, including clean air, a safe climate, access to safe water and adequate sanitation, healthy and sustainably produced food, and healthy biodiversity and ecosystems.[22]

These substantive and procedural elements of the right to a healthy environment clarify the standards of conduct expected of States, and so delineate when behaviour is likely not criminally wrongful on the part of individual decision-makers. For example, to protect the clean air component of the right to a healthy environment, States must (a) monitor air quality and impact on human health; (b) assess sources of air pollution; (c) make information publicly available, including public health advisories; (d) establish air quality legislation, regulations, standards and policies; (e) develop air quality action plans at the local, national and, if necessary, regional levels; (f) implement air quality action plans, and enforce the standards; and (g) evaluate progress and, if necessary, strengthen plans to ensure that the standards are met.[23] In an ecocide case against individual State officials involving damage to the environment resulting from air pollution, these steps provide useful benchmarks both to determine whether acts are 'unlawful', as well as to assess whether an individual has met the level of foresight or fault required under the proposed definition of ecocide.

This last point is relevant to two elements of the definition proposed by the Pacific Island States: the general *mens rea* requirement that acts be "committed with knowledge that there is a substantial likelihood of severe and either widespread or long-term damage to the environment being caused by those acts"; and the requirement that acts that are not unlawful be 'wanton', defined as "with reckless disregard for damage which would be clearly excessive in relation to the social and economic benefits

EU diplomacy; calls on the EU and the Member States to take bold initiatives to fight the impunity of environmental crimes at a global level". European Parliament 2021, para 49.

[20] See UN General Assembly Resolution 2022a.

[21] UN Human Rights Council 2018, 2019a.

[22] Ibid.

[23] UN Human Rights Council 2018, para 39.

anticipated". State actors who, in accordance with their individual level of responsibility, have met the benchmarks set by the international human rights system have solid ground for asserting that their actions meet neither of these two tests.

State responsibilities specifically with regard to climate change have also been elaborated by human rights bodies, providing benchmarks which could be used in a similar way. The UN High Commissioner for Human Rights has pointed out that the deadly impact that climate events have on the right to life:

> is no longer simply an argument of reasonable foreseeability, but of current, lived experience: individuals worldwide are drowning in climate change-induced flood waters, choking on more polluted and more dangerous air, starving in famines, and overheating in their own homes. [...] The law requires feasible steps to be taken to prevent such loss of life.[24]

Implementation of the obligation to respect and ensure the right to life depends on measures taken by States to preserve the environment and protect it against harm, pollution and climate change caused by public and private actors.[25] The standards elaborated by the UN human rights bodies and mechanisms have been cited authoritatively, notably by the Grand Chamber of the European Court of Human Rights in its groundbreaking judgment in *Verein Klimaseniorinnen Schweiz and Others v. Switzerland*.[26]

In a number of concluding observations on national periodic reports, the Human Rights Committee has underlined States' obligation to take precautionary measures to mitigate climate change and protect people, including those most at risk, from its negative impacts. The Committee has called for consistent implementation of climate commitments and the provision of information on measures taken with regard to such commitments; affirmed the right to an effective remedy for climate change-related violations; and highlighted the importance of ensuring the right to meaningful and effective participation in climate action.[27] The Committee on Economic, Social and Cultural Rights has highlighted States' obligation to act on the basis of the best scientific evidence available to prevent foreseeable harm caused by climate change; work together to mobilise the maximum available resources in an effort to do so, including finance to support rights-based climate action that benefits people in vulnerable situations; effectively regulate private actors to ensure that their actions do not worsen climate change; and adopt policies that can channel modes of production

[24] European Court of Human Rights, *Verein KlimaSeniorinnen and Others v. Switzerland*, Intervener Brief filed by the UN High Commissioner for Human Rights pursuant to leave granted by the Court on 20 July 2021, Application No. 53600/20, (Intervener Brief filed by the UN High Commissioner for Human Rights), para 12. In 2019, the UN Human Rights Committee underscored the "pressing and serious" threats posed by environmental degradation and climate change to the ability of present and future generations to enjoy the right to life, noting that States' obligations under international environmental law should therefore inform the content of that right, and vice versa. UN Human Rights Committee 2019, para 62.

[25] UN Human Rights Committee 2019, para 62.

[26] European Court of Human Rights, *Verein KlimaSeniorinnen Schweiz and others v. Switzerland*, Judgment, 9 April 2024, Application No. 53600/20.

[27] For a summary of relevant concluding observations of the Human Rights Committee, see Intervener Brief filed by the UN High Commissioner for Human Rights, above n 24.

and consumption towards a more environmentally sustainable pathway.[28] The High Commissioner has urged that human rights-based climate action by States include the development and implementation of plans to limit global warming to no more than 1.5 degrees, with immediate action to reduce dependency on fossil fuels and to address the negative human rights impacts that are already occurring.[29]

The UN Special Rapporteur on human rights and climate change added to this in his first report to the UNGA.[30] Highlighting the "catastrophically inadequate response" by States to reducing greenhouse gas emissions, he urged States, pursuant to their obligations under international human rights law, to take measures to eliminate the use of fossil fuels, address the funding gap on loss and damage, and increase participation and protect the rights of indigenous and environmental human rights defenders. His report further highlighted the accountability gap with regard to harms caused by climate change, outlining a list of recommended actions for States to remedy this gap including support for "an indictable offence of ecocide" under the International Criminal Court.[31]

It is clear from the foregoing that States are now provided with an increasingly detailed set of actions required in order to meet their human rights obligations in relation to climate change. While just 15 years ago in 2009, a UN report suggested that it was "virtually impossible to disentangle the complex causal relationships linking historical greenhouse gas emissions of a particular country with a specific climate change-related effect"[32] and that it was unclear whether such effects could be qualified as human rights violations, these developments in human rights law as well as advances in climate science mean that this is no longer the case. As outlined above, this framework is also relevant to individual criminal responsibility for ecocide, where State actors are concerned: in particular as regards either foresight of harm, or the lawfulness of the acts.

5.2.3 *Business and Human Rights Due Diligence*

The human rights framework can also guide businesses with respect to liability for the crime of ecocide.[33] The UN Guiding Principles on Business and Human Rights, which were endorsed by the UN Human Rights Council in a consensus resolution in 2011,[34] have become an authoritative global standard for preventing and addressing adverse business-related human rights impacts. The Guiding Principles elaborate on the State duty to protect, as well as outline the corporate responsibility to respect

[28] UN Human Rights Council 2022, para 40. See also UN OHCHR 2018, para 9.

[29] UN Human Rights Council 2021c, para 68(a).

[30] UN Human Rights Council 2021a.

[31] UN General Assembly 2022b, para 90(f).

[32] UN Human Rights Council 2009.

[33] For a more detailed overview, see Oldring and Robinson 2023.

[34] UN Human Rights Council 2011b.

human rights which requires that businesses "avoid causing or contributing to adverse human rights impacts through their own activities and address such impacts when they occur".[35] Transparency and disclosure regarding the human rights, climate and environmental impacts of business activities are recognised as fundamental to ensuring accountability, in view of their importance to the rights to access to information and public participation.

The Guiding Principles are not a legally binding instrument. Discussions towards an international legally binding instrument on 'transnational corporations and other business enterprises with respect to human rights', which began in 2014, are ongoing.[36] Meanwhile, in May 2024, the European Council adopted the long-awaited EU Directive on Corporate Sustainability Due Diligence, building on national legislation in a number of States and drawing upon the normative framework reflected in the Guiding Principles.[37]

The UN Guiding Principles describe *how* companies can identify, prevent, mitigate, and account for how they address their adverse human rights impacts through the exercise of human rights due diligence.[38] This process involves four steps: assessing actual and potential human rights impacts; integrating and acting upon the findings; tracking the effectiveness of responses; and communicating on how impacts are addressed.[39] Undertaking social and environmental impact assessments are an integral part of this process.[40] Due diligence processes include a business responsibility to consult and engage with rights holders, in particular those in situations of heightened vulnerability who often bear a disproportionate burden of the adverse impacts of environmental degradation.[41] The Special Rapporteur asserts that in order to ensure accountability, businesses must implement "operational-level grievance mechanisms

---

[35] UN Human Rights Council 2011a. Drawing on the Guiding Principles, the UN Special Rapporteur on human rights and the environment asserts that the responsibility to respect human rights applies "not only to businesses whose activities may directly damage the climate and environment, but also to the full array of enterprises supporting these businesses, including financial institutions, law firms, public relations firms, accounting firms, and consultancies". UN Human Rights Council 2024a, para 16.

[36] UN Human Rights Council 2024b.

[37] https://commission.europa.eu/business-economy-euro/doing-business-eu/corporate-sustainability-due-diligence_en. Accessed 3 July 2025. Observers have pointed out that while the EU Directive aligns substantially with international due diligence standards, it reflects important limitations with regard to the scope of companies covered and obligations in terms of 'downstream' impacts. See Bueno et al. 2024, pp. 1–7; Shift Project 2023; UN OHCHR 2020, 2021a.

[38] There are also corporate-driven demands for greater accountability. *See*, for example, the International Corporate Governance Network (ICGN) statements calling upon governments and standard-setters to 'mandate regulations and collaborate internationally to criminalise ecocide', among other measures to protect human rights and the environment. ICGN 2021.

[39] UN Human Rights Council 2011a, Guiding Principle 17.

[40] This due diligence requirement comprises both an ongoing practice and a standard of care expected of corporate actors. UN OHCHR 2021b, p. 36.

[41] UN Human Rights Council 2011b, para 19.

capable of providing effective remedies to rights holders whose right to a healthy environment they have adversely impacted".[42]

The requirement to exercise human rights due diligence can help in the assessment of whether environmentally harmful acts are 'wanton', one of the two alternate criteria in the definition of ecocide proposed by the Pacific Island States. The due diligence framework requires businesses to assess both the environmental and human rights impact of their actions,[43] providing a way to evaluate both the damage and the social and economic benefits of environmentally harmful corporate actions. This would provide clarity to businesses on the scope of their responsibility under ecocide law: individual decision-makers whose business has complied effectively with the requirements of international human rights due diligence standards should be protected against accusations of having acted "with reckless disregard for" excessive environmental damage.[44]

5.3 Interpreting Ecocide Through a Human Rights Lens to Contribute to Environmental and Climate Justice

5.3.1 Introduction

Using a human rights lens to interpret the crime of ecocide can highlight the disproportionate impact of environmental destruction on vulnerable and marginalised individuals and groups. Prosecutions that reflect this reality have the most potential to lead to jurisprudence that encompasses the full impact of the criminality, and can serve as a step towards environmental and climate justice. While there is no singular definition of these concepts, we understand the goal of climate and environmental justice to be halting environmental and climate destruction, mitigating and redressing the impact on vulnerable and marginalised communities, and holding to account those responsible, while also proactively seeking to protect against future degradation and rights violations.[45] As an approach which connects the environmental and climate crisis to the social, racial and economic injustices in which they are deeply entangled, climate and environmental justice have human rights concerns at their core.

[42] Ibid., para 22.

[43] UN Human Rights Council 2011a, Guiding Principles 17 and 18.

[44] While compliance with human rights due diligence may protect against a charge of ecocide, failure to comply would not equate to commission of the crime, unless all the elements of the crime were satisfied.

[45] Adelman and Kotzé 2021, pp. 30–43. See also Natarajan 2021.

5.3.2 Structural Inequalities and Disparate Impacts

An assessment of the climate crisis through a human rights lens reveals that the most vulnerable sectors of global society are affected in grossly unequal ways. The impacts of climate change and environmental destruction exacerbate existing poverty and inequalities, and compound intersecting forms of discrimination, leading one UN expert to warn of the risk of a 'climate apartheid', where the wealthy and privileged escape the worst effects of climate change, while vulnerable communities, people of colour and indigenous peoples, bear the greatest impacts.[46] Even conservative estimates suggest, for example, that without urgent climate action, 120 million more people will have been pushed into poverty by 2030.[47] Entrenched and systemic gender-based discrimination has intensified human rights harms related to serious environmental damage and led to gendered impacts, with women and girls suffering disproportionately from the impacts of climate breakdown.[48] Moreover, a racialised analysis demonstrates how the climate and biodiversity crisis is linked to colonialism and economic and political frameworks that have systematically disregarded the rights of indigenous peoples, people of African descent, and other racialised groups.[49] At the same time, individuals and communities that are profoundly affected by climate change have not had a meaningful voice in decision-making processes around climate change solutions—and yet their free and informed participation is both critical for effective climate action and the prevention of serious environmental damage, and a human rights imperative.

A racial justice analysis reveals that on a global scale those most affected by climate and environmental harms are located in Global South countries. As two leading scholars in this area have written,

> [t]he historical emissions of states of the Global North did not benefit all countries and their populations equally or promote universal global progress and development. Rather they enabled colonial suppression 'abroad' and class and racial suppression 'at home', which helped lay the foundations for the contemporary, unjust, and unequal international legal order.[50]

Climate change has a profound impact on Small Island Developing States, where communities with limited capacity to mitigate risks build climate-resilient economies and infrastructures, and absorb the economic and social aftershocks after already suffering the effects of extreme weather events.[51] Rising sea levels and intense weather systems have threatened the right to life and caused damage to infrastructure, jeopardising the rights to housing, water and sanitation, and health. Individuals, families and communities have been displaced, with further ripple effects on the right to education, cultural rights, and the right to development.

---

[46] UN Human Rights Council 2019b.

[47] Ibid., p. 4. *See* also World Bank 2016, p. 12.

[48] UNEP et al. 2021. See also CEDAW 2018.

[49] UN Human Rights Council 2021b.

[50] Mason-Case and Dehm 2021; see also UN General Assembly 2022c.

[51] Thomas et al. 2020.

Within nations, distribution of power along racial lines also sees racialised groups bearing the brunt of environmental burdens, including living in what the UN Special Rapporteur on human rights and the environment has called 'sacrifice zones': places where "residents suffer devastating physical and mental health consequences and human rights violations as a result of living in pollution hotspots and heavily contaminated areas".[52] The former Special Rapporteur on contemporary forms of racism added her support and emphasis to this concept, reframing them as 'racial sacrifice zones'.[53] In his report on toxic environments, the Special Rapporteur on human rights and the environment lists a wealth of examples from every region around the globe, such as the so called "Cancer Alley" in Louisiana, the United States, a location of over 150 refineries and petrochemical plants, where the predominantly Black local communities suffer cancer at significantly higher rates than the national average. Or the Pata Rât landfill in Romania, where marginalised Roma people, lacking basic amenities, are further exposed to arsenic, benzene, lead, mercury and other toxins, and suffer infections of the ears, eyes and skin, as well as asthma, bronchitis, high blood pressure, cancer and heart, liver and stomach ailments.[54]

Environmental destruction has had a devastating impact on the human rights of the many indigenous peoples around the world who depend on ecosystems that are particularly vulnerable to the effects of climate change and extreme weather events such as floods, droughts, heatwaves, wildfires and cyclones.[55] The legacies of colonialism, and the ecological destruction that has accompanied it also continue to threaten the cultural identity and survival of many indigenous peoples, often through resource extraction projects. To highlight one example, in Canada, the findings of the national inquiry into missing and murdered indigenous women and girls in 2019 recognised the link between resource extraction projects, the 'boomtown'[56] and 'man camp'[57] environments that these projects created, and violence against indigenous

---

[52] UN Human Rights Council 2022, para 29. The Special Rapporteur considers that "[t]he continued existence of sacrifice zones is a stain upon the collective conscience of humanity".

[53] UN General Assembly 2022c, para 2: "'Sacrifice zones,' as illustrated in this report, are more accurately described as 'racial sacrifice zones.' Racial sacrifice zones include the ancestral lands of indigenous peoples, territories of the Small Island Developing States (SIDS), racially segregated neighbourhoods in the Global North, and occupied territories facing drought and environmental devastation. The primary beneficiaries of these racial sacrifice zones are transnational corporations that funnel wealth, towards the Global North, and privileged national and local elites globally."

[54] UN Human Rights Council 2022, paras 30–46.

[55] UN Human Rights Council 2017. See also UN Human Rights Council 2022; UN General Assembly 2022c.

[56] Large-scale resource extraction projects can cause an influx of predominantly male workers to a rural or remote indigenous community, creating a sudden, often short-lived economic 'boom', with significant direct and indirect consequences for indigenous women and girls. See for example Amnesty International 2016.

[57] 'Man camps' are temporary housing facilities constructed for predominantly male workers on resource extraction projects.

women girls and 2SLGBTQQIA people.[58] The national inquiry cited the perspective of one indigenous woman to describe the linkages:

> The industrial system of resource extraction in Canada is predicated on systems of power and domination. This system is based on the raping and pillaging of Mother Earth as well as violence against women. The two are inextricably linked. With the expansion of extractive industries, not only do we see desecration of the land, we see an increase in violence against women. Rampant sexual violence against women and a variety of social ills result from the influx of transient workers in and around workers' camps.[59]

The reality reflected in the findings of the national inquiry was amplified by indigenous activists at the COP26, who urged greater awareness of the linkages between extractive industries, climate destruction and violence against indigenous women and girls, and asserted that "femicide is directly linked to the ecocide".[60]

The lack of respect for the human rights of indigenous peoples also disregards indigenous peoples' perspectives and knowledge of their environments, and the vital role of indigenous land stewardship.[61] Indigenous peoples play an invaluable part in sustainable environmental management of natural resources and biodiversity conservation in many areas of the world, as manifested through indigenous-led climate research and monitoring initiatives such as the Indigenous Guardians programmes.[62] Still, the voices of indigenous peoples continue to be marginalised and silenced through repressive measures, threats to their livelihood and even violence.[63]

A human rights assessment also reveals the particular vulnerability of children to the impacts of environmental destruction. While all children are vulnerable to the negative impacts of climate change, with the youngest being most at risk, nearly half of the world's children live at "extremely high risk" in places where poverty and a lack of access to clean water, healthcare and education intersect to diminish the likelihood of a child's ability to survive the climate crisis.[64] This dire situation

---

[58] National Inquiry into Missing and Murdered Indigenous Women and Girls 2019. See also Standing Committee on the Status of Women 2022. The National Inquiry has chosen to use the term '2SLGBTQQIA' (representing Two-Spirit, lesbian, gay, bisexual, transgender, queer, questioning, intersex and asexual people). See National Inquiry into Missing and Murdered Indigenous Women and Girls 2018.

[59] National Inquiry into Missing and Murdered Indigenous Women and Girls 2019, p. 586.

[60] Brooks 2021.

[61] The Kunming-Montreal Global Biodiversity Framework highlights the role of indigenous peoples and local communities as custodians of biodiversity and as partners in its conservation, restoration and sustainable use, and declares that the Framework's implementation must ensure that "the rights, knowledge, including traditional knowledge associated with biodiversity, innovations, worldviews, values and practices of indigenous peoples and local communities are respected, and documented and preserved with their free, prior and informed consent". Conference of the Parties to the Convention on Biological Diversity 2022, para 7(a).

[62] See, for example, Intergovernmental Panel on Climate Change 2023; Indigenous Leadership Initiative 2021.

[63] Indigenous peoples accounted for more than one third of the 227 environmental and land defenders killed in 2020 alone—reportedly the deadliest year on record. Global Witness 2021. See also UN Human Rights Council 2020.

[64] UNICEF 2021. UNICEF reports a major disconnect between the countries where greenhouse gas emissions are generated and those where children are enduring the most significant climate-driven

is eroding development gains and undermining the full spectrum of the rights of children, who are often unable to protect their own rights. The inter-generational impacts of environmental destruction are also being increasingly recognised and addressed by courts at the national level, where decision-makers are being held to account for actions or omissions that will impact the enjoyment of rights by both present and future generations.[65]

Ultimately, a human rights lens helps to reveal the human stories of the impacts of climate change and environmental destruction, and in so doing, to deepen our understanding of the interlinkages between people and the environment. This understanding will help to inform the crime of ecocide. By providing insights as to the grave impact of specific acts of ecocide on marginalised groups, or on "natural, cultural or economic resources", it will assist prosecutors to frame their indictments to reflect the full impact of the criminality. This is crucial to establishing a body of law which reflects lived experience and contributes to more just outcomes.

The way sexual and gender-based violence (SGBV) has been treated within international criminal law provides an illustration of this trajectory.

5.3.3 The Example of Sexual and Gender-Based Violence Prosecutions at International Courts

At both the International Criminal Tribunal for the former Yugoslavia (ICTY), and the International Criminal Tribunal for Rwanda (ICTR), judges intervened in early cases to raise the issue of sexual violence, which had not been specifically charged by the prosecutor.[66] Most famously, in the first case before the ICTR, *Prosecutor v. Akayesu*, the prosecutor applied for leave to amend the indictment to include sexual violence charges after evidence of this had emerged in court at the prompting of the judges, and a coalition of Rwandan and international women's organisations had filed an amicus brief on this point.[67] The advocacy of feminist and women's rights groups helped to amplify the harrowing lived experience and voices of the victims and surface aspects of the larger crime that had been obscured, telling a fuller story.

impacts, with the 33 countries listed as 'extremely high-risk', in terms of the impact on children, emitting only 9% of global CO_2 emissions. The 10 highest emitting countries collectively account for nearly 70% of emissions.

[65] See Chatham House 2021. The UN Committee on the Rights of the Child also recognizes the principle of intergenerational equity and the interests of future generations in its General Comment no 26 on children's rights and the environment with a special focus on climate change. See UN Committee on the Rights of the Child 2023. See also Intervener Brief filed by the UN High Commissioner for Human Rights, above n 24, para 23.

[66] See Van Schaack 2008, p. 7. Van Schaack discusses not only the Akayesu case at the ICTR but also Prosecutor v. Nikolic at the ICTY, where judges encouraged the prosecutor to amend the indictment to charge sexual violence, which they later did. See Van Schaack 2008, p. 7, fn 13.

[67] Ibid., pp. 5–11.

Akayesu was ultimately convicted of two sexual violence charges: rape as a crime against humanity as well as genocide through sexual violence.[68]

From this point on, actors both within and outside the courts worked to overcome the obstacles to investigating and prosecuting crimes of sexual violence.[69] Convictions accumulated for rape and sexual violence as genocide, crimes against humanity and war crimes.[70] It should be noted that no new law was required to criminalise acts of sexual violence in these categories. Evidence of sexual violence might even, as in the Akayesu case, have been presented in court as part of the prosecution case under a more general charge. But the explicit articulation of SGBV crimes led both to greater awareness and to a body of jurisprudence that can protect women and other victims of SGBV in a more robust fashion. By the time the ICC Statute was negotiated in 1998, and thanks in large part to feminist activism, rape, enforced prostitution, forced pregnancy, enforced sterilisation, sexual slavery, sex trafficking and other crimes of sexual violence were explicitly listed under its war crimes and crimes against humanity provisions.[71]

Charges of ecocide that are informed by a human rights analysis have a similar potential to generate awareness, accountability and protection for all victims of environmental destruction. When an indictment articulates the disparate impact of environmental destruction on marginalised groups, and a prosecution gives those experiences centre stage in its presentation of evidence, the result is jurisprudence protecting these groups. As these cases accumulate, they also build a detailed account that illuminates structural discrimination and the relationship between power and environmental harms. As prosecutions and convictions for wartime SGBV accumulated, so did measures aimed at prevention and reparations, as well as broader initiatives to address the structural exclusion of women from the maintenance of peace and security. The ground-breaking UN Security Council Resolution 1325, passed in 2000, not only calls for the protection of women and girls from gender-based violence, but also urges all actors to increase the participation of women and incorporate gender perspectives in all UN peace and security efforts.[72] Ecocide prosecutions informed by human rights can support and articulate the need for attention to the disparate impacts of environmental destruction. Just as the naming of gender-based violence in prosecutions and then judgements at international courts led to greater awareness of and accountability for those crimes, building a body of protective law towards

---

[68] Ibid., p. 19.

[69] For an account of this journey and the lessons learned at the ICTY, see Brammertz and Jarvis 2017. See also Askin 2003; Campbell 2007.

[70] Ibid.

[71] Rome Statute, above n 8, Articles 7(1)(g), 8(2)(b)(xxii), 8(2)(e)(vi). It should be said that there has been criticism of the ICC's record on implementing its progressive legal framework, see for example Altunjan 2021.

[72] UN Security Council 2000. The many subsequent institutional developments include, at international level, the creation of the Special Representative of the UN Secretary-General on Sexual Violence in Conflict in 2009. See UN Security Council 2009. See for the national level the UK government's Preventing Sexual Violence in Conflict Initiative, https://www.gov.uk/government/organisations/preventing-sexual-violence-in-conflict-initiative/about. Accessed 5 July 2025.

gender justice, an understanding of ecocide that centres on those most affected by the crime has the best potential to achieve environmental and climate justice.

5.3.4 *Limitations of a New International Crime to Contribute to Climate Justice*

One criticism of using the crime of ecocide to address climate harms is the inability of a new crime to deal with past injustice, owing to the non-retroactivity of criminal law. The principle of legality requires that the crime be forward-looking: no-one may be punished for an act that was not prohibited at the time it was committed. This skews accountability for global emissions towards today's polluters, ignoring the massive historic emissions of industrialised nations in the Global North. In other words, could it be said that criminalising ecocide directs efforts precisely away from climate justice?

There are a number of ways to answer this important enquiry. One is to note that leading industrialised countries such as the US, Russia and Germany still figure among the highest emitting states.[73] Another is to accept that prosecuting ecocide in the way we have discussed will be just one element of a human rights-based solution to the destruction of our environment, and will need to be accompanied by cooperative action on climate loss and damage[74] as well as other forms of reparations in order to achieve climate justice. A third answer involves the definition of the prohibited destruction in the proposed crime of ecocide, and in particular that it should be either unlawful or wanton.

'Wanton' is defined in the proposed amendment as "with reckless disregard for damage which would be clearly excessive in relation to the social and economic benefits anticipated". As the IEP explained in the commentary accompanying their draft:

> This introduces a proportionality test into the definition which reflects environmental law principles. Much national and international environmental law involves a balancing of environmental harms against social and economic benefits, which is expressed in the principle of sustainable development, and the Panel was mindful that socially beneficial acts, such as housing developments and transport links, can cause severe and either widespread or long-term damage to the environment.[75]

One ingredient of the principle of sustainable development is the concept of Common But Differentiated Responsibilities (CBDR), which was enshrined as Principle 7 of

[73] European Commission 2022.

[74] See Paris Agreement, adopted Paris Agreement, opened for signature 12 December 2015, 55 ILM 740, entered into force 4 November 2016, Article 8(3): "Parties should enhance understanding, action and support, including through the Warsaw International Mechanism, as appropriate, on a cooperative and facilitative basis with respect to loss and damage associated with the adverse effects of climate change."

[75] Stop Ecocide Foundation 2021.

the Rio Declaration on Environment and Development at the first Rio Earth Summit in 1992.[76] The declaration states:

> In view of the different contributions to global environmental degradation, States have common but differentiated responsibilities. The developed countries acknowledge the responsibility that they bear in the international pursuit of sustainable development in view of the pressures their societies place on the global environment and of the technologies and financial resources they command.

It has been summarised as expressing the need to evaluate responsibility for the remediation and mitigation of environmental degradation based on both historical contribution and present capabilities.[77] The 1997 Kyoto Protocol[78] drew on this principle to make a distinction between proposed goals for developed and developing countries, and it appears in the preamble to the 1992 UN Framework Convention on Climate Change (UNFCCC),[79] which acknowledges "that the global nature of climate change calls for the widest possible cooperation by all countries and their participation in an effective and appropriate international response, in accordance with their common but differentiated responsibilities and respective capabilities and their social and economic conditions[.]"

The IEP's suggestion that the principle of sustainable development be applied in assessing whether acts causing severe and widespread or long-term damage are also "wanton" therefore opens the door to consideration of the common but differentiated responsibilities principle. It allows for evaluation of economic and social benefits to take place within a context of both historic contribution and present capabilities. It also opens a space to examine where, on the one hand, the benefits and, on the other, the harms of extractive and other industrial activities, accrue.[80]

5.4 Conclusion

Adding ecocide to the ICC Statute, and thus to the list of "the most serious crimes of concern to the international community as a whole", would recognise the triple planetary crisis of climate change, loss of biodiversity and pollution among the greatest

---

[76] UN General Assembly 1992. The principle also appears in the International Law Association's (ILA) 2002 New Delhi Declaration of Principles of International Law Relating to Sustainable Development, Section 3, "The principle of common but differentiated responsibilities". See ILA 2002.

[77] De Lucia and Reibsten 2007.

[78] Kyoto Protocol to the United Nations Framework Convention on Climate Change, opened for signature 11 December 1997, 2303 UNTS 162, entered into force 16 February 2005.

[79] United Nations Framework Convention on Climate Change, opened for signature 9 May 1992, 1771 UNTS 107, entered into force 21 March 1994. See also ILA 2002, Section 3, "The principle of common but differentiated responsibilities".

[80] A concern arises under the principle of legality here, as it is unclear—in the absence of precedent or guidance—how such an assessment would be made. However, it is possible to imagine that clearer parameters could be developed, most likely through jurisprudence.

threats to human rights of our era. In this contribution, we explore two ways in which a human rights approach can flesh out the content of the proposed crime in a manner that supports the ultimate goals of prevention, protection and justice. The first draws upon standards of conduct and associated benchmarks for State and corporate actors which the international human rights system has begun to detail over the last few years, with relation to environmental destruction and climate change. These help to delineate the elements of the crime, in particular around issues of fault or foresight. Failure to comply with certain standards may also render acts that are not otherwise prohibited "unlawful", thus satisfying one element of the proposed ecocide definition. The second considers how a human rights approach centres affected individuals and groups, and so can highlight the disproportionate impacts of severe and widespread or long-term environmental damage on marginalised and disempowered populations. Such an approach can assist ecocide prosecutions to address the full impact of the criminality, and has the most potential to generate awareness, accountability and protection for all victims of environmental destruction, tracing a path towards environmental and climate justice.

Post Scriptum As this chapter was finalized in January 2025, it does not reflect significant developments including the Advisory Opinions issued subsequently by the International Court of Justice and the Inter-American Court of Human Rights on the obligations of States in respect of climate change. These Opinions further support and reinforce the analysis as presented in this chapter.

References

Articles, Books and Other Documents

Adelman S, Kotzé L (2021) Introduction: Climate Justice in the Anthropocene. Oñati Socio-Legal Series 11(1):30–43

Altunjan T (2021) The International Criminal Court and Sexual Violence: Between Aspirations and Reality. German Law Journal 22:878–893

Amnesty International (2016) Out of Sight, Out of Mind Report: Gender, Indigenous Rights, and Energy Development in Northeast British Columbia, Canada. https://www.amnesty.org/en/documents/amr20/4872/2016/en/. Accessed 3 July 2025

Askin K (2003) Prosecuting Wartime Rape and Other Gender-Related Crimes under International Law: Extraordinary Advances, Enduring Obstacles. Berkeley Journal of International Law 21(2):288–349

Brammertz S, Jarvis M (2017) Prosecuting Conflict-Related Sexual Violence at the ICTY. Oxford University Press, Oxford

Brooks L (2021) Indigenous women speak out at Cop26 rally: 'Femicide is linked to ecocide'. 10 November 2021. https://www.theguardian.com/environment/2021/nov/10/indigenous-women-speak-out-at-cop26-rally-femicide-is-linked-to-ecocide. Accessed 5 July 2025

Bueno N, Bernaz N, Holly G, Martin-Ortega O (2024) The EU Directive on Corporate Sustainability Due Diligence (CSDDD): The Final Political Compromise. Business and Human Rights Journal 9(2): 294–300

Campbell K (2007) The Gender of Transitional Justice: Law, Sexual Violence and the ICTY. International Journal of Transitional Justice 1(3):411–432

CEDAW (2018) General Recommendation No. 37 on Gender-related dimensions of disaster risk reduction in the context of climate change, UN Doc. CEDAW/C/GC/37

Chatham House (2021) Climate change and human rights-based strategic litigation. https://www.chathamhouse.org/2021/11/climate-change-and-human-rights-based-strategic-litigation Accessed 3 July 2025

Conference of the Parties to the Convention on Biological Diversity (2022) Decision adopted by the Conference of the Parties to the Convention on Biological Diversity on Kunming-Montreal Global Biodiversity Framework, CBD/COP/DEC/15/4

De Lucia V, Reibsten R (2007) Common but differentiated responsibility. In: Cleveland CJ (ed) Encyclopaedia of Earth. National Council for Science and the Environment, Washington D.C.

European Commission (2022) Emissions Database for Global Atmospheric Research (EDGAR) 2022 Report. https://edgar.jrc.ec.europa.eu/report_2022. Accessed 3 July 2025

European Parliament (2021) Human rights and democracy in the world and the European Union's policy on the matter – annual report 2021, 2021/2181(INI). https://oeil.secure.europarl.europa.eu/oeil/popups/ficheprocedure.do?lang=en&reference=2021/2181(INI). Accessed 3 July 2025

Global Witness (2021) Last Line of Defence: The industries causing the climate crisis and attacks against land and environmental defenders. https://globalwitness.org/en/campaigns/land-and-environmental-defenders/last-line-of-defence/. Accessed 3 July 2025

Government of Belgium (2020) Statement of Belgium to the 19th Session of the Assembly of State Parties to the Rome Statute of the International Criminal Court. https://static1.squarespace.com/static/5ca2608ab914493c64ef1f6d/t/5fe1e759b356721fce380f27/1608640346408/GD.BEL.14.12+%282%29.pdf. Accessed 3 July 2025

Government of the Republic of Vanuatu (2019) Government of the Republic of Vanuatu to the 18th Session of the Assembly of State Parties to the Rome Statute of the International Criminal Court, 2nd – 7th December 2019. https://asp.icc-cpi.int/sites/asp/files/asp_docs/ASP18/GD.VAN.2.12.pdf. Accessed 3 July 2025

Human Rights for the Planet (2022) The Strasbourg Principles of International Environmental Human Rights Law. Journal of Human Rights and the Environment 13:195–202

Indigenous Leadership Initiative (2021) Backgrounder: Indigenous-Led Conservation in the Boreal is Key to Climate Leadership. https://www.ilinationhood.ca/publications/backgrounderborealcarbonipca. Accessed 3 July 2025

Intergovernmental Panel on Climate Change (2023) Special Report on Climate Change and Land: Summary for policymakers. https://www.ipcc.ch/srccl/chapter/summary-for-policymakers/. Accessed 3 July 2025

International Corporate Governance Network (2021) Statement of Shared Climate Change Responsibilities to the United Nations Climate Change Conference of the Parties 26 (COP 26). https://www.icgn.org/sites/default/files/2023-10/23.%20UK%20-%20COP26%20-%20Statement%20of%20Shared%20Climate%20Change%20Responsibilities%2C%20October%202021.pdf. Accessed 3 July 2025

International Law Association (2002) New Delhi Declaration of Principles of International Relating to Sustainable Development. International Environmental Agreements: Politics, Law and Economics 2:209–216

Mackintosh K (2023) European Parliament Votes Unanimously for Ecocide. https://opiniojuris.org/2023/04/10/european-parliament-votes-unanimously-for-ecocide/. Accessed 3 July 2025

Mason-Case S, Dehm J (2021) Redressing Historical Responsibility for the Unjust Precarities of Climate Change in the Present. In: Mayer B, Zahar A (eds) Debating Climate Law. Cambridge University Press, Cambridge, pp 170–189

Natarajan U (2021) Climate Justice. In: Valverde M, Clarke KM, Smith ED, Kotiswaran P (eds) Routledge Handbook of Law and Society. Routledge, Oxon

National Inquiry into Missing and Murdered Indigenous Women and Girls (2018) Lexicon of Terminology. https://www.mmiwg-ffada.ca/wp-content/uploads/2018/02/NIMMIWG_Lexicon_ENFR-1.pdf. Accessed 5 July 2025

National Inquiry into Missing and Murdered Indigenous Women and Girls (2019) Reclaiming Power and Place: The Final Report of the National Inquiry into Missing and Murdered Indigenous Women and Girls. https://www.mmiwg-ffada.ca/final-report/. Accessed 3 July 2025

Oldring L, Robinson D (2023) Does Human Rights Due Diligence Offer the Key to Prosecuting Ecocide? https://ecocidelaw.com/wp-content/uploads/2023/08/11-Oldring-and-Robinson-Human-Rights-Due-Diiligence.pdf. Accessed 3 July 2025

Republic of Maldives (2019) Written Statement of the Republic of the Maldives to the 18th Session of the Assembly of State Parties to the Rome Statute of the International Criminal Court, 3 December 2019. https://asp.icc-cpi.int/sites/asp/files/asp_docs/ASP18/GD.MDV.3.12.pdf. Accessed 3 July 2025

Robinson D (2023) The Ecocide Wave is Already Here: National Momentum and the Value of a Model Law. https://www.justsecurity.org/85244/the-ecocide-wave-is-already-here-national-momentum-and-the-value-of-a-model-law/. Accessed 3 July 2025

Shift Project (2023) Aligning the EU Due Diligence Directive with International Standards: Key Issues in the Negotiations. https://shiftproject.org/resource/aligning-the-cs3d-with-the-international-standards/. Accessed 5 July 2025

Standing Committee on the Status of Women (2022) Responding to the calls for justice: addressing violence against indigenous women and girls in the context of resource development projects. https://www.ourcommons.ca/DocumentViewer/en/44-1/FEWO/report-5/. Accessed 3 July 2025

Stop Ecocide Foundation (2021) Independent Expert Panel for the Legal Definition of Ecocide, Commentary and Core Text. https://www.legal-tools.org/doc/pb375e/. Accessed 25 June 2025

Stop Ecocide International (2024) https://www.stopecocide.earth/2024/mass-destruction-of-nature-reaches-international-criminal-court-icc-as-pacific-island-states-propose-recognition-of-ecocide-as-international-crime#:~:text=Following%20notification%20of%20UN%20Secretary,co%2Dsponsored%20by%20fellow%20Pacific. Accessed 3 July 2025

Thomas A, Baptiste A, Martyr-Koller R, Pringle P, Rhiney K (2020) Climate Change and Small Island Developing States. Annual Review of Environment and Resources 45:1–27

UN Committee on the Rights of the Child (2023) General Comment No 26 on children's rights and the environment with a special focus on climate change, UN Doc. CRC/C/GC/26

UN General Assembly (1992) Report of the United Nations Conference on Environment and Development, UN Doc. A/CONF.151/26 (Vol. I)

UN General Assembly (2022a) Resolution 76/300 'The human right to a clean, healthy and sustainable environment', UN Doc. A/RES/76/300

UN General Assembly (2022b) Report of the UN Special Rapporteur on the promotion and protection of human rights in the context of climate change, UN Doc. A/76/226

UN General Assembly (2022c) Report of the Special Rapporteur on contemporary forms of racism, racial discrimination, xenophobia and related intolerance, UN Doc. A/77/549

UN Human Rights Committee (2019) General Comment No 36 on the right to life, UN Doc. CCPR/C/GC/36

UN Human Rights Council (2009) Report of the Office of the United Nations High Commissioner for Human Rights on the Relationship Between Climate Change and Human Rights, UN Doc. A/HRC/10/61

UN Human Rights Council (2011a) Report of the Special Representative of the Secretary-General on the issue of human rights and transnational corporations and other business enterprises, 'Guiding Principles on Business and Human Rights: Implementing the United Nations "Protect, Respect and Remedy Framework"', UN Doc. A/HRC/17/31

UN Human Rights Council (2011b) Resolution 17/4 'Human rights and transnational corporations and other business enterprises', UN Doc. A/HRC/RES/17/4

UN Human Rights Council (2017) Report of the UN Special Rapporteur on the rights of indigenous peoples, UN Doc. A/HRC/36/46

UN Human Rights Council (2018) Report of the Special Rapporteur on the Issue of Human Rights Obligations Relating to the Enjoyment of a Safe, Clean, Healthy and Sustainable Environment, UN Doc. A/HRC/37/59

UN Human Rights Council (2019a) Report of the Special Rapporteur on Human Rights and the Environment, Right to a Healthy Environment: Good Practices, UN Doc. A/HRC/43/53

UN Human Rights Council (2019b) Report of the Special Rapporteur on extreme poverty and human rights, 'Climate Change and Poverty', UN Doc. A/HRC/41/39

UN Human Rights Council (2020) Report of the UN Special Rapporteur on human rights defenders, 'Final warning: death threats and killings of human rights defenders', UN Doc. A/HRC/46/35

UN Human Rights Council (2021a) Resolution 48/14 'Mandate of the Special Rapporteur on the promotion and protection of human rights in the context of climate change', UN Doc. A/HRC/RES/48/14

UN Human Rights Council (2021b) Report of the UN Working Group of Experts on People of African Descent, 'Environmental justice, the climate crisis and people of African descent', UN Doc. A/HRC/48/78

UN Human Rights Council (2021c) Analytical study on the promotion and protection of the rights of older persons in the context of climate change, UN Doc. A/HRC/47/46

UN Human Rights Council (2022) Report of the Special Rapporteur on the issue of human rights obligations relating to the enjoyment of a safe, clean, healthy and sustainable environment, "The right to a clean, healthy and sustainable environment: non-toxic environment", UN Doc. A/HRC/49/53

UN Human Rights Council (2023) The human right to a clean, healthy and sustainable environment, UN Doc. A/HRC/52/L.7

UN Human Rights Council (2024a) Report of the Special Rapporteur on the issue of human rights obligations relating to the enjoyment of a safe, clean, healthy and sustainable environment: Business, planetary boundaries, and the right to a clean, healthy and sustainable environment, UN Doc. A/HRC/55/43

UN Human Rights Council (2024b) Draft Report on the tenth session of the open-ended intergovernmental working group on transnational corporations and other business enterprises with respect to human rights, UN Doc. A/HRC/58/XX

UN OHCHR (2018) Statement of the Committee on Economic, Social and Cultural Rights on Climate Change and the International Covenant on Economic, Social and Cultural Rights. https://www.ohchr.org/en/statements-and-speeches/2018/10/committee-releases-statement-climate-change-and-covenant. Accessed 5 July 2025

UN OHCHR (2020) UN Human Rights "Issues Paper" on legislative proposals for mandatory human rights due diligence by companies. https://www.ohchr.org/sites/default/files/Documents/Issues/Business/MandatoryHR_Due_Diligence_Issues_Paper.pdf. Accessed 5 July 2025

UN OHCHR (2021a) EU Mandatory Human Rights Due Diligence Directive: Recommendations to the European Commission. https://www.ohchr.org/sites/default/files/Documents/Issues/Business/ohchr-recommendations-to-ec-on-mhrdd.pdf. Accessed 3 July 2025

UN OHCHR (2021b) Fact Sheet No. 38: Frequently Asked Questions on Human Rights and Climate Change. https://www.ohchr.org/en/publications/fact-sheets/fact-sheet-no-38-frequently-asked-questions-human-rights-and-climate. Accessed 3 July 2025

UN OHCHR (2024) Keynote Speech to 'The Promise of International Law in the Face of Ecological Crises' Conference: 'Well past the hour' for countries to align climate laws with human rights obligations' https://www.ohchr.org/en/statements-and-speeches/2024/05/well-past-hour-countries-align-climate-laws-human-rights. Accessed 3 July 2025

UN Security Council (2000) Resolution 1325, UN Doc. S/RES/1325

UN Security Council (2009) Resolution 1888, UN Doc. S/RES/1888

UN Security Council (2024) Report of the Secretary General: Protection of Civilians in Armed Conflict - Report of the Secretary-General, UN Doc. S/2024/385

UNEP (2024) Draft ministerial declaration of the United Nations Environment Assembly at its sixth session, UN Doc. UNEP/EA.6/HLS/L.1

UNEP, UN Women, UN OHCHR (2021) Human Rights, Gender Equality and the Environment: Key Messages. https://www.unwomen.org/en/digital-library/publications/2022/06/policy-paper-human-rights-environment-gender-equality. Accessed 3 July 2025

UNICEF (2021) The Climate Crisis is a Child Rights Crisis: Introducing the Children's Climate Risk Index. http://www.unicef.org/reports/climate-crisis-child-rights-crisis. Accessed 3 July 2025

Van Schaack B (2008) Engendering Genocide: The Akayesu Case Before the International Criminal Tribunal for Rwanda. http://digitalcommons.law.scu.edu/facpubs/629 Accessed 3 July 2025

World Bank (2016) Shock Waves: Managing the Impacts of Climate Change on Poverty. https://openknowledge.worldbank.org/handle/10986/22787. Accessed 3 July 2025

Lisa Oldring is a Senior Fellow with the UCLA Law Promise Institute Europe and a doctoral candidate at the University of Amsterdam Faculty of Law. Her research focuses on the crime of ecocide from a human rights perspective. Oldring is an international human rights lawyer with over twenty years of practice at the global level, primarily with the United Nations Human Rights Office where she led work on issues including counter-terrorism, the use of force, and global surveillance practices. She has served as legal advisor to UN-mandated international commissions of inquiry on Darfur, Sudan and on Lebanon; Special Advisor to Mary Robinson (Chair, GAVI Board); advisor to the first UN Special Rapporteur on the right to health; and attaché to the International Committee of the Red Cross. She began her UN work in the post-conflict human rights field operation in Rwanda. Oldring is an active member of the Board of the Directors of Lawyers Without Borders (Canada) and serves on the Advisory Board of Stop Ecocide International.

Kate Mackintosh is Executive Director and Professor from Practice at the UCLA Law Promise Institute Europe. She has had an extensive career in human rights and international criminal justice, holding senior positions across civil society organizations, academia and the UN. She currently serves on the International Council of Experts on the Investigation of Crimes Committed in Armed Conflict in Ukraine, as well as the Advisory Group for the International Criminal Court Prosecutor's Policy on Environmental Crimes. She represented the State of Palestine at the ICJ in the context of the Request for an Advisory Opinion on States' responsibilities in the face of climate change. From 2020 to 2021 she was Deputy co-chair of the Independent Expert Panel for the Legal Definition of Ecocide.

Part III
Where?

Chapter 6
Ecocide as an International Crime? Perspectives on Prosecution at the ICC and in the Netherlands

Göran Sluiter, Barbara van Straaten and Ava Schuster

Contents

Abstract Ecocide, the causing of serious environmental harm, is gaining momentum as a potential international crime before the International Criminal Court. This chapter examines the ecocide definition proposed by the Independent Expert Panel and explores how—alternatively to an amendment of the International Criminal Court's Statute—ecocide could be prosecuted under existing international crimes. Although the Prosecutor seems open to addressing environmental crimes within this existing framework, significant legal and conceptual obstacles remain due to the anthropocentric nature of the core crimes. However, the residual category of crimes against humanity may offer a viable avenue for addressing crimes equivalent to

This publication is part of the NWO-funded VICI research project 'The Outer Limits of Secondary Liability'. The present book chapter is an adapted and updated version of Sluiter and Van Straaten 2020.

G. Sluiter (✉)
University of Amsterdam, Amsterdam, The Netherlands
e-mail: g.k.sluiter@uva.nl

Open University, Heerlen, The Netherlands

B. van Straaten
Prakken d'Oliveira Human Rights Lawyers Coöperatief U.A., Amsterdam, The Netherlands
e-mail: bvanstraaten@prakkendoliveira.nl

A. Schuster
University of Amsterdam, Amsterdam, The Netherlands
e-mail: avasofieschuster@gmail.com

L. Burgers et al. (eds.), *Ecocide: Criminalising Serious Harm against the Environment*, International Criminal Justice Series 38, https://doi.org/10.1007/978-94-6265-715-1_6

ecocide. Environmental harm could also prove contextual elements or be considered an aggravating factor in sentencing. Beyond the International Criminal Court, domestic jurisdictions can provide fora to prosecute such environmental offences. The Netherlands are a case in point, given its strong track record in international criminal law and ability to prosecute corporations. In the hope that the Dutch Prosecution Service will be inspired by progressive judgements on civil liability for environmental damage and the ICC Prosecutor's new focus on environmental crimes, we advocate for a more proactive policy, even if it entails complex cross-border investigations.

Keywords Independent Expert Panel · Crimes against humanity · Other inhumane acts · Netherlands Economic Offenses and International Crimes Acts · Ecocide · Environmental crimes · War crimes · Article 8(2)(b)(iv) ICC Statute

6.1 Introduction

Over the past years, initiatives have been emerging to include the causing of serious environmental harm in the *corpus* of international criminal law, particularly as a stand-alone international crime within the jurisdiction of the International Criminal Court (ICC or Court). The term 'ecocide' has been proposed to cover the relevant criminal conduct. Recently, this academic debate accumulated in a proposal for a universally recognised definition. On 22 June 2021, an independent expert group convened by the NGO *Stop Ecocide Foundation* presented a definition of 'ecocide', which is designed to be adopted as a new Article 8*ter* in the Statute for the International Criminal Court (ICC Statute).

One can think of several reasons as to why ecocide, or serious damage to the environment, deserves to be included in international criminal law, be it as a war crime, a crime against humanity or as an international crime in its own right. Ecocide causes considerable, perhaps even irreparable, harm to the environment, which affects the planet, the ecosystem, and humanity as a whole. One might argue that the seriousness of ecocide thus merits equivalence to existing international crimes. Indeed, from the point of view of the norm-expressive function of international criminal law, there is a strong case to be made for elevating ecocide to the status of an international crime and including it in the jurisdiction of the ICC.

The Netherlands prides itself as a vocal advocate for the further enhancement and development of international criminal law. It has undertaken several initiatives to hold States accountable for violations of international human rights law and international humanitarian law.[1] More importantly, the Netherlands has over the years prosecuted various cases involving war crimes and other international crimes at the national

[1] For example, in September 2020 the Netherlands issued a formal diplomatic notice to the Government of Syria in which it held the Assad government responsible for serious human rights violations, in particular torture, see Rijksoverheid [Central Government of the Netherlands] 2020. Furthermore, in July 2020, the Netherlands brought an inter-State application with the European Court of Human Rights (ECtHR) against Russia regarding its role in the downing of flight MH17: ECtHR *Ukraine*

level,[2] making it one of the countries with the best track record for the prosecution of international crimes globally. This makes the Netherlands an interesting case study to further assess the possibilities to prosecute ecocide as an international crime at the domestic level.

In the past, initiatives to bring ecocide under the jurisdiction of the ICC have also been launched in the Netherlands, although for the time being, the Dutch legislator does not seem to be inclined to directly penalise ecocide.[3] A parliamentary initiative[4] to persuade the Dutch government to undertake steps for the criminalisation of ecocide on a national and international level was dismissed by the government.[5] Similarly, in response to parliamentary questions raised after the publication of the above-mentioned new definition on ecocide, the responsible Ministers stated that they found that there is currently insufficient political will at the global level for amendment of the ICC Statute to include ecocide as a new crime.[6]

At the moment, it is impossible to predict whether and how ecocide as a new and stand-alone international crime will become part of international criminal law. This contribution therefore focuses on the question to what extent *current* international criminal law, as codified in the ICC Statute, offers points of departure for the prosecution of ecocide and how the Netherlands should take this into account in its national investigation and prosecution practice.

This contribution does not aim to answer the question at hand in its entirety but rather focuses on the following aspects. First, we will discuss the development of ecocide within the context of the ICC, including a few observations on the recent ecocide definition (Sect. 6.2). We will then outline some possibilities for including ecocide within the prosecution of existing international crimes at the ICC (Sect. 6.3). As a next step, we will discuss how the Netherlands could pay more attention to the protection of the environment in its investigation and prosecution of environmental harm (Sect. 6.4), before concluding with some final remarks (Sect. 6.5).

and the Netherlands v. Russia, Grand Chamber Hearing, 26 January 2022, Application No. 8019/16, 43800/14 and 28525/20.

[2] See e.g. The Hague District Court, 14 April 2022, ECLI:NL:RBDHA:2022:3410 regarding a case of war crimes committed in the Afghan Pul-e-Charkhi prison in 1983–1987; The Hague District Court, Judgment, 15 December 2017, ECLI:NL:RBDHA:2017:14782 regarding war crimes committed in Ethiopia during the Red Terror (1978); The Hague Court of Appeal, 9 May 2007, ECLI:NL:GHSGR:2007:BA4676 regarding complicity in war crimes by supplying raw materials used in the production of deadly gas for chemical attacks; and 's-Hertogenbosch Court of Appeal, 21 April 2017, ECLI:NL:GHSHE:2017:1760 regarding complicity for war crimes by supplying arms to the regime of Charles Taylor in Liberia.

[3] For an overview of States which have, at present, penalised ecocide under national law, see Ecocide Law, https://ecocidelaw.com/existing-ecocide-laws/. Accessed 13 July 2025.

[4] Tweede Kamer der Staten-Generaal [House of Representatives] 2020b.

[5] Tweede Kamer der Staten-Generaal [House of Representatives] 2020c.

[6] Tweede Kamer der Staten-Generaal [House of Representatives] 2020a.

6.2 Ecocide and International Criminal Law

Ecocide as a serious crime against the environment first emerged in the 1970s, in reaction to the use of the defoliant chemical Agent Orange by the US in the Vietnam War.[7] Since then, there have been several—unsuccessful—attempts to develop the crime of serious environmental damage as part of international criminal law.[8]

The most recently proposed definition, which has gained quite a bit of momentum, is the one developed by the 'Independent Expert Panel for the Legal Definition of Ecocide' (hereinafter: the Panel). A new definition on ecocide was proposed in an attempt to draft "a practical and effective definition of the crime of 'ecocide'. (…) It is the hope of the Panel that the proposed definition might serve as the basis of consideration for an amendment to the Rome Statute of the International Criminal Court (ICC)."[9] The new definition—which is envisaged to be included as a new Article 8*ter* in the Rome Statute—reads as follows:

Ecocide

1. For the purpose of this Statute, "ecocide" means unlawful or wanton acts committed with knowledge that there is a substantial likelihood of severe and either widespread or long-term damage to the environment being caused by those acts.
2. For the purpose of para 1:

   i. "Wanton" means with reckless disregard for damage which would be clearly excessive in relation to the social and economic benefits anticipated;
   ii. "Severe" means damage which involves very serious adverse changes, disruption or harm to any element of the environment, including grave impacts on human life or natural, cultural or economic resources;
   iii. "Widespread" means damage which extends beyond a limited geographic area, crosses state boundaries, or is suffered by an entire ecosystem or species or a large number of human beings;
   iv. "Long-term" means damage which is irreversible or which cannot be redressed through natural recovery within a reasonable period of time;
   v. "Environment" means the earth, its biosphere, cryosphere, lithosphere, hydrosphere and atmosphere, as well as outer space.

In the commentary to the definition, one finds the considerations and rationales underlying the choices made in the proposed definition.[10]

---

[7] In 1972 during the UN Stockholm Conference on the Human Environment, former Prime Minister of Sweden, Olaf Palme, referred to the Vietnam War as a form of ecocide; see Greene 2019, pp. 10–11.

[8] For a comprehensive overview and analysis of these attempts and the history of ecocide, see ibid., pp. 7–26.

[9] Stop Ecocide Foundation 2021.

[10] Ibid.

The work of the Panel is to be welcomed and applauded in many respects. Apart from the norm-setting function of the definition and its acknowledgement of the necessity for environmental protection at an international criminal level, the definition offers many interesting and useful elements. The proposal appears relatively realistic, by, for example, building in a certain threshold for qualification of certain acts as ecocide by incorporating the qualifiers 'severe', 'widespread' and 'long-term'. These—and other—terms are taken from the existing body of international (criminal) law,[11] implying a seamless alignment with other legal texts that can—together with available case law—assist in the interpretation of the various elements of the definition.[12]

Nonetheless, issues of interpretation persist, as the proposed ecocide definition diffuses the applicable *mens rea* standard. The default mental element provided under the Rome Statute requires 'knowledge' and implies a relative certainty of the result of one's actions.[13] Although Article 8*ter* explicitly incorporates the 'knowledge' element, the commentary notes that it should be interpreted closer to 'recklessness' or 'dolus eventualis'—a considerably lower standard.[14] Despite the fact that such a lower standard might be more suitable when prosecuting ecocide,[15] this mix of elements is not without problems. If embraced by state parties, the provision may inadvertently impose a higher mental element than intended by the Panel, particularly when considering that the Court has previously rejected an interpretation of 'knowledge' as encompassing 'dolus eventualis'.[16]

In addition, the explanations of elements such as 'widespread', 'long-lasting' and 'severe' seem to divert from the same or similar terms under Additional Protocol I and the Environmental Modification Convention.[17] In essence, no matter how compelling or imperative the justifications may be for incorporating distinct thresholds and definitions compared to existing international law, such deviations ultimately complicate the interpretation and application of ecocide.

---

[11] Protocol Additional to the Geneva Conventions of 12 August 1949, and relating to the Protection of Victims of International Armed Conflicts, opened for signature 8 June 1977, 1125 UNTS 3, entered into force 7 December 1978 (AP I), Articles 35(3) and 55(1). Rome Statute of the International Criminal Court, opened for signature 17 July 1998, 2187 UNTS 3, entered into force 1 July 2002 (Rome Statute), Article 8(2)(b)(iv). Convention on the Prohibition of Military or Any Other Hostile Use of Environmental Modification Techniques, opened for signature 10 December 1976, 1108 UNTS 151, entered into force 5 October 1978 (ENMOD). International Law Commission (ILC) 1991, Article 26. In relation to 'widespread' the Panel borrowed from the ICC's interpretation of 'widespread' within crimes against humanity, namely affecting large numbers of human beings. This last anthropocentric concept of 'widespread' was adapted for ecocide to include entire ecosystems or species, see Stop Ecocide Foundation 2021.

[12] ENMOD, above n 11, Annex.

[13] ICC, *The Prosecutor v Jean-Pierre Bemba Gombo*, Decision Pursuant to Article 61(7)(a) and (b) of the Statute, 15 June 2009, Case No. ICC-01/05-01/08-424, (Bemba Confirmation Decision), para 362.

[14] Stop Ecocide Foundation 2021.

[15] Minkova 2023, p. 78; Karnavas 2021.

[16] Bemba Confirmation Decision, above n 13, para 363.

[17] Compare Article 8*ter*(2) to the 'Understandings' of ENMOD, Article 1. See ICRC 2023.

Another point of criticism alleges that the Panel missed its chance to recognise ecocide as a truly eco-centric and stand-alone crime focusing exclusively on the environment as the victim or object of protection. By defining 'wanton' acts as damage that is 'clearly excessive in relation to the social and economic benefits anticipated',[18] the Panel de facto included a cost–benefit analysis.[19] This is problematic, as it suggests that acts normally amounting to ecocide can be legitimised due to their social and economic benefits.[20] Overall, such a distinction between human profit and environmental harm might be superfluous, as both people and the environment inevitably bear the costs of ecocide.[21] However, the inclusion of this human-centred element might be justified to enhance the proposal's chances of adoption, as it is believed that states are hesitant to endorse an exclusively eco-centric crime.[22]

There are further points of critique, or concerns, which entail, in our view, that the proposed ecocide-definition is not likely going to be part of the Rome Statute in the near, or even not so near, future.

First, owing to its relatively open-ended nature, it remains still rather unclear what conduct would be covered by the definition. In this regard, it should be noted that the proposed ecocide-definition contrary to all other core crimes in the ICC Statute, does not set out a list of punishable acts.

Second, building on the aforementioned concern regarding legality and legal certainty, the definition may overstretch criminal liability if one were to apply fully all existing modes of criminal liability under the Rome Statute. For example: applying aiding and abetting liability (Article 25(3)(c) of the Rome Statute) could under the present, rather vague, definition extend the scope of ecocide-liability to an extremely large group of relatively insignificant enablers and facilitators. This may be neither realistic nor desirable.[23]

Third, given the experience with negotiations on crimes falling within the jurisdiction of the ICC, it is not to be expected that countries will reach an agreement on the adoption of this new environmental crime in the ICC Statute in the short term. Moreover, states may be involved in environmental pollution reaching the threshold of ecocide themselves and thus may have little appetite for criminalising their own governmental policies and actions. Despite the new definition, there are large differences of perception between states when it comes to the concepts of 'environmental pollution' and 'environmental protection'. In this respect one can mention the extraction of shale gas and tar sands in the US and Canada, which is banned in most countries in Europe because of its large-scale environmental effects,[24] and which some

[18] Stop Ecocide Foundation, Article 8ter(2)(i).

[19] Minkova 2023, pp. 72, 73.

[20] Ibid., pp. 65, 76.

[21] Ibid., p. 76.

[22] Voigt 2021.

[23] See also Chaps. 8 and 9 in this volume.

[24] See for instance Article 13(a) Wasserhaushaltsgesetz (2016) [German Water Resources Act] stating that the exploration for and extraction of natural gas or crude oil using the so-called fracking

of them even consider a crime.[25] Another example is the regulation of deforestation, which is increasingly the subject of fierce debate between states and international action groups. Against these fundamental differences of opinion in what constitutes environmental damage, the open-ended nature of the definition and lack of concrete punishable acts may become particularly problematic.

Fourth, a new crime of ecocide being added to the ICC Statute may systematically and conceptually not sit well with the core crimes currently codified in the ICC Statute, namely genocide, war crimes, crimes against humanity and the crime of aggression. These crimes have in common that they are in essence 'state crimes'. They are either committed by the state (crime of aggression), by its national armed forces (war crimes),[26] or are part of a state policy (crimes against humanity and genocide). Even if the perpetrator cannot be linked to a state, he or she must be connected to an organisation with comparable features, such as a rebel group with a certain degree of organisation and authority over territory. As a consequence, the provisions in the ICC Statute are tailored to address state and state-like entities, as reflected in the general principles of international criminal law, such as command responsibility, no defence of superior orders, no statutes of limitations etc.[27]

In the case of ecocide, however, the intention seems to be not only to criminalise serious environmental harm caused by government action, but also to target companies guilty of the same conduct. Leaving aside the fact that until now there has not been criminal liability for—private—legal entities, such as companies, under the Rome Statute, the expansion of the ICC's scope beyond 'state crimes' can be criticised from the perspective of conceptual consistency within the Statute. Moreover, it is unclear to what extent the state-centred provisions will stand in the way of their application outside the context of commission by states or state-like actors.

In light of the aforementioned difficulties with the proposed ecocide-definition and the unlikelihood of ecocide becoming part of international criminal law as a new and stand-alone international crime in the near, perhaps even the not so near, future, we have opted to explore, in the following paragraphs, the possibilities for the prosecution of ecocide—serious damage to the environment—under *existing* international criminal law.

---

method is prohibited in shale, clay or marl rock or coal seam rock because of its detrimental effects on the environment.

[25] In several European jurisdictions where fracking is prohibited, constituent acts within the fracking process have been criminalized. In France, fracking without a prior declaration and authorization has been a criminal act for over a decade, as stipulated in Article 3, LOI n° 2011-835 du 13 juillet 2011 [Law No. 2011-835 of July 13, 2011]. Consequently, when the French National Assembly passed legislation prohibiting the issuance of new licenses for oil and gas exploration, de facto criminalizing fracking. See LOI n° 2017-1839 du 30 décembre 2017 [Law No. 2017-1839 of 30 December 2017].

[26] Note that in non-international or internal armed conflicts, war crimes may also be committed by armed groups.

[27] Rome Statute, above n 11, Articles 28, 33, 29.

6.3 Possibilities to Prosecute Ecocide in the Context of Existing International Crimes

The desire for a greater focus on environmental crimes within the framework of existing international crimes is evident from the 2016 Policy Paper on Case Selection and Prioritisation by the ICC Prosecutor: "(…) the Office will give particular consideration to prosecuting Rome Statute crimes that are committed by means of, or that result in, *inter alia*, the destruction of the environment, the illegal exploitation of natural resources or the illegal dispossession of land."[28]

This reference is widely regarded as an important development in the potential contribution of international criminal law to environmental protection.[29] It also raises the question: what are at present the possibilities under the Rome Statute to investigate and prosecute acts that cause serious damage to the environment?

Within the core crimes of the ICC Statute, only one explicit reference to the environment can be found. As part of the penalisation of war crimes, Article 8(2)(b)(iv) ICC Statute criminalises the following act committed within the framework of an international armed conflict:

> Intentionally launching an attack in the knowledge that such attack will cause incidental loss of life or injury to civilians or damage to civilian objects or <u>widespread, long-term and severe damage to the natural environment</u> which would be clearly excessive in relation to the concrete and direct overall military advantage anticipated. [emphasis added]

To our knowledge, this provision has never been used at the ICC, or at the national level. There are several issues with this, as of yet, only explicit international environmental crime in the ICC Statute. As the crime is limited to acts of violence committed as part of an international armed conflict, damage inflicted on the environment during an internal armed conflict or in peacetime therefore falls outside of its scope. Besides, the *actus reus* erects a high conviction threshold, considering the elements 'widespread, long-term and severe damage to the natural environment' and 'clearly excessive'. Finally, it is remarkable, and disappointing from the perspective of environmental protection, that even very serious damage[30] to the environment still has to be weighed against the expected military benefit. A successful prosecution of ecocide under Article 8(2)(b)(iv) ICC Statute seems therefore difficult.

That said, the Russian aggression against Ukraine showcases several incidents and attacks which could be categorised under this provision, such as attacks on or nearby the Chernobyl and Zaporidzje nuclear plants[31] or the destruction of the Kakhovka Dam.[32] Even if such attacks may not have—yet—resulted in widespread,

[28] Office of the Prosecutor of ICC 2016, para 41.

[29] See, for example, coverage in Bowcott and Vidal 2016 and the Guardian 2016.

[30] For a comprehensive analysis of environmental damage as a war crime, see Rauxloh 2011, pp. 426–434.

[31] For a number of instances of damaging the Ukrainian environment as a result of Russian attacks, see Keisler 2022.

[32] Gillett 2023. See also Chap. 7 in this volume.

long-term and severe damage to the environment, it could be interesting to explore whether certain attacks and methods of warfare deployed by the Russian armed forces amount to an attempt to commit the aforementioned war crime, as is penalised in Article 25(3)(f) of the ICC Statute.

Since no other war crimes in the ICC Statute explicitly reference the environment, any attempt to include environmental harm—let alone ecocide—under other provisions from Article 8(2)(b)(iv) would require some interpretative and argumentative efforts. Although Article 55(1) of the Additional Protocol I to the 1949 Geneva Conventions designates protection to the environment within the context of the protection granted to civilian objects—which are protected, inter alia, by Article 8(2)(b)(ii) ICC Statute—no such claims have been prosecuted before the ICC to date. Hence, we will now shift our focus to another core crime.

Prosecuting ecocide in the context of genocide seems difficult to imagine. Genocide requires the "intent to destroy, in whole or in part, a national, ethnical, racial or religious group, as such".[33] In certain situations, the infliction of serious harm to the environment may be carried out with this special intent.[34] For instance, the Court has previously found contamination of water pumps to also form part of a genocidal policy.[35] However, the inherent limitation of extending the crime of genocide to encompass ecocide lies in the human-centred nature of genocide. The provision's exclusive focus on harm inflicted upon human beings only tangentially acknowledges environmental harm as a consequence thereof and not as a crime in and of itself.[36] Consequently, the deliberate infliction of serious harm to the environment driven by genocidal intent is unlikely to be fulfilled in most cases involving serious environmental damage.[37]

The same reasoning applies to the crime of aggression, where the criminalisation focuses on inter-state violence.[38] Hence, genocide or the crime of aggression do not appear to be viable options for the prosecution of the (wilful) destruction of flora and fauna. That leaves us with the last core crime: crimes against humanity.

---

[33] Rome Statute, above n 11, art 6.

[34] The destruction of the Rohingya's environment, with accompanying severe environmental harm, could be an example of a situation in which severe environmental harm directed at one specific, ethnic, group contributes to the finding of genocide; see also Durney 2018, p. 425.

[35] ICC, *The Prosecutor v. Omar Hassan Ahmad Al Bashir*, Second Decision on the Prosecution's Application for a Warrant of Arrest, 12 July 2010, Case No. ICC-02/05-01/09-94, para 38.

[36] Minkova 2023, p. 65.

[37] For a discussion of the possible application of the crimes of genocide and war crimes to ecocide, see also Jägers 2017, pp. 365–372.

[38] For the purposes of para 1, 'act of aggression' means the use of armed force by a State against the sovereignty, territorial integrity or political independence of another State, or the use of armed force by a State that is otherwise incompatible with the Charter of the United Nations. See Rome Statute, above n 11, Article 8a.

6.3.1 Crimes Against Humanity

Crimes against humanity, unlike war crimes, do not require the existence of an armed conflict. They require the existence of a "widespread or systematic attack directed against any civilian population, with knowledge of the attack".[39] Possible underlying acts of an attack include murder, extermination, deportation or persecution. In addition to specific criminal acts listed in Article 7(1)(a) to (j), there also exists, in Article 7(1)(k), a residual category of crimes against humanity, consisting of "other inhumane acts of a similar character intentionally causing great suffering, or serious injury to body or to mental or physical health".[40]

Although the definition of crimes against humanity in the ICC Statute does not refer to the environment in any way, the residual category may be broad enough to offer more possibilities to prosecute ecocide than war crimes, the crime of aggression or genocide. A flexible interpretation of crimes against humanity would resonate with the background and development of this crime, where—in the absence of a clear definition—natural law was an important starting point.[41] Natural law, or the idea of universal principles of criminal law shared by all of humanity, delineates certain conduct as universally criminal.[42] Owing to such a vague premise, crimes against humanity have been compared to a 'chameleon'-like structure,[43] as universal understandings of criminal conduct are subject to change. Consequently, this framework might extend to encompass crimes related to the environment, particularly if they are deemed an integral part of a broader pattern of conduct constituting an attack on a civilian population.

We see three possibilities to include environmental crimes in the jurisdiction of the ICC, using crimes against humanity. The first is to prosecute environmental crimes as "other inhumane acts".[44] The second, which is more in line with the ICC Prosecutor's Policy Paper cited above, is to regard environmental harm as a means of committing or a result of various punishable acts within crimes against humanity. Finally, environmental harm can be taken into account in establishing the requirement of a "widespread or systematic attack directed against any civilian population", the threshold for the commission of the underlying acts.

---

[39] Rome Statute, above n 11, Article 7(1).

[40] Ibid., Article 7(1)(k).

[41] See Dubler 2008, pp. 87–88, who refers to natural law as the first stage of crimes against humanity.

[42] International Covenant on Civil and Political Rights, opened for signature 16 December 1966, 999 UNTS 171, entered into force 23 March 1976, Article 15(b) has been considered a strong foundation for crimes against humanity in the Nuremberg processes (see also ibid.):

> Nothing in this article shall prejudice the trial and punishment of any person for any act or omission which, at the time when it was committed, was criminal according to the general principles of law recognized by the community of nations.

[43] Dubler 2008, p. 106.

[44] Rome Statute, above n 11, Article 7(1)(k).

6.3.1.1 Other Inhumane Acts

As far as the first option is concerned, it could be argued that destruction of the environment constitutes an "other inhumane act" according to Article 7(1)(k) ICC Statute. This open-ended provision allows for the introduction of novel underlying acts.[45] However, such acts must be comparable—in terms of nature and gravity[46]—to the underlying acts in Article 7(1)(a) to (j) and intentionally "cause great suffering or serious injury to body or to mental or physical health."

The underlying acts adopted in case law under Article 7(1)(k) as other inhumane acts include *inter alia*: mutilation/dismemberment of corpses,[47] forced marriages,[48] and attempted murder (in the case law of international criminal tribunals that did not criminalise attempt).[49] Looking at these established and recognised "other inhumane acts", one may wonder whether they are of a similar character to the acts currently included in Article 7(1)(a) to (j).[50] In our view, the case law on "other inhumane acts"

---

[45] Compared to other definitions of crimes against humanity, the ICC Statute has included more specifically circumscribed criminal acts than, for example, the Statute of the International Criminal Tribunal for the former Yugoslavia. See UN Security Council 1993. There are eight underlying acts in the ICTY Statute and ten in the ICC Statute. Yet, in 1998, it was not considered that crimes against humanity were already exhaustively defined in letters (a) to (j) in para 1 of Article 7 of the Rome Statute; hence the addition of *other inhuman acts*. The same applies to the Draft Convention on the Prevention and Punishment of Crimes Against Humanity, of which 'other inhuman acts' also remains part. See ILC 2019. In short, the importance of this residual category is apparently still there even in the current codification of crimes against humanity. The residual category may therefore be used, otherwise it would no longer have any independent meaning. See in this sense also ICTY, Kupreškić Trial Judgement, 14 January 2000, Case No. IT-95-16-T, para 563: "(…) The phrase "other inhumane acts" was deliberately designed as a residual category, as it was felt undesirable for this category to be exhaustively enumerated. An exhaustive categorization would merely create opportunities for evasion of the letter of the prohibition. (…)".

[46] International Criminal Court (ICC), Elements of Crimes, reproduced in the Official Records of the Assembly of the States Parties to the Rome Statute of the International Criminal Court, First Session, New York, 3–10 September 2002, ICC-ASP/1/3 and Corr.1, part II.B, Article 7(1)(k).

[47] See ICTR, Niyitegeka Trial Judgement, 16 May 2003, Case No. ICTR-96-14, para 465, on the genital mutilation of a dead Tutsi woman: "The Chamber finds that the acts committed […] are acts of seriousness comparable to other acts enumerated in the Article, and would cause mental suffering to civilians, in particular, Tutsi civilians, and constitute a serious attack on the human dignity of the Tutsi community as a whole." In the Netherlands, there recently was a conviction for posing with corpses by IS fighters. It was not deemed a crime against humanity, but a war crime. See The Hague District Court, 23 July 2019, ECLI:NL:RBDHA:2019:7430.

[48] First recognised as other inhumane acts in the case law of the Special Court for Sierra Leone (SCSL); see SCSL, AFRC Appeals Judgement, 22 February 2008, Case No. SCSL-2004-16-A, paras 197–203. Thereafter also in the case law of the Extraordinary Chambers in the Courts of Cambodia (ECCC), see ECCC, Nuon Chea and Khieu Samphan Trial Judgement, 16 November 2018, Case No. 002/2, paras 740–749 and at the ICC, see The Prosecutor v. Dominic Ongwen, Trial Judgment, 4 February 2021, Case No. ICC-02/04-01/15, para 2751.

[49] This was the case with the ICTY; for recognition of attempted murder as other inhumane acts, see ICTY, Vasiljević Trial Judgement, 29 November 2002, Case No. IT-98-32-T, para 239.

[50] Critical on this: Jyrkkiö 2011, para 5.2.

demonstrates that there is certain flexibility in the *ejusdem generis* requirement.[51] For instance, forced circumcisions qualify as crimes against humanity as they are comparable in their nature and gravity to other form(s) of sexual violence as set out in 7(1)(g).[52] 'Similar character', as was said, allows for some flexibility, as it would be impossible for the Court to provide an exhaustive enumeration of inhumane acts.[53]

Therefore, accepting the infliction of serious harm to the environment under Article 7(1)(k) is defensible,[54] even if one were not to consider it to be fully of the same character compared to the harm that is described in the other subparagraphs of Article 7(1) ICC Statute. In light of this, the drafters of the Statute envisioned crimes against humanity to constitute crimes "of concern to the international community as a whole"[55] and to comprise "conduct which is impermissible under generally applicable international law".[56] Considering the potentially far-reaching and fatal consequences for humanity of ecocide-like crime, as well as current criminalisation of such acts, one can argue that severe damage to the environment appears worthy of inclusion.

The part of Article 7(1)(k) of the Rome Statute which requires that ecocide "intentionally caus[es] great suffering, or serious injury to body or to mental or physical health", may appear more problematic. It rules out a fully non-anthropocentric inclusion of ecocide under "other inhumane acts", as damage to the environment will—in this context—always need to be accompanied by human suffering or injury. This may indeed not be ideal, and a number of scholars and activists argue for a shift away from such anthropocentric handling of ecocide. That said, inclusion of some anthropocentric dimension in ecocide may assist in its development and acceptance. This comes also to the fore in another definition of ecocide, the one developed by Polly Higgins, in which criminal liability is made dependent on ecocide "[severely diminishing] peaceful enjoyment by the inhabitants [of their territories]".[57]

One can think of a variety of situations in which damage to the environment also constitutes suffering or injury to the—local—population, such as the detrimental effect that forced migration of indigenous peoples from forest areas to cities has on their mental health.[58] Hence, the inclusion of human interests in the crime of ecocide does not undermine the project *per se*; rather, it could enhance the development of the

[51] *Ejusdem generis rule*: literally 'of the same rule'. An interpretation rule for articles of law that refers to the situation where an enumeration of specific terms or categories is followed by a more general term. That general term must then be interpreted restrictively, in accordance with the concepts or matters specifically mentioned in the article of law, and may therefore not be applied or interpreted (too) broadly (in other words: must be read as meaning 'of the same').

[52] ICC, *The Prosecutor v. Uhuru Muigai Kenyatta*, Decision on the Confirmation of Charges, 23 January 2012, Case No. ICC-01/09-02/11 (Kenyatta Confirmation of Charges), para 277.

[53] ICC, *The Prosecutor v. Dominic Ongwen*, Judgment on Appeal, 15 December 2022, Case No. ICC-02/04-01/15-2023 (Ongwen Judgment on Appeal), para 1017.

[54] See also Gillett 2023, in relation to the destruction of the Kakhovka Dam.

[55] ICC Elements of Crimes, above n 46, art 7.

[56] Ibid.

[57] See Ecocide Law, https://ecocidelaw.com/polly-higgins-ecocide-crime/. Accessed 13 July 2025.

[58] Ceretta et al. 2023, p. 7.

law in a more anthropocentric context.[59] Article 7(1)(k) offers a pathway for doing just that.

In addition, the recognition of serious environmental harm as an "other inhumane act" resonates with the current climate in which environmental harm is increasingly threatening humanity (and already for that reason it is quite fitting within the category of crimes against *humanity*). The advantage of recognising serious environmental harm as "other inhumane acts" will also lie in the norm-expressive function of international criminal law. It can be argued that qualifying environmental harm as an independent crime against humanity, albeit under the umbrella of "other inhumane acts", does more justice to the seriousness of such an act than including it as a means of commission or as a result of other underlying acts (to be discussed below, under Sect. 6.3.1.2).

In practice, prosecuting serious environmental harm as a crime against humanity under Article 7(1)(k) will not be easy. The same contextual and intent requirements continue to apply. Thus, it would have to be proven that serious environmental harm was part of a "widespread or systematic attack on a civilian population". Furthermore, the prosecution would have to prove *intent* to cause great suffering, or serious injury to body, mental or physical health as a result of the environmental harm.[60] It is to be expected that for many environmental crimes it can be argued that they follow from accidents or miscalculations—in other words: that they have not been committed intentionally and hence that the strict intent requirement of Article 30(2) ICC Statute has not been met.[61] But these obstacles can be addressed if the facts and evidence in a given case allow for it.

In short, although the residual category under Article 7(1)(k) requires acts comparable to existing crimes and intentional infliction of great suffering or serious injury to body or mental/physical health, its interpretative flexibility allows for potential inclusion of serious environmental harm as a crime against humanity. The anthropocentric aspect of the provision might actually aid its development and acceptance, while recognising environmental harm within this framework aligns with the pressing global environmental concerns and serves a normative function in international criminal law. Nevertheless, challenges in prosecution persist, including proving intent and demonstrating a widespread or systematic attack on a civilian population.

---

[59] This consideration is particularly relevant given that the distinction between human and environmental interests is more conceptual than substantive.

[60] ICC Elements of Crimes, above n 46, Article 7(1)(k).

[61] This provision reads as follows:

> For the purposes of this Article, a person has intent where:
>
> a. In relation to conduct, that person means to engage in the conduct;
> b. In relation to a consequence, that person means to cause that consequence or is aware that it will occur in the ordinary course of events.

Thus, the ICC does not recognise conditional intent. But national systems, such as the Netherlands, can apply their own *mens rea* approach, including constructions of conditional intent.

6.3.1.2 Environmental Harm as a Means of Committing or a Result of Certain Crimes Against Humanity

The second option would be to address environmental harm not as such but as a method or consequence in the commission of crimes against humanity, which can potentially result in aggravated sentencing. In line with the Prosecutor's Policy Paper, the Prosecutor may charge environmental harm as a means of committing a crime against humanity or as the result of a crime against humanity.[62] In our view, there are several crimes against humanity that would suit the inclusion of environmental harm in this way. Prominent examples are extermination (Article 7(1)(b)), deportation or forcible transfer of population (Article 7(1)(d)), and persecution against any identifiable group (Article 7(1)(h)).[63] In all three instances, destruction of the environment can either be a means to or a result of committing the offence. An example cited in literature concerns the harrowing situation of the Rohingya population in Myanmar, where their extermination, deportation and persecution go hand in hand with serious harm, even destruction, of their living environment.[64] Another example is 'land grabbing' in Cambodia, as a result of which tens of thousands of farmers are driven from their land (deportation), causing very serious harm.[65]

Another example that comes to mind—although not derived from practice—would be when certain attacks, such as carpet bombings or widespread chemical attacks, would be carried out over a large array of land; it is to be expected that in addition to human loss the collateral damage would exist of widespread destruction of flora and fauna.[66]

In case, as we hope, there will be more attention to damage to the environment as a means to commit a crime against humanity or as a consequence thereof, the question arises as to what the effect will be on individual liability and punishment. At the level of liability, there will be no immediate visible effect, as the qualification will remain one of guilt for one of the existing crimes against humanity. However, at the level of punishment, the law of the ICC is quite flexible in the determination and use of—aggravating—factors in the determination of an appropriate sentence.[67] Arguably, severe damage to the environment that occurred in the context of the

[62] Jägers 2017.

[63] Rome Statute, above n 11, Article 7(1). Some of these options are also discussed in Gillett 2023.

[64] Durney 2018, pp. 425–426.

[65] Ibid., pp. 426–429. In 2021, the non-governmental organisations Global Witness, the International Federation for Human Rights (FIDH) and Climate Counsel sent an open letter to the ICC Prosecutor in which they asked the Prosecutor to pursue the widespread practice of land grabbing in Cambodia as a crime against humanity. In the letter, the organisations explicitly referred to the serious environmental destruction that is paired with the practice of land grabbing and called the situation an "climate and environmental emergency", see Alley et al. 2021.

[66] Such conduct could of course also qualify as a war crime, either the environment-specific war crime or another war crime when the attack would lead to a serious violation of the laws and customs of war. However, depending on the context and circumstances, such attacks can also amount to crimes against humanity.

[67] See on the determination of sentences, Rome Statute, above n 11, Article 78. ICC Rules of Procedure and Evidence, reproduced in the Official Records of the Assembly of States Parties to

commission of a crime against humanity should be recognised and used as an—important—aggravating factor in sentencing.[68]

It is important to note that also in the context of commission of one of the other core crimes—war crimes, genocide and the crime of aggression—severe damage to the environment can occur and, thus, deserves equal attention, for example as an aggravating factor in sentencing.

6.3.1.3 To Establish the Widespread or Systematic Attack

Finally, as a third option, environmental harm could be taken into account in determining whether a widespread or systematic attack on a civilian population has taken place. An attack on a civilian population is understood as: "a course of conduct involving the multiple commission of acts referred to in paragraph 1 [of Article 7 ICC Statute] against any civilian population, pursuant to or in furtherance of a State or organizational policy to commit such attack".[69]

As we have previously established, serious damage to the environment may be an underlying act (above, Sect. 6.3.1.1), the means to or the result of a crime against humanity (above, Sect. 6.3.1.2). As such, it may also be relevant for the determination that a widespread or systematic attack on civilians was committed. Large-scale environmental damage, with serious consequences for the civilian population, may

---

the Rome Statute of the International Criminal Court, First Session, New York, 3–10 September 2002, ICC-ASP/1/3 and Corr.1, part. II.A, Rule 145.

[68] See ICC, Rules of Evidence and Procedure, above n 67. Rule 145 provides good starting points for such recognition. Rule 145(1)(c) refers to the extent of damage caused and to the means used to commit the crime as relevant factors to determine the sentence, and in both cases damage to the environment can play an important role. In addition, Rule 145(2)(b)(iii) mentions explicitly 'commission of the crime where the victim is particularly defenceless' as an aggravating factor that the Court must take into account. The 'environment' should in our view be regarded, by definition, as such a particularly defenceless victim. See also Chap. 10 in this volume.

[69] Rome Statute, above n 11, Article 7(2)(a). For application in ICC jurisprudence, see ICC, *The Prosecutor v. Bosco Ntaganda*, Trial Judgment, 8 July 2019, Case No. ICC-01/04-02/06, paras 662 and 663: "An 'attack' for the purpose of crimes against humanity is distinct from an 'attack' referred to in Article 8 of the Statute for the purpose of determining whether a war crime was committed. It may be, but need not be, part of a military operation. The requirement that the acts form part of a 'course of conduct' indicates that Article 7 is meant to cover a series or overall flow of events, as opposed to a mere aggregate of random or isolated acts. In addition, the statutory requirement that the 'course of conduct' must involve the 'multiple commission of acts' sets a quantitative threshold involving a certain number of acts. Each of the acts must fall within the course of conduct and cumulatively they must satisfy the required quantitative threshold. To demonstrate the multiple commission of acts, only those acts enumerated in Article 7(1)(a) to (k) may be relied upon, but acts not listed in Article 7(1) may nevertheless be considered for other purposes. For instance, they can assist the determination whether the attack was directed against a civilian population, or whether it was pursuant to, or in furtherance of, a State or organisational policy [original footnotes omitted]."

For an analysis of the 'chapeau elements' of crimes against humanity, see Sluiter 2011, pp. 102–141.

meet the 'attack on civilians' threshold for the following two reasons. First, environmental damage will often occur as "a series or overall flow of events",[70] rather than "a mere aggregate of random or isolated acts", as required by ICC case law. In addition, in a significant number of instances, environmental damage may result from the policies of a state or organisation, therefore meeting the other requirement for an attack on the civilian population.

It follows from the above requirements that serious environmental damage caused by state policy, or organised actions from a state-like organisation, could well qualify as an attack against a civilian population. On the other hand, it will be more difficult to qualify a single or a few incidents of environmental damage as an "attack against the civilian population".[71]

6.4 What Can the Netherlands Do?

The Netherlands has quite a good international reputation for prosecuting international crimes. Well-known examples are the Van Anraat[72] and Kouwenhoven[73] cases, both of which ended in a conviction. The Public Prosecution Service decided to set up a specialised team to prosecute international crimes early on, which eventually led to the current Team International Crimes (TIC) of the Public Prosecution Service.[74] The Netherlands therefore forms a good case study to assess the possibilities for the prosecution and trial of ecocide as an international crime at the national level.

One of the main advantages of prosecuting ICC offences at the domestic level under Dutch law is that corporations can also be prosecuted. Article 51 of the Dutch Criminal Code allows for the prosecution of legal entities. This is a major and important difference in the context of ecocide compared to the ICC, which does not recognise the criminal liability of legal persons. Furthermore, like the criminal codes in many other countries, the Dutch Criminal Code includes specific environmental offences which could be used as a basis for the prosecution of ecocide-like incidents. Examples include drinking water pollution (Article 173 Criminal Code), soil and surface water pollution (Article 173a and 173b Criminal Code) and exposure

---

[70] Ibid.

[71] A single incident or operation in which multiple crimes are committed could amount to a crime against humanity provided that the relevant contextual elements are met (see ICC, *The Prosecutor v. Germain Katanga*, Judgment pursuant to Article 74 of the Statute, 7 March 2014, Case No. ICC-01/04-01/07 (Katanga Trial Chamber Judgment) para 1101).

[72] Netherlands Supreme Court 30 June 2009, LJN: BG4822, Strafkamer Nr. 07/10742.

[73] 's-Hertogenbosch Court of Appeal, 21 April 2017, ECLI:NL:GHSHE:2017:1760.

[74] Named after the International Crimes Act (ICA), which includes the criminalisation of international crimes, see Openbaar Ministerie 2023. In addition to the ICC *core crimes* (genocide, Article 3 ICA; crimes against humanity, Article 4 ICA; war crimes, Articles 5–7 ICA; aggression, Article 8b ICA) the ICA also contains penal provisions regarding torture (Article 8 ICA) and enforced disappearances (Article 8a ICA). The criminalisation of *core crimes* in the ICA follows the ICC Statute.

to radioactive substances (Articles 161quater to 161d Criminal Code).[75] Article 304 Criminal Code provides for the aggravating circumstance of committing a (serious) assault by administering substances that are harmful to life or health.

However, most prosecutions for environmental offences take place based on the Economic Offences Act (*Wet op de Economische Delicten*) (EOA).[76] For instance, Section 1a of the EOA criminalises the violation of a number of provisions in the Environmental Management Act, the Nature Conservation Act, the Transport of Dangerous Substances Act, the Soil Protection Act and the Water Act. If provisions listed in Article 1a sub 1 ° and 2 ° are violated intentionally, these economic offences qualify as crimes (Article 2 EOA).[77] Thus, there are several *leges speciales* that can be applied to (serious) environmental harm. The question is, however, whether application of only these specialised national laws does justice to instances of severe environmental damage, ecocide. Arguably, a narrow focus on isolated or limited instances of environmental harm indeed falls short of adequately addressing the nature and severity of ecocide-like incidents.

A potential solution would be to also use grave 'ordinary' offences in the prosecution of serious environmental harm such as (attempted) manslaughter or the (attempted) infliction of serious bodily harm. Large-scale destruction of a living environment may often cause serious health issues, such as respiratory problems, skin irritation or cancer. As long as the symptoms are sufficiently severe, an injury of this nature could qualify as 'serious bodily harm'.[78] In very serious cases, it could even constitute an attempted manslaughter or culpable homicide. The prosecution of these kinds of criminal offences might do more justice to the scale and seriousness of the circumstances, certainly if environmental harm is accompanied by great human suffering.

Coming back to our discussion above, the potential for prosecution hinges on various factors, notably the scale of damage to the environment, the existence of a "widespread or systematic attack on the civilian population", and causing of (human) suffering or injury. In these scenarios, prosecution could be based on "other inhumane act", as a crime against humanity under the International Crimes Act (ICA). Yet, it would be safe to work with alternative charges in the event that the high threshold of crime against humanity could not be met. For instance, in addition to each domestic offence, an alternative charge could be formulated with the corresponding offence from the ICA. Such a 'double' approach would ultimately assist in the goal of preventing impunity.

---

[75] See also Lam and Linden 2022, p. 165.

[76] See also Lopik and Stax 2020, pp. 117–126, 120.

[77] In light of the focus of this article and it being part of a collected volume on ecocide, we will not discuss the national criminal offences any further here.

[78] Netherlands Supreme Court, 03 July 2018, ECLI:NL:HR:2018:1051, with commentary by R. Silver, paras 2.5 and 2.7.

6.4.1 Expediency

Aside from the strength and feasibility of a potential case based on the available evidence, the expediency principle (*opportuniteitsbeginsel*) always plays a role in Dutch prosecutorial decisions.[79] This means that the prosecution service can refuse investigation or prosecution if this were not to be desirable, the latter being assessed on the basis of what is in the public interest. When making that assessment, the scarce investigative capacity of qualified investigators and the available resources will play a role as well.[80] These considerations would certainly also apply to cases involving ecocide. Such cases will often feature a cross-border dimension, for example when a Dutch corporation intentionally commits a chemical spillage whose effects are also measured abroad. Or when one of the subsidiaries of a Dutch multinational commits an environmental crime in the country of its operation. This raises questions as to what extent it is appropriate for the Dutch Public Prosecutor to devote its limited resources to a potentially lengthy and complex investigation that could—in theory—also be conducted by the authorities in the country where the incident occurred.

That said, in the context of ecocide as an international crime the expediency rule does not fully apply. The principle of complementarity, as enshrined in Articles 1 and 17 of the ICC Statute, means that the ICC can only exercise jurisdiction if state parties are unwilling or unable to prosecute a case at national level. Hence, the starting point of the ICC Statute is that states, such as the Netherlands, will take the lead in the investigation and prosecution of crimes under the ICC Statute.[81] To the extent that damage to the environment will become a more significant part of the ICC's investigation and prosecution of international crimes, this can have an effect on Dutch prosecutorial policy as well, with no or a reduced role for the expediency principle. The Dutch prosecutors will generally follow the ICC's lead in its prosecutorial policies, meaning that once there is more consensus about the legal possibilities and grounds to prosecute crimes as (part of) ecocide, the Dutch prosecutor will have a clearer instruction to align their prosecutorial decisions with the ICC framework and policy.[82]

As far as we are aware, there has not yet been a case in which environmental harm was reported as a crime against humanity in the Netherlands. However, an example of the past which involved serious environmental harm is the criminal complaint

---

[79] Pieterman 1985; Brouwer 2010 pp. 207–216.

[80] See, *inter alia*,'s-Hertogenbosch Court of Appeal, 22 February 2000, ECLI:NL:GHSHE:2000:AD3143.'s-Hertogenbosch Court of Appeal, 25 September 2002, ECLI:NL:GHSHE:2002:AE8415.

[81] For the view that the principle of complementarity entails a duty to prosecute the ICC's core crimes, see Kleffner 2003, pp. 86–113.

[82] Until 2012 a prosecutorial directive applied for handling criminal complaints for international crime Directive: *Aanwijzing afdoening van aangiften op basis van de wet internationale misdrijven* [Instruction on disposal of declarations under the International Crimes Act]. However, this directive was revoked on 1 January 2012 and has not been replaced since then.

and following appeal procedure in the case against Trafigura/Probo Koala.[83] The case revolved around the question of whether the Dutch company Trafigura B.V. (among others) should be prosecuted for the intentional spillage of chemical waste in Côte d'Ivoire, which caused large scale environmental pollution (Article 173a Penal Code). In the criminal complaint that started the case it was argued that the spillage also constituted the crimes of manslaughter, aggravated assault, culpable homicide and infliction of grievous bodily harm.[84]

In the appeals procedure[85] that followed the prosecutor's decision to dismiss the case, the Court of Appeal ruled that the plaintiffs did not have standing to the extent that the complaint related to the crimes of manslaughter and grievous bodily harm.[86] However, the Court of Appeal—in an *obiter dictum*—did look at the merits of the case when it considered the non-prosecution of environmental offences, and came to a conclusion of dismissal as well.[87] The Court of Appeal explicitly assessed the feasibility of a criminal investigation into the facts that was to be conducted outside the Netherlands. The Court of Appeal concluded that the feasibility of such a prosecution was 'doubtful'. It was noted that the authorities in Côte d'Ivoire had not responded to requests for mutual legal assistance submitted by the Netherlands. The Court of Appeal therefore anticipated that future requests for mutual legal assistance, which were necessary to complete the investigations and to question possible witnesses, would also remain unanswered. In view of these circumstances, the Court of Appeal found that the Public Prosecution Service was right in refusing to prosecute Trafigura for the events in Côte d'Ivoire.

The considerations of the Court of Appeal regarding the possibility of international cooperation are not convincing. After all, cross-border investigations are often a considerable challenge. In this respect, the MH17 trial is a good example. There were a number of fruitless requests for mutual legal assistance to Russia and many witnesses and evidence were located in an area to which the Dutch investigative authorities had little or no access. Nevertheless, this has not prevented the Prosecutor from completing the criminal investigation against at least some suspects and bringing the case to court, eventually resulting in three life sentences and one

---

[83] The Hague Court of Appeal, 12 April 2011, ECLI:NL:GHSGR:2011:BQ1012, with commentary by Van Ham.

[84] Trafigura had already been prosecuted for offences relating to the same complex of offences (in short, the illegal export of toxic substances from the Netherlands with the ship Probo Koala and subsequent dumping in Côte d'Ivoire), but each of these cases related to offences allegedly committed in the Netherlands. The Public Prosecutor had therefore not prosecuted Trafigura Beheer B.V. and others for offences allegedly committed in Côte d'Ivoire.

[85] Pursuant to Article 12 Wetboek van Strafvordering [Dutch Code of Criminal Procedure].

[86] See above n 84. The complainant was Greenpeace, a non-governmental organisation whose objective, according to its articles of association, is the promotion of nature conservation. The Court found that reporting about manslaughter, aggravated assault, culpable homicide, grievous bodily harm or a misdemeanour in office or profession fell outside the purpose of the articles of association. In view of the limited focus of this chapter, this admissibility aspect will not be discussed further.

[87] Ibid.

acquittal.[88] The question is thus whether an equally substantive (investigative) effort can be expected in case of serious environmental harm, even if the victims do not have the Dutch nationality and the harm occurs outside the Netherlands.

A re-evaluation of serious environmental harm within the prosecution policy of the Public Prosecution Service seems thus necessary, even if the harm occurs outside the Netherlands. After all, environmental harm is not bound by national borders and a serious chemical spillage elsewhere will implicate the global environment and therefore also the Netherlands. Moreover, serious environmental harm will lead to loss of habitat, causing great human suffering in the short and longer term. As far as we are concerned, a review of the prosecution policy for cross-border serious environmental harm is particularly appropriate for situations of serious environmental harm that could be classified as crimes against humanity or that come close to such crimes because of the extent and serious suffering of the victims. We are optimistic that in this day and age the Dutch Prosecution Service will share that view.

In this regard it is worth mentioning that recent developments in civil litigation show that the legal landscape for the responsibility for environmental harm and climate change is rapidly changing. In a ground-breaking civil case, the Supreme Court of the Netherlands has confirmed that the Dutch State is under a legal obligation to reduce the CO_2-emissions of the Netherlands by the end of 2020 with at least 25% compared to 1990.[89] Equally progressive is a judgment of The Hague District Court which ordered Royal Dutch Shell (RDS) to reduce the CO_2-emissions of the Shell group by net 45% in 2030, compared to 2019 levels, through the Shell group's corporate policy.[90] Finally, in 2021 the Court of Appeal in The Hague ruled that the parent company RDS was liable for oil spillages in Nigeria that were caused under responsibility of its Nigerian subsidiary.[91] The Court of Appeal held that the parent company had violated its duty of care for its Nigerian subsidiary (foreign direct liability claim), which had caused severe environmental damage to the plaintiffs. We believe that in comparison with such judgements, criminal litigation cannot stay behind and has its share and responsibility in the protection of the environment.

6.5 Conclusion

The central question in this contribution is to what extent current international criminal law, as codified in the ICC Statute, offers starting points for the prosecution of ecocide and how the Netherlands could contribute to the prosecution of ecocide in

[88] The Hague District Court, 17 November 2022, ECLI:NL:RBDHA:2022:14039 (Kharchenko), ECLI:NL:RBDHA:2022:14036 (Dubinsky), ECLI:NL:RBDHA:2022:14037 (Girkin), ECLI:NL:RBDHA:2022:14040 (Pulatov).

[89] Netherlands Supreme Court, 20 December 2019, ECLI:NL:HR:2019:2007.

[90] The Hague District Court, 26 May 2021, ECLI:NL:RBDHA:2021:5337.

[91] The Hague Court of Appeal, 29 January 2021, ECLI:NL:GHDHA:2021:132, ECLI:NL:GHDHA:2021:133, ECLI:NL:GHDHA:2021:134.

its national practice. This question is not easy to answer because, first of all, ecocide is not yet universally accepted or recognised as an existing crime; the laudable and welcome effort of the proposed ecocide definition in 2021 by the Panel is unlikely to be included as a new crime within the Rome Statute in the near future. We have therefore opted to explore the options under international criminal law as it is today. If we consider ecocide to be the infliction of serious harm to the environment, we have to acknowledge that the core crimes within the ICC Statute only refer to environmental harm (or in that provision: environmental damage) as an element of crime in one specific war crime. However, in practice this provision does not—yet—contribute effectively to the (international) criminal protection of the environment.

Looking at the other core crimes, specifically the category of crimes against humanity offers possibilities for the prosecution of environmental harm. Serious environmental harm could be prosecuted as "other inhumane acts", a residual category within crimes against humanity that leaves room for further development. In addition, environmental harm could be taken into account when determining the existence of a widespread or systematic attack on a civilian population, the threshold requirement for crimes against humanity. Finally, the ICC prosecution policy could pay special attention to the prosecution of crimes against humanity, such as deportation or persecution against any identifiable group, where environmental harm is the means of commission or a serious (collateral) consequence thereof; in that case it should be considered as an important aggravating factor in sentencing.

The latter option is now in the spotlight. Indeed, in 2016, the then ICC Prosecutor Fatou Bensouda indicated that she would like to pay more attention to environmental harm in the context of existing crimes within the ICC Statute. This is a welcome development that fits with the need for increasing attention towards environmental protection. In our opinion, however, the ICC Prosecutor was still slightly cautious in her ambitions, given that ecocide could also be included as "other inhumane acts" within crimes against humanity. Moreover, the Prosecutor's ambitions have not yet been converted into practice, namely a concrete and ongoing case at the ICC.

We hope that the Netherlands will be inspired by the (admittedly limited) ambitions of the ICC Prosecutor and will pay more attention to the prosecution of serious environmental offences. Of course, various national penal provisions already offer possibilities for the prosecution of environmental harm under Dutch law. However, these focus mainly on harm occurring in the Netherlands. But what about serious environmental harm committed outside Dutch territory, for example by a Dutch multinational?

Previous case law, such as the Trafigura-case, shows that the Public Prosecution Service and the Dutch courts have been rather hesitant and—with reference to expected problems in interstate cooperation—decided to dismiss such investigations and prosecutions. We believe that this should be avoided in the future. Taking into account the principle of complementarity and the position of the Netherlands as host country of the ICC, the importance of prosecuting environmental harm as an international crime—or in connection with an international crime—in the Netherlands is crucial. Even if serious environmental harm were not to qualify as a crime against humanity, for example because it is not part of an attack on the civilian population as a state policy, it may well be quite close to it in terms of seriousness. In such a scenario, active investigation and prosecution is imperative, even if it entails complex cross-border investigations. Hopefully, the Dutch Prosecution Service will be inspired by progressive judgements on civil liability for environmental damage.

References

Articles, Books and Other Documents

Alley P et al. (2021) Open Letter: Supporting the Cambodian Land Grabbing Case. https://www.fidh.org/IMG/pdf/cambodia_open_letter_to_icc_pros_16_march_2021.pdf. Accessed 16 May 2025

Bowcott O, Vidal J (2016) ICC widens remit to include environmental destruction cases. https://www.theguardian.com/global/2016/sep/15/hague-court-widens-remit-to-include-environmental-destruction-cases. Accessed 16 May 2025

Brouwer HN (2010) Met inachtneming van het opportuniteitsbeginsel: de politiek en de vrije beleidsruimte van het Openbaar Ministerie. Strafblad

Ceretta LP et al. (2023) Climate change and mental health of Indigenous peoples living in their territory: a concept mapping study. Frontiers in Psychiatry. https://doi.org/10.3389/fpsyt.2023.1237740

Dubler R (2008) What's in a name? A Theory of Crimes Against Humanity. Australian International Law Journal 15:85–107

Durney J (2018) Crafting a Standard: Environmental Crimes as Crimes Against Humanity Under the International Criminal Court. Hastings Environmental Law Journal 24(2):413–430

Gillett M (2023) The Kakhovka Dam and Ecocide. https://verfassungsblog.de/the-kakhovka-dam-and-ecocide/. Accessed 16 May 2025

Greene A (2019) The Campaign to Make Ecocide an International Crime: Quixotic Quest or Moral Imperative? Fordham Environmental Law Review 30(3):1–48

ICRC (2023) Understandings of ENMOD - Article 1. https://ihl-databases.icrc.org/en/ihl-treaties/enmod-1976/understandings. Accessed 14 November 2023

International Law Commission (1991) Draft Code of Crimes against the Peace and Security of Mankind: Titles and texts of articles adopted by the Drafting Committee, UN Doc. A/CN.4/L.459/Add.1

International Law Commission (2019) Draft Convention on the Prevention and Punishment of Crimes Against Humanity, UN Doc. A/CN.4/L.935

Jägers N (2017) Vernietiging van het milieu: een internationaal misdrijf? [Destruction of the environment: an international crime?]. ArsAequi 66(5):365–372

Jyrkkiö T (2011) 'Other inhumane acts' as crimes against humanity. Helsinki Law Review 1:183–207

Karnavas M (2021) Ecocide: Environmental Crime of Crimes or Ill-Conceived Concept? http://opiniojuris.org/2021/07/29/ecocide-environmental-crime-of-crimes-or-ill-conceived-concept/. Accessed 21 November 2023

Keisler S (2022) Environmental Warfare in Ukraine: Should We Prosecute Eco-Crimes Like War Crimes? https://georgetownsecuritystudiesreview.org/2022/05/16/environmental-warfare-in-ukraine-should-we-prosecute-eco-crimes-like-war-crimes/. Accessed 16 May 2025

Kleffner JK (2003) The Impact of Complementarity on National Implementation of Substantive International Criminal Law. Journal of International Criminal Justice 1(1):86–113

Lam V, Linden M (2022) Wat is nodig voor een duurzaam milieu(straf)recht? Vereniging van Milieurecht 2022-2:165–174

Lopik SJ, Stax SH (2020) Klimaatverandering en strafrecht: een verkenning. Boom Strafblad. https://doi.org/10.5553/Bsb/266669012020001003002

Minkova LG (2023) The Fifth International Crime: Reflections on the Definition of "Ecocide". Journal of Genocide Research 25(1):62–83

Office of the Prosecutor of International Criminal Court (2016) Policy Paper on Case Selection and Prioritisation. https://www.icc-cpi.int/sites/default/files/itemsDocuments/20160915_OTP-Policy_Case-Selection_Eng.pdf. Accessed 16 May 2025

Openbaar Ministerie [Netherlands Public Prosecution Service] (2023) Team Internationale Misdrijven. https://www.om.nl/onderwerpen/internationale-misdrijven/team-internationale-misdrijven. Accessed 16 May 2025

Pieterman R (1985) Opportuniteit; een uniek kenmerk van de strafvervolging in Nederland. Sociologisch Tijdschrift 12(2):339–367

Rauxloh R (2011) The role of international criminal law in environmental protection. Natural Resource Investment and Africa's Development 13:423–461

Rijksoverheid [Central Government of the Netherlands] (2020) Kamerbrief over aansprakelijkstelling Syrië voor grove mensenrechtenschendingen. https://www.rijksoverheid.nl/documenten/kamerstukken/2020/09/18/kamerbrief-over-aansprakelijkstelling-syrie-voor-grove-mensenrechtenschendingen. Accessed 16 May 2025

Sluiter G (2011) "Chapeau Elements" of Crimes against Humanity in the Jurisprudence of the UN Ad Hoc Tribunals. In: Sadat LN (ed) Forging a Convention for Crimes Against Humanity. Cambridge University Press, Cambridge, pp 102–141

Sluiter G, Van Straaten B (2020) Ecocide als internationaal misdrijf? Perspectieven op vervolging en berechting in Nederland. Strafblad 2020, nr. 3, pp. 127–135

Stop Ecocide Foundation (2021) Independent Expert Panel for the Legal Definition of Ecocide: Commentary and Core Text. https://www.stopecocide.earth/legal-definition. Accessed 9 July 2025

The Guardian (2016) ICC widens remit to include environmental destruction cases. https://www.theguardian.com/global/2016/sep/15/hague-court-widens-remit-to-include-environmental-destruction-cases. Accessed 15 May 2025

Tweede Kamer der Staten-Generaal [Netherlands House of Representatives] (2020a) Kamerstukken [Parliamentary Papers] II 2020–2021, 35690, Aanhangsel van de Handelingen 6 oktober 2021, Antwoord op vragen van de leden Van Raan en Teunissen over de publicatie van de juridische definitie van ecocide door een internationaal panel van experts [Appendix to the Bulletin Oct. 6, 2021, Answer to Questions by Members Van Raan and Teunissen on the publication of the legal definition of ecocide by an international panel of experts]. https://www.tweedekamer.nl/kamerstukken/kamervragen/detail?id=2021Z11849&did=2021D37175. Accessed 9 July 2025

Tweede Kamer der Staten-Generaal [Netherlands House of Representatives] (2020b) Kamerstukken [Parliamentary Papers] II 2020–2021, 35690, Nr. 2: Initiatiefnota van het lid Van Raan: «Ecocide: de ontbrekende misdaad tegen de vrede» [Initiative note by Member Van Raan: «Ecocide: the missing crime against peace»]. https://www.tweedekamer.nl/kamerstukken/detail?did=2020D53898&id=2020Z25653. Accessed 9 July 2025

Tweede Kamer der Staten-Generaal [Netherlands House of Representatives] (2020c) Kamerstukken [Parliamentary Papers] II 2020–2021, 35690, Nr. 3: Brief van de Ministers van Buitenlandse Zaken en voor Buitenlandse Handel en Ontwikkelingssamenwerking [Letter from the Ministers of Foreign Affairs and for Foreign Trade and Development Cooperation]. https://zoek.officielebekendmakingen.nl/kst-35690-3.html. Accessed 13 July 2025

UN Security Council (1993) Statute of the International Criminal Tribunal for the Former Yugoslavia (as amended on 17 May 2002), UN Doc. S/RES/827

Voigt C (2021) «Ecocide» as an international crime: Personal reflections on options and choices. https://www.ejiltalk.org/ecocide-as-an-international-crime-personal-reflections-on-options-and-choices/. Accessed 14 November 2023

Cases

ECCC, *Nuon Chea and Khieu Samphan,* Trial Judgement, 16 November 2018, Case No. 002/2
ECtHR, *Ukraine and the Netherlands v. Russia*, Grand Chamber Hearing, 26 January 2022, Application No. 8019/16, 43800/14 and 28525/20)
ICC, *The Prosecutor v Jean-Pierre Bemba Gombo*, Decision Pursuant to Article 61(7)(a) and (b) of the Statute, 15 June 2009, Case No. ICC-01/05-01/08-424
ICC, *The Prosecutor v. Bosco Ntaganda*, Trial Judgment, 8 July 2019, Case No. ICC-01/04-02/06
ICC, *The Prosecutor v. Dominic Ongwen*, Judgment on the Appeal, 15 December 2022, Case No. ICC-02/04-01/15-2023
ICC, *The Prosecutor v. Dominic Ongwen*, Trial Judgment, 4 February 2021, Case No. ICC-02/04-01/15
ICC, *The Prosecutor v. Germain Katanga*, Judgment pursuant to article 74 of the Statute, 7 March 2014, Case No. ICC-01/04-01/07
ICC, *The Prosecutor v. Omar Hassan Ahmad Al Bashir*, Second Decision on the Prosecution's Application for a Warrant of Arrest, 12 July 2010, Case No. ICC-02/05-01/09-94
ICC, *The Prosecutor v. Uhuru Muigai Kenyatta*, Decision on the Confirmation of Charges, 23 January 2012, Case No. ICC-01/09-02/11
ICTR, *Niyitegeka Trial Judgement*, 16 May 2003, Case No. ICTR-96-14
ICTY, *Kupreškić Trial Judgement*, 14 January 2000, Case No. IT-95-16-T
ICTY, *Vasiljević Trial Judgement*, 29 November 2002, Case No. IT-98-32-T
Netherlands Supreme Court 30 June 2009, LJN: BG4822, Strafkamer Nr. 07/10742
Netherlands Supreme Court, 03 July 2018, ECLI:NL:HR:2018:1051
Netherlands Supreme Court, 20 December 2019, ECLI:NL:HR:2019:2007
SCSL, AFRC Appeals Judgement, 22 February 2008 (Case No. SCSL-2004-16-A)
'S-Hertogenbosch Court of Appeal, 21 April 2017, ECLI:NL:GHSHE:2017:1760
'S-Hertogenbosch Court of Appeal, 22 February 2000, ECLI:NL:GHSHE:2000:AD3143
'S-Hertogenbosch Court of Appeal, 25 September 2002, ECLI:NL:GHSHE:2002:AE8415
The Hague Court of Appeal, 12 April 2011, ECLI:NL:GHSGR:2011:BQ1012
The Hague Court of Appeal, 29 January 2021 (ECLI:NL:GHDHA:2021:132), (ECLI:NL:GHDHA:2021:133), (ECLI:NL:GHDHA:2021:134).
The Hague Court of Appeal, 9 May 2007, ECLI:NL:GHSGR:2007:BA4676
The Hague District Court, 14 April 2022, ECLI:NL:RBDHA:2022:3410
The Hague District Court, 15 December 2017, ECLI:NL:RBDHA:2017:14782
The Hague District Court, 17 November 2022 (ECLI:NL:RBDHA:2022:14039, Kharchenko), (ECLI:NL:RBDHA:2022:14036, Dubinsky), (ECLI:NL:RBDHA:2022:14037, Girkin), (ECLI:NL:RBDHA:2022:14040, Pulatov).
The Hague District Court, 23 July 2019, ECLI:NL:RBDHA:2019:7430
The Hague District Court, 26 May 2021, ECLI:NL:RBDHA:2021:5337

Treaties and other Legal Documents

Convention on the Prohibition of Military or Any Other Hostile Use of Environmental Modification Techniques, opened for signature 10 December 1976, 1108 UNTS 151, entered into force 5 October 1978
International Covenant on Civil and Political Rights, opened for signature 16 December 1966, 999 UNTS 171, entered into force 23 March 1976
International Criminal Court, Elements of Crimes, reproduced in the Official Records of the Assembly of the States Parties to the Rome Statute of the International Criminal Court, First Session, New York, 3–10 September 2002, ICC-ASP/1/3 and Corr.1, part II.B

International Criminal Court, Rules of Procedure and Evidence, reproduced in the Official Records of the Assembly of States Parties to the Rome Statute of the International Criminal Court, First Session, New York, 3–10 September 2002, ICC-ASP/1/3 and Corr.1, part. II.A

Protocol Additional to the Geneva Conventions of 12 August 1949, and relating to the Protection of Victims of International Armed Conflicts, opened for signature 8 June 1977, 1125 UNTS 3, entered into force 7 December 1978

Rome Statute of the International Criminal Court, opened for signature 17 July 1998, 2187 UNTS 3, entered into force 1 July 2002

Prof. Göran Sluiter is Professor of International Criminal Law at the University of Amsterdam and Professor of Criminal Law and Procedure at the Open University in the Netherlands. He studied law at the University of Maastricht (1996) and obtained his PhD in international criminal law at Utrecht University (2002). Apart from practising before various international courts and tribunals, including the ECCC and the ICC, Göran worked as Partner at Prakken D'Oliveira Human Rights Lawyers until 1 January 2024. Göran is the principal investigator in the VICI-funded research project 'Rethinking the Outer Limits of Secondary Liability for International Crimes and Serious Human Rights Violations' which runs from September 2018 until September 2025. Between 2006 and 2011, he was the principal investigator in the VIDI-funded research project 'International criminal procedure - In search of General Rules and Principles'.

Barbara van Straaten is a criminal lawyer and partner at Prakken D'Oliveira Human Rights Lawyers. Barbara focuses on business and human rights cases, as well as international criminal law, extradition and surrender cases. Among other things, she helps (legal) persons in reporting crimes, assists victims of serious violent and moral crimes and regularly lectures students on criminal law. Barbara obtained an LL.M in International Criminal Law and Criminal Law at the University of Amsterdam, while completing part of her studies at Cambridge University and Columbia University. During her studies, she gained experience at the ICTY, the UN Human Rights Council and the European Commission. Prior to this, Barbara worked as a lawyer at a large commercial law firm where she gained experience in assisting and advising companies.

Ava Schuster holds an LL.M. in International and Transnational Criminal Law from the University of Amsterdam and an LL.B. in International and European Law from the University of Groningen. Parallel to her studies, Ava worked as a Research Assistant at the UCLA Promise Institute Europe and at the VICI research project 'Rethinking the Outer Limits of Secondary Liability for International Crimes and Serious Human Rights Violations'. Currently, Ava works as a Legal Trainee at the European Center for Constitutional and Human Rights.

Chapter 7
Lawfare Against Ecocide: How Ukraine Prosecutes Environmental Crimes Committed During Armed Conflict

Borys Babin and Oleksii Plotnikov

Contents

Abstract Nature is a silent victim of the armed conflict between the Russian Federation and Ukraine, which began in 2014 as a proxy war, led to the occupation of parts of Ukrainian territory and in 2022 escalated into a full-scale war unseen in Europe since 1945, with attacks in the vicinity of nuclear objects, natural reserves becoming battlegrounds, air, land, and water becoming contaminated with debris and chemical substances, and with animal species being decimated. At the same time, Ukraine is one of the few nations in the world to have criminalised ecocide as a crime distinct from other crimes against nature. This chapter will address the investigations of ecocide in the context of the armed conflict in Ukraine. It will open with an overview of the environmental damage caused by the conflict resulting from the Russian aggression against Ukraine and will proceed with the description and analysis of the Ukrainian legislation on ecocide. It will then address the investigations of ecocide run by Ukraine and explain the challenges encountered by the Ukrainian authorities in the investigation of environmental damage resulting from

B. Babin (✉)
Association of Reintegration of Crimea, Kyiv, Ukraine
e-mail: babinb@ukr.net

O. Plotnikov
The Tenth of April, Odesa, Ukraine

L. Burgers et al. (eds.), *Ecocide: Criminalising Serious Harm against the Environment*, International Criminal Justice Series 38, https://doi.org/10.1007/978-94-6265-715-1_7

armed conflict. Finally, the chapter will attempt to demonstrate how this experience may be beneficial for the international efforts to criminalise ecocide.

Keywords Ecocide · Environmental crimes · War crimes · Russo-Ukrainian armed conflict · Rome Statute · Environmental protection

7.1 Introduction: Combating Warfare with Lawfare

Richard Rogers, a deputy co-chair of the Independent Expert Panel for the Legal Definition of Ecocide, described Ukraine as a champion in the establishment of the crime of ecocide, noting the historical importance of Ukraine for the definition of crimes against humanity and the crime of genocide.[1] Just as eight decades ago, the reasons for Ukraine's championing are more than sinister. Also now, Ukraine is the battleground of a full-scale armed conflict, entailing countless and unimaginable crimes.

Since 24 of February 2022, the Russian invasion of Ukraine has been on the frontlines of the media worldwide. However, this armed conflict began much earlier, in February 2014, when the Russian Federation occupied the Ukrainian Autonomous Republic of Crimea following the victory of the Maidan protests in Kyiv. Frequently (and incorrectly)[2] perceived as bloodless, this occupation was only the first step in a proxy conflict involving Russian attempts to undermine Ukrainian sovereignty and force the country into subjugation using military and non-military means. It was followed by an invasion of the Donetsk and Luhansk Oblasts (regions) of Ukraine by armed bands and mercenaries supported by Russian regular armed forces, resulting in eight years of conflict of varying intensity. Despite being characterised as frozen by some commentators,[3] the conflict never was. Both its Crimean and East Ukrainian elements have been described as an international armed conflict and occupation by one state of a territory of another state by international bodies, including the Office of the United Nations High Commissioner for Human Rights (OHCHR),[4] the EU,[5] and the Prosecutor of the International Criminal Court (ICC).[6] The year 2022 was the year when the hostilities escalated into a full-scale invasion.

Ukraine stands on the defensive on the battlefield, limiting its ambitions to regaining control over the occupied territories. On the legal field, however, Russia

[1] Rogers did so at the conference 'United for Justice', held in Lviv, Ukraine on 13 March 2023. Stop Ecocide International 2023.

[2] At least two Ukrainian servicemen have been killed and several wounded in the process of establishing Russian control over the Crimean Peninsula, while civilians suffered a campaign of intimidation, including murders, torture, enforced disappearances and other human rights abuses. For details see Zayets et al. 2016.

[3] For example, Bebler 2015.

[4] Office of the High Commissioner for Human Rights (OHCHR) 2017.

[5] European Union 2016.

[6] ICC Office of the Prosecutor 2016.

seeks to legitimise and defend its actions[7] whereas Ukraine actively attacks the aggressor,[8] relying on 'lawfare'[9] as opposed to warfare waged by Russia. Ukraine's objective is to make the aggressor 'pay the price', while Russia on several occasions (and not without some success) relied on legal mechanisms to assert its control over the occupied territories and minimise the losses.[10]

One of the elements of the Ukrainian lawfare was the submission of declarations on the acceptance of the ad hoc jurisdiction of the ICC in relation to the 'Maidan crimes' and crimes committed in Crimea and Eastern Ukraine starting 20 February 2014, and onwards.[11] In December 2020, the ICC Prosecutor concluded the preliminary examination, finding that "there is a reasonable basis at this time to believe that a broad range of conduct constituting war crimes and crimes against humanity within the jurisdiction of the Court have been committed in the context of the situation in Ukraine".[12] On 2 March 2022, the ICC Prosecutor announced the opening of another investigation "into the Situation in Ukraine from 21 November 2013 onwards, thereby encompassing within its scope any past and present allegations of war crimes, crimes against humanity or genocide committed on any part of the territory of Ukraine by any person".[13]

[7] In general, since 2014 Russia has relied on the doctrine of remedial secession to justify its occupation of Crimea, Donetsk and Luhansk Oblasts. For the Russian perspective, see Kapustin 2015. Tolstykh 2015. For an independent analysis, see Lundstedt 2018; Radpey 2022. It further justified its right to invade Ukraine by alleging that the Ukrainian government committed genocide against the Russian-speaking population. On 27 February 2022 Ukraine instituted proceedings in the ICJ asking the Court to find that no genocide is taking place and that the Russian Federation may not invoke the Genocide Convention to justify its invasion. *See* International Court of Justice (ICJ) 2022. See also Schabas 2022. In order to legitimise occupation under Russian internal law, the occupiers held a sham referendum in Crimea immediately denounced by the UN General Assembly (UNGA) 2014 and a Kafkaesque-style referenda in the Donetsk, Luhansk, Kherson, and Zaporizhzhia Oblasts. Remarkably, the latter was held when Russia controlled about two thirds of the Oblast's territory, not including the city of Zaporizhzhia itself, which is home to approximately half of the region's population. The General Assembly condemned these "referenda" by 143 votes with 5 votes against and 35 abstentions. See UNGA 2022a.

[8] Russia was labelled aggressor by the UN General Assembly resolution at the request of the Security Council under the "Uniting for Peace" procedure. See UNGA 2022b.

[9] For an extensive description of different aspects of lawfare between Ukraine and Russia, see, for example, Goldenziel 2022.

[10] As exemplified by the ICJ judgement in the Application of the International Convention for the Suppression of the Financing of Terrorism and of the International Convention on the Elimination of All Forms of Racial Discrimination (Ukraine v. Russian Federation), where Russia managed to rebut virtually all Ukraine's claims. See ICJ, *Application of the International Convention for the Suppression of the Financing of Terrorism and of the International Convention on the Elimination of All Forms of Racial Discrimination* (Ukraine v. Russian Federation), Judgment of 31 January 2024, ICJ Rep 2024.

[11] See Marchuk 2016. For more information about the conflict in Ukraine, including the Maidan events, see T.M.C. Asser Instituut, MATRA Ukraine, 'Conflict in Ukraine'. https://www.asser.nl/matra-ukraine/ukraine-international-crimes/conflict-in-ukraine. Accessed 23 May 2023.

[12] ICC 2022a.

[13] ICC 2022b.

In parallel, both Ukraine and Russia run domestic criminal investigations into acts allegedly committed by the agents of the opposing party. According to the Ukrainian Office of the Prosecutor General (OPG), as of 6 June 2024, 133,484 alleged Russian war crimes were under investigation.[14] As of 13 March 2023, 104 investigations concerned environmental damage caused during the conflict, and eleven of them were classified under Article 441 of the Criminal Code of Ukraine (CCU)—ecocide.[15]

This chapter will examine the investigation of ecocide in the context of the conflict in Ukraine. It will first provide an overview of environmental damage caused by conflict in Ukraine, followed by a description and analysis of Ukrainian legislation on ecocide and information on ecocide investigations. The chapter will further examine the challenges encountered by Ukrainian authorities in the investigation of environmental damage resulting from armed conflict and will attempt to demonstrate how this experience may be beneficial to international efforts to criminalise ecocide.

7.2 Environmental Damage Caused by the Russo-Ukrainian Armed Conflict

On 25 January 2023, the Parliamentary Assembly of the Council of Europe passed a resolution on the environmental impact of armed conflicts, which opened with a statement of an obvious fact: "environmental damage resulting from armed conflicts can be multifaceted, severe, long-lasting and mostly irreversible".[16] Lawrence et al. observe quite pessimistically that "while a large body of knowledge of the consequences of war on the ecological dynamics of a variety of biological systems is known, a comprehensive assessment of these impacts has yet to be conducted".[17] They conclude that "there seems to be little evidence that military strategists consider environmental consequences of military activities when planning or executing military actions related to conflict".[18]

The Russo-Ukrainian armed conflict started as a proxy war and continues as a full-scale war between two armies employing all the contemporary arsenal except nuclear weapons. Various (international) reports have established that the Russian Federation has neglected and is still neglecting the limitations established by international law in the planning and execution of military operations, leading to "staggering" human rights violations and "unspeakable atrocities".[19]

---

[14] Office of the Prosecutor General of Ukraine, 'Crimes Committed During the Full-Scale Invasion of the RF'. https://www.gp.gov.ua/en. Accessed 25 May 2024.

[15] Interfax-Ukraine 2023.

[16] Parliamentary Assembly of Council of Europe (PACE) 2023.

[17] Lawrence et al. 2015, p. 3.

[18] Ibid.

[19] Terms used by the Council of Europe Commissioner for Human Rights, Dunja Mijatović after a country visit in May 2022. Council of Europe 2022.

Nature is one of the victims of this conflict, and there exists overwhelming evidence that Russian commanders not only fail to consider the environmental consequences of military actions, but in fact exploit adverse environmental impacts to gain a military advantage.

Arguably, the most obvious manifestation of such tactics is the use of nuclear objects for military purposes. On the first day of the invasion, Russian units marched directly into the Chornobyl[20] exclusion zone in a futile attempt to reach Kyiv from the north. The lack of protective equipment and the unexplainably reckless conduct of the Russian soldiers indicate that the nature of the radioactively contaminated area has not been taken into account during the planning and execution of military manoeuvres.[21] Nuclear objects like the Zaporizhzhia Nuclear Power Plant were turned into military bases and potential battlegrounds,[22] while others, like the RADON radioactive waste management facility in the city of Kharkiv, are situated in areas that regularly come under missile attacks and heavy shelling.[23]

The absence of serious nuclear accidents is nothing short of a miracle, but sadly, chemical pollution has occurred. There were several conflict-related chemical accidents during the 'frozen' stage of the conflict,[24] but the damage they caused is incomparably less than that caused by full-scale hostilities. Debris from munitions, such as aerial bombs, artillery, phosphorus munitions, unexploded ordnance, mines, ruined buildings, destroyed vehicles, fuel and oil spills, as well as human and animal remains may turn some of Ukraine's territories into a scorched earth, similar to the Zone Rouge,[25] some parts of which are still uninhabitable a century after the war.[26]

Since 2014, entire landscapes have deteriorated drastically as a result of hostilities in the Donetsk and Luhansk oblasts and predatory exploitation of industries and natural resources both in the eastern regions[27] and in Crimea.[28] The 2022 invasion affected 20% of nature reserves and three million hectares of forests and put 2.9

[20] The correct Ukrainian pronunciation of the name of this geographical object is "Chornobyl" as opposed to the common Russian pronunciation "Chernobyl" widely used in English texts. This chapter will employ the Ukrainian names of geographical objects located in Ukraine.

[21] Among other things, Russian soldiers established positions in the 'Red Forest'—one of the most radioactively contaminated locations in the world. For a detailed account see Strick 2022; Kamenev 2022.

[22] See, for example, Farmer 2022; Prokip 2022.

[23] IAEA experts assess damage to Kharkiv nuclear research facility. World Nuclear News (WNN) 2022.

[24] One of them will be addressed in more detail below.

[25] A zone in France considered unliveable as a result of fighting during the First World War. See Heiderscheidt 2018.

[26] For a detailed description of conflict-related chemical pollution, see UN Environment Programme (UNEP) 2022. See also Maksymiv 2023.

[27] For details on the deterioration of the environment in the Donetsk and Luhansk Oblasts after 2014 *see* Organization for Security and Co-operation in Europe (OSCE) 2017.

[28] For details on the ecological crisis in Crimea see Babin and Plotnikov 2022.

million hectares of the Emerald Network[29] at risk. Sixteen Ramsar sites[30] encompassing a total of 600,000 hectares came under threat of destruction. Eight natural reserves and nine national parks[31] remain under occupation.[32] There are reports that Russian troops use natural reserves for military purposes,[33] establishing military positions and hunting animals there.[34] According to the Ministry of Environmental Protection and Natural Resources of Ukraine, the conflict has affected 600 animal species and 750 plant and mushroom species.[35]

The environmental effects of the conflict extend far beyond the borders of Ukraine. According to Ukrainian marine biologist Ivan Rusev, at least 50,000 dolphins perished in the Black and Azov Seas due to mines, underwater explosions and sonars of the Russian vessels, and it could take up to 50 years to restore the population to pre-war levels.[36] Ukrainian carbon emissions rose by 23% due to wildfires, combat operations, and the migration of internally displaced persons and refugees.[37] A less obvious aspect is that the destruction of forests and wetlands as well as other conflict-related damage is likely to lead to long-term effects on the global climate,[38] while post-war reconstruction will require significant natural resources, which may result in a notable increase in greenhouse gas emissions.[39]

On 27 April 2023, the European Economic and Social Committee (EESC) adopted an own-initiative opinion concluding that:

> Russia's actions appear to amount to ecocide based on a definition proposed by legal experts and published in June 2021. The EESC has called for "ecocide" as defined by the Independent Panel for the Legal Definition of Ecocide, to be codified as a criminal offence under EU

---

[29] The Emerald Network is an ecological network made up of areas of special conservation interest (ASCIs) located in 18 Contracting Parties and Observer States to the Bern Convention in the neighbouring areas of the European Union. https://emerald.eea.europa.eu. Accessed 24 May 2023.

[30] Sites protected under the Convention on Wetlands of International Importance especially as Waterfowl Habitat. See Convention on Wetlands of International Importance Especially as Waterfowl Habitat, Ramsar, opened for signature 02 February 1971, RN 14583, entered into force 21 December 1975, as amended by the Protocol of 3 December 1982 and the Amendments of 28 May 1987.

[31] According to a Facebook post published by WWF-Ukraine on 6 November 2022, there were 10 national parks under occupation, but the Kamianska Sich National Nature Park was de-occupied several days later.

[32] We are Ukraine, https://www.weareukraine.info/the-war-has-already-affected-20-of-reserves-and-3-million-hectares-of-forest-in-ukraine/. Accessed 24 May 2023.

[33] Belousova 2018.

[34] Belousova 2023a.

[35] International Fund for Animal Warfare (IFAW) 2023.

[36] Gembranska 2023.

[37] Belousova 2022a.

[38] Kicaj et al. note that the increase in greenhouse gas emission combined with the increasing amounts of soot from burning cities and towns, fields, wildfires, and combat activities may have a dramatical impact on the speed of melting of glaciers and hasten the rising of the planet's temperature globally. See Kicaj et al. 2023.

[39] Ibid., p. 3.

> law. The recognition of the crime of ecocide in the revised EU Environmental Crime Directive will lead to developments in legislation beyond EU, in particular in the International Criminal Court, which may aid in bringing a degree of accountability for Russia, reflecting the environmental and ecological harm caused.[40]

Perhaps this statement is necessary as it acknowledges that crimes against the environment committed during a conflict may amount to ecocide, as this crime is now recognised in international doctrine. However, even if the EU and its Member States promptly adopted ecocide laws, these laws would still be unsuitable for the prosecution of perpetrators of crimes that have already been committed due to the principle of non-retroactivity of criminal law. However, both Ukraine and Russia had already recognised ecocide as a crime in their respective criminal codes, and Ukraine has a history of prosecution of alleged ecocide perpetrators in the context of the conflict.

7.3 Ecocide Under Ukrainian Law: A Comparison with the Proposed Amendment to the Rome Statute

Many states have included offences against the environment in their criminal laws, but only very few use the term 'ecocide'. It seems that Russia was the first state to include the crime of ecocide into its criminal legislation in 1996.[41] Some of the post-Soviet states followed that example and added similar or identical definitions to their respective criminal codes.[42] The Ukrainian definition, which remains unchanged since the adoption of the CCU in 2001, is "Mass destruction of flora and fauna, poisoning of air or water resources, and also any other actions that may cause an environmental disaster".[43] This crime is punishable by imprisonment for a term of eight to fifteen years, placing it in the category of 'special grave offences', the gravest category of crimes under Ukrainian law. Interestingly, Section VIII of the CCU is dedicated to offenses against the environment, including violations of environmental safety regulations, contamination of soil, air pollution, water pollution, etc. However, ecocide is part of Section XX 'Criminal offences against peace, security of mankind and international legal order', and the crime of ecocide is followed immediately by an article on the crime of genocide. It appears that the authors of the Ukrainian Criminal Code somehow shared a similar mindset with the Independent Expert Panel,[44] since they clearly had a parallel between ecocide and genocide in mind.

The description of the crime under Article 441 of the CCU contains a list of natural objects: flora, fauna, air, and water resources. However, the *actus reus* of ecocide is based more on the type and intensity of the action. Central to the definition are actions

[40] European Economic and Social Committee (EESC) 2023.

[41] Criminal Code of the Russian Federation, Article 358.

[42] See Ecocide Law in National Jurisdictions. https://ecocidelaw.com/existing-ecocide-laws. Accessed 24 May 2023.

[43] Criminal Code of Ukraine, Article 441.

[44] Stop Ecocide Foundation 2021.

like "*mass destruction* of flora and fauna", "*poisoning* of air or water resources" and "any other *actions*" that "*may cause* an environmental disaster" (our emphasis). In view of the words "and also *any other actions* that may cause" (an environmental disaster), the *actus reus* of his provision focuses on the *potential* of certain actions, including mass destruction of flora and fauna and poisoning of air or water resources, to cause an environmental disaster. Hence, even though certain specific actions must take place, it is not necessary for an environmental disaster to occur for the definition to be met; the mere possibility suffices.

Remarkably, Section VIII of the CCU, titled 'Criminal offences against the environment', contains a much more comprehensive list of protected objects, including land, soil, mineral resources, air, water, sea, continental shelf, flora, plants, animals subject to hunting and fishing, protected territories, and conservation areas, etc. It describes a variety of negative actions, such as contamination, deterioration, pollution, wasteful use, illegal mining, illegal transportation, illegal hunting, and illegal fishing. Furthermore, some sanctions for crimes described in the section mention "death of people or other grave consequences" as aggravating circumstances. Article 242 of the CCU refers to "mass destruction of flora and fauna or any other grave consequences", echoing the language of Article 441. It therefore appears that the potential of an "environmental disaster" is the only element distinguishing ecocide from other crimes against the environment.

The legislation of Ukraine lacks a definition of the term 'environmental disaster'. The Big Ukrainian Encyclopaedia (BUE), edited by the Academy of Sciences of Ukraine, defines environmental disaster as:

> a negative modification of environmental balance to the state of disappearance of conditions of existence of a living organism, population, species of biosphere. It is mostly a quick destructive irreversible event connected to infliction of damage to ecosystems and biological diversity accompanied by the collapse of biota (including humans).[45]

The definition may be considered semi-official since its publication was supported by a Decree of the President of Ukraine.[46] Proceeding from this definition, adverse impacts on nature must reach a certain degree of severity to be considered ecocide. From the point of view of Article 441 of the CCU, that threshold may be reached when the mass destruction is such that it may cause a natural disaster, namely the disappearance of conditions of existence of a living organism, population, species of biosphere. This is similar to the definition offered by the Independent Expert Panel (IEP), which points at a "substantial likelihood". On the other hand, the latter definition contains a seemingly closed list of objects that may be adversely affected, as opposed to the open list contained in the Ukrainian definition.[47] At that, even if

---

[45] Big Ukrainian Encyclopedia, Environmental Disaster (in Ukrainian), vue.gov.ua/Екологічна_катастрофа. Accessed 24 May 2023.

[46] Questions of preparation and publication of the Big Ukrainian Encyclopedia. Decree of the President of Ukraine of 12.01.2015 No 7/2015 (in Ukrainian). https://zakon.rada.gov.ua/laws/show/7/2015?lang=en#Text. Accessed 24 May 2023. Although the publication itself was ordered by a Decree, the text has not been officially approved, and it should in no way be considered a legal act.

[47] Several additional parallels can be drawn between the definitions of the BUE and that of the IEP. The severity criteria can be compared to the "disappearance of conditions of existence", as both

the list of protected objects provided by the IEP is not necessarily exhaustive, it does not explicitly provide for the inclusion of further objects.

Under Ukrainian law, the *mens rea* of ecocide is always characterised as intent. Under Article 24 of the CCU, intent may be direct or indirect. The intent is deemed direct if "a person was conscious of the socially injurious nature of his or her action (act or omission), foresaw its socially injurious consequences, and wished them",[48] whereas indirect intent means that "a person was conscious of the socially injurious nature of his/her action (act or omission), foresaw its socially injurious consequences and anticipated, though did not wish them".[49]

Indirect intent can be roughly compared with the wanton criteria of the IEP definition, taking into account that both acts and omissions under Ukrainian law foresee a certain degree of knowledge, which makes them comparable to the 'with knowledge element' of the IEP definition.

Thus, although the definition of ecocide in Article 441 of the CCU and that proposed by the IEP are not identical, there are some similarities, which makes the Ukrainian experience possibly beneficial for the international efforts to criminalise ecocide.

At this point one could notice that the formula utilised by the Criminal Code of Ukraine lacks an important aspect, namely whether it entails a balancing exercise. If it does, then the notion of ecocide in Ukrainian law is similar to a war crime in international law, which is usually evaluated against the military necessity considerations. If it does not, this makes the notion of ecocide similar to the notion of genocide, where the mere idea of balancing is blasphemous. At first glance, Article 441 of the CCU does not provide for a balancing exercise. However, the same can be said about Article 438 (war crimes), which does not provide for a balancing exercise, but which refers to the norms of international law, including those of the Rome Statute, which do provide for it. If a norm of international law existed, this could give a hint on the need of a balancing exercise in Ukrainian law. However, in the absence of such a norm, as well as in the absence of a relevant judicial practice, one cannot definitely conclude whether the notion of ecocide in Ukrainian law entails a balancing exercise.

7.4 Ukraine's Investigations of Conflict-Related Ecocide

Although Article 441 was present in the CCU since 2001, the evidence of its application prior to 2016 is scarce. Open sources provide information about around a dozen criminal proceedings instituted under Article 441 in relation to the armed conflict since 2016. One can outline three categories of such sources: (1) press-releases

definitions explain that damage must affect entire ecosystems (the 'widespread' criterion from the IEP definition), and both definitions note the irreversibility of the damage in question ('long-term' criterion from the IEP definition).

[48] Criminal Code of Ukraine, Article 24.

[49] Ibid., Article 24(2).

and other official notifications of public bodies, (2) the Unified State Register of Court Decisions,[50] a government-run electronic resource comprising the texts of all judicial decisions rendered by the Ukrainian courts since 2007, and (3) commentaries and interviews with officials, experts, and NGOs involved in ecocide-related investigations. Virtually all of this information is only accessible in Ukrainian.

7.4.1 Crimean Titan and Related Enterprises

Ukraine's first investigation on conflict-related ecocide commenced in 2016 and touched upon the activities of Crimean Titan, the largest titanium dioxide producer in Europe located near the Perekop Isthmus in Crimea. Initially, the case was classified under Article 364 of the CCU (abuse of authority) due to improper documentation of the disposal of hazardous waste on Ukraine-controlled territory immediately adjacent to the plant.[51] In September 2018, a significant chemical emission occurred at the plant, prompting the partial evacuation of the nearby town of Armyansk.[52] In 2019, the extant Ukrainian criminal case was reclassified under Articles 441 (Ecocide) and 241 (Air pollution) of the CCU.

Available procedural decisions reveal that the case now involves two other enterprises registered in Russia: the Crimean Soda Plant and the Brom Plant, which are part of the same industrial cluster as Crimean Titan. The alleged unlawful activities are claimed to be causing grave consequences, including misuse of natural resources "by the occupying authorities for their own needs".[53] In 2019, the case was expanded to include the operations of a pumping station that transports water from Western Syvash, an artificial lake created during the Soviet era to meet the needs of the aforementioned industrial cluster, to the natural bay of Eastern Syvash, thereby altering its ecological system.[54] As of May 2023, no further information on this case is available from open sources.

7.4.2 Nuclear Objects

The first conflict-related ecocide investigation concerning damage to a nuclear object appears to have been opened in connection with the so-called "Klivazh" object, an underground cavern created by an industrial nuclear explosion near the town

[50] Unified State Register of Judicial Decisions, https://reyestr.court.gov.ua. Accessed 25 May 2023.

[51] Procedural decisions in this case are available in Ukrainian from Ukraine's State Register of Judicial Decisions. https://reyestr.court.gov.ua. Accessed 25 May 2022. Criminal proceedings No 42016010000000238, Court cases 752/13071/17, 766/22955/19, and others.

[52] For details see Coynash 2018.

[53] https://reyestr.court.gov.ua/Review/88261641. Accessed 25 May 2022.

[54] For more information on the pumping station see Association of Reintegration of Crimea 2023.

of Yenakieve in 1979. After Russian proxies occupied the town in 2014, the so-called Donetsk People's Republic (DPR) ceased draining water from the mine, thus creating a risk of leakage of radioactive materials into surface waters. On 23 May 2018, the Donetsk Oblast Prosecutor's Office announced that an investigation had been launched under Article 441 (Ecocide). However, no further information was ever published or found in open sources.[55] The outcome of the investigation remains unknown.

On 3 March 2022, an investigation was initiated under Articles 258 (Act of terrorism) and 441 (Ecocide) of the CCU in connection with the occupation of the Chornobyl nuclear power plant, flooding of nuclear waste storages, and disruption of the upper layer of the ground on the radioactively contaminated territories.[56] On 1 June 2022, *Uryadovyi Kurier*, an official gazette of the Cabinet of Ministers of Ukraine, published summons[57] addressed to certain nationals of the Russian Federation, demanding that they appear before the court in a criminal proceeding with the same number.[58] However, the summons includes charges under neither of the abovementioned articles, but under Article 438 of the CCU (War crimes).

On 4 March 2022, an investigation was opened into the attack and seizure of the Zaporizhzhia nuclear power facility,[59] the sixth largest in the world and the largest in Europe, which has been under Russian occupation since that date. The initial charges were also based on Articles 258 and 441 of the CCU. On 18 May 2022, the OPG published information identifying a Russian commander suspected of attacking and seizing the power plant. However, the charges were again based on Article 438 of the CCU rather than Article 441.[60] On 6 August 2022, the OPG classified another shelling of the power plant as a war crime (Article 438).[61]

On 7 March 2022, the OPG opened a third investigation into the damaging of a nuclear facility as ecocide. It concerned a missile strike on the premises of the Kharkiv Institute of Physics and Technology, which administers a research facility that contained 37 nuclear fuel elements at the time of the attack. As of April 2024, the investigation is ongoing.[62]

---

[55] Truth Hounds 2021.

[56] https://reyestr.court.gov.ua/Review/105216859. Accessed 25 May 2022.

[57] In accordance with the procedure established by the Criminal Procedural Code of Ukraine, in case the whereabouts of a person are unknown, that person may be summoned to court via a publication in an official media.

[58] https://ukurier.gov.ua/media/newspaper/adv/2022-05-31/121_7242r.pdf. Accessed 25 May 2022.

[59] Office of the Prosecutor General of Ukraine 2022a.

[60] Office of the Prosecutor General of Ukraine 2022b.

[61] Office of the Prosecutor General of Ukraine 2022c.

[62] Interfax-Ukraine 2024.

7.4.3 Fuel and Oil Storage Facilities

A second group of cases emerged in March 2022 and concerned the consequences of missile strikes against fuel and oil storage facilities. Three such investigations have been reported on the website of the OPG concerning attacks against fuel and oil facilities with subsequent fires resulting in contamination of air and soil.[63] All attacks were classified under Articles 438 and 441 of the CCU. No further information on these investigations is available.

7.4.4 Mass Extermination of Animals

One of the most remarkable ecocide investigations based on Article 441 of the CCU relates to the mass deaths of sea mammals observed during the conflict. Thousands of corpses of dolphins and porpoises have been found on the shores of the Black and Azov Seas, and it is estimated that at least 20% of the sea mammals' population died during the conflict.[64] The possible reasons are underwater explosions and extensive use of sonars by warships, which negatively affect the health and the ability of dolphins and other sea mammals to navigate. According to the information published on the OPG website, biological materials obtained during the autopsy of the discovered mammals were sent for further analysis to the University of Padova and the University of Hannover. Further, the OPG declared its intention to contact its counterparts in Bulgaria, Romania, and Türkiye asking for information about similar instances of mass deaths of sea mammals.[65]

Another notable ecocide investigation was opened on 10 December 2022 in respect to the deaths of around 4 million chickens at a poultry farm de-energised as a result of fighting and occupation. The decomposition of millions of bird corpses resulted in uncontrolled pollution of soil with biological hazards. Here, the object of investigation is not the murrain of the poultry itself but the pollution of the environment as a result of these deaths.[66]

---

[63] Office of the Prosecutor General of Ukraine 2022d, 2022e, 2022f.

[64] Belousova 2022b.

[65] Odesa Region Prosecutor's Office 2022.

[66] Office of the Prosecutor General of Ukraine 2022g.

7.5 Challenging Investigations: How to Bring Ecocide Out of the Dark

Available information on ecocide investigations in Ukraine indicates that at least some of these cases will never reach the court. According to the former Prosecutor General of Ukraine Iryna Venedyktova, as of 21 June 2022, there were 12 cases of ecocide under investigation.[67] On 13 March 2023, the deputy Prosecutor General Viktoria Litvinova mentioned that there had been 11 conflict-related ecocide investigations by that date.[68] Finally, in an interview on 16 June 2023 the advisor to the Prosecutor General of Ukraine Maksym Popov spoke about 14 investigations.[69] These fluctuating numbers are likely to point out the complexities the Ukrainian investigators are confronted with in ecocide cases. There are several possible explanations for this.

The first reason derives from the nature of ecocide, which is not a typical crime against nature but rather the intentional mass destruction of nature (flora, fauna, air, water) that may cause an environmental disaster. As indicated above, it is not a coincidence that both the Ukrainian legislator and the international experts put ecocide in the same category of international crimes, including genocide. Not every attack that impairs the environment can be characterised as ecocide. According to Maksym Popov, there have been over 190 investigations into war crimes that caused harm to the environment, but only 14 into ecocide. Therefore, it is plausible to assume that some incidents initially investigated under Article 441 of the CCU have subsequently been reclassified as other environmental crimes. For example, the attacks against fuel storage facilities may have caused certain environmental damage, however, it appears problematic to demonstrate how exactly such attacks could cause an environmental disaster capable of wiping out entire biotas. The same appears to be true for the case of the poultry farm, which undoubtedly contaminated the ground, but there seems to be little evidence of the potential of an environmental disaster. The fact that in most of the known instances of ecocide investigations, the offence is originally classified under multiple articles is likely to confirm this hypothesis. The initial classification of an act as ecocide may be combined with other environmental crimes like air or water pollution, charges of terrorism or war crimes. As the investigation progresses, the investigators may seek a different classification, which may be easier to prove to the detriment of the more complicated notion of ecocide.

Proceeding with the genocide parallel, and coming back to what was already discussed above, one can wonder whether ecocide should be seen more as a war crime (whose qualification is dependent on a balancing between humanity and military necessity) or as a genocide (whose qualification is not dependent on such balancing).

---

[67] Ukrinform, Ukraine's prosecutor general meets with U.S. counterpart. https://www.ukrinform.net/rubric-polytics/3512163-ukraines-prosecutor-general-meets-with-us-counterpart.html. Accessed 25 May 2022.

[68] Interfax-Ukraine 2023.

[69] Ecocide in Ukraine: What Should We Do Now? https://www.youtube.com/watch?v=LspvZh8O7wI. Accessed 17 June 2023.

In the context of war crimes, considerations of military necessity become relevant. Thus, the passage of Russian troops through the Chornobyl zone was obviously a result of military necessity because this offered the attacker the most expedient route to attack the Ukrainian capital. Indeed, this caused some environmental damage, but from the point of view of the war crime approach, in order to claim individual criminal responsibility, such damage must be weighed against the military advantage gained. However, if ecocide should be more seen as a genocide, there can be no military necessity justifying it. A war crime is simpler to prove, but a judge would have to undertake a balancing exercise to establish guilt. If this is a stand-alone crime, it will be more difficult to prove, at least in terms of threshold, but the balancing exercise would be excluded from this process.

The problem of classification is strongly connected to the problem of a threshold to be proven in order for an act to meet the definition of ecocide. Article 441 of the CCU contains vague terms that the existing apparatus of criminal law cannot explain, in part due to the absence of pertinent case law and in part due to the need for specialised expertise. What should the scale of the destruction of flora and fauna be to be considered 'mass'? Despite some clarification derived from the BUE, what is an environmental disaster and how can a certain action lead to an environmental disaster? How to establish a causal link between an action and the subsequent disaster? There is hardly a definitive response, not only in Ukraine but worldwide.

It appears that the Government of Ukraine realises the significance of this challenge. In August 2021, the OPG established a Specialized Environmental Prosecutor's Office (SEPO),[70] which became a leading institution in the investigation of crimes against nature, including ecocide. The new body is tasked with investigating criminal offences in the sphere of environmental protection. It cooperates closely with Ukrainian and international experts[71] in investigations and training of the prosecutors to investigate crimes against the environment and ecocide.

The first result came in April 2023, when the SEPO sent an indictment of ecocide to a court against two individuals accused of dumping industrial discharges into the water, resulting into the destruction of the local biota.[72] Although this case is unrelated to the conflict, it may indicate an important shift in the mindset of Ukrainian officials, demonstrating their readiness to treat the environment as an object deserving protection by means of criminal law.[73] Another intriguing issue of this case is that the investigators used a quite low threshold of ecocide. The pollution in question affected around 4 square kilometres, where fish, benthic animals, and flora perished. If the case results in a guilty verdict, this may lead to recognition that an ecocide can also occur in the context of very local ecosystems.

---

[70] Regulation on the Specialized Environmental Prosecutor's Office of 02.02.2021, No 247 [in Ukrainian].

[71] See, for example Environment People Law 2023.

[72] Belousova 2023b.

[73] This is not the first time when a case on the protection of the environment reaches the court, however previously such cases were investigated within civil or administrative procedures, or (rarely) under different articles of the CCU unrelated to ecocide.

7.6 Nova Kakhovka: More Questions Than Answers

On 6 June 2023 the dam in Nova Kakhovka collapsed.[74] Approximately 8,600 square kilometres were inundated. The catastrophe affected at least 48 protected sites established by the Nature Reserves Fund. Unknown quantities of fish and animals perished, including endangered species like red salamanders.[75] Wildlife habitats, including in nature reserves, have been affected or destroyed.[76] The Dnipro River and the Black Sea were contaminated with chemicals and industrial waste. Thirty-two settlements, including major cities like Kherson, were partially or fully flooded.[77] The number of human casualties remains unknown, but it numbers in the dozens if not hundreds.[78]

Long-lasting consequences may include the collapse of agriculture in the Kherson Oblast and Crimea, which is dependent on water from the Nova Kakhovka reservoir, shortages in drinking water, and a reduction in agricultural production. Without water from the reservoir, the region may become an arid steppe or even a semidesert.

The OPG launched an ecocide investigation,[79] and later submitted data on the accident to the ICC.[80] Nova Kakhovka was seen by many as a chance of becoming a showcase ecocide trial and the first case before the ICC on conflict-related environmental crimes.[81]

Yet it has apparently not. A year after the disaster, there is very little information about the progress of the investigation. Apart from the early reports of 2023 about Ukraine allegedly pioneering prosecution for ecocide,[82] no further information appeared in the public space either in English or Ukrainian, except the information that the investigation is still in progress and that Ukraine seemingly does not prepare a case file for the ICC. It thus appears that the Nova Kakhovka case has become another ecocide investigation that went into the darkness with unclear perspectives of getting into the light again.

[74] The authors will refrain from elaborating on the reasons of the collapse. The general opinion in Ukraine is that the Russian forces blew up the dam to slow down the Ukrainian offensive. A tentative investigation by the New York Times confirms this assumption. See: Glanz et al. 2023.

[75] Hybrid Warfare Analytical Group 2023.

[76] Prokip 2023.

[77] Visit Ukraine, Blowing up the Kakhovka dam: how russian terror will damage Ukraine's ecology https://visitukraine.today/blog/2035/blowing-up-the-kakhovka-dam-how-russian-terror-will-damage-ukraines-ecology. Accessed 10 June 2024.

[78] The Kyiv Independent 2023.

[79] Stetsenko 2023.

[80] RFE/RL 2023.

[81] Hansen 2023.

[82] Petit 2023.

7.7 Conclusions

Environmental crimes have become emblematic of the Russo-Ukrainian armed conflict after the full-scale Russian invasion of Ukraine in 2022, and nature is exactly that silent victim that needs a voice. Some publicity was given to the issue, especially after the Nova Kakhovka disaster. Yet the focus seems to have disappeared again.

Ukraine is one of the few countries recognising ecocide as a crime distinct from other crimes against nature, and it does not seem to hesitate to use the instruments of its domestic law to initiate conflict-related ecocide investigations, examples of which have been described above. The emergence of the SEPO seemed to have confirmed the country's determination to investigate and prosecute ecocide, thus not only using this instrument as a legal means for combating the aggressor, but also paving the way for the global movement on the prosecution of ecocide.

Yet none of the investigations initiated, even in extreme cases like Nova Kakhovka, reached the court or even received significant media coverage. Moreover, officials routinely (and sometimes confusingly) report the number of cases under investigation, but not their progress. The explanation can follow from two different types of response to a complexity posed by ecocide investigations.

The first type of response (and the easiest explanation for the silence surrounding the silent victim) is the difficulty of the investigation of ecocide faced by the Ukrainian prosecutors and the absence of domestic or international practice that they could rely on to overcome this difficulty. This may lead to reluctance in the qualification of certain acts as ecocide and attempts to investigate these acts as other crimes against nature. However, this does not explain the fact that the number of ecocide investigations remains relatively stable and that some cases may be investigated as ecocide not only for legal, but also for political reasons.

Another possible type of response is that the Ukrainian authorities may treat ecocide as a crime so unique that it warrants a longer and deeper investigation than ordinary crimes. This is where the question of the parallel between ecocide and genocide comes into play, and the issue of balancing. Seeing ecocide as a crime similar to genocide, no balancing is required before the label can be attached. However, if acts amounting to ecocide are considered ordinary types of attacks (and are thus requalified under other Articles of the CCU) one should carefully establish whether the damage to the environment outweighs the military advantage.

The 6th of June 2024 marked the first anniversary of the Nova Kakhovka disaster. Despite some promises, no further information on the investigation appeared in the public space. What is known is that the investigation is ongoing, thus there is still hope for a landmark outcome, not only clarifying important aspects related to the Ukrainian legal system, but also assisting international efforts to criminalise ecocide.

References

Articles, Books and Other Documents

Association of Reintegration of Crimea (2023) Environmental Challenges of Occupation of Crimea and Other Forms of Russian Aggression. https://arcrimea.org/en/analytics/2023/06/13/environmental-challenges-of-occupation-of-crimea-and-other-forms-of-russian-aggression/. Accessed 13 June 2022

Babin B, Plotnikov O (2022) Prosecution of Ecocide as a Weapon in Armed Conflict: Reflections on Crimea. https://www.internationalcrimesdatabase.org/Commentary/IcdBriefs2022. Accessed 24 May 2023

Bebler B (2015) Ukraine vs. Russia. In: Bebler B (ed) "Frozen Conflicts" in Europe. Verlag Barbara Budrich, pp 189–207

Belousova K (2018) The Occupiers Turned the Protected Island of the Kherson Region into a Military Base. https://ecopolitic.com.ua/en/news/okupanti-peretvorili-zapovidnij-ostriv-herson shhini-na-vijskovu-bazu-2/. Accessed 23 May 2024

Belousova K (2022a) Due to the war in Ukraine, the amount of carbon emissions increased by a quarter. https://ecopolitic.com.ua/en/news/v-ukraini-cherez-vijnu-kilkist-vikidiv-vuglecju-zrosla-na-chvert-2/. Accessed 23 May 2024

Belousova K (2022b) The Black Sea washed ashore thousands of dead dolphins. https://ecopolitic.com.ua/en/news/chorne-more-vikinulo-na-bereg-tisyachi-mertvih-delfiniv-video-2/. Accessed 23 May 2024

Belousova K (2023a) Russia destroys Ukrainian nature reserves. https://ecopolitic.com.ua/en/news/rosiya-znishhuie-ukrainski-zapovidniki-strilec-2/. Accessed 23 May 2024

Belousova K (2023b) The first case of ecocide brought to court in Ukraine. https://ecopolitic.com.ua/en/news/v-ukraini-podali-do-sudu-pershu-spravu-za-ekocid-2. Accessed 25 May 2023

Council of Europe (2022) Visit to Ukraine: Commissioner Mijatović calls for continuous support and justice for victims of the war. https://www.coe.int/en/web/portal/-/visit-to-ukraine-commis sioner-mijatovic-calls-for-continuous-support-and-justice-for-victims-of-the-war. Accessed 21 May 2023

Coynash G (2018) Factory behind Crimea Chemical Disaster in Armyansk demands Russia prosecutes Ukraine. https://khpg.org/en/1537105770. Accessed 25 May 2023

Environment People Law (2023) News on the session "Accountability for War Crimes against the Environment". http://epl.org.ua/en/announces/united-for-justice-prytyagnennya-do-vidpov idalnosti-za-voyenni-zlochyny-proty-dovkillya. Accessed 6 June 2023

European Economic and Social Committee (2023) Right to a healthy environment in the European Union especially in the context of the war in Ukraine, NAT/885-EESC-2022. https://www.eesc.europa.eu/en/our-work/opinions-information-reports/opinions/right-healthy-environment-european-union-especially-context-war-ukraine. Accessed 24 May 2023

European Union (2016) EU statement on "Russia's Ongoing Aggression against Ukraine and Illegal Occupation of Crimea". https://www.eeas.europa.eu/node/14165_en. Accessed 23 May 2023

Farmer M (2022) Zaporizhzhia Nuclear Plant: A timeline of events since Russia's invasion. https://www.power-technology.com/features/ukraine-zaporizhzhia-timeline-nuclear-plant. Accessed 21 May 2023

Gembranska L (2023) 50,000 dolphins died in the Black Sea during the war: an interview with the biologist of the Tuzlivski Lymany. https://ecopolitic.com.ua/en/news/50-000-dolphins-died-in-the-black-sea-during-the-war-an-interview-with-the-biologist-of-the-tuzlivski-lym any/. Accessed 23 May 2024

Glanz J et al. (2023) Why the Evidence Suggests Russia Blew Up the Kakhovka Dam. https://www.nytimes.com/interactive/2023/06/16/world/europe/ukraine-kakhovka-dam-collapse.html?fbclid=IwAR1sgbqj0DM9glf20UfLmarRrGWlYH0h_nhBEf_MXJqP_0lXaX2Zf1OPNsM. Accessed 17 June 2023

Goldenziel J (2022) An alternative to Zombieing: Lawfare between Russia and Ukraine and the Future of International Law. https://live-cornell-law-review.pantheonsite.io/wp-content/uploads/2023/01/Goldenziel-online-essay-final.pdf. Accessed 21 May 2023

Hansen T (2023) Could the Nova Kakhovka Dam Destruction Become the ICC's First Environmental Crimes Case? https://www.justsecurity.org/86862/could-the-nova-kakhovka-dam-destruction-become-the-iccs-first-environmental-crimes-case/. Accessed 21 May 2024

Heiderscheidt D (2018) The Impact of World War one on the Forests and Soils of Europe. The Undergraduate Research Journal at the University of Northern Colorado 7(3). https://digscholarship.unco.edu/cgi/viewcontent.cgi?article=1175&context=urj. Accessed 23 May 2023

Hybrid Warfare Analytical Group (2023) Ecocide by Russia Puts Endangered Animals on the Edge of Extinction. https://uacrisis.org/en/ecocide-by-russia-puts-endangered-animals-on-the-edge-of-extinction. Accessed 15 June 2023

Interfax-Ukraine (2023) Prosecutor General's Office investigates 11 cases of ecocide committed since start of war. https://en.interfax.com.ua/news/press-conference/895832.html. Accessed 23 May 2023

Interfax-Ukraine (2024) Shelling by Russians of Kharkiv Institute of Physics and Technology in 2022 aimed at causing damage to nuclear facility; they're qualified as ecocide – prosecutor's office. https://en.interfax.com.ua/news/press-conference/982478.html. Accessed 23 May 2024

International Court of Justice (2022) Allegations of Genocide under the Convention on the Prevention and Punishment of the Crime of Genocide (Ukraine v. Russian Federation), Application Instituting Proceedings, 27 February 2022. https://www.icj-cij.org/sites/default/files/case-related/182/182-20220227-APP-01-00-EN.pdf. Accessed 21 May 2023

International Criminal Court (2022a) Statement of the Prosecutor, Fatou Bensouda, on the conclusion of the preliminary examination in the situation in Ukraine. https://www.icc-cpi.int/Pages/item.aspx?name=201211-otp-statement-ukraine. Accessed 10 January 2022

International Criminal Court (2022b) Statement of ICC Prosecutor, Karim A.A. Khan QC, on the Situation in Ukraine: Receipt of Referrals from 39 States Parties and the Opening of an Investigation. https://www.icc-cpi.int/news/statement-icc-prosecutor-karim-aa-khan-qc-situation-ukraine-receipt-referrals-39-states. Accessed 23 May 2023

International Criminal Court Office of the Prosecutor (2016) Report on Preliminary Examination Activities. https://www.icc-cpi.int/iccdocs/otp/161114-otp-rep-PE_ENG.pdf. Accessed 21 May 2023

International Fund for Animal Warfare (2023) War in Ukraine has devastating consequences for biodiversity. https://www.ifaw.org/international/press-releases/war-ukraine-biodiversity. Accessed 23 May 2024

Kamenev M (2022) How Russia took over Chernobyl. https://www.opendemocracy.net/en/odr/chernobyl-russian-occupation-nuclear-radiation-effects. Accessed 21 May 2023

Kapustin A (2015) Crimea's Self-Determination in the Light of Contemporary International Law. Zeitschrift für ausländisches öffentliches Recht und Völkerrecht 75:101–118

Kicaj H, Polukarov Y, Prakhovnik N, Polukarov O, Kachynska N (2023) How war in Ukraine is affecting the climate. International Journal of Environmental Studies 80(2):277–283

Lawrence M, Stemberger H, Zolderdo A, Struthers D, Cooke S (2015) The effects of modern war and military activities on biodiversity and the environment. https://tspace.library.utoronto.ca/bitstream/1807/69913/1/er-2015-0039.pdf. Accessed 21 May 2023

Lundstedt T (2018) 'Peaceful' and 'remedial' annexations of Crimea. https://voelkerrechtsblog.org/peaceful-and-remedial-annexations-of-crimea. Accessed 21 May 2023

Maksymiv S (2023) Russian Ecocide: How the Russian Invasion has Led to Heavy Metal Pollution in Ukraine's Environment. https://ukraineworld.org/articles/analysis/russian-ecocide. Accessed 21 May 2023

Marchuk I (2016) Ukraine and the International Criminal Court: Implications of Ad Hoc Jurisdiction Acceptance and Beyond. Vanderbilt Journal of Transnational Law 49(2):323–370

Odesa Region Prosecutor's Office (2022) Mass death of dolphins in the Black Sea as a result of the armed aggression of rf –public prosecutors commence criminal proceedings into the facts of ecocide (in Ukrainian). https://od.gp.gov.ua/ua/news.html?_m=publications&_t=rec&id=319340 Accessed 25 May 2022

Office of the Prosecutor General of Ukraine (2022a) The Enemy creates a threat of environmental disaster in Ukraine and in Europe – an investigation of ecocide has begun (in Ukrainian). https://www.gp.gov.ua/ua/posts/vorog-stvoryuye-zagrozi-ekokatastrofi-v-ukrayini-ta-yevropi-rozpochato-rozsliduvannya-ekocidu-2. Accessed 25 May 2023

Office of the Prosecutor General of Ukraine (2022b) The occupation of the Zaporizhzhia NPP – a commander of a military unit of RF is notified of charges (in Ukrainian). https://www.gp.gov.ua/ua/posts/zaxoplennya-zaporizkoyi-aes-komandiru-viiskovoyi-castini-rf-povidomleno-pro-pidozru. Accessed 25 May 2023

Office of the Prosecutor General of Ukraine (2022c) Shelling by the Russian military of the Zaporizhzhia NPP – proceedings initiated (in Ukrainian). https://www.gp.gov.ua/ua/posts/obstril-rosiiskimi-viiskovimi-zaporizkoyi-aes-rozpocato-provadzennya. Accessed 25 May 2023

Office of the Prosecutor General of Ukraine (2022d) Air strikes against oil depots in the Zhytomyr region – ecocide under investigation (in Ukrainian). https://www.gp.gov.ua/ua/posts/aviacini-udari-po-naftobazax-na-zitomirshhini-rozslidujetsya-skojennya-ekocidu. Accessed 25 May 2022

Office of the Prosecutor General of Ukraine (2022e) Shelling by the occupiers of an oil depot in the Rivne Region – investigation initiated (in Ukrainian). https://www.gp.gov.ua/ua/posts/obstril-okupantami-naftobazi-na-rivnenshhini-rozpocato-rozsliduvannya. Accessed 25 May 2022

Office of the Prosecutor General of Ukraine (2022f) Missile attack of an oil depot in the Rivne region – investigation of ecocide initiated (in Ukrainian). https://www.gp.gov.ua/ua/posts/raketnii-obstril-naftobazi-na-rivnenshhini-rozpocato-rozsliduvannya-za-faktom-ekocidu. Accessed 25 May 2022

Office of the Prosecutor General of Ukraine (2022g) Mass pest of poultry in the Kherson Region – public prosecutors confirm new consequences of the armed aggression of the RF (in Ukrainian). https://www.gp.gov.ua/ua/posts/masovii-mor-ptaxiv-u-cornobayivci-prokuratura-zafiksuvala-cergovi-naslidki-zbroinoyi-agresiyi-rf. Accessed 25 May 2022

Organization for Security and Co-operation in Europe (2017) Environmental Assessment and Recovery Priorities for Eastern Ukraine. https://www.osce.org/files/f/documents/4/3/362566_0.pdf. Accessed 23 May 2023

Parliamentary Assembly of Council of Europe (2023) Environmental Impact of Armed Conflicts, Resolution 2477. https://pace.coe.int/en/files/31600/html. Accessed 21 May 2023.

Petit F (2023) Kakhovka dam: Ukraine pioneers prosecution for ecocide. https://www.justiceinfo.net/en/119148-kakhovka-dam-ukraine-pioneers-prosecution-ecocide.html. Accessed 30 June 2023.

Prokip A (2022) Why the Zaporizhzhia Nuclear Power Plant Matters…for the Whole World. https://www.wilsoncenter.org/blog-post/why-zaporizhzhia-nuclear-power-plant-mattersfor-whole-world. Accessed 21 May 2023.

Prokip A (2023) The Kakhovka Dam Disaster: Responsibility and Consequences. https://www.wilsoncenter.org/blog-post/kakhovka-dam-disaster-responsibility-and-consequences. Accessed 30 June 2023.

Radpey L (2022) Remedial Peoplehood: Russia's New Theory on Self-Determination in International Law and its Ramifications beyond Ukraine. https://www.ejiltalk.org/remedial-peoplehood-russias-new-theory-on-self-determination-in-international-law-and-its-ramifications-beyond-ukraine. Accessed 21 May 2023

RFE/RL (2023) Ukraine's Prosecutor To Provide ICC With Data On Kakhovka Dam Destruction.https://www.rferl.org/a/ukraine-prosecutor-icc-kakhovka/32449051.html. Accessed 10 June 2024

Schabas W (2022) Preventing Genocide and the Ukraine/Russia case. https://www.ejiltalk.org/preventing-genocide-and-the-ukraine-russia-case. Accessed 21 May 2023

Stetsenko S (2023) Thousands Of Fish Dead In Kakhovka Reservoir As Ukraine Launches 'Ecocide' Probe Over Dam. https://www.rferl.org/a/thousands-dead-fish-kakhovka-reservoir-ukraine-ecocide-probe-dam/32452124.html. Accessed 10 June 2024

Stop Ecocide Foundation (2021) Independent Expert Panel for the Legal Definition of Ecocide: Commentary and Core Text. https://www.stopecocide.earth/legal-definition. Accessed 24 May 2023

Stop Ecocide International (2023) Ukraine justice conference addresses ecocide law. https://www.stopecocide.earth/breaking-news-2023/ukraine-justice-conference-addresses-ecocide-law. Accessed 21 May 2023

Strick B (2022) Digging in Danger: How Russian Forces Built an Outpost in Chernobyl's Exclusion Zone. https://www.info-res.org/post/digging-in-danger-how-russian-forces-built-an-outpost-in-chernobyl-s-exclusion-zone. Accessed 21 May 2023

The Kyiv Independent (2023) Interior Ministry: Kakhovka Dam death toll rises to 16, with 31 missing. https://kyivindependent.com/kakhovka-dam-death-toll-rises-to-16-with-31-missing. Accessed 10 June 2024

Tolstykh V (2015) Three Ideas of Self-Determination in International Law and the Reunification of Crimea with Russia. Zeitschrift für ausländisches öffentliches Recht und Völkerrecht 75:119–139

Truth Hounds (2021) Donbass Environment: Invisible Front. https://truth-hounds.org/wp-content/uploads/2021/09/donbas-ecology-report-2021-truth-hounds_en.pdf. Accessed 25 May 2022

UN Environment Programme (2022) The Environmental Impact of the Conflict in Ukraine: A Preliminary Review. https://wedocs.unep.org/bitstream/handle/20.500.11822/40746/environmental_impact_Ukraine_conflict.pdf?sequence=3&isAllowed=y. Accessed 23 May 2023

UN General Assembly (2014) Territorial Integrity of Ukraine, UN Doc. A/RES/68/262

UN General Assembly (2022a) Territorial integrity of Ukraine: defending the principles of the Charter of the United Nations, UN Doc. A/RES/ES-11/4

UN General Assembly (2022b) Aggression against Ukraine, UN Doc. A/RES/ES-11/1

UN Office of the High Commissioner of Human Rights (2017) Situation of human rights in the temporarily occupied Autonomous Republic of Crimea and the city of Sevastopol (Ukraine), UN Doc. A/HRC/36/CRP.3

World Nuclear News (2022) IAEA experts assess damage to Kharkiv nuclear research facility. https://www.world-nuclear-news.org/Articles/IAEA-experts-assess-damage-to-Kharkiv-nuclear-rese. Accessed 10 January 2022

Zayets S, Matviychuk O, Pechonchyk T, Svyrydova D, Skrpnyk O (2016) The Peninsula of Fear: Chronicle of the Occupation and Violation of Human Rights in Crimea. KBC, Kyiv

Prof. Borys Babin is a chief scientific expert at the Dragomanov Ukrainian State University and a lector at the National Aviation University. He holds a Juris Doctor degree from the Institute of Legislation of the Verkhovna Rada of Ukraine. He acts as an expert with the UN bodies, OSCE, Council of Europe, Minority Rights Group International and Crimean Tatar Resource Center. He was an Agent of Ukraine before the European Court of Human Rights in 2015 and a Representative of the President of Ukraine in the Autonomous Republic of Crimea in 2017–2018. In 2020, he was a primary founder of the Association of Reintegration of Crimea.

Dr. Oleksii Plotnikov is a senior lawyer with the Civic Organization "The Tenth of April". He holds a PhD from the National University "Odesa Academy of Law" (Ukraine), and was a Fulbright visiting researcher at Cardozo School of Law (USA). He was an expert of the Expert Council with the Representative of the President of Ukraine in the Autonomous Republic of Crimea in 2018. He acts as an expert with the UNDP and the Crimean Tatar Resource Center, and was a co-founder of the Association of Reintegration of Crimea.

Part IV
Who?

Chapter 8
Climate Change as the Ultimate Form of Ecocide: Are Producers and Consumers 'Partners in Crime'?

Harmen van der Wilt

Contents

Abstract Against the backdrop of an elaborate proposal of an Independent Expert Panel to insert ecocide as a fifth international crime under the jurisdiction of the International Criminal Court, this article addresses the question of who should be held criminally responsible for this crime. To be more precise: is it fair to only prosecute representatives of large business corporations and state officials, while letting consumers of polluting products off the hook? In addressing the issue, one is bound to take into consideration two arguments that pull in contrary directions. On the one hand, one must admit that large entities have the (organisational) power and capacities to cause widespread and disastrous damage to the environment, while private consumers are fragmented, and their causal contributions are futile. On the other hand, however, one cannot deny that the most serious, if not apocalyptic, forms of ecocide, like climate change through greenhouse emissions, are caused by common action of producers and consumers, in accordance with the economic laws of supply and demand. While it cannot be denied that there is a power gap between producers and consumers, both in terms of knowledge of the pernicious effects of carbon emissions and capacity to prevent global cataclysm, that difference is narrowed by the notion of mutual interdependence, inherent to the market mechanism. The conclusion is therefore that exclusive criminal responsibility of representatives of large corporations or state officials would not be justified.

Keywords Ecocide · International crimes · Climate change · International Criminal Court · Criminal responsibility · Corporate producers · Consumers

H. van der Wilt (✉)
University of Amsterdam, Amsterdam, The Netherlands
e-mail: H.G.vanderwilt@uva.nl

L. Burgers et al. (eds.), *Ecocide: Criminalising Serious Harm against the Environment*, International Criminal Justice Series 38, https://doi.org/10.1007/978-94-6265-715-1_8

8.1 Introduction

It has probably not escaped the broader public's attention that eco-activists have been quite vocal in demanding that ecocide is added as a fifth international crime to the jurisdiction of the International Criminal Court (ICC).[1] In view of the rapid degradation of the environment, the ongoing climate change and the callous disregard of states, corporations etc. for the present and imminent disastrous consequences of their irresponsible activities, such claims are understandable and sympathetic. The more precarious and pertinent question is whether the elevation of ecocide to the status of international crime is warranted, both from a practical perspective—is it an effective measure to increase deterrence of future violations and in doing so reduce the danger of climate change?—and from a theoretical perspective: is it conceptually sound to consider ecocide on the same par as aggression, genocide, crimes against humanity and war crimes?

At the behest of the Stop Ecocide Foundation, an Independent Expert Panel of renowned legal experts (Panel) has engaged in drafting a legal definition of ecocide that might be inserted in the Rome Statute.[2] The proposal includes an addition to the Preamble of the Rome Statute,[3] an addition of a new article on the jurisdiction *ratione materiae* of the ICC, and a definition of ecocide, to be included in the Statute as Article 8*ter*: "*For the purpose of this Statute, 'ecocide' means unlawful or wanton acts committed with knowledge that there is a substantial likelihood of severe and either widespread or long-term damage to the environment being caused by those acts.*"[4]

In conformity with the standard systematic approach in the Rome Statute, the Panel next provides definitions of the elements of the crime—"severe and either widespread or long-term damage", "unlawful or wanton acts", "environment"—and follows with a careful account in which it explains where and why it borrowed or deviated from established norms of international criminal and humanitarian law. In particular, the Panel points out that the insertion of "severe and either widespread *or* long-term damage" [emphasis added] and "unlawful or wanton acts" serves to raise the threshold for prohibited conduct, justifying its qualification as an international crime.[5] In respect of the first mentioned element, which obviously aims to emphasise the gravity of the consequences, the Panel steers a middle course between the cumulation of the adjectives that features, among other things, in Article 8, s.2, sub b

---

[1] Apart from the numerous declarations and publications, a more spectacular manifestation was the occupation of the ICC premises by eco activists in 2019. See Cockburn 2019.

[2] Stop Ecocide Foundation 2021. Rome Statute of the International Criminal Court, opened for signature 17 July 1998, 2187 UNTS 3, entered into force 1 July 2002.

[3] Ibid., para 2*bis*. "Concerned that the environment is daily threatened by destruction and deterioration, gravely endangering natural and human systems worldwide".

[4] Rome Statute, above n. 2, Article 5(1)(e). 'The crime of ecocide'.

[5] Ibid., p. 7.

(iv) of the Rome Statute,[6] and the disjunctive phrasing ("widespread, longlasting or severe effects") that is used in Article I of the 1976 Convention on the Prohibition of Military or any other Hostile Use of Environmental Modification Techniques.[7] In the opinion of the Panel, the former would be too demanding and raise unsurmountable problems of evidence, while the latter would cast the net too wide by including, for instance, long-term damage that would not be so serious. In the second element, the qualification 'wanton' is particularly interesting, as it links a specific *mens rea* standard—to wit, recklessness—to a consequence of the act. In accordance with the definition, as presented by the Panel, 'wanton' means "with reckless disregard for damage which would be clearly excessive in relation to the social and economic benefits anticipated".[8] The provision thus introduces a balancing exercise between serious damage to the environment and social/economic advantages. While such a trade-off reveals a candid realism towards current world opinion, it also casts doubts on the Panel's resolve to move away from anthropocentrism and put the environment first.[9] The Panel's publication ends with two brief reflections on *mens rea*—basically reiterating the choice for the recklessness standard—and on ecocide as a crime of endangerment which emanates in the phrasing "(knowledge of) substantial likelihood" and is not foreign to international criminal law.[10]

Despite the shortcomings that some critical scholars have been quick to notice, but that are inevitable, in view of the highly complex and contested subject matter, the Panel is to be commended for presenting a thoughtful and constructive proposal. It has at least succeeded in dispelling qualms of—mainly—criminal lawyers that ecocide would develop into a crime of strict liability, a suggestion that was made by the most ardent advocates for criminalisation.[11]

A comprehensive discussion of all the elements that have been briefly highlighted above would clearly exceed the scope of this chapter. Instead, it will focus on one

[6] Article 8(2)(b) Rome Statute depicts the "Other serious violations of the laws and customs applicable in international armed conflict, within the established framework of international criminal law" as war crimes under the jurisdiction of the ICC and para (iv) reads "Intentionally launching an attack in the knowledge that such attack will cause (…) widespread, long term *and* severe damage to the natural environment which would be clearly excessive in relation to the concrete and direct overall military advantage anticipated" (emphasis added).

[7] Stop Ecocide Foundation 2021, p. 8.

[8] The qualification 'wanton' features in Article 8(2)(a) of the Rome Statute that lists the 'grave breaches' of the Geneva Conventions. Sub (iv) reads: "Extensive destruction and appropriation of property, not justified by military necessity and carried out unlawfully and *wantonly*". Emphasis added. The broader *mens rea* standard, including recklessness, has been confirmed by the International Criminal Tribunal for the former Yugoslavia in ICTY, *Prosecutor v. Kordić and Čerkez*, Judgment, 26 February 2001, IT-95-14/2, paras 346–347.

[9] For critical comments in this respect, see Heller 2021.

[10] As the Panel points out, it is for instance not a requirement for genocide that an entire group or part of it is actually destroyed. See Stop Ecocide Foundation 2021, p. 12.

[11] See especially Higgins 2010, p. 68: "It is proposed that ecocide be a crime of strict liability, one without the requirement of a mens rea". The late Scottish lawyer Polly Higgins has been rightly praised as the godmother of the concept of ecocide, but not being a criminal lawyer, she did not share the latter's innate allergy against any introduction of strict liability in criminal law.

aspect that has hitherto slightly been ignored, both by the Panel and by subsequent commentaries, to wit: who can or should be held criminally responsible for ecocide as an international crime?[12] The choice of the topic has been inspired by the author's continuous struggle with the question whether it is fair to only prosecute (the representatives of) large business corporations or state officials, while letting consumers of polluting products off the hook.[13] A negative answer to that question would obviously entail that anyone of us could potentially incur responsibility for an international crime and would probably imply the demise of the initiative. After all, where all are guilty, no one is, as the familiar commonplace goes. In addressing the issue, one is bound to take into consideration two arguments that pull in contrary directions. On the one hand, one must admit that large entities have the (organisational) power and capacities to cause widespread and disastrous damage to the environment, while private consumers are fragmented and their causal contributions are futile. On the other hand, however, one cannot deny that some of the most serious, if not apocalyptic, forms of ecocide are caused by common action of producers and consumers, in accordance with the economic laws of supply and demand. For two reasons, climate change through greenhouse emissions serves as a paradigmatic case for our discussion. First, it features amongst the 'planetary boundaries', the transgression whereof increases the risks to people and ecosystems.[14] The gravity element in the ecocide definition of the Panel is therefore easily satisfied. Secondly, climate change is the dire harmful consequence of the accumulation of daily activities by producers and consumers.[15] The inquiry into the potential (criminal) responsibility of both sides of the bargain is therefore made with climate change as an arguable case of ecocide in mind. Throughout this chapter, I will touch upon specific legal aspects, like causality, functional capacity to commit (international) crimes, *mens rea* and—especially—the nature of the crime of ecocide, as these elements shed light on the central topic of research. I propose to structure my discourse along the following lines. Section 8.2 discusses the conspicuous absence of a further specification of the (potential) suspect in the Panel's proposal on ecocide, against the backdrop of a different approach with respect to other international crimes that stresses the capacity to engage in those crimes. Section 8.3 reflects on the legitimacy of prohibiting harmful effects on the environment, as a result of economic exchange between producers and consumers, by comparing such an initiative with criminal policy in respect of other market transactions like traffic in illicit drugs and selling and reception of stolen goods. In both situations sellers and buyers incur criminal responsibility, despite the fact that socio-psychological relations in terms of knowledge and interdependence are often more 'unequal' in case of drugs traffic, when compared with money laundering.

---

[12] A conspicuous exception is the careful analysis by Hamilton and Tiernan 2022.

[13] An earlier attempt to address the issue was published in a Dutch legal journal, see Van der Wilt 2021, pp. 267–270.

[14] For the concept of planetary boundaries, presenting a set of nine planetary boundaries within which humanity can continue to develop and thrive for generations to come, *see* https://www.stockholmresilience.org/research/planetary-boundaries/the-nine-planetary-boundaries.html. Accessed 20 July 2025.

[15] For the notion of 'accumulative harm', see Feinberg 1984, pp. 228 ff; Kernohan 1993.

Assuming that oil and gas producers are better organised and more knowledgeable than consumers, it raises the question whether such a differentiation in capacities is relevant at all for the attribution of responsibility and if so, whether the commercial transaction between producers and consumers of fossil fuels resembles the configuration of illicit drugs trade or rather is more similar to money laundering. In Sect. 8.4 the emphasis shifts to the nature of ecocide, in terms of the good or value that needs to be protected and the harm that is to be averted. In this respect, two elements are of particular interest for the central issue in this contribution. Firstly, the elusiveness of the concept of ecocide is at odds with the notion of the *nullum crimen* principle in general and the *lex certa* principle in particular. It raises the question whether impaired knowledge of the prospect of being held responsible for ecocide is common to both consumers and producers. Or would a finding of privileged expertise within the realm of large oil corporations warrant their exclusive criminal responsibility? In the second place, and relatedly, one wonders who or what is actually the victim of ecocide. Any perspective that pitches affluent economic players against disadvantaged people and nature will arguably be conducive to a division of (criminal) responsibility that differs from a position presenting ecocide as a largely self-inflictive disaster. Section 8.5 rounds off with a couple of (cautious and provisional) conclusions.

8.2 On the Democratisation of Perpetration: Ecocide as the Odd Man Out?

The Panel's proposal for a definition of ecocide does not indicate who can be held criminally responsible for the crime. At this point, the Panel's definition deviates from an earlier draft that was presented by the Scottish lawyer Polly Higgins to the International Law Commission (ILC). According to this definition, ecocide comprises "acts or omissions committed in times of peace or conflict by any *senior person within the course of State, corporate or any other entity's activity* (…)".[16] The message is clear: powerful actors, operating within large institutions that steer economic and political developments and—by doing so—pollute our planet on a massive scale, bear the brunt of the (imminent) tragedy and will be held to account as 'the most responsible'.

It is not uncommon in international criminal law to link responsibility to the culprit's capacity to commit international crimes. The most conspicuous example is the definition of aggression in the Rome Statute that limits the circle of perpetrators to "person[s] in a position effectively to exercise control over or to direct the political or military action of a State."[17] On the occasion of the amendment of the Rome Statute that followed the Review Conference in Kampala in 2010, expanding the jurisdiction of the ICC with the crime of aggression, the provision on individual criminal responsibility (Article 25 Rome Statute) was enriched with a new section,

[16] Higgins 2010, p. 68. Emphasis added.

[17] Rome Statute, above n. 2, Article 8bis (1).

Article 25(3)bis. It stipulates that only the persons wielding control over the State apparatus can incur criminal responsibility in respect of the crime of aggression. At first blush, this provision may appear to be repetitive, but on closer scrutiny it is highly important, because it imparts that the restriction of addressees applies also to secondary perpetrators/accomplices. This implies that those lacking the powers to control and direct the policy of a state cannot incur responsibility on the basis of other modes of liability, like inducing or aiding and abetting, either. The crime of aggression is therefore a leadership crime par excellence. It is quite obvious that the introduction of aggression as an international crime in the Rome Statute is indebted to the post-war trials at the International Military Tribunals at Nuremberg and Tokyo, where the Nazi kingpins, belonging to the inner circle of Hitler, and members of the Japanese political and military elite were prosecuted and convicted on account of planning, initiating and waging crimes against peace. However, it has been correctly observed that the 'control and direct' test that has been incorporated in the Rome Statute is a departure from the more lenient 'shape and influence' test that had been applied by the Tokyo Tribunal.[18] Arguably, the application of such a broader criterion would include CEOs of large industrial companies who did not participate in the conspiracy to wage war and might therefore not have been privy to the initial decision, but whose material contributions in terms of arms and logistics might surely have influenced the length and course of the war.[19] For the purpose of this chapter, these legal refinements need not detain us further here, because they detract from the central point that I wish to make. Criminal responsibility for the crime of aggression is predicated on the culprit's power to unleash a macro-event that affects the lives of numerous people or, at least, to give shape to its course or influence its outcome. As O'Keefe aptly notes: "A humble functionary or foot-soldier cannot commit a crime of aggression".[20]

In the realm of crimes against humanity, the capacity to engage in atrocities as a precondition for criminal responsibility is a vital element as well. In this context, however, not as a 'quality' of an individual perpetrator, but as a feature of a collective. Article 7(2)(b) of the Rome Statute stipulates that an attack on a civilian population—the core element of crimes against humanity—must be in furtherance of the policy of a State or an organisation. When seized with the question what characteristics an 'organisation' should have in order to meet the standard of this provision, the majority of the ICC Pre-Trial Chamber in the Kenya case held that a group did not have to possess state-like features. Decisive would be its capabilities to perform acts which

---

[18] Heller 2007, p. 496. It should be emphasised, however, that the Nuremberg Tribunal adhered to the stricter 'control and direct' test, which implies that the Rome Statute adopted the Nuremberg approach.

[19] Compare Boister and Cryer 2008, p. 153. Industrialists were not amongst the accused at the Tokyo Trial, so the assumption was not put to the test. The leadership of the huge German companies IG Farben and Krupp, however, were acquitted from the charges of crimes against peace, which suggests that the Nuremberg Tribunal harboured the more stringent 'direct and control' test.

[20] O'Keefe 2007, p. 158.

infringe basic human values.[21] The late Judge Kaul disagreed with the majority's point of view. In his opinion, the organisation within the meaning of Article 7(2)(a) of the Rome Statute at least had to partake in a number of features of a State.[22] The majority's opinion, while slightly tautological, puts the issue plainly on the table. Each assessment whether a person or entity may qualify as a (potential) perpetrator of an international crime starts with the question whether that person/entity has the capability to perform the impugned act in the first place.

In the case of genocide, the emphasis on the collective dimension is less prominent. Undoubtedly, this has to do with the criminal provision's singular preoccupation with its *mens rea*—the special intent to destroy a group as such—and the underlying resolve to prevent genocide, which implies that the destruction of the group need not have materialised to create criminal responsibility.[23] It would therefore be theoretically possible that an individual, imbued by hatred against a specific racial group, through his or her isolated acts, would incur responsibility for genocide.[24] However, commentators have denounced the possibility of a single génocidaire as a far-fetched option, observing that genocide usually occurs within a context of systemic violence and implicitly suggesting that a single person would never be able to accomplish the crime.[25]

The unified power of a collective as a prerequisite for the commission of international crimes is arguably least pronounced in the case of war crimes. Indeed, civilians that are not affiliated to States or non-state armed groups can be held responsible for war crimes.[26] However, this general statement is perhaps in need of some qualification, as the most conspicuous contextual element of war crimes requires that

[21] ICC, *Situation in the Republic of Kenya, Decision Pursuant to Article 15 of the Rome Statute on the Authorization of an Investigation into the situation in the Republic of Kenya*, Pre-Trial Chamber II, Case No. ICC-01/09, 31 March 2010, para 90. In elaborating on this general standard, the PTC offered a number of indicia, para 93: "(i) whether the group is under a responsible command, or has an established hierarchy; (ii) whether the group possesses, in fact, the means to carry out a widespread or attack against a civilian population; (iii) whether the group exercises control over part of the territory of a State; (iv) whether the group has criminal activities against the civilian population as a primary purpose; (v) whether the group articulates, explicitly or implicitly, an intention to attack a civilian population; (vi) whether the group is part of a larger group, which fulfils some or all of the abovementioned criteria" (footnotes omitted).

[22] ICC, *Situation in the Republic of Kenya*, n. 21, Dissenting Opinion of Judge Hans Peter Kaul, para 51.

[23] Compare Werle and Jessberger 2020, p. 339.

[24] Compare ICTR, *Prosecutor v. Kayishema and Ruzindana*, Trial Chamber Judgment, 21 May 1999, ICTR-95-1-T, para 94 and ICTY, *Prosecutor v. Jelisić*, Trial Chamber Judgment, 14 December 1999, IT-95-10-T, para 100.

[25] See Werle and Jessberger 2020, p. 355 (footnote 146): "However, this case (of the prosecution of single, isolated individual for genocide), is unlikely to have practical significance, as the criminal acts will typically be part of a systematic attack"; Cassese and Gaeta 2013, p. 128: "(…) although they (*id est*: crimes against humanity and genocide) need not be perpetrated by State officials or by officials of entities such as insurgents, they are usually carried out with the complicity, connivance, or at least the toleration or acquiescence of the authorities".

[26] O'Keefe 2007, p. 134.

they have a nexus with an armed conflict.[27] In a landmark decision that dealt with the topic, the ICTY's Appeals Chamber elucidated that "the existence of an armed conflict must, at a minimum, play a substantial part in the perpetrator's ability to commit the crime, his decision to commit it, the manner in which it was committed or the purpose for which it was committed".[28] Elaborating on this still rather elusive standard, the Appeals Chamber instructed the Trial Chamber to take a number of factors into account:

> *the fact that the perpetrator is a combatant*; the fact that the victim is a non-combatant; the fact that the victim is a member of the opposing party; *the fact that the act may be said to serve the ultimate goal of a military campaign; and the fact that the crime is committed as part of or in the context of the perpetrator's official duties.*[29]

These parameters display the conventional—and probably realistic—perspective that war crimes are usually committed by members of—regular or irregular—armed forces.

The brief discourse on the relevance of power and capacity in the taxonomy of international crimes reveals the essence of system criminality. The *auctores intellectuales* of international crimes cannot accomplish their devious plans on their own. They are in need of the (loyal) assistance of scores of assistants and executioners that do the 'dirty work'. This interaction and collaboration—usually structured along hierarchical lines—foments the power to engage in atrocities.

The pertinent question is whether the interrelationship between perpetrators of the crime of ecocide complies with this socio-legal characterisation of international crimes as system criminality *stricto sensu*. In answering that question, it is inevitable to distinguish between an entity's internal organisation and the interactions between producers and consumers. The former aspect is rather self-evident and uncontroversial. It is quite obvious that states and large corporations, by virtue of their abundant financial and human resources, have the capacity to inflict immense damage to the environment.

However, if we are willing to accept the premise that some of the most egregious and life-threatening forms of ecocide, in particular climate change, are caused by (business transactions between) producers and consumers, we are bound to address their interaction as well. And it is at this point that the analogy with the 'familiar' core crimes runs astray. It is a stretch of imagination—if not ludicrous—to portray the relationship between big oil companies and car drivers as a conspiracy to commit environmental crimes. For one thing, neither of the two really desires or intends to damage the ecosystem; it is rather a deplorable consequence of their actions. Although, as we have noticed before, such a *dolus directus* is diluted into recklessness

[27] In the Elements of Crimes, annexed to the Rome Statute, the nexus-element is expressed in the condition that "the conduct took place in the context of and was associated with an – international or internal – armed conflict". See International Criminal Court, Elements of Crimes, reproduced in the Official Records of the Assembly of the States Parties to the Rome Statute of the International Criminal Court, First Session, New York, 3–10 September 2002, ICC-ASP/1/3 and Corr.1, part II.B.

[28] ICTY, *Prosecutor v. Kunarac et al.*, Judgment, 14 June 2002, IT-96-23 and 23/1, para 58.

[29] Ibid., para 59. Emphasis added.

in the Panel's proposal, the draft also provides for the safety valve of 'social or economic benefits' that can be invoked as a justification. Moreover, the relations between producers and consumers do not even meet the lowest standards of cohesion that are required for system criminality. Their fleeting transactions take place in an abstract context of mutual anonymity, from which only in the most general terms a 'common purpose' or a 'joint agreement' can be inferred.

The conclusion that ecocide does not fit the mould of the existing international crimes does not imply, however, that individual criminal responsibility cannot be limited to those agents that have the greatest capacity to inflict severe damage to the environment.[30] After all, it is precisely their power to create havoc that might justify their being considered as 'the most responsible', rather than their feeble clients, whose individual contributions to the (impending) disaster are negligible. This argument requires some further reflections on the question why consumers' activity is an aggregation of fragmented decisions that cannot be legally attributed to a 'collectivity'. Moreover, we should inquire how and why power differentiation in the relationship between producer and client is relevant for the assessment of their respective (criminal) responsibility, if the outcome of their transaction is harmful. To that purpose, we will engage in a short comparative analysis between ecocide on the one hand and drugs offences and theft/reception of stolen goods on the other hand. After all, as will transpire in the next section, criminal legislation does not differentiate between producers/sellers and consumers/buyers in both latter situations, for the purpose of attributing criminal responsibility. Yet, especially in the case of narcotic offences, power dissimilarities are usually considerable. It raises the question whether there are good reasons to deviate from this practice in case of ecocide, by singling out representatives of corporations and state officials for incurring criminal responsibility.

8.3 Ecocide as the Outcome of Daily Commercial Transactions

The proposition of Higgins to focus on state officials and (representatives of) large corporations as the main or even sole culprits of the crime of ecocide (see above, n. 16) has found wide acclaim. Criminologist Rob White, for instance, holds that individual consumers should not incur criminal responsibility for global warming. Rather, state officials and corporate leaders should be held accountable, as they are the ones that effectively plan and control the capitalist system that generates the problem.[31] The argument reminds us vividly of the discussion on the capacity of political and

[30] At the risk of stating the obvious, I wish to bring to mind that the International Criminal Court has only jurisdiction over natural persons, which implies that only representatives of states and corporations can be prosecuted and tried for international crimes. See the Rome Statute, above n. 2, Article 25, s.1.

[31] White 2017, p. 63.

economic powerholders as an important reason for holding them 'the most responsible' for international crimes *stricto sensu* (see the previous section). It still begs the question, however, whether the contributions of producers and consumers—and hence their (criminal) responsibility—can artificially be severed, as they are intrinsically connected in causing the fateful harm.

A possible—affirmative—answer might be that individuals in their exploitation of the 'common good' (the environment) do not act in furtherance of the public interest—as Adam Smith famously and optimistically postulated in his defence of the free market economy—, but rather as calculating enterprisers. They lack the natural incentive to join forces and create a collective organisation for the pursuit of their common interest, unless they can reap a clear and visible benefit from such an initiative. In a brief but seminal essay, Garrett Hardin has demonstrated why this is the case.[32] While Hardin addresses the 'tragedy of the commons' in the context of the population problem and the challenges of birth control, he exemplifies his point of view with the pollution of the environment, which is according to him a consequence of unchecked population growth (and increased welfare). Referring to polluting activities (putting sewage, chemical substances or heat wastes into the water, noxious and dangerous fumes in the air), Hardin continues:

> The rational man finds that his share of the costs of the wastes he discharges into the commons is less than the cost of purifying his wastes before releasing them. *"Since this is true for everyone, we are locked into "fouling our own nest", so long as we behave only as independent, rational, free-enterprisers".*[33]

The second sentence in italics is particularly illuminating to understand the quandary of the aspirant buyer of (especially polluting) consumer goods. Confronted with the options of being a 'responsible' citizen and indulging in the guilty pleasures of eating juicy red meat and taking the airplane to far-off holiday destinations, many people—sometimes grudgingly—choose the latter. After all, any—even moderate—success of environmental protection by means of consumer abstention is predicated on other members of the community's compliance with the self-imposed asceticism. Reciprocal suspicion that the other(s) will be less circumspect is likely to spoil the arrangement in the first place. This typical application of classic game theory is aggravated by (wo-)man's sense of futility of his or her own activities in light of gigantic and highly complicated problems. An appeal to conscience is not a solution either, as Hardin argues, because it sends a double message that is contradictory, hypocritical and even pathogenic:

> The intended communication (i) is: "If you don't do as we ask, we will openly condemn you for not acting as a responsible citizen". The unintended communication (ii) is: "If you do

[32] Hardin 1968. Hardin has been criticized for presenting an oversimplification of population growth, based on Malthusian logic, *see* Hunter and Prakash 2019, pp. 78–79. However, in my view this criticism does not detract from the soundness of his reasoning in respect of the obstacles to collective action for consumers. I am indebted to Ms. Merle Kooijman, PhD candidate at the University of Amsterdam, who drew my attention to the article of Hunter and Prakash.

[33] Hardin 1968, p. 1245, italics added.

> behave as we ask, we will secretly condemn you for a simpleton who can be shamed into standing aside while the rest of us exploit the commons".[34]

There seems no other option than coercive regulation of the problem of worldwide environmental damage by considerable reduction of the production and consumption of polluting goods. This can be accomplished by forcible limitation of the supply which, primarily, affects the economic position of producers and, subsequently—through price increases—has influence on consumers. Or, alternatively, by heavily taxing consumer goods, in which the order and weight of the effects on the respective economic players is the reverse. As a lay person in economic science, I am not equipped nor authorised to judge the effectiveness of either of those measures. However, if we translate fiscal measures to criminal legislation and policy, the analogy with the question who should be held responsible—producers, consumers or both?—is rather obvious. As indicated before, scholars like Higgins and White have defended the exclusive penalisation of corporations (and state officials), because they wield control over the system, while the array of consumers is fragmented and their individual causal contribution to the damage is negligible. The concept of the 'tragedy of the commons' offers a convincing explanation for this state of affairs.

There is yet another argument that sustains the claim that consumers are not to be held (criminally) responsible for global environmental disasters like climate change, at least not integrally. The persuasiveness of Hardin's discourse is largely due to its applicability in an ideal situation of agents having more or less equal capacity to harm the environment. In the global context, however, the ecological footprints of consumers are hugely disparate. According to a report, compiled by Oxfam and the Stockholm Environment Institute, the world population's wealthiest 1% were responsible for more carbon emissions than the poorest 50%, while the richest 10% were responsible for 52% of emissions in the period from 1990 to 2015.[35] Such a large discrepancy in contributory fault would militate against considering consumers as a homogenous group that would deserve condemnation on the same footing. Any proposal that advocates the criminal responsibility of both producers and consumers must therefore not only take into account that individual contributions are slight, but also that the share in the environmental degradation of rich consumers exceeds that of poor people to a large extent. In view of the complications inherent to the dual criminal responsibility of producers and consumers, the alternative that focuses on liability of corporations has a certain intuitive appeal. However, it does not correspond with the common practice of penal policy to hold both parties in a criminal bargain responsible. Drugs offences are a clear example. Article 36, s. 1 sub (a) of the Single Convention on Narcotic Drugs provides that

> Subject to its constitutional limitations, each Party shall adopt such measures as will ensure that (…) production, manufacture (…), *offering for sale, distribution, purchase* (…) (of narcotics) shall be punishable offences when committed intentionally, and that serious

[34] Hardin 1968, p. 1246.

[35] The Guardian 2020.

> offences shall be liable to adequate punishment particularly by imprisonment or other penalties of deprivation of liberty.[36]

Hence, the production, manufacture, sale and purchase of drugs are presented as separate offences, committed by distinct individuals, and both (should) fall under the purview of criminal law.[37] Whereas the Single Convention therefore highlights the distinctiveness of selling and buying narcotics, international legal instruments of more recent date sometimes tend to lump both elements of the transaction together under the label of 'illicit traffic'.[38] Producer/seller and consumer are thus presented as partners in a harmful activity that deserves a criminal response.

In our inquiry why both participants in the transaction should incur criminal responsibility—in contradistinction to the proposals to focus attention on the providers-, we should ponder on the question what exactly the harm is and on whom it is inflicted. It is probably not a stretch to argue that concern for the mental and physical welfare of the user is the prime reason for penalisation. Obviously, there are derivative or secondary harmful consequences, affecting broader society, like the commission of offences under the influence of narcotics, crimes against property committed for the purpose of purchasing the drugs and increased pressures on the national health system, but for the sake of poignancy we should leave them aside.

If we accept that the criminal law prohibition on drug use is primarily inspired by the objective to persuade (aspiring) consumers to abstain from their bad and self-destructive habits, penalisation of drug use can be qualified as a typical example of *legal paternalism.* In the introduction to his groundbreaking study *The Moral Limits of the Criminal Law,* Joel Feinberg paraphrases the liberty-limiting principle of legal paternalism as the conviction that "it is always a good reason in support of a prohibition that it is probably necessary to prevent harm (physical, psychological,

[36] Single Convention on Narcotic Drugs, as amended by the Protocol amending the Single Convention on Narcotic Drugs, opened for signature 30 March 1961, 520 UNTS 151, entered into force 13 December 1964. Italics added.

[37] It is interesting in this respect that Article 36, s. 2(a)(i) stipulates that "Each of the offences enumerated in paragraph 1, if committed in different countries, shall be considered as a distinct offence". The provision wishes to underscore that the interests of several states can be impaired by the distinct components of continuous illegal transaction. 'Import' and 'export' of the same narcotic, though factually the same and each other's mirror image, are separate harmful events when considered from the perspective of the affected community.

[38] See, for instance, Article 1 of the United Nations Convention against Illicit Traffic in Narcotic Drugs and Psychotropic Substances, opened for signature 19 December 1988, 1582 UNTS 95, entered into force 11 November 1990, that includes the container concept of 'illicit traffic' in its definitions (under (m)). By immediately defining 'illicit traffic' in terms of its composite elements that are verbatim and explicitly derived from the 1961 Single Narcotics Convention, the novelty is no more than a cosmetic operation. See, however, also the EU Council Framework Decision of 13 June 2002 on the European Arrest Warrant and the Surrender Procedures between the Member States, 2002/584 JHA, OJL 190, 18 July 2002, Article 2, section 2 which lists 'illicit trafficking in narcotics drugs and psychotropic substances', comprising evidently both the selling and the purchase of drugs, as one of the offences in respect of which dual criminality should not be checked by the executing State that assesses the European Arrest Warrant.

or economic) to the actor himself."[39] He immediately adds that the liberal position, of which he is avowedly an adherent, does not acknowledge legal paternalism as a legitimate reason for restricting liberty. Criticism of legal paternalism raises interesting but complicated questions in respect of the 'liberal position's' view on the criminal responsibility of the supplier. Freely given consent appears to be a pivotal concept in this quandary. After all, if one respects the autonomy of the individual to dispose over his/her body, consistency demands that one should also acknowledge his/her right to freely engage in business transactions that sustain such endeavour, even if that would be conducive to physical or mental ruin. The supplier of the—detrimental—instrumentalities should not be punished for his/her actions, because the bargain is directly linked to the consumer's autonomous choices. The liberals will probably rebut that free choice of the consumer is an illusion and that power relations between producers and consumers are therefore unequal. The individual drug user is no match for mighty drug cartels that ruthlessly exploit the user's addiction and increase his/her dependence. From this perspective, it is perfectly legitimate to portray the provider of drugs as the sole wrongdoer who administers harm to others and who should on that account be held criminally responsible.[40]

At first sight, the liberal position's acknowledgement of the legitimacy of punishing only the seller of drugs, while letting the consumer off the hook, lends support to similar claims in the context of environmental crimes, as we discussed before. However, it requires further reflection to find out whether the analogy is entirely fitting. For one thing, it may be a bit of a stretch to compare our addiction to kerosene to the predicament of the drug user. In other words, the latter may be more dependent on his/her business partner than the former. Moreover, in case of use of narcotics the harm is concrete and tangible, whereas environmental damage can be much more elusive, especially in the case of long term and gradual degradation of the environment. It begs the question who or what actually suffers from the demise of the environment and whether this issue in any way has a bearing on the division of responsibility between producers and consumers of polluting goods.

Within the configuration of drugs trafficking, the self-inflicted harm (from the perspective of the consumer) and the unequal relationship between seller and buyer are inter-related, if not inseparable. Such a social context is less self-evident in the case of transactions that are conducive to serious environmental damage. We will therefore briefly address a crime pattern involving exchange of goods, in which business parties act on equal footing and detrimental consequences are purposely externalised. Crimes against property and (subsequent) reception of stolen goods or (money) laundering seem to offer a good example. The thief, embezzler or burglar and the person who buys the loot, for his/her own material satisfaction or in order to disguise its criminal provenance, are certainly 'partners in crime' who inflict harm

[39] Feinberg 1984, p. 26. On p. 24, Feinberg explicitly asserts that "legal paternalism would provide support for criminal prohibitions of (…) possession and use of Psychoactive drugs".

[40] It complies with the famous premise of Mill 1859, p. 13: "the only purpose for which power can be rightfully exercised over any member of a civilized community, against his will, is to prevent harm to others".

on a third person, but they are not accessories in the narrow, formal sense of criminal law. The reason for this apparent anomaly is that the initial crime against property has been completed, which implies that the receiver cannot have facilitated the offence.[41] Crimes against property, like theft, extorsion and embezzlement, are therefore defined in specific titles and articles within the legal taxonomy of penal codes, separately from those on 'facilitation of crimes'.[42] Some legal systems acknowledge the possibility of an accessory *after* the fact, which is from a semantic perspective an apt description, but doctrinally slightly spurious.[43] It is an interesting question whether a person who provides assistance to a crime by taking care of the getaway car in the neighbourhood of the locus delicti can be properly qualified as an 'aider and abettor' of the crime. The Dutch Supreme Court has accepted the possibility, provided that the main perpetrator had reached a prior agreement with the accomplice on the division of labour.[44] Apparently, the promise of an easy and quick escape had strengthened the resolve of the principal, and the accomplice had therefore also been helpful before and during the crime.[45] In common law criminal systems the fact pattern would typically meet the requirements of a conspiracy.

The legal niceties of the precise reading of the partnership between the offender against property and his/her business partner (the receiver of stolen goods or money launderer) need not detain us further. What is essential for our discussion is that the perpetrator of the predicate crime and the receiver or money launderer act on an equal footing, for their mutual advantage, and to the prejudice of a third person or entity. The latter is usually by no means subservient to or an accomplice of the former. This hierarchical parity is exemplified by their respective contributions being covered by distinct criminal law provisions.[46] The configuration is definitely different

[41] The Dutch Penal Code distinguishes between simultaneous complicity (Article 48, sub 1 DPC) and preceding complicity (Article 48, sub 2 DPC), referring to those who 'intentionally provide opportunity, means or information' for the commission of a crime.

[42] The Dutch Penal Code exemplifies the structural distinction. Titles XXII, XXIII, XXIV and XXV of the Second Book of the DPC cover respectively 'theft and poaching', 'extorsion', 'embezzlement' and 'fraud', while Titles XXX and XXXA address respectively 'favouring/ facilitation' and '(money) laundering'. It should be emphasised in this context that the acquisition of stolen goods and money laundering do not necessarily and always coincide. The receiver of a stolen good may just crave the possession of the item, without intending to conceal its illegal provenance, while the (money) launderer may have devices to cover or disguise the initial criminal acts (forgery of documents, for instance), without obtaining possession of stolen property. However, these crimes can obviously concur.

[43] Compare United States' federal criminal legislation. 18 U.S. Code, § 3 defines an accessory after the fact as 'the person who, knowing that an offense against the United States has been committed, receives, relieves, confronts or assists the offender in order to hinder or prevent his apprehension, trial or punishment'.

[44] Dutch Supreme Court, 15 December 1987, NJ 1988, 835.

[45] See also Kelk and de Jong 2013, p. 478.

[46] Compare the UN Convention against Transnational Organized Crime, opened for signature 15 November 2000, 2225 UNTS 209, entered into force 29 September 2003, p. 209. Articles 6 and 7 dedicate special provisions to the repression of the laundering of proceeds of organised crime, thus calling attention to their vital importance. Article 6, s. 2(b)(i) explicitly qualifies as 'laundering': "*the acquisition*, possession or use of property, knowing, at the time of receipt, that such property

from the average transaction between supplier and consumer in the case of narcotics, both in terms of power relations and injured party. However, for (criminal) law the distinctions are largely immaterial, because, as we have noticed, in both cases the supplier and the receiver incur criminal responsibility. Consent to engage in harmful and criminal conduct appears to be the essential lynchpin between the parties, and the different contexts in which the crimes take place are to a large extent ignored.[47] However, as the proclivity of lumping providers and consumers of narcotics together for the purposes of the application of criminal law has been fiercely criticized by the 'liberal position', it is important to distinguish between the two crime patterns.

The question is whether ecocide, in the form of the consequence of wasteful human practices and as a result of numerous transactions between producers and consumers, is comparable to illicit traffic in narcotics or rather mirrors the paradigm of the offender against property and the (money) launderer. Being presented in this slightly provocative way, the reader will understand that I am especially interested in power relations and the question whose rights or interests are especially considered to be impaired by serious environmental crime. The next section will address these issues.

8.4 Ecocide: Legality Principle and Victims

As already briefly indicated in the introduction, the definition of ecocide as proposed by the Panel is very broad. It does not contain any specific acts that are likely to cause severe damage to the environment. Moreover, the affected entity—the 'environment'—is defined in all-encompassing terms.[48] Accordingly, ecocide is purely qualified by the (likely) consequences of certain activities ("*knowledge that there is a substantial likelihood of severe and either widespread or long-term damage to the environment being caused by those acts*") that need not have (yet) materialised, nor even have to materialise in the future.[49] In this respect, the crime of ecocide radically deviates from the redaction of existing core crimes under the jurisdiction of the ICC. The provision on Crimes against Humanity (Article 7 Rome Statute), for instance, enumerates a number of specific acts—murder, enslavement, torture,

---

is the proceeds of crime" (italics mine). In other words, the provision confirms that the purchase of stolen good can serve as a device to conceal its criminal provenance.

[47] Not entirely, though. Article 3, s. 4(b-d) of the UN Convention against Illicit Traffic in Narcotic Drugs and Psychotropic Substances, above n. 38, makes allowance for a different approach of drugs consumers by suggesting measures in the area of health care, education and rehabilitation/ social integration, either as an alternative or in combination with criminal punishment. It signifies an acknowledgement of the consumer being the more vulnerable party, but it does not deflect from the essentially punitive approach.

[48] According to the proposed new Article 8*ter*, s. 2(e) of the Rome Statute, 'Environment' means the earth, its biosphere, cryosphere, lithosphere, hydrosphere and atmosphere, as well as outer space. Stop Ecocide Foundation 2021, p. 5.

[49] Let us recall that ecocide is a crime of endangerment.

rape—that have struck (numerous) concrete people of flesh and blood and links those acts to the contextual element of a—widespread or systematic—attack on a civilian population.

Some previous initiatives to define ecocide remained closer to this conventional approach. It would exceed the scope of this contribution to elaborate on the history of the concept of ecocide.[50] By way of example, we might point at Richard Falk's proposal for an International Convention on the Crime of Ecocide that contains specific acts, like the "use of chemical herbicides to defoliate and deforest natural forests for military purposes" and the "use of bulldozing equipment to destroy large tracts of forest or cropland for military purposes."[51] While Falk intended his proposed Convention to apply in time of peace and in time of war, some of the provisions clearly betray his dismay of the environmental warfare in Vietnam.

The comprehensive approach of the Panel reveals its ambitions and commitment and makes sense for those who aim for the broadest possible protection of the environment. However, one may wonder whether such an open formulation conforms with the axiom that criminal law provisions should be sufficiently precise. This *lex certa* principle, being a corollary of the legality principle (*nullum crimen sine lege*), enables the individual to freely organise his/her own life, without the unexpected interference of the state, and therefore vindicates personal autonomy and protection against public arbitrariness.[52] If ecocide is only defined in terms of the consequences to the environment, without any elucidation of the *actus reus*, it is questionable whether an agent is capable of organising his/her course of action in order to escape punishment. The introduction of a justificatory ground—"social and economic benefits"—adds another layer of uncertainty, as it may not be clear when such benefits would prevail over the concern for the environment.[53]

The quintessential question is whether it is fair that only (representatives of) states and large corporations are exposed to such an uncertain fate—by potentially incurring criminal responsibility for an international crime of ecocide—, while individual consumers are left untouched, although the aggregate of their actions equally contributes to the ecological cataclysm. The hypothesis is that such a skewed division of responsibility would only be justified if the former—major economic and political actors—possess superior knowledge of the detrimental consequences of their actions and/or the latter—the consuming public—would (also) suffer from the harm of ecocide. These configurations imply a power inequality between 'producers' and 'consumers' that, according to the liberal position, warrants a unilateral criminal responsibility of the dominant business partner (see the discussion on criminal responsibility in case of drugs offences in the previous section). The subsequent

[50] For an excellent survey, see Greene 2019, pp. 7–26.

[51] See Falk 1973, p. 21.

[52] For a concise discussion of the roots and elements of the legality principle in criminal law, see Peristeridou 2016, pp. 35–55.

[53] The problem is slightly mitigated by the insertion of the qualifier that the damage must be 'clearly' excessive to social and economic benefits but it still invites a very difficult balancing exercise. Stop Ecocide Foundation 2021, p. 5.

inquiry will focus on climate change as the consequence of greenhouse emissions and will specifically address the issue who or what is/are the victim(s) of this menacing disaster.

The investigation into the question of who or what suffers from climate change should, in my view, distinguish between actual and prospective victims and between humans and non-human species. It cannot be gainsaid that, as this chapter is written, both humans and nature already suffer from the effects of climate change or from man-made ecological disasters that will result in climate change. We need only point at the massive deforestation in the Amazon region that affects indigenous people's rights of subsistence and habitat and forces them to leave their native grounds,[54] the excessive droughts in African countries and the Middle East that threaten small-farmers' livelihoods, and the dramatic rise of the sea-level, menacing the lives of island dwellers in the Pacific.[55] While the Panel's definition of ecocide does not require that humans fall victim, these examples represent fairly easy cases, because both people and nature are affected. Many of these dismal assaults on people and nature involve concrete acts that are the outcome of deliberate corporate or governmental policy and yield tangible harm. It would generally be relatively easy to identify the main culprits, whereas holding consumers that indirectly benefit from these activities criminally responsible would be far-fetched, in view of the ignorance of their causal contribution.[56] Some of the most flagrant human rights violations that coincide with these environmental crimes could even be subsumed under the category of 'crimes against humanity' as they involve killings, forced transfer or persecution. For the prosecution of such mass crimes, the introduction of ecocide as a fifth crime under the jurisdiction of the ICC would therefore be unnecessary.[57]

In respect of the huge consequences of climate change that still are hidden in the future, but will probably affect all life on earth, the (criminal) responsibility is much harder to assess. In substance, they easily meet the standard of being "of concern to the international community as a whole" which is the qualifier for international crimes under the Rome Statute.[58] The Preamble of the Rome Statute elucidates *why* these crimes are of concern to the international community as a whole by pointing out that they "threaten the peace, security and well-being of the world".[59] Although it is a matter of controversy what—and how drastic—the social/political consequences

---

[54] See Ferrante and Fearnside 2021.

[55] Mimura 2013.

[56] We are not talking here, of course, of the moral choice to become a vegetarian or abstain from taking the airplane.

[57] See the complaint that has been filed at the ICC against the Brazilian president Bolsonaro, by the Austrian environmental group AllRise in October 2021, petitioning an investigation into his involvement in crimes against humanity, on account of his alleged destruction of the Amazon rainforest; Profiri 2021.

[58] Compare the Preamble of the Rome Statute, above n. 2, sub (4): '*Affirming* that the most serious crimes of concern to the international community as a whole must not go unpunished and that their effective prosecution must be ensured by taking measures at the national level and by enhancing international cooperation.'

[59] Rome Statute, above n. 2, Preamble, sub (3).

of climate change will be,[60] one could cautiously assert that they probably will fit that description.

However, the quest to find those who are responsible for this awkward—imminent—situation is hampered by the multiplication of—unassociated—perpetrators which inevitably results in dilution of responsibility. Moreover, ecocide in general and climate change in particular are arguably examples of crimes that are 'self-inflicted'. Anastacia Greene has poignantly observed that "climate change is an "ecocide" in the making, but a crime without a criminal. We are all both perpetrator and victim".[61] The rhetorical force of this one-liner predictably invites the objection that some are more responsible and others more victimised. But that is precisely the claim that Greene seeks to dispel. While the producer–consumer dynamic in the context of climate change bears a superficial resemblance to the relationship between contracting parties in the context of illicit drug trade, in the former case the parties are—for several reasons—much more on a par. For one thing, both large corporations and their customers have the uneasy feeling, itching at their conscience, that their transactions aggravate the situation, but the precise scope and seriousness of the consequences largely defy the human imagination. Recent information reveals that oil giant Exxon's scientists already in the 1970s precisely predicted global warming, while the corporation subsequently disguised these findings and made all efforts to discredit urgent warnings of climate scientists.[62] Such advanced privileged knowledge, connoting bad faith to engage in cover-up, clearly strengthens the case for prioritizing the prosecution of corporate representatives. However, in view of the current knowledge of the detrimental effects of carbon emissions for the climate, having become part of the public domain, it does not preclude the co-responsibility of consumers. Secondly, the self-pitying contention that 'the general public' is the victim of an evil conspiracy of large corporations is insincere and hypocritical, because it denies the plain fact that all abstract entities are ultimately composed of human beings. In other words: in the face of apocalyptic disaster, we are all in it together.

The argument that corporations and states have superior—organisational—capacity to address the situation and should therefore be held primarily responsible is admittedly the hardest nut to crack. But even here the postulated power gap between producers and consumers is effaced—or at least narrowed—by the notion of mutual interdependence that is inherent to the market mechanism. The representation of the relationship between producers and consumers as being structurally unequal belittles the autonomy and liberty of the latter in a free market economy. When sufficiently hard-pressed, consumers can join hands and force large petrol producing companies out of business. My interim conclusion would therefore be that the power gap

[60] See, for instance, Buhaug et al. 2010, p. 75.

[61] Greene 2019, p. 34.

[62] Milman 2023. An article in Science has corroborated these findings and asserted that the corporation's knowledge dated back to the 1950s, see Supran et al. 2023.

between producers and consumers is insufficiently large—both in terms of knowledge and capacity—to justify exclusive criminal responsibility of large corporations for the *prospective* consequences of climate change.

Finally, I will briefly pay attention to the question whether environmental degradation that is caused by humans should only qualify as an international crime when human rights and interests are at stake, or whether the environment deserves protection as a self-standing *Rechtsgut*. The issue has divided anthropocentrists and non-anthropocentrists (eco-centrists) and a comprehensive discussion obviously goes beyond the scope of this contribution.[63] However, the topic bears some relevance to the division of responsibility, because both approaches offer different perspectives on the perpetrator victim divide. The eco-centric paradigm locates the antagonism mainly between wasteful humankind and vulnerable nature, while anthropocentrism stresses the contrast between powerful and affluent agents on the one hand and disadvantaged people suffering from environmental degradation on the other hand. While the analogy may sound a little contrived, one could argue that eco-centricism mirrors the money laundering configuration, whereas anthropocentrism is more on a par with drugs offences by portraying human beings as both perpetrators and victims.

It is noteworthy that the Panel has apparently embraced the non-anthropocentric position. In an interview with the Dutch newspaper *De Volkskrant*, renowned author and lawyer Philippe Sands, one of the frontmen of the Expert Panel, avowed his admiration for an essay by Christopher Stone.[64] In a contribution with the telling title 'Should Trees have Standing?', Stone presents the expanding circle of rights holders in the world's history, gradually including women, black people, (unborn) children and corporations (sic!), as a token of increasing human civilization and legal ingenuity.[65] In addressing the question whether the scope of rights holders could be further extended to, for instance, trees and lakes, he refutes the objection that animals, flowers, rivers and seas cannot properly communicate their (legal) interests with the observation that the same holds true for the unborn, senile persons, legal entities and 'the American People'. And he proposes the analogue construction of 'guardianship' as a device to represent non-human species and components of the natural environment before the courts. I must admit that I share Sands' infatuation and I find the line of argument quite convincing. However, I am less optimistic that the Assembly of States Parties will accept the introduction of ecocide as a fifth crime under the Rome Statute, if it also were to include assaults on nature without human casualties. The predominant atmosphere in international (criminal) law is (still) largely anthropocentric.

What is especially interesting for the discussion at hand is that the eco-centric position (implicitly) portrays the environment as being under fire by the agency of both producers and consumers of polluting goods. Rather than exemplifying a (partially) self-inflicted crime, ecocide, in this representation, reflects the paradigm

[63] The eco-centric position is mainly—but not exclusively—defended by moral philosophers, see especially Taylor 2011; Callicott 2014.

[64] Sitalsing 2021.

[65] Stone 1972.

of stealing and receiving stolen goods in which business partners conspire to harm a third party. Obviously, this does not imply that eco-centrists would be insensitive to a further differentiation between consumers, on the basis of contributory fault. Concern for both nature and (disadvantaged) humans would likely prompt them to be in favour of (criminal) responsibility for affluent and well-informed consumers who are also capable of protecting themselves from the most vicious consequences of climate change (at least temporarily). The gist of the issue is that the eco-centric position cannot be reconciled with exclusive criminal responsibility for corporations and state officials.

8.5 Some Final Reflections

While ecocide and the international crimes that are currently under the jurisdiction of the ICC share some common features and may even overlap, it is markedly distinctive in the way and by whom it is committed. Much large scale and irreversible environmental degradation is caused by the daily transactions between producers and consumers, especially if we consider climate change, massive deforestation, decline of biodiversity and pollution of the oceans. Such gradual but very serious disasters would easily meet the definition of ecocide, as proposed by the Panel, because they are (very) severe, widespread *and* long-term.

The pivotal question that was addressed in this chapter is whether it is fair to hold only the providers of consumer goods criminally responsible, while leaving the customers untouched. After due consideration, I find that it is not. I reach that conclusion on the basis of a comparative analysis of other 'criminal' transactions—illicit drug trade and crimes against property/money laundering—in which both parties to the contract incur criminal responsibility. The strongest case for exclusive criminal responsibility for the provider—at least according to the liberal position—can arguably be made for illicit drug trade, both in view of the unequal power relations between the business partners and because penalisation of the drugs consumer smacks of legal paternalism. However, as the hierarchical relations between providers and consumers that are conducive to environmental disasters like climate change are more akin to those within the configuration of money laundering, a distinction in criminal responsibility would not be warranted. A subsidiary argument that sustains the plea for 'shared responsibility' (or none at all) is that both providers and consumers labour under the rather elusive wording of the definition of ecocide, as proposed by the Panel. They are bereft of 'fair notice' whether they will incur criminal responsibility. In other words, their shared predicament in the realm of *mens rea* confirms their parity in ignorance.

I do acknowledge that climate change as an ecocide 'in the making' and the trade in narcotics/money laundering are not entirely comparable, because the latter lack the collective dimension of the former. But the interaction between collectivities in the commercial context results in a balance of power. After all, one might contend that the general public is seduced by 'big business' to purchase consumer goods that destroy the environment. But it is equally true that corporations are under pressure to provide the items that enable the public to lead their life of luxury.

At the end of this chapter, a few caveats are in order. For one thing it bears emphasis that my apprehensions against exclusive criminal responsibility for (representatives of) corporations and state officials should not be interpreted as a plea for prosecution of consumers. I do realize that this would be inconceivable, for practical, political and moral reasons. The argument rather works the other way round: because unilateral responsibility for suppliers of consumer goods would be unfair, neither of the contracting parties should incur responsibility which implies that climate change must remain beyond the ambit of ecocide as an international crime. Secondly, my findings are only meant to be applicable in the realm of structural, global and (largely) imminent ecological disasters, like climate change. I definitely see some room for the introduction of a fifth international crime of ecocide, provided that it relates to concrete environmental disasters, caused by human agency, that resulted in palpable harm to humans, other species and/or the environment.[66] I have no issue with qualifying ecocide as a crime of endangerment, but only in the limited sense that the environmental damage must have been foreseeable for the accused at the time of commission, not that the damage has yet to materialise. The new crime would especially have additional value for the protection of the environment—irrespective of the infringement of human interests—and in that respect I welcome the Panel's ecocentric approach. However, as already suggested above, I find the proposal wanting in the design of the *actus reus*. The current definition of ecocide falls short of the exigencies of criminal law. The Panel would be well-advised to reconsider the draft and identify specific acts that amount to ecocide, in line with the enumerative method that is followed in respect of crimes against humanity, genocide and aggression. The Panel might wish to opt for the open-ended approach that has been followed in the drafting of crimes against humanity.[67] While this strategy is questionable from the perspective of the legality principle, it is probably inevitable in view of the novelty of the crime and the wish to maintain some flexibility in order to address future devices that seriously impair the environment.

Finally, I wish to make clear that I by no means underestimate the seriousness of climate change and comparable forms of global environmental degradation. These are probably the biggest challenges for mankind in the next century in which the survival of the planet may be at stake. I simply wish to point out that criminal law is not the right tool to tackle these structural problems, if it cannot provide a fair

---

[66] An example would arguably be the current proceedings against the Dutch chemical concern Chemours, which has recently been convicted in tort proceedings for dumping poisonous PFAS for decades, which has caused the pollution of soil and groundwater and has severely affected the health of their neighbours. Criminal prosecution of the concern and its management is still under consideration. The elements of 'severe' and 'long term' would certainly be satisfied and the malicious intent of the management can probably be proven, in view of their attempts to cover up both their knowledge and the event. See https://www.parool.nl/nederland/rechtbank-chemours-aansprakelijk-voor-schade-veroorzaakt-door-uitstoot-van-pfas~b95e84ba/. Accessed 20 July 2025.

[67] Article 7, s. 1 (k) of the Rome Statute refers to 'other inhumane acts of a similar character intentionally causing great suffering, or serious injury to body or to mental or physical health'.

solution for the convoluted, shared responsibility of producers and consumers in the case of climate change.

References

Articles, Books and Other Documents

Boister N, Cryer R (2008) The Tokyo International Military Tribunal: A Reappraisal. Oxford University Press, Oxford

Buhaug H, Gletisch NP, Theisen OM (2010) Implications of Climate Change for Armed Conflict. In: Mearns R, Norton A (eds) Social Dimensions of Climate Change: Equity and Vulnerability in a Warming World. World Bank Publications, Washington DC, pp 75–101

Callicott JB (2014) Thinking like a Planet: The Land Ethics and the Earth Ethics. Oxford University Press, Oxford

Cassese A, Gaeta P (2013) Cassese's International Criminal Law. Oxford University Press, Oxford

Cockburn H (2019) Climate change activists who occupied International Criminal Court arrested by Dutch police. https://www.independent.co.uk/climate-change/news/climate-change-protest-extinction-rebellion-international-criminal-court-the-hague-a8872621.html. Accessed 16 January 2023

Falk R (1973) Environmental Warfare and Ecocide: Facts, Appraisal and Proposals. Bulletin of Peace Proposals 4(1):80–96

Feinberg J (1984) The Moral Limits of the Criminal Law, Volume One; Harm to Others. Oxford University Press, New York

Ferrante L, Fearnside P (2021) Brazilian Government violates Indigenous Rights: What could induce a Change? Die Erde 152(3):200–211

Greene A (2019) The Campaign to Make Ecocide an International Crime: Quixotic Quest or Moral Imperative? Fordham Environmental Law Review 30:1–48

Hamilton T, Tiernan M (2022) Who could be held responsible for ecocide under the Rome Statute? Rethinking Secondary Liability for International Crimes. https://rethinkingslic.org/blog/criminal-law/115-%20who-could-be-held-responsible-for-ecocide-under-the-rome-statute. Accessed 23 January 2023

Hardin G (1968) The Tragedy of the Commons. Science New Series 162(3859):1243–1248

Heller KJ (2007) Retreat from Nuremberg: The Leadership Requirement in the Crime of Aggression. European Journal of International Law 18:477–496

Heller KJ (2021) Skeptical Thoughts on the Proposed Crime on "Ecocide" (That Isn't). https://opiniojuris.org/2021/06/23/skeptical-thoughts-on-the-proposed-crime-of-ecocide-that-isnt/. Accessed 16 January 2023

Higgins P (2010) Eradicating Ecocide: Exposing the Corporate and Political Practices Destroying the Planet and Proposing the Laws Needed to Eradicate Ecocide. Shepheard-Walwyn, London

Hunter L, Prakash A (2019) Hardin's oversimplification of population growth. https://doi.org/10.1038/s41893-019-0230-5

Kelk C, De Jong F (2013) Studieboek materieel strafrecht [Textbook Substantive Criminal Law]. Kluwer, Deventer

Kernohan A (1993) Accumulative Harms and the Interpretation of the Harm Principle. Social Theory and Practice 19(1):51–72

Mill JS (1859) On Liberty, https://socialsciences.mcmaster.ca/econ/ugcm/3ll3/mill/liberty.pdf. Accessed 19 January 2023

Milman O (2023) Revealed: Exxon made ' breathtakingly' accurate climate predictions in 1970s and 80s. https://www.theguardian.com/business/2023/jan/12/exxon-climate-change-global-warming-research. Accessed 19 January 2023

Mimura N (2013) Sea-level Rise caused by Climate Change and its Implications for Society. Proceedings of the Japanese Academy, Series B Physical and Biological Sciences 89(7): 281–301
O'Keefe R (2007) International Criminal Law. Oxford University Press, Oxford
Peristeridou C (2016) The Principle of Legality. In: Keiler J, Roef D (eds) Comparative Concepts of Criminal Law. Intersentia, Cambridge/Antwerp/Portland, pp. 35–55
Profiri I (2021) Brazil president accused of 'crimes against humanity' for rainforest destruction. https://www.jurist.org/news/2021/10/environmental-group-announces-icc-suit-against-bolsonaro-for-rainforest-destruction/. Accessed 19 January 2023
Sitalsing S (2021) Rechten voor bomen, zeeën en rivieren: het kan heel goed [Rights for trees, seas and rivers: it is very well possible]. https://www.volkskrant.nl/columns-opinie/rechten-voor-bomen-zeeen-en-rivieren-het-kan-heel-goed~bce21704/. Accessed 19 January 2023
Stone C (1972) Should Trees have Standing? Southern Californian Law Review 45:450–501
Stop Ecocide Foundation (2021) Independent Expert Penal for the Legal Definition of Ecocide, Commentary and Core Text. https://www.stopecocide.earth/legal-definition. Accessed 18 January 2023
Supran G, Rahmstorf S, Oreskes N (2023) Assessing ExxonMobil's global warming projections. Science. https://doi.org/10.1126/science.abk0063
Taylor P (2011) Respect for Nature: A Theory of Environmental Ethics. Princeton University Press, Princeton, New Jersey
The Guardian (2020) World's richest 1% cause double CO2 emissions of poorest 50%, says Oxfam. https://www.theguardian.com/environment/2020/sep/21/worlds-richest-1-cause-double-co2-emissions-of-poorest-50-says-oxfam. Accessed 18 January 2023
Van der Wilt H (2021) Grootschalige Milieuvervuilers voor het Internationale Strafhof: (g)een Schijn van Kans? [Large-scale Polluters of the Environment before the International Criminal Court: Any Chance of Success?] Delikt en Delinkwent 51:263–270
Werle G, Jessberger F (2020) Principles of International Criminal Law. Oxford University Press, Oxford
White R (2017) Carbon Criminals, Ecocide and Climate Justice. In: Holley C, Shearing C (eds) Criminology and the Anthropocene. Routledge, London, pp 50–81

Prof. Harmen van der Wilt is professor emeritus of international criminal law. From 2004 to 2022 he was associated with the Amsterdam Center for International Law, University of Amsterdam. His research interests lie in the concepts of criminal responsibility in International Criminal Law, the nature of international crimes, domestic prosecutions of international crimes, legal reaction to terrorism, history in the courtroom and extradition. He has been a member of the editorial board of the Journal of International Criminal Justice, the Netherlands Yearbook of International Law, the major Dutch journal on criminal law 'Delikt and Delinkwent' and 'Militair Rechtelijk Tijdschrift'. Van der Wilt has been an ad litem Judge in the Criminal Court of Roermond and ad litem judge in the Special Chamber for International Criminal Cooperation in Criminal Matters of the District Court in Amsterdam. He is vice-president of the Antonio Cassese Foundation. His latest publications include 'The Law and Practice of Extradition', Routledge: London/ New York 2022 and L. Yanev and H. van der Wilt (eds.) 'Law and Practice on Universal Jurisdiction over Core International Crimes: Universality without Uniformity', Edward Elgar Publishers 2025 (forthcoming).

Chapter 9
Who Could Be Responsible for Ecocide Under the Rome Statute?

Tomas Hamilton and Marc Tiernan

Contents

Abstract The proposal of the Stop Ecocide Foundation's Independent Panel of Experts to amend the Rome Statute with a crime of ecocide seeks to bring accountability to those who wreak environmental destruction. Yet the definition leaves questions as to which individuals could be held liable. In this chapter, we examine how the modes of liability in Rome Statute Articles 25 and 28 would assign individual responsibility for ecocide. Like genocide, war crimes, crimes against humanity and the crime of aggression, environmental destruction is frequently brought about by the compounding actions of many individuals. The development of international criminal law has taken place in response to this collective nature, with modes of liability that are specifically tailored to address mass action. Using a hypothetical scenario involving the establishment and operation of a coal mine, the chapter assesses how the Rome Statute's liability framework might hold individuals

T. Hamilton
Guernica 37 Chambers, London, UK
e-mail: tomas.hamilton@pm.me

M. Tiernan (✉)
Faculty of Law, University of Amsterdam, Amsterdam, The Netherlands
e-mail: m.b.tiernan@uva.nl

L. Burgers et al. (eds.), *Ecocide: Criminalising Serious Harm against the Environment*, International Criminal Justice Series 38, https://doi.org/10.1007/978-94-6265-715-1_9

responsible for perpetrating, aiding and abetting, failing to prevent and punish, and attempting the crime of ecocide. The chapter offers an opportunity to reflect on the potential scope of the crime of ecocide in its practical application and its adherence to fundamental principles of criminal law. Ultimately, the chapter identifies concerns that the currently proposed definition of ecocide may be too broad and vague, thereby undermining the principle of legality.

Keywords Rome Statute · International Criminal Court · Modes of liability · Ecocide · Criminal law

9.1 Introduction

The destruction of the natural environment is probably one of the most harmful activities ever carried out by humans. Although environmental destruction from mining, forest clearances, pollution and hunting dates back thousands of years,[1] today's massive harm to nature, principally through changes in land and sea use and direct exploitation of organisms, is only accelerating.[2] We also continue to consume vast amounts of fossil fuels at an alarming rate, releasing billions of tons of carbon dioxide and other harmful pollutants on a yearly basis.[3] The question "who is responsible?" can be answered reflexively: we all are. But some are far more responsible than others, and the recognition of our unequal destructive roles is consistent with increasing calls for criminalisation. Identifying who should be criminally liable for environmental destruction requires us to normatively justify the criminalisation of specific acts, untangle collective and ongoing harms, and pinpoint individual responsibility. In this context, the Stop Ecocide Foundation's Independent Expert Panel (IEP) proposed a draft amendment to the International Criminal Court's (ICC) Rome Statute. For this to happen, the Assembly of States Parties to the Rome Statute would need to vote to adopt the amendment by two-thirds majority.[4] The proposal sets out parameters to expand the Court's subject matter jurisdiction, which would determine the range of acts of environmental destruction that could be criminalised. With this proposal

[1] Brahic 2008.

[2] United Nations Sustainable Development 2019: "the assessment's authors have ranked, for the first time at this scale and based on a thorough analysis of the available evidence, the five direct drivers of change in nature with the largest relative global impacts so far. These culprits are, in descending order: (1) changes in land and sea use; (2) direct exploitation of organisms; (3) climate change; (4) pollution and (5) invasive alien species." Concerns over biodiversity loss were reflected in the United Nations Convention on Biological Diversity, opened for signature 5 June 1992, 1760 UNTS 79, entered into force 29 December 1993.

[3] SEI et al. 2023, pp. 4–5.

[4] Rome Statute of the International Criminal Court, opened for signature 17 July 1998, 2187 UNTS 3, entered into force 1 July 2002 (Rome Statute), Article 121(3).

on the table, a new question crops up: "who could be held liable for ecocide if this proposal becomes law?"

The IEP's proposal posits an urgent need to address impunity for severe environmental destruction through the adjudicative mechanism of a(n) (international) tribunal.[5] To that end, the IEP has provided an important benchmark in a much-needed conversation on the possibilities (and limitations) of criminal accountability for serious environmental harms. However, one aspect of the IEP's proposal that has received insignificant attention is the potential scope of individual liability when applied to crimes of ecocide. A thorough assessment of the value and practicality of the IEP's definition however rests not only on discussion of the substantive activities that would be covered, but also requires understanding who could be held liable. Our examination of how liability could be assigned to individuals begins with a look at the collective nature of ecocide. We draw comparisons with other international crimes and identify challenges that arise when assigning liability to individuals for collective acts (Sect. 9.2). Next, we apply the IEP's proposed law to a hypothetical scenario of ecocide involving the creation and operation of a coal mine, in conjunction with the Rome Statute's framework for individual criminal liability set out in its Articles 25 and 28. We consider how different actors in the hypothetical scenario could be held responsible through several modes of liability: perpetration, aiding and abetting, command responsibility, and attempts. This exercise provides an opportunity to assess the law's application in practice, its scope of liability, and its adherence to principles of criminal law (Sect. 9.3). Following this, we identify several aspects of the IEP's proposed definition of ecocide that could render it overly broad and vague (Sect. 9.4). Finally, we offer some brief concluding thoughts on the IEP's proposal (Sect. 9.5).

9.2 The Collective Nature of Ecocide

The IEP did not give specific factual examples of ecocide in the proposal or its accompanying commentary. In an interview subsequent to the publication of the proposal, IEP Co-Chair Philippe Sands KC stated "the authorization, for example, in an industrialized country of a massive new coal field and a massive new coal fired power plant without properly taking into account impacts on the climate system, I think, could arguably come within this definition."[6] While IEP members must have considered other examples of ecocide, we are yet to come across a well-developed analysis of how the ICC's modes of liability, particularly secondary liability, would apply to hypothetical examples of environmental destruction. It seems unworkable,

[5] This urgency has been emphasised in the Vanuatu-led proposal in October 2024 to the Assembly of States Parties that ecocide be formally classified as an international crime. See Harvey 2024.

[6] Surma and Talmazan 2021. Kevin Jon Heller analysed this example, concluding that it was unlikely to fall under the IEP's definition. Heller 2021a.

from the perspective of international criminal law practice, to properly understand what is being proposed by the IEP without engaging in such an analysis.

The most egregious examples of environmental destruction, from changes in land and sea use, to direct exploitation of organisms, to climate change, are best characterised as collective acts.[7] In this sense, environmental destruction often shares similarities with occurrences of traditional international crimes. The Rome Statute crimes are in essence "an expression of collective criminality".[8] The very definitions of these crimes contain overarching contextual requirements, which mean that the conduct for which an individual can be held responsible usually takes place amid attacks, armed conflicts, plans, and policies. In other words, these crimes invariably involve people acting in concert through organisational structures and hierarchies. As such, international criminal law has often faced conceptual problems associated with the attribution of individual action. Lawyers and scholars have long struggled with how to determine criminal liability for international crimes that take place in contexts of mass atrocities, armed conflicts, or systematic violence. To address these difficulties, doctrines of modes of liability have evolved to assign responsibility to individuals acting within collective systems.[9]

Many of these difficulties would arise when attributing liability for ecocide. Based on the IEP's current definition, contributions that collectively lead to a "substantial likelihood of severe and either widespread or long-term damage to the environment being caused by those acts" would be criminalised.[10] Notably, some of the most commonly-mooted instances of ecocide concern the excessive burning of fossil fuels. In such cases, there is a distinctiveness to the relationship between the criminal conduct involved and the harm caused due to the society-wide extent of participation in these activities. The desirability of criminalising a broad range of 'ecocidal conduct' then quickly leads to normative questions about who is causally responsible for the harm that arises from environmental damage committed on such a global scale and accumulated over decades.[11] For example, global warming has arisen from the collective accumulation of uncountably numerous separate instances of fossil fuel use by individuals, whether directly as they sit in traffic jams or switch on their gas-powered central heating, or more indirectly when they switch on electric lights that are powered by coal plants, or much more remotely when they consume products or services with a high carbon footprint. Still, while innumerable individuals have contributed to climate change throughout history, some contributions are calculably much greater than others and more proximate to destructive impacts.

Corporations are among some of the worst offenders of environmental destruction.[12] This further complicates the attribution of liability to individuals for acts of

[7] United Nations Sustainable Development 2019.

[8] Cassese 2007, p. 110.

[9] For a description of ICC modes of liability, see Sect. 9.3.

[10] Stop Ecocide Foundation 2021, Article 8ter(1).

[11] For a thorough and detailed treatment of the variety of ICC prosecutorial issues arising from a broad range of environmental harms, see Gillett 2022.

[12] Watts 2024; Riley 2017.

ecocide. Currently, the ICC framework does not allow for corporate entities to be held liable for crimes.[13] Even where an individual corporate employee is the target of prosecution, it may be difficult to establish the *mens rea* and *actus reus* elements of individual liability in cases of environmental destruction that result from the activities of complex organisational structures. But this issue is not unique to ecocide, nor unique to corporate involvement. International crimes are often carried out by governments, militaries, or non-state actors which have complex organisational structures like those found in large corporations. Moreover, corporate actors have been held liable—in their individual capacity—for past international crimes.[14] German industrialists were prosecuted by the U.S. Military Tribunals in Nuremberg for their participation in Nazi crimes.[15] Domestic courts have also prosecuted businessmen for their contributions to international crimes.[16] While the ICC has yet to prosecute any individual for crimes carried out through corporate activities, there are no legal barriers to doing so *per se*, and such prosecutions may emerge.

Serious environmental destruction can arise from the production and consumption of consumer goods, such as fossil fuels[17] or farm produce.[18] This raises the question of how to distinguish the potential criminal responsibility of those who produce these goods, from those who collectively consume the goods. In this same volume, Harmen van der Wilt argues "that the power gap between producers and consumers is insufficiently large – both in terms of knowledge and capacity - to justify exclusive criminal responsibility of large corporations for the *prospective* consequences of climate change."[19] Put differently, he suggests that criminalising ecocide would imply that both consumers and producers be held liable, criminally, for such environmental destruction. We agree to the extent that there is no principled reason to prevent an individual from being held responsible, even criminally responsible, based merely on their normative status as a consumer. However, in most cases, the level of contribution of individual consumers to major acts of environmental destruction often appears so diminutive as to obviate criminal responsibility (think of the Chief Executive of a beef-producing company involved in illegal logging, versus the owner of fractional shares in the company, versus the purchaser of a single steak). The contributions of individual consumers will infrequently reach the causal threshold necessary to trigger criminal liability, whereas a key individual on the supply side of an industry is more likely to make a much larger and more proximate contribution. Nonetheless, liability will be assessed on a case-by-case basis, requiring a factual analysis of an individual's actions and intent in relation to the crime.

---

[13] "The Court shall have jurisdiction over natural persons pursuant to this Statute." Rome Statute, above n 4, Article 25(1).

[14] Aksenova 2021, pp. 256–258; Huisman and van Sliedregt 2010, pp. 804–805.

[15] Jessberger 2010, pp. 783–802; Kaleck and Saage-Maaß 2010, pp. 701–702.

[16] Huisman and van Sliedregt 2010, pp. 807–815; Sluiter and Yau 2020, pp. 316–324.

[17] Readfearn and Cox 2022.

[18] Phillips et al. 2019.

[19] See Chap. 8 of this volume.

The current IEP definition encompasses a vast range of different acts. Not all punishable occurrences of ecocide under the IEP's proposal will be large-scale collective harms like global warming. Severe and widespread or long-term environmental damage may occur through acts of destruction which fall more clearly into classic forms of attribution, to a military or political leader through a hierarchical group of perpetrators. For example, a state's military attack on a nuclear power plant could cause an environmental disaster qualifying as an act of ecocide.[20] It may be easier to prosecute acts of ecocide where the resulting harm is attributable to a single act or limited number of actors. But if the focus of ecocide prosecutions was centred on less complex attributive pathways, this could leave unpunished the most serious environmental threats, like climate change, ocean pollution, and the destruction of the Amazon rainforest.

The broad scope of the IEP's definition raises an interesting quandary. Where the most serious forms of environmental destruction are causally diffuse in time and space (e.g., global warming), a far greater number of actors will have been involved in contributing to the destruction, and their individual contributions may be more evenly matched (compared to, say, the centralised control that a military commander exerts over troops). Responsibility for the harm must be shared across the actors involved, but "the sharing of responsibility can lead to a diffusion of responsibility that makes it more difficult to determine who is responsible for what."[21] So, for the most serious acts of environmental destruction, prosecutors may struggle to establish the elements necessary to assign liability to any one individual. In that scenario, it may end up being easier to assign liability to less serious acts of environmental destruction with fewer actors involved.

Due to the plethora of potential contributors to the worst instances of ecocide, it is critical to identify which individuals will be implicated by the proposed crime. In view of its broadly-worded scope of liability, there is nothing in the IEP's definition that would limit liability to the actors most responsible for ecocide.[22] This is to an extent true of all other 'core crimes' in the Rome Statute, where the Statute does not conscribe ICC prosecutions to the highest echelons of command (with the exception of the so-called 'leadership requirement' for the crime of aggression).[23] Although sometimes misconstrued in commentary on the ICC, the Rome Statute does not restrict prosecutions to those most responsible, irrespective of prosecutorial policy that may indicate that a particular prosecutor wishes to focus on higher-ranking individuals.[24] It is prosecution policy within the OTP to select cases for investigation and prosecution in light of the gravity of the crimes, the degree of responsibility of the

[20] Ecocide Law Alliance 2022.

[21] Nollkaemper 2018, p. 524.

[22] The IEP's definition requires certain thresholds to be met before acts of environmental destruction trigger liability. This ensures that only serious acts of environmental destruction will be prosecuted. However, as with genocide, crimes against humanity, and war crimes, the IEP's definition does not limit the prosecution of the crime to any specific actors, like those most responsible. See Stop Ecocide Foundation 2021.

[23] Rome Statute, above n 4, Articles 8(*bis*)(1) and 25(3)(*bis*).

[24] Ferdinandusse and Whiting 2021, p. 759.

alleged perpetrators and the potential charges. Such policies are open to change by the Prosecutor of the day.[25] A future Prosecutor may decide to follow a different approach to target-prioritisation that could remain equally consistent with the Rome Statute and regulations.[26] Punishment for genocide, crimes against humanity, and war crimes can therefore be imposed not only on the upper echelons of political, military, and corporate hierarchies, but also on those who make less significant contributions to the crimes.[27] In the absence of limitations to the liability models applicable under Article 25 of the Rome Statute, liability for a crime of ecocide could similarly extend to a vast array of persons with differing levels of involvement in environmental destruction.

So far, we have identified that environmental destruction is often collective in nature and that concerns indeed exist that a crime of ecocide, as currently drafted, could impose criminal liability on a very broad range of actors. But these problems of collective criminality are not unique to ecocide. The fact that numerous individuals may contribute to the crime, while complicated, does not in and of itself pose a barrier to prosecution. To go further, we must consider the ICC's modes of liability.

9.3 Examining the Ecocide Proposal in Light of the ICC's Modes of Liability

A holistic understanding of any law requires consideration of how it would apply in practice. There are at least two gaps in the (already quite expansive) commentary on the IEP's proposal. First, there is a lack of factual hypotheses about the types of conduct that could amount to the crime of ecocide.[28] Second, there is limited discussion as to how Rome Statute Article 25(3) and Article 28 would apply to this crime.

Article 25(3) and Article 28 of the Rome Statute set out the modes of liability that link individuals to crimes based on their level of involvement in the criminality. Article 25(3)(a) provides for doctrines of direct, indirect, and co-perpetration that assign liability to individuals who perpetrate crimes by themselves, through others, or with others. Article 25(3)(b) provides for liability for ordering, soliciting, or inducing the commission of crimes. Articles 25(3)(c) and 25(3)(d) set out secondary modes of liability, including aiding and abetting and contribution to a group's activities. Secondary modes of liability determine whether individuals can be held liable for their complicity in the crimes of others. Article 25(3)(e) prohibits incitement to commit genocide. Article 25(3)(f) describes how individuals can be held liable for

[25] See ICC Office of the Prosecutor 2016.

[26] See Hamilton 2025, sect. 9.6.

[27] Note here the distinction between, on the one hand, the Rome Statute, above n 4, Article 1, reference to "the most serious crimes of international concern", and on the other hand, the issue of who is to be prosecuted for their involvement in those crimes.

[28] With the exception of Heller 2021a.

attempting to commit crimes. Article 28 provides for the responsibility of commanders and other superiors. Military and civilian leaders can be held liable for failing to prevent or punish the crimes of their subordinates.

To examine how the Rome Statute modes of liability could apply, we begin with a hypothetical scenario concerning the operation of a coal mine that we have invented for the purposes of discussion. In this scenario, we consider a company that is authorised to mine an area of land for coal. The company consists of directors, senior management, middle management, and employees. The operation of this mine requires government officials to approve the mining site. Contracted geologists and engineers help to plan and develop the mine's operations. The mining company purchases or rents mining materials, machinery, and other infrastructure to operate the mine. Employees mine coal under the management's supervision. Management reports the mine's activities back to the company's directors. The company sells the coal to a powerplant which burns the coal to produce electricity that is then sold to consumers.[29]

Real-world examples of coal mines share similarities to this hypothesis, including the Aberpergwm mine in the U.K.,[30] the Parsa East and Kante Basan mines in India,[31] and the Narrabri mine in Australia.[32] Undoubtedly, there are many more examples of this kind. In the following sub-sections, we examine how the ICC's liability models of co-perpetration and indirect perpetration, complicity, attempt, and command responsibility might assign liability to the actors in this hypothesis.

9.3.1 Perpetration

The Rome Statute holds individuals criminally responsible for committing crimes through the doctrine of perpetration under Article 25(3)(a). Perpetration occurs when a person "[c]ommits […] a [Rome Statute] crime, whether as an individual, jointly with another or through another person, regardless of whether that other person is criminally responsible." Article 25(3)(a) includes direct perpetration, co-perpetration, indirect perpetration, and indirect co-perpetration forms of liability.[33]

[29] This hypothesis is based on the example provided by IEP Co-Chair Philipe Sands KC. We have chosen to focus on the mining part of Sand's example. See Surma and Talmazan 2021.

[30] BBC 2022.

[31] Cassey 2020.

[32] Readfearn and Cox 2022.

[33] ICC, *Prosecutor v Bosco Ntaganda*, Trial Chamber VI Judgment, 8 July 2019, Case No. ICC-01/04-02/06 (Ntaganda Trial Judgment), paras 771–772. ICC, *Prosecutor v Dominic Ongwen*, Judgment on the appeal of Mr Ongwen against the decision of Trial Chamber IX of 4 February 2021 entitled 'Trial Judgment', 15 December 2022, Case No. ICC-02/04-01/15 A (Ongwen Appeal Judgment) paras 627–630, 635–638.

Perpetrators at the ICC must have control over the crime, that is, the ability to frustrate the crime.[34]

Regarding co-perpetration, the Pre-Trial Chamber in *Lubanga* explained:

> [T]he concept of co-perpetration is originally rooted in the idea that when the sum of the coordinated individual contributions of a plurality of persons results in the realisation of all the objective elements of a crime, any person making a contribution can be held vicariously responsible for the contributions of all the others and, as a result, can be considered as a principal to the whole crime.[35]

According to prevailing ICC jurisprudence, co-perpetration requires that the accused shares a common plan with two or more people to commit a crime and provides an essential contribution to the common plan.[36] The accused must fulfil the mental element for the crime[37] and intentionally provide their essential contribution with awareness that the crime will occur.[38]

As to the indirect form of perpetration, the Trial Chamber explained in *Ongwen* that "[a]n indirect perpetrator controls the persons or persons who execute the material elements of the crime by subjugating their will."[39] An indirect perpetrator can commit a crime through a person or an organisation which they control.[40] The accused must fulfil the mental elements of the crime and be aware of the factual circumstances that give rise to their control over the crime.[41]

According to ICC caselaw, Article 25(3)(a) also provides for indirect co-perpetration liability.[42] The Appeals Chamber found that indirect co-perpetration "constitutes an integrated mode of liability provided for in the Statute that combines the constitutive elements of indirect perpetration and co-perpetration."[43] Indirect co-perpetration occurs when "the objective elements of the crime are executed by other

---

[34] ICC, *Prosecutor v Thomas Lubanga Dyilo*, Judgment on the appeal of Mr Thomas Lubanga Dyilo against his conviction, 1 December 2014, Case No. ICC-01/04-01/06 A5 (Lubanga Appeal Judgment), para 469, 473. ICC, *Prosecutor v Bosco Ntaganda*, Judgment on the appeals of Mr Bosco Ntaganda and the Prosecutor against the decision of Trial Chamber VI of 8 July 2019 entitled 'Judgment', 30 March 2021, Case No. ICC-01/04-02/06 A A2 (Ntaganda Appeals Judgement), para 1041. Ongwen Appeal Judgment, above n 33, paras 629–632, 637–638.

[35] ICC, *Prosecutor v Thomas Lubanga Dyilo*, Decision on the confirmation of charges, 29 January 2007, Case No. ICC-01/04-01/06 (Lubanga Confirmation of Charges), para 326.

[36] ICC, *Prosecutor v Thomas Lubanga Dyilo*, Judgment pursuant to Article 74 of the Statute, 14 March 2012, Case No. ICC-01/04-01/06 (Lubanga Trial Judgment), paras 979–1006. Lubanga Appeal Judgment, above n 34, paras 445, 469, 473.

[37] Rome Statute, above n 4, Article 30; Lubanga Trial Judgment, above n 36, paras 1007, 1012.

[38] Lubanga Confirmation of Charges, above 35, paras 331, 349–355. Lubanga Trial Judgment, above n 36, paras 1007–1012.

[39] ICC, *Prosecutor v Dominic Ongwen*, Trial Judgment, 4 February 2021, Case No. ICC-02/04-01/15 (Ongwen Trial Judgment), para 2783.

[40] Ibid., paras 2783–2784. Ntaganda Trial Judgment, above n 33, paras 777–778. Ongwen Appeal Judgment, above n 33, paras 630–631.

[41] Ongwen Trial Judgment, above n 39, para 2788.

[42] Ntaganda Trial Judgment, above n 33, para 772; Ongwen Appeal Judgment, above n 33, paras 635–636.

[43] Ongwen Appeal Judgment, above n 33, para 636.

persons who are utilized by the co-perpetrators for the commission of the crime."[44] The indirect co-perpetration doctrine, not explicitly provided for in the Rome Statute but developed through the Court's caselaw, remains highly controversial among ICC judges[45] and academics.[46]

To determine who may have perpetrated ecocide in the coal mine hypothesis, we must first identify the *actus reus*, that is, the conduct that caused "a substantial likelihood of severe and either widespread or long-term damage to the environment".[47] Notably, the definition criminalises conduct that creates "a dangerous situation, rather than a particular outcome".[48] Depending on what is considered damage to the environment in the hypothetical mine situation, individuals may have committed ecocide in different ways. The operation of the mine could directly cause significant and long-term environmental damage to a particular area of land or ecosystem through the extraction process or pollution associated with mining activities. Alternatively, coal mining could indirectly contribute to global warming if the coal is sold and later burned as a fossil fuel. This raises two initial questions regarding the definition. What is "the environment"? And does the definition criminalise conduct that indirectly creates a risk of harm? We explore both questions in greater detail in Sect. 9.4, but some initial thoughts are offered here as we work through the hypothesis.

If the harm is construed as damage to the local environment, perhaps stemming from geological damage or waste pollution, it could be argued that those directors and upper management who authorised and operate the mine may have perpetrated or co-perpetrated ecocide. It is not hard to conceive of their direct and essential contributions to the destruction of the local environment around the mine. Alternatively, those who control the mining company might face liability for ecocide as indirect perpetrators based on their control over the mining organisation that carries out the environmental destruction.

If the harm is construed as global warming—a macroscopic dimension of environmental harm to the earth's atmosphere—it will be far more difficult to demonstrate that those same individuals co-perpetrated ecocide. While the coal produced in the mine will undoubtedly contribute to global warming in some way once burned, it will be hard to qualify the mining operation as an essential contribution to global warming for the purpose of imposing liability through doctrines of co-perpetration. Even though the mine might contribute to a substantial risk of global warming in a

---

[44] ICC, *Prosecutor v Dominic Ongwen,* Decision on the Confirmation of Charges, 23 March 2016, Case No. ICC-02/04-01/15 (Ongwen Confirmation of Charges), para 39.

[45] See Ntaganda Appeals Judgment, above n 34, paras 1039–1048. ICC, *Prosecutor v Bosco Ntaganda,* Separate opinion of Judge Luz Del Carmen Ibáñez Carranza on Mr Ntaganda's appeal, 30 March 2021, Document Number ICC-01/04-02/06-2666. ICC, *Prosecutor v Bosco Ntaganda,* Separate opinion of Judge Howard Morrison on Mr Ntaganda's appeal, 30 March 2021, Document Number ICC-01/04-02/06-2666.

[46] Van Sliedregt 2021.

[47] Stop Ecocide Foundation 2021, Article 8ter(1).

[48] Ibid., sect. III. 4.

factual sense, it is unlikely that the mine could frustrate global warming by not operating, making the acts too remote from the large-scale risk of harm to satisfy requirements of legal causation.[49] This is the apparent conundrum of collective contributions to a large-scale environmental atrocity. Criminal law might be ill-suited to holding anyone responsible for minor, yet ultimately accumulative, contributions to massive carbon emissions.

Nedeski and Nollkaemper argue that attribution science offers a solution to the "problem of collective causation".[50] Rather than frame the harm in broad terms, like global warming, we could focus on specific harms which result from carbon emissions. Global warming causes numerous harms, including hotter temperatures, drought, loss of species, sea level rise, floods, extreme weather, and much more.[51] Developments in the field of attribution science could allow us to demonstrate that a company's emissions contributed to a specific environmental harm or risk of harm associated with global warming. For example, it might be possible to attribute a particular heatwave or drought to a company or state's emissions.[52] Criminal law could then consider individuals' contributions to this harm to determine whether liability should arise.

Next, if the harm must be direct, depending on an ICC judicial bench's interpretation of the crime's broad *actus reus* and causation requirements, then the production of coal and its sale to a power plant or consumers might not qualify as an act of ecocide. By producing and selling coal, the mine is unlikely to cause directly risks of harm related to global warming. The power plant would cause the most direct, least remote, risks of harms associated with global warming by burning the fuel to produce electricity and releasing harmful pollutants into the atmosphere.[53] ICC judges might determine that the independent acts of a power plant or consumers break the chain of causation between the acts of those in charge of the mining company and the creation of a risk of harm to the atmosphere. Alternatively, one could examine whether individuals in charge of the mine share a common purpose with those who control the power plant to profit from the extraction and use of coal in a manner that involves harming the atmosphere. In such a scenario, co-perpetration or indirect co-perpetration may be appropriate to assign liability if it can be demonstrated that persons behind the mining activities provided essential contributions to the risk of environmental harm.

---

[49] The co-perpetrator must make an "essential contribution" to the crime for liability to arise. Lubanga Confirmation of Charges, above n 35, para 347. Lubanga Trial Judgment, above n 36, paras 996–999. Lubanga Appeal Judgment, n 34, para 473. ICC, *Prosecutor v Jean-Pierre Bemba Gombo et al.*, Trial Chamber VII Judgment pursuant to Article 74 of the Statute, 19 October 2016, Case No ICC-01/05-01/13 (Bemba et al. Trial Chamber Judgment), para 69.

[50] Nedeski and Nollkaemper 2022.

[51] Causes and Effects of Climate Change, https://www.un.org/en/climatechange/science/causes-effects-climate-change. Accessed 30 April 2024.

[52] Nedeski and Nollkaemper provide the following example, "[f]or instance, thirty-seven per cent of the total increase in likelihood of the Argentinian heatwave in 2013-2014 was attributed to emissions of the member states of the European Union." Nedeski and Nollkaemper 2022.

[53] We discuss the difference between direct and indirect harm requirements below in Sect. 9.4.

Ecocide must involve an unlawful or wanton act under the IEP's definition. We will assume, in the absence of any international laws against coal mining, that the mine was authorised by local government and operates lawfully. Thus, the operation of the mine must be wanton to qualify as ecocide. Wanton is defined as an act undertaken "with reckless disregard for damage which would be clearly excessive in relation to the social and economic benefits anticipated".[54] Whether the mine's operation is wanton will require weighing its social and economic benefits against these environmental harms. The wanton requirement, discussed further in Sect. 9.4, is perhaps the most heavily criticised aspect of the IEP's definition.[55] For the purpose of this exercise, we will assume that the mine's operation is wanton, and that the economic benefits of the coal are outweighed by harms to either the local geological environment or the atmosphere, considering the availability of cleaner, renewable energies.

There is the fundamental issue of whether the co-perpetrators, directors and senior managers of the coal mine project have the requisite *mens rea*. Doctrines of co-perpetration require a 'meeting of minds' over a common plan or purpose to commit crimes.[56] Notably, the IEP proposed "a *mens rea* of recklessness or *dolus eventualis*, requiring awareness of a substantial likelihood of severe and either widespread or long-term damage."[57] As Kai Ambos points out, there are two major issues with this description of the *mens rea*.[58] First, some commentators argue that *dolus eventualis* and recklessness are distinct *mens rea* requirements.[59] Second, the wording in the crime's proposed definition, "*knowledge* that there is a substantial likelihood" (emphasis added), suggests a higher threshold than *dolus eventualis* or recklessness.[60] For the purpose of our analysis, we will proceed with the understanding that *dolus eventualis* is the *mens rea* requirement.[61]

If we consider the development and operation of the mine as acts that could cause environmental damage, any persons who intentionally provide essential contributions to these activities could be held liable as co-perpetrators, provided they have the adequate *mens rea*. While the directors and managers involved in the development and operation of the mine might plan to extract and sell coal with the aim of generating profit, arguably, they will also be well-aware of the substantial likelihood that their activities will cause severe and widespread or long-term environmental damage, either directly to mined land or indirectly to the atmosphere when the coal is burned. The virtual certainty of environmental destruction inherent to the mining process would mean that their plans to operate a coal mine would necessarily encompass these

[54] Stop Ecocide Foundation 2021, Article 8ter(2)(a).

[55] Heller 2021b; Ambos 2021; Robinson 2022, pp. 332, 344.

[56] Kevin Jon Heller identified difficulties with establishing the *mens rea* for ecocide, as well as challenges with the wanton requirement, based on the IEP's proposal. Heller 2021b.

[57] Stop Ecocide Foundation 2021, sect. III.3.

[58] Ambos 2021.

[59] Ibid. See also Fletcher and Ohlin 2005, p. 554.

[60] Ambos 2021. See also Heller 2021b.

[61] Stop Ecocide Foundation 2021, sect. III.3.

criminal results. Those individuals will have the adequate *mens rea* to co-perpetrate ecocide.

9.3.2 Secondary Liability

The Rome Statute includes secondary modes of liability in Articles 25(3)(c) and 25(3)(d). Aiding and abetting under Article 25(3)(c) of the Rome Statute provides for criminal responsibility if an individual "[f]or the purpose of facilitating the commission of such a crime, aids, abets or otherwise assists in its commission or its attempted commission, including providing the means for its commission." Article 25(3)(d) assigns liability for any other contribution to a crime committed by a group acting with a common purpose.

The jurisprudence of the ICC has already begun to wrangle with the outer limits of criminal liability for accomplices.[62] Liability under Article 25(3)(c) arises when an accomplice intentionally provides help or encouragement to a principal crime. While the assistance must contribute to the principal crime in some way, there is some recent ICC caselaw that suggests that the Article 25(3)(c) "does not require the meeting of any specific threshold".[63] The Trial Chamber justified this low causal requirement based on "the enhanced *mens rea* requirement",[64] referred to as the 'purposive intent' requirement. According to the Trial Chamber, the wording of Article 25(3)(c) necessitates "a higher subjective mental element and means that the accessory must have lent his or her assistance with the aim of facilitating the offence."[65]

To trigger liability under 25(3)(d), an accused must provide any other contribution to a group carrying out criminal conduct, with a *mens rea* as low as knowledge of the crimes to which they are contributing under subsection (d)(ii). The wording of Article 25(3)(d), "any other contribution", suggests even minor contributions could trigger liability.[66] But according to Pre-Trial Chamber jurisprudence,

---

[62] Ventura 2019, pp. 208–217. See also Hamilton 2021.

[63] Bemba et al. Trial Chamber Judgment, above n 49, para 93. The Appeals Chamber appeared to confirm that Article 25(3)(c) requires the assistance has some effect on the principal crime but remained silent as to whether this effect must reach a certain threshold. ICC, *Prosecutor v Jean-Pierre Bemba Gombo et al.*, Appeals Chamber Judgment pursuant to Article 74 of the Statute, 8 March 2018, Case No ICC-01/05-01/13 A A2 A3 A4 A5 (Bemba et al. Appeals Judgment), para 1327.

[64] Bemba et al. Trial Chamber Judgment, above n 49, para 95.

[65] Ibid., para 97.

[66] ICC, *Prosecutor v Callixte Mbarushimana*, Judgment on the appeal of the Prosecutor against the decision of Pre-Trial Chamber I of 16 December 2011 entitled "Decision on the confirmation of charges", Separate Opinion of Judge Silvia Fernandez de Gurmendi, 30 May 2012, Case No ICC-01/04-01/10 OA 4 (Mbarushimana, Separate Opinion of Judge de Gurmendi), para 9.

an accomplice must provide a significant contribution to the crime.[67] In a separate opinion in the *Mbarushimana* case, Judge Fernández de Gurmendi disagreed with the Pre-Trial Chamber's establishment of a significant contribution threshold for Article 25(3)(d), recognising the possibility that so-called 'neutral' contributions might trigger liability.[68]

If the mine's destructive extraction processes or pollution constitute ecocide, it is likely that many individuals in our hypothesis will assist the crime. Employees, contractors, and government officials will have all contributed, to varying degrees, to the mine's operation by providing labour, goods, regulatory approval, and other services. These contributions could satisfy the relatively low causal thresholds of 25(3)(c) and 25(3)(d).

Regarding the *mens rea* requirements, at the very least, one could envisage that employees and contractors would intentionally carry out their work and services for the mine. Government officials would have intentionally authorised the mine. It is less clear whether these actors would have either purposive intent, under Article 25(3)(c), or simple knowledge, under Article 25(3)(d), that they are contributing to the crime of ecocide through their actions. Most individuals are aware that coal mines pose inherent environmental risks to local environments. The *mens rea* requirement of knowledge under 25(3)(d) could be established if secondary actors know that they are contributing to mining operations that carry a substantial risk of severe and long-term or widespread harm to the environment, and they are aware that this risk of harm outweighs the mine's potential social or economic benefits.

The purposive intent requirement under Article 25(c) may be more difficult to prove. Employees, contractors, and government officials could argue that they provided assistance for the purpose of pursuing economic or political gains, not the purpose of facilitating ecocide. Still, it would be difficult to separate a person's purpose to facilitate the mining activities, for whatever reason, from his or her purpose to facilitate ecocide if they are aware of the intrinsic risks of environmental destruction associated with the mining extraction process. Framed in this way, it would be likely that employees, contractors, and government officials who aim to facilitate the mining process could satisfy the purposive intent requirement of 25(3)(c).

A more complex question is whether secondary liability could arise for contributions to global warming in our hypothesis. A fundamental aspect of secondary liability at the ICC is its derivative nature.[69] In most atrocity situations, the identification of principal perpetrators is rarely at issue, and prosecution case theories against accomplices are usually clear as to who those individuals were assisting. It is not necessary to convict or even identify the principal perpetrator before convicting an accomplice through secondary modes of liability, but it is necessary to prove that a crime, to which the accomplice contributed, was committed or attempted. Some

---

[67] ICC, *Prosecutor v Callixte Mbarushimana*, Decision on the confirmation of charges, 16 December 2011, Case No ICC-01/04-01/10 (Mbarushimana Confirmation of Charges), paras 282–285.

[68] Mbarushimana, Separate Opinion Judge de Gurmendi, above n 66, paras 11–12. See also Burchard 2010, pp. 919–921.

[69] Van Sliedregt 2012, p. 74.

forms of ecocide could present the possible scenario of 'principal-less' complicity. As discussed in the previous sub-section, it will be difficult, but not impossible, to prove that specific individuals provided essential contributions to large scale environmental harms, like global warming, for the purpose of assigning liability under 25(3)(a).[70] Accordingly, this could raise the challenge of assigning secondary liability for a crime that no one perpetrated.

Secondary modes of liability would perhaps be the most appropriate way of assigning liability for ecocide to individuals who provide indirect contributions that are not essential to the risk of environmental harm. If we were to construe the environmental destruction in the coal mine hypothesis as risks associated with global warming stemming from the burning of fossil fuels, those in charge of the mine might assist the creation of such risks. It may be demonstrable that a mine, particularly a large one, contributed to risks associated with global warming to a degree that would satisfy the relatively low causation requirements under 25(3)(c) or 25(3)(d). The directors and upper management of the mine will likely know that they are contributing to global warming. And considering coal is being sold as fuel that will undoubtedly produce carbon emissions, one could even argue that the mine's higher-ups also provide their assistance for the purpose of facilitating activities that contribute to global warming.

Finally, the contribution to environmental damage made by the consumers who eventually purchase and use the electricity cannot be overlooked. Consumers of fossil fuels are often aware that their actions are contributing to environmental destruction. And indeed, by buying and using the fossil fuel powered electricity, consumers are contributing to some degree to harmful mining activities and global warming. But the actions of the average consumer in our hypothetical scenario are likely to have minimal effects on the environmental damage. It is therefore unlikely that their contributions would qualify even under the low causal requirements of 25(3)(c) or (d).[71]

9.3.3 Command Responsibility

The basis for liability through command responsibility, or superior responsibility, under Article 28 stems from the duty of a leader to reasonably control the acts of those over whom they hold influence. Notably, liability is triggered by an omission, either a failure to prevent or punish.[72] The duties to prevent and punish crimes are distinct from one another. The duty to prevent arises before and during the crime's occurrence, and the duty to punish arises after a crime has been carried out by the subordinates. There is some debate among international criminal law scholars over

[70] See above, Sect. 9.3.1.

[71] See above, Sect. 9.2. We do not rule out the possibility that some consumer activities could reach a threshold to trigger liability, either as a co-perpetrator or, more likely, as an accomplice.

[72] Jackson 2019a, p. 410.

whether command responsibility amounts to some form of derivative liability for the crime committed by the subordinates or whether the doctrine punishes a superior's failure to carry out duties of prevention or punishment as a separate offence.[73] At the ICC, the superior must have effective authority and control over the criminal activities, and the superior must know of or consciously disregard information regarding the crimes.[74]

The doctrine of command responsibility is typically thought-of as a way to hold leaders, usually those in military positions, accountable for their subordinates' misconduct. A CEO or other corporate leader could be held liable through Article 28 for failing to prevent or punish crimes carried out by his or her employees as non-military superiors. Previous international criminal tribunals have established that the doctrine of superior responsibility applies to non-military superiors in commercial positions. A notable instance of a non-military commercial superior being held responsible for the actions of non-military subordinates is the case of Alfred Musema, who was convicted as a superior at the International Criminal Tribunal for Rwanda (ICTR) under Article 6(3) of the ICTR Statute.[75] Musema was the director of the Gisovu Tea Factory during the Rwandan genocide. The ICTR Trial Chamber found that Musema exercised *de jure* and *de facto* authority over the employees of the tea factory, highlighting his legal and financial control over those employees.[76] He was convicted for failing to prevent crimes of extermination and genocide committed by his employees.[77]

In most scenarios that we have considered in our hypothesis above, the doctrine of command responsibility would not be relevant since those at the top of the coal mine are themselves orchestrating the mining operations and the sale of coal. However, it could be the case that a subordinate of a coal mine is responsible for triggering an environmental harm that was not directly ordered by the senior management of the company and perhaps falls outside the mine's regular business operations. By way of example, the doctrine of command responsibility could be relevant if the coal mine employees illegally dump waste causing severe pollution that was not part of the senior management's plans. The question in a case such as this would be whether the senior management could be held criminally responsible for failing to take adequate measures in relation to the actions of their subordinates, the low-ranking coal mine workers.

Other modes of liability, such as indirect perpetration, ordering, aiding and abetting or instigation, would usually be the most appropriate ways to hold senior corporate management responsible for crimes committed through business operations. Nonetheless, there are conceivable crimes that could occur at our hypothetical coal mine that are not orchestrated by senior management but stem from their failure to

[73] Ibid., p. 411.

[74] Rome Statute, above n 4, Article 28.

[75] ICTY, *Prosecutor v Alfred Musema*, Judgment and Sentence, 27 January 2000, Case No. ICTR-96-13-T (Musema Judgment).

[76] Ibid., para 880.

[77] Ibid., paras 899–900, 950–951.

prevent or punish the activities of subordinates, such that command responsibility would be an appropriate mode of liability to charge.

9.3.4 Attempts

The Rome Statute prescribes attempts as an "independent mode of liability" for international crimes.[78] Article 25(3)(f) states that an individual can be held responsible for "[a]ttempts to commit such a crime by taking action that commences its execution by means of a substantial step, but the crime does not occur because of circumstances independent of the person's intentions." Given the nature of attempt, the crime itself does not need to occur.

In *Ongwen*, the ICC Trial Chamber convicted the accused of attempted murder as a crime against humanity and a war crime.[79] According to the Trial Chamber, Dominic Ongwen, through and with the Lord's Resistance Army, committed various acts of violence against civilians at camps for internally displaced persons.[80] Some acts of violence, which included shooting, beating, and burning victims, "represented a substantial step commencing the execution of the crime against humanity and the war crime of murder, whereas the completion of the crime, i.e. the death of the victims, did not occur due to independent circumstances."[81] With regard to the *mens rea*, the Trial Chamber noted that attempt "is characterized by the fact that the perpetrator did not fulfil all objective elements despite his or her intention to do so."[82] The Chamber thus held that "there are no distinctions to be drawn between the mental elements required for [a crime] in its consummated form and those required for its attempted form."[83]

According to the IEP, ecocide is a crime of endangerment.[84] The crime punishes conduct that is substantially likely to cause severe and either widespread or long-term damage to the environment. No actual harm need materialise. This raises a question as to how someone might attempt ecocide. Reading the proposed definition in conjunction with 25(3)(f), individuals could attempt ecocide by taking a substantial step towards creating a substantial risk of severe harm to the environment.

In our hypothesis, acts leading up to the operation of the mine might qualify as acts of ecocide since there is no requirement of actual harm.[85] It is unclear at what point the development of the coal mine would give rise to "the creation of

---

[78] De Hemptinne 2019, p. 351.

[79] Ongwen Trial Judgment, above n 39, para 3116.

[80] Ibid., paras 2881, 2934, 2980.

[81] Ibid., paras 2882, 2935, 2981.

[82] Ibid., para 2699.

[83] Ibid.

[84] Stop Ecocide Foundation 2021, sect. III. 4. See also our discussion below regarding the harm requirement, Sect. 9.4.

[85] Ibid.

a dangerous situation".[86] But whenever this point does occur, the mine's directors and upper management could potentially be prosecuted for committing ecocide. Conceivably then, those same directors and upper management could be prosecuted for attempting ecocide at an even earlier stage of the mine's development where the completion of the crime did not occur due to independent circumstances. Perhaps individuals could attempt ecocide when they purchase land, draw up plans for the mine, or lobby governments to authorise the mine. If such preparatory acts were to constitute a "substantial step" towards the completion of ecocide in the sense of Article 25(3)(f), this would raise the interesting but perhaps concerning scenario of convictions for attempted ecocide in the early stages of planning or preparing potentially environmentally harmful activity. On the one hand, this might offer an innovative way of preventing very harmful environmental destruction long before it occurs. At the same time, liability for attempted ecocide could lead to premature convictions for acts that are far-removed from any actual harm, overextending the application of international criminal law.

Finally, attempt convictions largely rely on the fulfilment of a crime's *mens rea* in the absence of a completed *actus reus*. The proposed *mens rea* for ecocide, "recklessness or *dolus eventualis*",[87] could further extend liability for attempted ecocide.[88] Concerns with imposing liability for attempting endangerment are considered further in Sect. 9.4.

9.3.5 Summary

Our preliminary analysis above suggests that a broad range of corporate behaviour that causes or contributes to serious environmental harms could give rise to liability for ecocide under the Rome Statute's provisions on co-perpetration and accomplice liability. In addition, some modes of liability (viz. superior responsibility and attempts) would be of relevance in narrow circumstances where there is a lack of evidence to prove a superior's contribution to crimes or an inability to establish the completion of the crime.

The coal mine hypothesis reiterates the need to first understand the descriptive question of who could be implicated by the proposed legal provisions in the IEP's text before any definition of ecocide becomes putatively operable as an amendment to the Rome Statute. By exploring the question of who could be liable for ecocide, we can then have a more meaningful and precise discussion on whether this criminalisation is merited at the societal level. Discussions such as this would foster better engagement with the principle of legality, moving away from a more aspirational approach to Rome Statute amendment towards proposals that take heed of the maxim *nulla poena sine lege*. This would also enable State Parties to better assess the stakes of agreeing

[86] Ibid.

[87] Ibid., sect. III. 3.

[88] De Hemptinne 2019, p. 348, fn. 67.

to the definition, and individuals would be able to better understand how to comply with the legal standards that would be imposed on them by a fifth Rome Statute crime.

9.4 Interpreting the Scope of Liability as Per the Terms of the IEP Definition

Our preceding analysis of the modes of liability is, in essence, an attempt (incomplete and preliminary as it is) to understand the likely scope of the IEP's proposed crime of ecocide. We now move to consider three issues that stood out during our analysis of the hypothetical scenario. Underlying these issues is a concern that the definition of ecocide could be impermissibly broad and vague, undermining the principle of legality.[89] Each of the issues, when properly clarified, could alter the range of individuals who would be implicated for the crime.

9.4.1 The Terms "Environment" and "Any Element of the Environment" Lack Specificity

The proposed definition of 'environment' lacks specificity. The crime of ecocide can be triggered by "severe and either widespread or long-term damage" to "any element of the environment".[90] The commentary states that the environment is "the earth, its biosphere, cryosphere, lithosphere, hydrosphere and atmosphere, as well as outer space."[91] The definition suffers from undetermined scalability, and it is unclear how the lines of criminality would be drawn. Depending on what one considers "the environment" or "any element of the environment", different acts could be criminalised by ecocide.

If we consider the environment to mean macro concepts such as "the earth, its biosphere, cryosphere, lithosphere, hydrosphere and atmosphere, as well as outer space", the threshold requirement of "severe and either widespread or long-term damage" becomes extremely high. The world's largest coal mine may only cover a tiny fraction of the lithosphere or be responsible for a fraction of yearly carbon dioxide emissions into the atmosphere. At this scale, it would be difficult to establish that the mine caused the requisite damage to the environment. On the other hand, if ecocide criminalises damage to "any element of the environment", say a forest or

[89] The principle of legality is reflected in Article 22 of the Rome Statute and represents a fundamental rule of international law. It enjoys additional protection under the Rome Statute through Article 21(3). The principle of legality requires that criminal laws are defined with sufficient specificity and provide legal certainty. See Dias 2022, pp. 4–5, 42–43, 48, 160.

[90] Stop Ecocide Foundation 2021, Article 8ter.

[91] Ibid., Article 8ter(2)(e).

animal subspecies, we immediately lower the scope and scale of damage required. Acts such as deforestation or poaching could amount to ecocide. While the threshold requirement of "severe and widespread or long-term damage" attempts to filter out smaller scale acts, this threshold relates only to the damage required. The damage scale is dependent on what constitutes "the environment" or "any element of the environment". It would be much easier to cause "severe and either widespread or long-term damage" to a limited "element of the environment" than a macroscopic understanding of the environment.

So, for example, if a forest ("any element of the environment") that crosses two state boundaries ("widespread") is destroyed ("severe"), or if a small forest ("any element of the environment") is destroyed ("severe") to build a holiday resort ("long term"), then these acts would appear to satisfy the elements of ecocide according to the definition.[92] But these examples of damage are relatively small in comparison to much more grave acts of environmental destruction. By way of a different example, if the object of damage is a much larger part of the environment, like the Pacific Ocean ("any element of the environment"), then immediately the threshold requirements for damage of "severe and either widespread or long-term damage" become much harder to fulfil. The scale of damage required to trigger liability ("severe and either widespread or long-term damage") is relative to the scale of the "element of the environment" that is subjected to the damage.

Without clearer guidance as to what constitutes "the environment" or "any element of the environment" under the IEP definition, it is difficult to predict what acts might amount to ecocide, and who might be liable for them. Indeed, jurists will likely agree that the principle of legality calls for such an enhanced level of definitional precision to comply with fundamental tenets of criminal law theory.

9.4.2 No Actual Harm Is Required

Our second concern is that the definition of ecocide could punish acts that are too remote from any actual environmental harm. This stems from the proposed crime being one of endangerment. As the commentary notes:

> Culpability for the crime of ecocide attaches to the creation of a dangerous situation, rather than to a particular outcome. It is the commission of acts with knowledge of the substantial likelihood that they will cause severe and either widespread or long-term damage that is criminalized. The crime of ecocide is thus formulated as a crime of endangerment rather than of material result.[93]

Thus, the IEP's definition of ecocide does not require the environment to suffer actual harm. This makes ecocide a somewhat blunt tool when it comes to assigning blame.

---

[92] Ibid., Article 8ter. Recall that the crime according to the IEP definition requires one of two alternate elements—either widespread *or* long-term.

[93] Ibid., sect. III. 4.

The crime does not differentiate between culpability for acts that cause harm from acts that do not cause any harm.

Consider two oil tankers that leave a shipyard, and on both ships the captains know that crucial safety procedures have not been followed. Both captains have knowledge of a substantial likelihood that severe and long-term damage could occur. Ship A ruptures causing a catastrophic oil spill. Ship B sails safely to port. Without the requirement for actual harm, both ship captains are equally guilty of ecocide. It is worth considering whether ecocide should recognise a difference between these two ships. Moreover, it can be extremely difficult to predict what constitutes a risk, and incorrect determinations of risks could lead to premature prosecutions. Imagine a third ship, Ship C, that has similar safety issues but is stopped by port authorities just as the captain is about to set sail. Could the captain of Ship C also be prosecuted for creating a risk of harm? Heightened concerns arise when assigning liability for risks through peripheral or inchoate modes of liability under the Rome Statute, like complicity and attempt. According to the current definition of ecocide, individuals could be held liable for assisting the creation of a risk of environmental damage or for attempting to create a risk of environmental damage.

There is also a question of whether the definition of ecocide under the IEP's proposal criminalises indirect endangerment. Secondary modes of liability could give rise to liability for indirect contributions to ecocide, but clarification is needed as to whether the *actus reus* of the crime itself has an indirect causal requirement such that perpetrators could be held liable for causing a risk of indirect harm. To the best of our knowledge, the IEP has yet to clarify whether indirect endangerment would be criminalised under their proposal. The terms "being caused by those acts" in the definition and "will cause" in the commentary suggest that the conduct must directly cause "a substantial likelihood" of environmental damage, i.e., the conduct must create the risk without interventions.[94] But further clarification would be welcome given the open nature of the definition and the broad range of acts that could qualify as the crime's *actus reus*.

The distinction between direct and indirect endangerment could have drastic impacts on the scope of liability.[95] Direct endangerment involves an act that is substantially likely to cause direct damage to the environment without any intervening acts (e.g., operating a coal mine could directly damage the surrounding land), whereas indirect endangerment involves an act that is substantially likely to create a risk that could result in others causing harm (e.g., mining coal could indirectly damage the atmosphere if that coal is later burned by others).[96] Indirect endangerment could significantly expand what acts constitute ecocide and allow for the prosecution of acts that create remote risks of harm. Whether the endangerment can be indirect or direct is also important for determining who could be liable as a perpetrator for ecocide, and for delineating the difference between perpetrators and accomplices.

---

[94] Ibid., Article 8ter(1), sec. III. 4.

[95] Duff 2005, pp. 963–964. See also Cornford 2012, pp. 497–505.

[96] Duff 2005, p. 963.

As the IEP notes in its commentary, there are other international crimes of endangerment.[97] Notably, certain war crimes found in Article 8(2)(b) of the Rome Statute require an attack but no actual harm. The IEP also identifies genocide a crime of endangerment.[98] The IEP argues that making ecocide a crime of endangerment "avoids the problems of having to await materialization of ecological catastrophe."[99] While this concern is justifiable, greater clarity should be provided as to what acts constitute ecocide if it is to be punished as a crime of endangerment. Current crimes of endangerment in the Rome Statute, such as genocide under Article 6 and war crimes found in Article 8(2)(b), clearly stipulate the risk creating acts that can give rise to liability.[100] In contrast, the IEP's definition of ecocide sets out the *actus reus* in very broad terms.[101]

Finally, crimes of endangerment in the Rome Statute require a higher *mens rea* threshold than what is required under the IEP's definition of ecocide. War crimes found in Articles 8(2)(b)(i) to (iii) require "intentionally directing attacks" against civilian and humanitarian personnel and infrastructure. Genocide requires an even higher *mens rea* threshold of specific intent to destroy, in whole or in part, a protected group.[102] By contrast, when it comes to the IEP's definition, "the Panel proposes a *mens rea* of recklessness or *dolus eventualis*, requiring awareness of a substantial likelihood of severe and either widespread or long-term damage."[103] If ecocide is defined as a crime of endangerment, a higher *mens rea* element, in line with Article 30 of the Rome Statute or perhaps incorporating some form of special intent (*dolus specialis*), would better accord with the requirement thresholds of other Rome Statute endangerment crimes. A higher *mens rea* would also negate risks of over-criminalisation where the objective *actus reus* and causation requirements involve the creation of a risk, a comparatively lower objective threshold than actual harm.

9.4.3 The Wanton Requirement May Be Unnecessary

According to the IEP's definition, ecocide involves "unlawful or wanton acts". The requirement provides an "anthropocentric safety valve", preventing the punishment of environmental destruction that benefits humans in some way.[104] As the IEP notes in

[97] Stop Ecocide Foundation 2021, sect. III 4.

[98] Ibid.

[99] Robinson 2022, p. 332.

[100] The IEP notes that genocide does not require the actual destruction, in whole or in part, of a protected group. They describe this as endangerment. The acts which constitute genocide are very clearly set out in the Rome Statute. This provides greater clarity as to what acts risking genocide can trigger liability. Stop Ecocide Foundation 2021, Sect. III 4.

[101] See also Chap. 6 in this volume.

[102] Rome Statute, above n 4, Article 6.

[103] Stop Ecocide Foundation 2021, sect. 3. Above, in Sect. 9.3.1, we highlight concerns that the IEP's *mens rea* threshold lacks clarity.

[104] Heller 2021b.

its commentary, the requirement ensures that ecocide will only criminalise "damage to the environment which would be clearly excessive in relation to the social and economic benefits anticipated."[105] The IEP describes the wanton requirement as "a proportionality test" that balances environmental harms against social and economic benefits.[106] Some scholars favour a more ecocentric approach, criticising the IEP's definition for failing to value the environment as an end in itself.[107]

The wanton requirement raises an interesting question regarding the purpose and scope of criminal liability for ecocide. The IEP's definition includes gravity thresholds (like severe, widespread, and long-term) to ensure that only serious acts of environmental destruction are criminalised.[108] The inclusion of a wanton element suggests that liability for ecocide is not assigned for the purpose of protecting the environment in and of itself. Rather, liability is assigned to those who carry out environmentally destructive acts that fail to provide proportionate economic and social benefits.

The possibility to evade liability under the IEP's definition by demonstrating acts were carried out for economic benefits raises particular concerns. No other international crime can be justified based on economic benefits. The normative seriousness of international crimes does not comport with a special liability exemption based on economic justifications for the harm. Moreover, the wanton requirement may unequally protect those individuals who can demonstrate that their activities produce economic benefits. Economic value can be based on dynamics that are inherently discriminatory and unfair, and it does not always signify societal value or worth. Of course, the wanton requirement necessitates weighing "economic and social benefits", with the conjunctive "and" in the Commentary suggesting both factors must be considered together.[109] Economic benefits alone may not be enough to justify environmental destruction under the IEP definition. Still, concerns remain as to how economic factors will be weighed in the wanton balancing exercise and how dissonance between economic and social benefits will be resolved.

Safety mechanisms already exist under international criminal law to protect against the prosecution of virtuous or necessary acts which, technically, qualify as criminal acts.[110] The defence, or justification, of necessity is well-established in domestic jurisdictions and permits individuals to carry out conduct which is necessary to prevent death or serious harm. Article 31(d) of the Rome Statute excludes liability for:

> conduct which is alleged to constitute a crime within the jurisdiction of the Court that has been caused by duress resulting from a threat of imminent death or of continuing or imminent serious bodily harm against that person or another person, and the person acts necessarily

---

[105] Stop Ecocide Foundation 2021, sect. 2.b.ii.

[106] Ibid.

[107] See, e.g., also Chap. 6 of this volume.

[108] Although, as noted above, we have concerns with the current construction of these thresholds in the IEP's definition.

[109] Stop Ecocide Foundation 2021, sect. 2.b.ii.

[110] Jackson 2019b, p. 835.

> and reasonably to avoid this threat, provided that the person does not intend to cause a greater harm than the one sought to be avoided. The threat may arise from other persons or uncontrollable circumstances.

As Jackson notes, Article 31(d) appears to exclude criminal responsibility for acts which are justified as necessary.[111] If it is necessary to produce and burn some fossil fuels to ensure essential societal functions, then such acts could likely be justified under Article 31(d) and non-punishable as ecocide.[112]

Understandably, the defence of necessity only applies to a very narrow set of situations under international criminal law, and indeed the threshold of what qualifies as necessary to prevent harm or death is extremely high. Still, as a pre-existing and well-established legal concept, the defence of necessity could address situations where other interests justify carrying out environmental destruction. And while a defence of necessity sets a high bar, it is broader in the sense that it is not restricted to only economic and social interests. The defence of necessity also offers an interesting lens to consider the IEP's definition of ecocide as an international crime. One might ask whether the wanton element is necessary when the defence of necessity could prevent undesirable convictions? If ecocide is serious enough to qualify as an international crime, should individuals who can demonstrate social and economic benefits be exempt from liability? Or should the environment only be destroyed when completely necessary?

Arguably, the discussion here points towards a larger issue with the definition of ecocide. It is too broad. Understandably, there are many legal harms that are not criminalised on the basis that the benefits of criminalisation are outweighed by costs of criminalisation. But rarely are broad harms criminalised with exceptions to limit the potential costs of criminalisation in the definition of a crime. Criminal courts are not optimal venues to weigh the costs and benefits of activities that risk causing environmental destruction. Environmental crimes in domestic jurisdictions are normally defined as specific acts which have been predetermined to cause greater harm than good—e.g., illegal fishing or illegal dumping. These laws recognise the permissibility of environmental destruction in some contexts and punish failures to carry out the harm within the parameters of what has been sanctioned. Arguably, this construction of criminalisation provides greater certainty than the IEP's approach and upholds fair labelling.

[111] Ibid., pp. 828, 829.

[112] Jackson provides and analyses the example of "a humanitarian agency that provides safe transport for a population that is being deported from occupied territory in an international armed conflict—the deportation constituting a war crime." He argues that the humanitarian workers will not be liable for assisting the terrorist organization's crime of forced deportation on the basis that they acted justifiably to protect the civilians' lives from danger. Jackson 2019b, pp. 819, 827–829.

9.5 Conclusion

Underlying the concerns highlighted in this chapter is a lack of clarity as to how ecocide will apply in practice and to whom it will apply. The current definition proposed by the IEP does not sit well with the principle of legality, particularly the principle of specificity. Criminal laws should be sufficiently precise to guide behaviour and put potential defendants on notice as to which acts are indeed criminal. Moreover, the over-broadness and lack of clarity in the current definition proposed by the IEP may lead to over-criminalisation. That is, the definition may lead to over-inclusivity of actors who are unworthy of criminal punishment.[113] Liability for an international crime is a very serious matter, and it should not be imposed on individuals without careful justification.

Of course, the definition is likely to develop over time through expert input, and it could be made more specific. Belgium recently adopted a new law criminalising ecocide, albeit in a much narrower sense than the IEP's definition.[114] Notably, the Belgian definition criminalises unlawful acts (not wanton acts) that cause "serious, widespread *and* long-term damage to the environment" (emphasis added), with a mental requirement of knowledge rather than *dolus eventualis*.[115] Without commenting on the merits of the Belgian definition of ecocide (it is arguably too narrow), the approach there suggests that governments may find the IEP's definition too broad to enact domestically, instead opting for more limited definitions.

We are not the first to recognise that the harms of severe environmental destruction require urgent attention, posing perhaps a greater existential threat to humanity and nature than any of the existing core international crimes. There is no doubt that in realising the normative aims of the project to criminalise ecocide, a vast toolkit of national and international legal mechanisms could be deployed. The Rome Statute is one such tool, offering the potential for distinctive, symbolic prosecutions that could contribute to the deterrence and punishment of the most serious forms of environmental harm. The IEP's initiative has kindled an evolving discussion about how to extend international criminal law to provide meaningful protection against environmental harm. Yet there are significant hurdles in criminal law theory and practice that would need to be addressed before the IEP's definition could be workable in actual cases. Our aim through this chapter has been to contribute to refining the definition, in a constructive way, so that one day, the Assembly of States Parties may adopt ecocide as an amendment to the Rome Statute.

Acknowledgements The authors presented earlier versions of this work at a panel event organised by the Sustainable Global Economic Law Centre on 8 October 2021 and an event organised by the Rethinking Secondary Liability for International Crimes project on 13 December 2021. Both events were held at the University of Amsterdam. The authors are thankful for the valuable feedback

[113] For discussion regarding the risks of over-criminalisation, see Husak 2009.

[114] Savard 2024.

[115] Ibid. Heller 2022.

they received during these events. The authors would also like to thank the book's editors and Kate Mackintosh for their valuable feedback and comments on previous drafts, and Ava Schuster for her helpful comments and assistance formatting the chapter.

Postscript This chapter was drafted prior to the publication of the Manual for a National Criminalisation of Ecocide by the Working Group on the National Criminalisation of Ecocide in partnership with Ecocide Law Advisory on 12 February 2025. The authors are pleased to note that some concerns and recommendations they raised in this chapter and elsewhere are also reflected in the Manual. See https://www.promiseeurope.law.ucla.edu/working-group.

References

Articles, Books and Other Documents

Aksenova M (2021) Corporate Complicity in International Criminal Law: Potential Responsibility of European Arms Dealers for Crimes Committed in Yemen. Washington International Law Journal 30(2):255–284

Ambos K (2021) Protecting the Environment through International Criminal Law. https://www.ejiltalk.org/protecting-the-environment-through-international-criminal-law. Accessed 23 April 2024

BBC (2022) Coal: Aberpergwm colliery gets OK to mine 40 million tonnes. https://www.bbc.com/news/uk-wales-politics-60147423. Accessed 17 June 2024

Brahic C (2008) The five oldest acts of environmental destruction. https://www.newscientist.com/article/dn15102-the-five-oldest-acts-of-environmental-destruction. Accessed 22 April 2022

Burchard C (2010) Ancillary and Neutral Business Contributions to 'Corporate–Political Core Crime': Initial Enquiries Concerning the Rome Statute. Journal of International Criminal Justice 8(3):919–946

Cassese A (2007) The Proper Limits of Individual Responsibility under the Doctrine of Joint Criminal Enterprise. Journal of International Criminal Justice 5(1):109–133

Cassey B (2020) India's ancient tribes battle to save their forest home from mining. https://www.theguardian.com/environment/2020/feb/10/indias-ancient-tribes-battle-to-save-their-forest-home-from-mining. Accessed 17 June 2024

Cornford A (2012) Indirect crimes. Law and Philosophy 32(4):485–514

De Hemptinne J (2019) Attempt. In: de Hemptinne J, Roth R, van Sliedregt E, Gal T, Roseen D, Van Poecke T, Cupido M, Ventura MJ, Yanev L (eds) Modes of Liability in International Criminal Law, 1st edn. Cambridge University Press, Cambridge, pp 339–354

Dias T (2022) Beyond Imperfect Justice – Legality and Fair Labeling in International Criminal Law. Brill-Nijhoff, Leiden

Duff AR (2005) Criminalizing Endangerment. In: Duff AR, Green S (eds) Defining Crimes: Essays on The Special Part of the Criminal Law, 1st edn. Oxford University Press, Oxford, pp 43–64

Ecocide Law Alliance (2022) Ukraine to prosecute Russia for ecocide following attack on Europe's largest nuclear power plant. https://www.ecocidelawalliance.org/ukraine-to-prosecute-russia-for-ecocide-following-attack-on-europes-largest-nuclear-power-plant/. Accessed 17 June 2024

Ferdinandusse W, Whiting A (2021) Prosecute little fish at the ICC. Journal of International Criminal Justice 19(4):759–781

Fletcher GF, Ohlin JD (2005) Reclaiming Fundamental Principles of Criminal Law in the Darfur Case. Journal of International Criminal Justice 3(3):539–561

Gillett M (2022) Prosecuting Environmental Harm Before the International Criminal Court. Cambridge University Press, Cambridge

Hamilton T (2021) An Arms Trade Case at the International Criminal Court: Would the Article 25(3)(c) 'purpose' requirement really matter? https://rethinkingslic.org/blog/criminal-law/93-an-arms-trade-case-at-the-international-criminal-court-would-the-article-25-3-c-purpose-requirement-really-matter. Accessed 17 June 2024

Hamilton T (2025) The Arms Trade and International Criminal Law. Oxford University Press, Oxford

Harvey F (2024) https://www.theguardian.com/law/article/2024/sep/09/pacific-islands-ecocide-crime-icc-proposal. Accessed 9 February 2025

Heller KJ (2021a) The Crime of Ecocide in Action. https://opiniojuris.org/2021/06/28/the-crime-of-ecocide-in-action/. Accessed 24 April 2024

Heller KJ (2021b) Skeptical Thoughts on the Proposed Crime of "Ecocide" (That Isn't). https://opiniojuris.org/2021/06/23/skeptical-thoughts-on-the-proposed-crime-of-ecocide-that-isnt. Accessed 17 June 2024

Heller KJ (2022) Belgium Set to Criminalise Ecocide (Kinda Sorta). https://opiniojuris.org/2022/11/08/belgium-set-to-criminalise-ecocide-kinda-sorta/. Accessed 17 June 2024

Huisman W, van Sliedregt E (2010) Rogue Traders: Dutch Businessmen, International Crimes and Corporate Complicity. Journal of International Criminal Justice 8(3):803–828

Husak D (2009) Overcriminalization: The Limits of the Criminal Law. New Criminal Law Review 12(2):237–240

ICC Office of the Prosecutor (2016) Policy paper on case selection and prioritisation. https://www.icc-cpi.int/sites/default/files/itemsDocuments/20160915_OTP-Policy_Case-Selection_Eng.pdf. Accessed 12 February 2025

Jackson M (2019a) Command Responsibility. In: de Hemptinne J, Roth R, van Sliedregt E, Gal T, Roseen D, Van Poecke T, Cupido M, Ventura MJ, Yanev L (eds) Modes of Liability in International Criminal Law, 1st edn. Cambridge University Press, Cambridge, pp 409–432

Jackson M (2019b) Virtuous Accomplices in International Criminal Law. International and Comparative Law Quarterly 68(4):817–835

Jessberger F (2010) On the Origins of Individual Criminal Responsibility under International Law for Business Activity: IG Farben on Trial. Journal of International Criminal Justice 8(3):783–802

Kaleck W, Saage-Maaß M (2010) Corporate Accountability for Human Rights Violations Amounting to International Crimes: The Status Quo and its Challenges. Journal of International Criminal Justice 8(3):699–724

Nedeski N, Nollkaemper A (2022) A guide to tackling the collective causation problem in international climate change litigation. https://www.ejiltalk.org/a-guide-to-tackling-the-collective-causation-problem-in-international-climate-change-litigation/. Accessed 30 April

Nollkaemper A (2018) The duality of shared responsibility. Contemporary Politics 24(5):524–544

Phillips D, Camargos D, Campos A, Wasley A, Heal A (2019) Revealed: rampant deforestation of Amazon driven by global greed for meat. https://www.theguardian.com/environment/2019/jul/02/revealed-amazon-deforestation-driven-global-greed-meat-brazil. Accessed 17 June 2024

Readfearn G, Cox L (2022) Narrabri mine expansion would make it dirtiest thermal coalmine in Australia, environmentalists say. https://www.theguardian.com/environment/2022/feb/14/narrabri-mine-expansion-would-make-it-dirtiest-thermal-coalmine-in-australia-environmentalists-say. Accessed 17 June 2024

Riley T (2017) Just 100 companies responsible for 71% of global emissions, study says. https://www.theguardian.com/sustainable-business/2017/jul/10/100-fossil-fuel-companies-investors-responsible-71-global-emissions-cdp-study-climate-change. Accessed 17 June 2024

Robinson D (2022) Ecocide - Puzzles and Possibilities. Journal of International Criminal Justice 20(2):313–347

Savard C (2024) Belgium Recognizes the Crime of Ecocide: A (Lukewarm) European First. https://ohrh.law.ox.ac.uk/belgium-recognises-the-crime-of-ecocide-a-lukewarm-european-first/#:~:text=Article%2094%20of%20Belgium's%20new,an%20infringement%20of%20federal%20legislation. Accessed 27 June 2024

SEI, Climate Analytics, E3G, IISD, UNEP (2023) Production Gap Report: Phasing down or phasing up? https://www.sei.org/publications/production-gap-report-2023/. Accessed 21 July 2025

Sluiter G, Yau S (2020) Aiding and Abetting and Causation in the Commission of International Crimes – The Cases of Dutch Businessmen Van Anraat and Kouwenhoven. In: Jørgensen NHB (ed) The International Criminal Responsibility of War's Funders and Profiteers, 1st edn. Cambridge University Press, Cambridge, pp 304–328

Stop Ecocide Foundation (2021) Independent Expert Panel for the Legal Definition of Ecocide: Commentary and Core Text. https://www.stopecocide.earth/legal-definition. Accessed 21 July 2025

Surma K, Talmazan Y (2021) In a Growing Campaign to Criminalize Widespread Environmental Destruction, Legal Experts Define a New Global Crime: "Ecocide". https://insideclimatenews.org/news/22062021/ecocide-definition-panel-international-crime. Accessed 22 April 2023

United Nations Sustainable Development (2019) UN Report: Nature's Dangerous Decline 'Unprecedented'; Species Extinction Rates 'Accelerating'. https://www.un.org/sustainabledevelopment/blog/2019/05/nature-decline-unprecedented-report/. Accessed 22 April 2022

Van Sliedregt E (2012) Individual Criminal Responsibility in International Law. Cambridge University Press, Cambridge.

Van Sliedregt E (2021) The ICC Ntaganda Appeals Judgment: The End of Indirect Co-perpetration? https://www.justsecurity.org/76136/the-icc-ntaganda-appeals-judgment-the-end-of-indirect-co-perpetration/. Accessed 5 April 2023

Ventura MJ (2019) Aiding and Abetting. In: de Hemptinne J, Roth R, van Sliedregt E, Gal T, Roseen D, Van Poecke T, Cupido M, Ventura MJ, Yanev L (eds) Modes of Liability in International Criminal Law, 1st edn. Cambridge University Press, Cambridge, pp 173–256

Watts J (2024) Just 57 companies linked to 80% of greenhouse gas emissions since 2016. https://www.theguardian.com/environment/2024/apr/04/just-57-companies-linked-to-80-of-greenhouse-gas-emissions-since-2016. Accessed 26 June 2024

Treaties, Cases and Other Legal Documents

ICC, *Prosecutor v Bosco Ntaganda,* Separate opinion of Judge Howard Morrison on Mr Ntaganda's appeal, 30 March 2021, Document Number ICC-01/04-02/06-2666

ICC, *Prosecutor v Bosco Ntaganda,* Separate opinion of Judge Luz Del Carmen Ibáñez Carranza on Mr Ntaganda's appeal, 30 March 2021, Document Number ICC-01/04-02/06-2666

ICC, *Prosecutor v Bosco Ntaganda,* Judgment on the appeals of Mr Bosco Ntaganda and the Prosecutor against the decision of Trial Chamber VI of 8 July 2019 entitled 'Judgment', 30 March 2021, Case No. ICC-01/04-02/06 A A2

ICC, *Prosecutor v Bosco Ntaganda*, Trial Chamber VI Judgment, 8 July 2019, Case No. ICC-01/04-02/06

ICC, *Prosecutor v Callixte Mbarushimana*, Decision on the confirmation of charges, 16 December 2011, Case No ICC-01/04-01/10

ICC, *Prosecutor v Callixte Mbarushimana*, Judgment on the appeal of the Prosecutor against the decision of Pre-Trial Chamber I of 16 December 2011 entitled "Decision on the confirmation of charges," Separate Opinion of Judge Silvia Fernandez de Gurmendi, 30 May 2012, Case No ICC-01/04-01/10 OA 4

ICC, *Prosecutor v Dominic Ongwen*, Decision on the Confirmation of Charges, 23 March 2016, Case No ICC-02/04-01/15

ICC, *Prosecutor v Dominic Ongwen*, Judgment on the appeal of Mr Ongwen against the decision of Trial Chamber IX of 4 February 2021 entitled 'Trial Judgment', 15 December 2022, Case No. ICC-02/04-01/15 A

ICC, *Prosecutor v Dominic Ongwen*, Trial Judgment, 4 February 2021, Case No ICC-02/04-01/15

ICC, *Prosecutor v Jean-Pierre Bemba Gombo et al.*, Appeals Chamber Judgment pursuant to Article 74 of the Statute, 8 March 2018, Case No ICC-01/05-01/13 A A2 A3 A4 A5

ICC, *Prosecutor v Jean-Pierre Bemba Gombo et al.*, Trial Chamber VII Judgment pursuant to Article 74 of the Statute, 19 October 2016, Case No ICC-01/05-01/13

ICC, *Prosecutor v Thomas Lubanga Dyilo*, Decision on the confirmation of charges, 29 January 2007, Case No ICC-01/04-01/06

ICC, *Prosecutor v Thomas Lubanga Dyilo*, Judgment on the appeal of Mr Thomas Lubanga Dyilo against his conviction, 1 December 2014, Case No ICC-01/04-01/06 A 5

ICC, *Prosecutor v Thomas Lubanga Dyilo*, Judgment pursuant to Article 74 of the Statute, 14 March 2012, Case No ICC-01/04-01/06

ICTY, *Prosecutor v Alfred Musema*, Judgment and Sentence, 27 January 2000, Case No. ICTR-96-13-T

Rome Statute of the International Criminal Court, opened for signature 17 July 1998, 2187 UNTS 3, entered into force 1 July 2002

United Nations Convention on Biological Diversity, opened for signature 5 June 1992, 1760 UNTS 79, entered into force 29 December 1993

Dr. Tomas Hamilton is a Barrister at Guernica 37 Chambers specialising in international criminal and human rights law. With expertise in corporate accountability, Tomas has worked on arms trade cases and on environmental issues concerning the development of ecocide as a potential crime in English law. He was previously assistant professor in international criminal law at the University of Amsterdam on the Steering Board of the project Rethinking Secondary Liability for International Crimes (funded by the Dutch Organization for Scientific Research, NWO).

Marc Tiernan is a lecturer in international criminal law at the University of Amsterdam. He is currently completing his PhD as part of the project Rethinking Secondary Liability for International Crimes (funded by the Dutch Organization for Scientific Research, NWO). He previously worked as a legal consultant with defence teams at the Extraordinary Chambers in the Courts of Cambodia.

Chapter 10
Ecocide: The Environment as Victim at the International Criminal Court

Giovanna Maria Frisso

Contents

Abstract One of the most innovative provisions of the Rome Statute of the International Criminal Court (ICC) concerns victims' rights to participate in the proceedings and to have the harm suffered repaired. The definition of ecocide proposed by the Independent Expert Panel (IEP) convened by the Stop Ecocide Foundation aims to protect the environment as an end in itself. As such, the definition seems to acknowledge the victimisation of nonhumans. Bringing to the fore the different meanings associated with the term victim in the ICC, including the different interpretations of the criteria provided for by the definition of the term victim under Rule 85 of the ICC Rules of Procedure and Evidence (RPE), this chapter argues that the existing legal framework allows for the recognition of nonhumans as victims of ecocide.

Keywords Ecocide · Environment · Victimisation · International Criminal Court · Rules of Procedure and Evidence · Victim

---

G. M. Frisso (✉)
University of Lincoln, Lincoln, UK
e-mail: GFrisso@lincoln.ac.uk

L. Burgers et al. (eds.), *Ecocide: Criminalising Serious Harm against the Environment*, International Criminal Justice Series 38, https://doi.org/10.1007/978-94-6265-715-1_10

10.1 Introduction

In 2016, the Office of the Prosecutor (OTP) of the International Criminal Court (ICC) published a Policy Paper on Case Selection and Prioritisation, indicating its intent to consider crimes committed through, or resulting in, "the destruction of the environment, the illegal exploitation of natural resources or the illegal dispossession of land".[1] The reference to the environment in the Policy Paper revitalised the debates about the international criminalisation of environmental destruction.[2] A few years later, in 2020, the Stop Ecocide Foundation convened an Independent Expert Panel for the Legal Definition of Ecocide (IEP). The definition was presented as a starting point for the consideration of an amendment to the Statute of the ICC (Rome Statute).[3] Whilst it still remains uncertain whether the IEP proposal will result in an amendment to the Rome Statute,[4] it has certainly promoted the debate concerning the prosecution of environmental damage in the ICC. In this regard, in 2024 the Prosecutor of the ICC, acknowledging that "damage to the environment poses an existential threat to all life on the planet",[5] has called for input to shape a new policy initiative to advance accountability for environmental crimes under the Rome Statute.[6]

Within this overall context, this chapter focuses on the potential recognition of victims of environmental crimes within the ICC. As explained by White, three different levels of victimisation in light of environmental harm can be identified: environmental justice (where the victims are humans); ecological justice (where the victims are specific environments), and species justice (where the victims are animals and plants).[7] Whilst White's levels of victimisation remains silent towards specific victims, such as human and non-human communities or future generations,[8] it introduces the diffuse ramifications of environmental harm into the discussion of environmental victimisation, bringing to our attention the harm suffered by nonhumans. The extent to which we focus on human victims of environmental harm, specific environments, communities or animals and plants reflects, to a certain degree, our ability to recognise that "'matter matters' or, put differently, (…) that entanglements of the

---

[1] Office of the Prosecutor of the International Criminal Court (ICC) 2016, para 41.

[2] Pereira 2020, p. 179.

[3] Previous efforts to criminalise offences against the environment and to define ecocide have been undertaken. See Falk 1973, p. 80; Gray 1996, p. 215; Higgins 2012, p. 9; Higgins et al. 2013, p. 251; Gaujer et al. 2012. The proposal to include a new crime to the jurisdiction of the ICC has been related to the declaratory impact and potential deterrent effect of any resulting conviction. As explained by Gillett, using "genocide and crimes against humanity to substitute for the direct prosecution of environmental harm would not signal the international community's condemnation of environmental harm itself". Gillett 2017, p. 227.

[4] See, for instance, Castellos 2024.

[5] Office of the Prosecutor of the ICC 2024.

[6] Ibid.

[7] White 2018, p. 244.

[8] Some of the limits of White's categorisation have been brought to my attention in an earlier version of this chapter by Laura Burgers. Regarding human communities and future generations, see Sknnider 2011, pp. 36, 38.

human and the nonhuman, of organic and inorganic matter, are deeply enmeshed in the interdependent web of life".[9]

Even though the recognition of humans as environmental victims still raises various issues,[10] this chapter will focus on the potential recognition of nonhumans as environmental victims by the ICC.[11] Despite debates concerning the adequacy of the IEP definition,[12] this chapter will rely on it, as a working definition, to illustrate some of the challenges related to the recognition of the environment as a victim before the ICC. In other words, this chapter will consider whether nonhumans can, within the existing legal framework of the ICC, be considered victims of "unlawful or wanton acts committed with knowledge that there is a substantial likelihood of severe and either widespread or long-term damage to the environment being caused by those acts".[13]

Whilst the separation between nonhumans and humans can be considered artificial within an ecocentric approach,[14] the distinction is adopted in this chapter to highlight the challenges related to the articulation of the intrinsic value of nonhumans and the due consideration of the complexity of ecological relationships within international criminal law.[15] In this perspective, the term 'environment' is hereby used to refer to biotic (plants, animals, bacteria, fungi) and abiotic components (air, water, soil) and their interactions. Due to the anthropocentric foundations of our existing legal system,[16] including international environmental law,[17] an analysis solely grounded in the prevailing jurisprudence limits our ability to acknowledge the environment as a victim on its own right. Therefore, this chapter originally examines the interpretation of existing legal categories in light of insights from green criminology and critical theory to advance the discussion about the recognition of nonhumans as victims in their own right within the ICC.

As highlighted by Killean and Dempster, green criminology draws attention to speciesism and other inequalities that render those most affected by environmental harm voiceless, prompting us to consider the rights of ecosystems and non-human animals.[18] To the extent that these inequalities have been built upon "assumptions

---

[9] Schilz 2017, p. 130.

[10] See Hall 2013.

[11] Broad references to the environment as a victim can already be found in the literature. See Leebaw 2014; Doran et al. 2021.

[12] See, for instance, Heller 2021.

[13] Stop Ecocide Foundation 2021. The terms wanton, severe, widespread, long-term, and environment were also defined.

[14] As summarised by Brisman and South, ecocentrism is "based on the idea that humans and their activities are inextricably interconnected with the rest of the natural world". Brisman and South 2018.

[15] See Grear 2015, p. 80.

[16] See Gellers 2020, p. 1.

[17] Kotzé and French 2018, p. 5.

[18] Killean and Dempster 2022, pp. 54–64.

about the core of personhood as disembodied, immaterial, and calculatingly rational",[19] our shared materiality becomes essential for a comprehensive recognition of environmental victims. In this context, Grear's work will be referenced to broaden the discussion of materiality beyond human confines.

Within the ICC, the recognition of the status of victims opens up "opportunities for the concerns of nature to be asserted by a legal representative and for reparations to be sought on behalf of ecosystems".[20] In this chapter, the recognition of the environment as a victim is, by itself, considered an important step in understanding what kind of knowledge about the environment international criminal justice produces.[21] As such, it is decoupled from the analysis of victims' right to participate in the proceedings before the ICC as well as victims' right to reparations.

Whilst the potential amendment of the Rome Statute to establish the ICC's jurisdiction over ecocide should ideally be followed by amendments aimed at the recognition of the environment as a victim, this aspect was not clearly addressed by the IEP. As such, this chapter explores the potential recognition of the environment as a victim within the ICC's current legal framework. This approach acknowledges that the Rome Statute already contains, even if only in a limited way, provisions for which the recognition of the environment as a victim might be relevant.[22] The prosecution of "intentionally launching an attack in the knowledge that such attack will cause [...] widespread, long-term and severe damage to the natural environment", for instance, opens the space to the discussion of which living and non-living components of the damaged natural environment could be recognised as a victim.[23] More importantly, though, the ICC framework does not require a correlation between being the object of a crime and being a victim of such crime.[24] As such, it "opens the door for the environment to be considered a victim when it has suffered harm as a result of the commission of whatever crime under the jurisdiction of the Court".[25]

Bringing to the fore specific challenges related to the recognition of the environment as a victim within the ICC's existing legal framework, this chapter contributes to the identification of aspects that should be the focus of future amendments. In a context of paradigmatic change, it enriches the literature on victim recognition by the ICC, critically examining the limits of the criteria established by RPE Rule 85(b) for recognising the environment as a victim. Adopting an interdisciplinary approach, it provides new insights into how the criteria of RPE Rule 85(a) can be

[19] Valverde 2017, p. 553.

[20] Doran et al. 2021.

[21] Houge 2019, p. 277.

[22] See Mistura 2018, p. 221. In relation to provisions relevant to the potential recognition of animals as victims, see Lostal 2021, p. 583.

[23] See Rome Statute of the International Criminal Court, opened for signature 17 July 1998, 2187 UNTS 3, entered into force 1 July 2002, Article 8(2)(b)(iv). The prosecution of environmental harm based on this provision has been considered extremely hard due to the cumulative criteria—widespread, long-term and severe damage—and the introduction of a balancing test in the evaluation of the environmental harm caused during the international conflict. Gillett 2017, p. 229.

[24] Lostal 2024.

[25] Ibid.

developed to acknowledge the environment as a victim, advancing our understanding of environmental victimisation.

For this purpose, Sect. 10.2 of this chapter addresses the different meanings attributed to the term victim within the legal framework of the ICC. Within this discussion, it highlights the limits that the criteria of RPE Rule 85(b) present to the acknowledgement of the environment as a victim. Section 10.3 furthers the analysis of the potential recognition of the environment as a victim within the existing legal framework through the analysis of the different interpretations of the criteria that inform the definition of the term victim provided for in RPE Rule 85(a).[26] Drawing attention to the overall ambiguity that characterises the meaning of the term victim within the ICC, this chapter highlights the fact that ascribing victimhood is not a neutral process. It involves weighing up the costs of victimhood against competing interests.[27] This process can be identified, for instance, in the definition of the term 'wanton' in the IEP proposal, which requires assessing whether the damage to the environment is "clearly excessive in relation to the social and economic benefits anticipated".[28] It can also be noted within the international criminal procedure when weighing the potential success of prosecuting specific charges against others or considering the extent to which processing victims' applications impacts the accused's right to a prompt trial.[29]

Ultimately, this chapter argues that, in a context in which the efforts related to the criminalisation of ecocide can be considered a part of a paradigmatic change that

[26] International Criminal Court, Rules of Procedure and Evidence, reproduced in the Official Records of the Assembly of States Parties to the Rome Statute of the International Criminal Court, First Session, New York, 3–10 September 2002, ICC-ASP/1/3 and Corr.1, part. II.A (RPE), Rule 85(a).

[27] According to White, at the basis of this process lies the understanding that "the intrinsic and worth and value of non-human environmental entities is vital from the point of view of an ecocentric approach, but this does not mean that instrumental uses of these by humans are, thereby, rendered unimportant". White 2018, p. 249. This understanding has rendered environmental harm unarticulated in light of potential benefits to humans.

[28] Heller, for instance, points out that "the Panel was mindful that socially beneficial acts, such as housing developments and transport links, can cause severe and either widespread or long-term damage to the environment" [and insisted] that "not all acts likely to cause severe and widespread or long-term damage to the environment are illegitimate, or even undesirable." In other words, it's fine to cause "severe and widespread or long-term damage to the environment" as long as humans benefit enough from the destruction. Heller 2021.

[29] Article 68(3) of the Rome Statute attempts to address the potential impact of victims' participation on the rights of the accused to a fair trial. See, for instance, Jonhson 2010, p. 495.

re-orients the law away from anthropocentrism,[30] this process involves the resignification of the criteria established by RPE Rule 85(a); a challenging, but certainly not inconceivable, process, if one considers that the environment is "a fundamental driver of disciplinary evolution, shaping legal concepts in seminal ways".[31]

10.2 Victims in the International Criminal Court

The Rome Statute has been considered a progressive instrument regarding victims' rights in international criminal law.[32] The Statute, however, does not define the term victim. The analysis of its negotiation process indicates that the involvement of victims in the proceedings was considered by different working groups throughout the negotiations.[33] As a result, the term victim refers "to different persons at different times, as specific victims interact in distinct ways with different parts of the [c]ourt at different phases of the proceedings".[34]

In the Rome Statute, the term victim is used, for instance, to describe those who have sent communications or information of crimes to the prosecutor[35] as well as those allowed to submit 'representations' or 'observations' before the commencement of the trial.[36] In these contexts, the status of a victim does not depend on a previous ruling of the ICC.[37] It is based on the interpretation of the Rome Statute by those submitting communications, representations, or observations. An example of the constraints imposed by the Rome Statute to the recognition of the environment as a victim can be seen in the communication submitted by the Human Rights Advocacy Collective and the Dom Paulo Evaristo Arns Commission for Human

[30] In accordance with Article 31 (1) of the Vienna Convention on the Law of Treaties, a treaty shall be interpreted in good faith in accordance with the ordinary meaning to be given to the terms of the treaty in their context and in the light of its object and purpose. Article 31(2) further clarifies that the context for the purpose of the interpretation of a treaty shall comprise, in addition to its text, its preamble. In this context, an amendment to the Preamble of the Rome Statute, endorsing an ecocentric approach, could enable a redefinition of the criteria related to the recognition of the status of victim within the ICC. In this regard, one should note that as the concept of victim is socially constructed and reflect social realities, its ordinary meaning is not static. See Mandi and Panitzer 2022, p. 49. See Vienna Convention on the Law of Treaties, opened for signature 23 May 1969, 1155 UNTS 331, entered into force 27 January 1980.

[31] Natarajan and Khoday 2014, p. 576.

[32] See Baumgartner 2008; Stahn et al. 2006; Trumbull 2008.

[33] UN Doc Preparatory Committee on the Establishment of an International Criminal Court 1998a, Part 4, Articles 36 and 37. UN Preparatory Committee on the Establishment of an International Criminal Court 1998b, Proposal by France and the United Kingdom of Great Britain and Northern Ireland. On the negotiation process of the Rome Statute, in relation to victims, see Baumgartner 2008, pp. 409–440.

[34] ICC Assembly of States Parties 2009, p. 2.

[35] See Rome Statute, above n 23, Article 15(3).

[36] Ibid., Article 19(3).

[37] Stahn et al. 2006, p. 225.

Rights. The communication pointed out alleged offenses perpetrated by Jair Messias Bolsonaro, then Brazilian President, against the environment—land, forests, wildlife, and rivers. Despite that, due to the non-criminalisation of offenses against the environment during peaceful times by the Rome Statute, the communication framed the acts that destroyed the environment as elements of crimes of extermination perpetrated against human beings. In this regard, the communication reads:

> Although the facts presented here highlight a key element in the offenses perpetrated by President Jair Messias Bolsonaro against the environment, whose consequences will be felt worldwide, this Informative Note is not intended to extend the types of crimes listed in the Rome Statute. Here, practices destroying the environment are elements of crimes of extermination perpetrated against human beings, as addressed in Article 7. This is because the means of existence of the indigenous peoples are grounded on their relationships to the land, the forest, wildlife and water. Consequently, trespassing on their lands, polluting rivers, illegal burn-offs in order to log timber and take possession of lands – which helps spread the flames through the forest – all contribute to putting these indigenous peoples at risk of falling victim to crimes against humanity.[38]

When related to Article 68(3) of the Rome Statute, which provides for the participation of victims in various stages of the proceedings before the ICC, a decision of the judges on whether or not a person is a victim from a legal point of view is required.[39] In this context, the status of a victim is assigned in light of the definitions of the term victim in RPE Rule 85. Based on the United Nations Victim Declaration, RPE Rule 85(a) defines victims as "natural persons who have suffered harm as a result of the commission of any crime within the jurisdiction of the Court".[40] In addition to the victimisation of natural persons, RPE Rule 85(b) provides for the victimisation of legal persons, stating that "victims may include organisations or institutions that have sustained direct harm to any of their property which is dedicated to religion, education, art or science or charitable purposes, and to their historic monuments,

[38] Human Rights Advocacy Collective (CADHu) and the ARNS Commission São Paulo 2019, para 11.

[39] Article 68(3) of the Rome Statute establishes that: "Where the personal interests of the victims are affected, the Court shall permit their views and concerns to be presented and considered at stages of the proceedings determined to be appropriate by the Court and in a manner which is not prejudicial to or inconsistent with the rights of the accused and a fair and impartial trial. Such views and concerns may be presented by the legal representatives of the victims where the Court considers it appropriate, in accordance with the Rules of Procedure and Evidence".

[40] The broad reference to harm in RPE, above n 26, Rule 85(a) concealed the disagreements during the negotiation process about the relevance of the types of harm considered in the United Nations Victims Declaration to the ICC. An agreement could not be reached over the types of harm included in the UN Victims Declaration, i.e., physical or mental injury, emotional suffering, economic loss or substantial impairment of their fundamental rights. There were also reservations with respect to indirect harm and the inclusion of collective harm. See Timm 2001, p. 290.

hospitals and other places and objects for humanitarian purposes".[41] These provisions highlight that not only victimhood, but also personhood, are legal constructs, which are historically and politically contingent.

It is, therefore, interesting to note that even though the negotiation process of the Rome Statute led to the criminalisation of intentionally causing widespread, long-term and severe damage to the natural environment during an international armed conflict, it did not address the victimisation of nonhumans. A similar silence can be noted in the negotiations of the ICC RPE. It seems, therefore, that the ICC's legal framework took into account only one level of environmental victimisation, acknowledging mainly humans as potential victims.[42]

More recently, new understandings of the term victim seem to be developing at the ICC. In the *Al Mahdi* case, Trial Chamber VIII expanded the concept of victims beyond the faithful and inhabitants of Timbuktu to include the people throughout Mali and the international community as victims of the destruction of world heritage sites by Al Mahdi.[43] The recognition of national and international communities as victims was directly linked to the cultural value assigned to the mausoleums, which were, most of them, designated as world heritage sites.[44] The recognition of the international and national communities as victims in the *Al Mahdi* case occurred outside the scope of the definition of victims in the RPE and the application process outlined therein.[45] Considering that the community of Timbuktu was the one which had undergone "disproportionately more harm",[46] Trial Chamber VIII focused its assessment of the various kinds of harm to the harm suffered by or within the community of Timbuktu, "i.e. organisations or persons ordinarily residing in Timbuktu at the time of the commission of the crimes or otherwise so closely related to the city that they can be considered to be part of this community at the time of the attack".[47]

Despite the prioritisation of people-centred approaches to heritage law,[48] the recognition of organisations as victims of heritage destruction in the *Al Mahdi* case has opened the space for the discussion of the recognition of the environment as a victim within the framework of Rule 85(b). As pointed out by Lostal, to the extent that "natural areas designated by humans, such as national parks, protected forests …

---

[41] Even though it was broadly acknowledged that legal entities are often the target of certain war crimes, the adoption of RPE Rule 85(b) was controversial. "Delegations opposed to the inclusion of legal persons feared a diversion of the Court's resources, better used for individual victims, and potential misuse of the participation scheme by multinational companies". Baumgartner 2008, p. 417.

[42] See White's discussion of the different environmental harm levels referred to above n 27, at p. 2.

[43] ICC, *Prosecutor v Ahmad Al Faqi All Mahdi,* Trial Chamber VIII, Reparation order, 17 August 2017, ICC-01/12-01/15-236, para 53.

[44] Ibid., para 17.

[45] Ibid., para 52.

[46] Ibid., paras 52, 56.

[47] Ibid., para 56.

[48] See Sterling 2020.

or biodiversity hotspots" could be considered to fulfil a goal, such as conservation,[49] the environment could be indirectly reflected in the definition of victim provided by RPE Rule 85(b).[50] Furthering this discussion, Gillett suggests the adoption of an environmentally-protective approach to the concept of ownership that informs our understanding of property.[51] This approach should enable the RPE Rule 85(b) to encompass "de jure and de facto forms of control, as well as concepts of ownership according to customary laws of the affected communities".[52] This, he explains, would enable "a trust or similar charitable, educational or scientific organisation, which is responsible for safeguarding an area in which environmental facets are damaged" to receive victim status under Rule 85(b).[53] Within this context, the "victim would be the organisation or institution [that owns the environment], and not the environment per se".[54]

Despite acknowledging that "the environment does not lend itself directly and unequivocally to being recognised as a victim if one adheres strictly to the wording of rule 85(b) RPE",[55] Lostal suggests that a broad interpretation of the term 'institutions and organisations' could encompass juridical entities,[56] allowing environmental areas recognised as juridical persons to qualify as victims. Such understanding would require not only extending property rights to the environment, but also reconceptualising these rights, so that they could be meaningfully applied to the environment.

Attempts to expand the right to property to the environment can already be found in the literature. Wesche, for instance, argues for the recognition of "nature's property rights" based on the creation of value by nature through ecosystem services.[57] To

---

[49] Lostal 2024. See references to protected environmental zones as a frontier for improved environmental protection in armed conflict in Gieseken and Murphy 2023.

[50] Lostal 2024.

[51] Gillett 2024. Lostal suggests, more broadly, that "as it is common for national legal systems to declare that natural resources are owned by the State" the term 'property' in Rule 85(b) should not be an obstacle to the application of this provision to the environment. Lostal 2024. It should, nonetheless, be noted that within this perspective the oceans and the atmosphere remain ownerless. See Sands 1989, p. 398.

[52] Gillett 2024.

[53] Lostal 2024.

[54] Ibid.

[55] Ibid.

[56] Lostal refers to the term 'legal entities', ibid. The phrase legal person, legal entities can refer to a bundle of legal positions as well as to an entity that meets certain criteria. See Kurki 2019, p. 128. In this chapter, the term is used to refer to legal positions. When referring to the entities, the phrases 'natural person' and 'juridical person' are used. As such, legal personality is used as the umbrella concept that encompasses both natural and juridical persons.

[57] Wesche 2022. Wesche differs his proposal to concretise the rights of nature as their property rights from that of Stone in the following terms: "while I am concerned with the grounding of nature's rights from existing property law, for Stone property rights serve to bioeconomically tie natural goods to a price". Both approaches seem, nonetheless, to enable the continuous commodification of nature.

the extent that ecosystem services are understood as "the direct and indirect contributions of ecosystems to human well-being",[58] his proposal remains informed by human perception. Such interpretation of the right to property when applied to the environment reiterates the utilitarian perspective reflected in the definition of victims of RPE Rule 85(b), according to which only properties with an intended function are to be protected. The recognition of the victimisation of the environment within these parameters would, therefore, be based on its assigned value to humans.[59] As such, the needs and capacities of nonhumans within these 'properties' would remain unacknowledged. In addition to that, areas whose potential value to human beneficiaries have not been identified would remain unprotected.[60] As pointed out by Natarajan, within this perspective, "the wealthy and powerful remain best positioned to define ecological health and integrity based on selfinterest, with the opportunity to decide which people and species merit conservation and those that will be silently sacrificed."[61]

To enable the recognition of the environment as a victim on its own right within RPE Rule 85(b) would require "the dissociation of the legal entity from the predetermined set of purposes its property must be dedicated to".[62] This would, nonetheless, mean the adoption of a new definition of victim through case-law, one that would simply refer to juridical entities. In this regard, Blanco and Grear point out that, despite the undoubted potential of legal personhood for imaginative juridical projects, "it is perfectly possible to foresee a world populated by myriad forms of legal persons/entities, in which familiar and long-standing patterns of marginalization and predation *persist*".[63]

Besides paving the way for the *indirect* recognition of the environment as a victim within RPE Rule 85(b), the *Al Mahdi* case prompt us to reflect upon the concept of community as a victim of heritage destruction and the extent to which it can encompass nonhumans.[64] After all, developments in the field of heritage law are increasingly recognising that heritage sites "are not made up of isolated natural or cultural attributes split into separate realities, but are intertwined, connected and constituted of relationships".[65] As such, any discussion related to the destruction of heritage law requires us to consider not only humans, but also nonhumans and

---

[58] Ibid.

[59] Lostal acknowledges that such interpretation of RPE Rule 85(b) could lead, at most, to the recognition of the victimisation of "environmental areas, such as a conservation area, that have been recognised as a legal person". Lostal 2024.

[60] Porto-Gonçalves and Leff 2015, p. 69.

[61] Natarajan 2022, p. 224.

[62] Lostal 2024.

[63] Blanco and Grear 2019, p. 99. See also Natarajan 2022, p. 208.

[64] In this regard, it is important to note that the notion of community within international law is highly contentious, even more so is the notion of an international community. See Villalpando 2010; Simma and Paulus 1998. Additionally, as explained by Kooijman, in the field of international criminal law, humanity seems to have been the sole focus of the international community up until now. See Kooijman 2022, p. 111.

[65] Larsen and Wijesuriya 2017, p. 145.

their relationships.[66] In this perspective, Fredengren points out that once nonhuman entities are acknowledged as "vital co-workers in the making of the word",[67] they should be acknowledged not only in political and bureaucratic heritage practices, but also more broadly as a part of the political web.[68] Proposals to broaden our understanding of community have been also put forward outside the field of heritage law. In this context, Wienhues suggests that "all living beings should be included into the community of justice" as they constitute a "community of fate".[69]

Another understanding of the term victim that might contribute to the discussion of the recognition of the environment as a victim within the ICC was put forward by Trial Chamber V, in the differentiation among the victims "who wished to appear directly before the Chamber", registered victim participants, and "victims who choose not to register or who are, for practical or security reasons barred from doing so".[70] In the first category, an application form needs to be completed and assessed by the Chamber.[71] The Chamber is responsible for granting the status of a victim. In the second category, victim participants submit their names, contact information, and information regarding the harm suffered to the Registry. Without any individualised review by the parties or a decision from the Chamber, this information is entered into a database. The database is shared with the common legal representative, who would then verify which victims are eligible to participate in the case.[72] In the third category, the identification of non-registered victims also falls under the responsibility of the legal representative.[73] The Chamber decided that the views and concerns of registered and non-registered victims should be expressed, in a general way, through common legal representation.[74]

When creating these categories, the Chamber acknowledged the negative impact that the administrative process, in particular the challenges related to the completion of a detailed application form, can have on the recognition of the victims.[75] As the recognition of the nonhumans as victims will certainly pose administrative challenges to the ICC, this jurisprudential development might facilitate the recognition of the environment as a victim, once it enables the recognition of the environment as a non-registered victim by a common legal representative.

---

[66] Fredengren 2015, p. 121.

[67] Ibid., p. 116.

[68] Ibid.

[69] Wienhues 2017, p. 367. See also Youatt 2014.

[70] ICC, *Prosecutor v Uhuru Muigai Kenyatta,* Trial Chamber V, Decision on Victims' Representation and Participation, 03 October 2012, ICC-01/09-02/11, paras 24, 51. To Kendall and Nouwen, victims in categories two and three become part of an amorphous category of victims. See Kendall and Nouwen 2013, p. 249.

[71] Ibid., para 24.

[72] Ibid., para 48.

[73] Ibid., para 51.

[74] Ibid., para 38.

[75] Ibid., paras 23, 30, 50.

The extent to which the term victim can refer to the environment in the ICC might, therefore, vary. At different times, different actors are responsible for conveying and acknowledging the nature of nonhumans' victimisation. In this context, the discussion of who should convey and acknowledge the nature of nonhumans' victimisation within the international criminal procedure has a direct impact on the knowledge that can be produced about the environment at the ICC. As illustrated by White,

> a 'river' may be defined in spiritual and cultural terms by an Indigenous community; be viewed primarily in terms of water flow according to the narrow Eurocentric conceptions (…); be seen as being constituted by its channel banks and channel bed according to the science of geomorphology; and be conceptualised as inclusive of riparian zones, which relate to the observed influence of the river on the biota within and adjacent to the river, from an ecological perspective.[76]

As the views of these various actors about the status of the environment as a victim are informed by the ICC legal framework, the definition of the term victim in RPE Rule 85(a) and RPE Rule 85(b) of the ICC RPE become relevant. Section 10.3 focuses on RPE Rule 85(a). This choice is informed by the potential application of the notion of indirect harm to the characterisation of harm as severe, long-term or widespread harm in the IEP definition of ecocide.[77] The discussion of indirect harm seems essential to a comprehensive understanding of environmental harm. The focus on RPE Rule 85(a) also takes into account that in contrast to institutions and corporations, that are both a human construct and a fictionalised human person, the biotic and abiotic components of the environment exist independently of human construction and imagination.[78] In addition to that, they should have the right to exist, flourish, regenerate its vital cycles irrespective of their relevance to humans. Within this perspective, RPE Rules 85(b) contributes to the discussion of the recognition of the environment as a victim to the extent that it demonstrates that personhood is a legal construct.

10.3 The Definition of Victim Included in Rule 85(a) and the Environment

To be granted the status of a victim of ecocide by the ICC under RPE Rule 85(a), three criteria need to be met: to be considered a natural person, to have suffered harm, and the establishment of the nexus between the harm suffered and the crime within the jurisdiction of the ICC (in this case, ecocide). These criteria are assessed against the information provided in applications for participation in the proceedings. The application process is provided for in RPE Rule 89.

---

[76] White 2017, p. 13; see also Bertenthal 2019, p. 357.

[77] RPE Rule 85(b) refers exclusively to direct harm. See ICC, *Prosecutor v Thomas Lubanga Dyilo*, Trial Chamber I, Decision on Victims' Participation, 18 January 2008, ICC-01/04-01/06, para 91.

[78] Clark et al. 2018, p. 831. In addition to that, the reference to institutions and organisations with specific objectives in RPE Rule 85(b) questions the extent to which the intrinsic value of the environment can be encompassed by RPE Rule 85(b).

RPE Rule 89(1) establishes that "to present their views and concerns, victims shall make written application to the Registrar, who shall transmit the application to the relevant Chamber". The defence and the prosecutor are allowed to comment on the application form. RPE Rule 89(2) grants the Chamber the power to reject the application, on its own initiative, or based on the comments of the parties, if it considers that the person is not a victim or that the criteria set forth in Article 68(3) of the Rome Statute are not fulfilled. RPE Rule 89(3) provides that an application "may be made by a person acting with the consent of the victim, or a person acting on behalf of a victim, in the case of a victim who is a child or, when necessary, a victim who is disabled". Potential amendments to the RPE should, therefore, consider the representation of nonhumans at the application stage to avoid it becoming an impediment to the recognition of the environment as a victim.[79] Similarly, new application forms, capable of capturing the harm suffered by the environment, will need to be developed.[80] Nonetheless, as seen in the previous section, within the existing legal framework, the recognition of the environment as a victim might be enabled by the legal representative, following the above-mentioned jurisprudence of Trial Chamber V.

As the recognition of victims and their rights to participate in the proceedings are interrelated per Article 68(3) of the Rome Statute, the latter provision imposes further constraints on the recognition of the environment as a victim. When considering the applications for participation, in addition to the criteria of RPE Rule 85(a), ICC Chambers have also "examined whether participation would be prejudicial to the rights of the accused or a fair and impartial trial, whether the victim's personal interests are affected, and at what stage participation would be most appropriate" when granting the status of a victim.[81] As the scope of participation of potential environmental victims is not the focus of this chapter, the next section will focus on whether each criterion established in RPE Rule 85(a) allows for the recognition of the environment as a victim.

10.3.1 Natural Person

There has not been much reflection on the notion of legal personhood in the jurisprudence of the ICC. Natural persons have been interpreted to refer mainly to human beings.[82] Nonetheless, it has also been defined in opposition to juridical persons.[83]

---

[79] For decisions related to the representation of the environment and the challenges they might put forward, see Clark et al. 2018; Tănăsescu 2020.

[80] Regarding the challenges related to the design of an application form, see War Crimes Research Office 2013.

[81] McDermott 2009, p. 28.

[82] Olásolo and Kiss 2010. See also Lostal 2021, p. 590.

[83] ICC, *Situation in the Democratic Republic of Congo*, Pre-Trial Chamber I, Decision on the Applications for Participation in the Proceedings of VPRS1, VPRS2, VPRS3, VPRS4, VPRS5, VPRS 6, 17 January 2006, ICC-01/04-101-tEN-Corr, para 80.

This approach, in a context of paradigmatic change, arguably opens the space for the application of the concept of 'natural person' to the environment.

The thematisation of environmental legal personhood has started to take place through the recognition of the rights of nature. References are commonly made to the 2008 Constitution of Ecuador,[84] the adoption of the Framework Law of Mother Earth and Integral Development to Live Well by Bolivia in 2012,[85] the recognition of the legal personhood of the Te Urewera, a New Zealand body of land formerly classified as a national park, in 2014,[86] and of the Whanganui River by New Zealand in 2017,[87] and the recognition of the legal personality of the Magpie River by Canada in 2021.[88] Various decisions at the domestic level have also acknowledged the rights of natural systems.[89] At the international level, the Inter-American Court of Human Rights' advisory opinion on the environment and human rights stated that the right to a healthy environment:

> protects the components of the environment, such as forests, rivers and seas, as legal interests in themselves, even in the absence of certainty or evidence of a risk to individuals. This means that it protects nature and the environment, not only because of the benefits they provide to humanity or the effects that their degradation may have on other human rights, such as health, life or personal integrity, but because of their importance to the other living organisms with which we share the planet that also merit protection in their own right.[90]

More recently, in the *Indigenous Communities Members of the Lhaka Honhat Association v. Argentina* case, the Inter-American Court of Human Rights confirmed its recognition of nature's independent rights.[91] It reasserted the understanding that the right to a healthy environment protects components of the environment "as legal interests in themselves, even in the absence of the certainty or evidence of a risk to individuals".[92] In fact, the protection of the environment was related to its importance to other living organisms, rather than to its usefulness to or effects on human beings.[93]

---

[84] Ecuador, Constitution of the Republic of Ecuador (2008). Gordon points out that in the Ecuadorian constitution, nature is given rights by analogy to persons and people. Gordon 2018, p. 52.

[85] Bolivia, Plurinational Legislative Assembly, "Framework Law of Mother Earth and Integral Development for Living Well" (2012).

[86] New Zealand, Te Urewera Act (2014).

[87] New Zealand, Te Awa Tupua (Whanganui River Claims Settlement) Act (2017).

[88] Canada, Reconnaissance de la personnalité juridique et des droits de la rivière Magpie – Mutehekau Shipu, Resolution 025-21 (2021). See, in general, Boyd 2015, p. 182; Shelton 2015; Darpö 2021.

[89] See, for example, Constitutional Court of Colombia, *Judgment T-622-16*, 10 November 2016, paras 9.27–9.31; Constitutional Court of Ecuador, *Judgment No. 218-15-SEP-CC*, 9 July 2015, 9–10, and High Court of Uttarakhand at Naintal of India, *Decision of 30 March 2017*. Petition (PIL) No. 140 of 2015, 61–66.

[90] Inter-American Court of Human Rights, *The Environment and Human Rights*, Advisory Opinion OC-23/17, 15 November 2017, para 62.

[91] Inter-American Court of Human Rights, *Indigenous Communities Members of the Lhaka Honhat Association v Argentina*, Judgment (Merits, reparations and costs), Series C No 420, 17 November 2020.

[92] Ibid., para 203.

[93] Ibid.

In these references, the recognition of the rights of nature has been articulated in broad terms or related to the concept of juridical personhood. As such, they do not provide a straightforward pathway to the recognition of the environment as a natural person. Despite that, these developments should not be underestimated. As pointed out by De Vido, "they challenged laws that have been created to protect the environment for the benefit of human beings without considering two key aspects: first, that human beings are themselves part of nature, and second, that the existence of nature per se, independently from human beings, matters".[94] Within this broader context, arguments have been put forward to enable the understanding of the environment in relation to other international instruments. Fischer-Lescano has, for instance, argued that the concept of the individual is "sufficiently open to interpretation to endow non-human entities with rights and with possibilities for their enforcement".[95] This understanding is particularly relevant to the discussion of environmental personhood within international human rights instruments, such as the International Covenant on Civil and Political Rights.[96]

The attribution of environmental personhood within the boundaries established by the binomen natural person and juridical person has not been without its challenges. The judgments in the *Ganges and Yamuna* case[97] and in the *Glaciers* case[98] by the High Court of Uttarakhand (the Court) illustrate some of them. Both decisions acknowledged rights to the environment through the recognition of its juridical personhood, Nonetheless, by comparing the environment to a living person, the Court, in both cases, seems to conflate the concept of a juridical person with that of a natural person.[99] In the *Ganges and Yamuna* case, the Court ruled that the two rivers are "living entities having the status of a legal person with all corresponding rights, duties and liabilities of a living person".[100] In the *Glaciers* case, the Court found that

> the Glaciers, including Gangotri & Yamunotri, rivers, streams, rivulets, lakes, air, meadows, dales, jungles, forests wetlands, grasslands, springs and waterfalls [are] legal entity/legal person/juristic person/juridical person/moral person/artificial person having the status of a legal person, with all corresponding rights, duties and liabilities of a *living person*, in order

[94] De Vido 2021, p. 107.

[95] Fischer-Lescano 2020, p. 252.

[96] According to Fischer-Lescano, such an interpretation of the International Covenant on Civil and Political Rights, does not necessarily "entitle non-humans in the same way as humans, but rather allows us to distinguish between the personal rights of humans and non-humans. Where non-human forms of personhood are recognized, the rights of non-human persons are no longer understood as embedded in the rights of human individuals, but can instead be developed specifically in relation to the persons to be protected. This enables the differentiation of non-subjective rights and thereby the clarification of the differences between human and non-human legal persons", Ibid. As seen in relation to the right to property, the extension of human rights to the environment raises further questions. See Natarajan 2022.

[97] High Court of Uttarakhand, *Mohd Salim v State of Uttarakhand & others*, WPPIL 126/2014, 2017 [19] (hereinafter, the Ganges and Yamuna case).

[98] High Court of Uttarakhand, *Lalit Miglani v State of Uttarakhand & others*, WPPIL 140/2015, 2017 64 (hereinafter, the Glaciers case).

[99] O'Donnell 2018, p. 138.

[100] Ganges and Yamuna case, above n 97, para 19.

> to protect and conserve them. They are also accorded rights akin to fundamental rights/legal rights.[101] [emphasis added]

Furthermore, in the *Glaciers* case, the Court explicitly stated that the rights of these legal entities "shall be equivalent to the rights of *human beings* and the injury/harm caused to these bodies shall be treated as harm/injury caused to the *human beings*" [emphasis added].[102] The attribution of juridical personality together with the analogy between these living entities and a living person, a human being, seems to suggest a certain discomfort with, on the one hand, the expansion of the concept of natural persons to include the environment and, on the other hand, the application of the concept of juridical personhood in light of the environment's intrinsic value.[103]

To address these challenges within the international criminal context, amendments aimed at the inclusion of crimes against the environment to the Rome Statute should, ideally, be followed by amendments to the RPE. Nonetheless, the application of the notion of natural personhood to the environment might not be inconceivable. As suggested by Grear, such application would require a (new) juridical imaginary that understands that "matter matters", that the human legal subject is not the autonomous, abstract human of traditional international human rights universalism, but a living, flesh and blood being.[104] Within this new imaginary, the term natural could be considered more broadly to refer to beings,[105] to the biotic and abiotic components of an ecosystem, such as plants, animals, soil, water, minerals, and gases. In other words, the word natural within the phrase 'natural person' in RPE Rule 85(a) could assume a broader meaning,[106] ensuring that the interpretation of the provisions related to the rights of victims could be applied to the environment.

Even if a requirement of a paradigmatic shift, the reconstruction of the meaning attributed to the phrase 'natural person' is certainly challenging. It could, however, be facilitated by the adoption of amendments to the Rome Statute that clearly reflect an ecocentric perspective regarding crimes against the environment. Such amendments would provide not only a clear indication of such a paradigmatic change but also a new legal context against which the ordinary meaning of the phrase 'natural person' would need to be assessed. In this regard, it is interesting to note that the IEP did suggest amendments to the Preamble of the Rome Statute, one of the constitutive elements of a treaty context, in accordance with Article 31(2) of the Vienna Convention on the Law of Treaties. The reconsideration of the automatic association between the

---

[101] Glaciers case, above n 98, para 64.

[102] Ibid., para 65.

[103] As explained by Pietrzykowski, the recognition of organisational entities "as separate holders of rights and duties is derivative and based on essentially pragmatic grounds. Namely, such recognition is supposed to serve as a tool to better realize some of the needs and interests of human beings. The goal of the recognition of any organizational entity as a legal person is the satisfaction of the interests of human persons." Pietrzykowski 2017, pp. 59–71. See also the overall criticism to the application of juridical personhood pointed out above.

[104] Grear 2015, p. 88.

[105] Lostal 2021, p. 590.

[106] This has been one of the points put forward by the Rights of Nature movement. See Gellers 2020, p. 1.

concept of natural persons and humans could, therefore, be derived from a new, less anthropocentric context.

Without an ecocentric perspective embedded in the Rome Statute, the potential reconstruction of the notion of a natural person would need to be motivated by the impact that overall developments in international and domestic law might have on the arguments put forward by the various actors responsible for the articulation of victimhood in the ICC. As seen, the first steps related to the definition of a victim might, therefore, be undertaken by non-specialised actors, those sending a communication to the OTP. They might also be the ones submitting applications for victims' participation on behalf of the environment. The legal representative of the victims can also put forward the characterisation of the environment as a victim and, therefore, address the extent to which the environment can be considered a natural person. The decisions of the judges within this context will need to take into account the convincing force of the legal arguments put forward by all these different actors within a broader context of paradigmatic change. In other words, whilst the concept of a natural person might be informed by previous decisions of the ICC, one should not disregard the impact of the overall (legal) background.

Due attention to the materiality that characterises human and nonhuman biotic elements as well as abiotic elements might provide the basis for the expansion of the concept of natural person within a less anthropocentric legal framework. In such a context, the recognition of the environment as a victim will need to take into account its concrete components. Their complex interactions will, therefore, need to be explored under the idea of harm.

10.3.2 The Notion of Harm

There is no definition of the term harm in the Statute of the ICC or in its RPE. According to the Appeals Chamber in the *Lubanga Dyilo* case, "[t]he word "harm" in its ordinary meaning denotes hurt, injury and damage [and] it carries the same meaning in legal texts, including in the RPE".[107] Various ICC Chambers have interpreted the notion of harm broadly to include physical or mental injury, emotional

[107] ICC, Appeals Chamber, *Prosecutor* v *Thomas Lubanga Dyilo*, Judgment on the appeals of The Prosecutor and The Defence against Trial Chamber I's Decision on Victims' Participation, 18 January 2008, ICC-01/04-01/06-1432, para 31.

suffering, and economic damage.[108] The determination of a single instance of harm suffered has been considered sufficient for the fulfilment of this criterion.[109]

Regarding environmental damage, De La Fayette notes that in the majority of international environmental law instruments "the concept of damage does not refer to damage to the environment, but damage through the environment to persons, property, and economic interests".[110] The influence of such an approach can also be felt in the IEP definition of ecocide. Relying on the 1976 Convention on the Prohibition of Military or any other Hostile Use of Environmental Modification Techniques, the IEP definition of severe damage involves "grave impacts on human life or natural, cultural or economic resources".[111] As a result, to ensure that the definition of ecocide embraces not only damage *through* the environment, but also damage *to* the environment, the IEP added the phrase "very serious adverse changes, disruption or harm to any element of the environment" to its definition of severe damage.

When the focus is on damage to the environment, French explains that "there is often agreement as to a term's core meaning to justify broad consensus, there is rarely agreement as regards a term's exact content".[112] The current interpretation of harm to humans by the ICC seems to reflect such an approach, allowing for the gradual articulation of various dimensions of harm. Regarding the environment, this approach enables the development of our understanding of harm not only in light of scientific knowledge, but also of Indigenous Traditional Knowledge.[113] As environmental harm does not necessarily follow a linear conception of cause and effect, Indigenous Peoples' "interpretation of reality as a world made up of constantly forming multidimensional cycles in which all elements are part of an entangled and complex web of interactions"[114] can further our ability to assess environmental harm.

It is, nonetheless, important to note that the types of harm already acknowledged by the ICC can contribute to the discussion of environmental harm. Wildman, for

---

[108] See, ICC, Pre-Trial Chamber III, *Prosecutor v Jean-Pierre Bemba Gombo*, Fourth Decision on Victim's Participation, 12 December 2008, ICC-01/05-01/08-320; ICC, Pre-Trial Chamber II, *Prosecutor v William Samoei Ruto, Henry Kiprono Kogsey and Joshua Arap Sang*, 5 August 2011, ICC-01/09-01/11-249, para 50; ICC, Appeals Chamber, *Prosecutor v Thomas Lubanga Dyilo*, Judgment on the appeals of The Prosecutor and The Defence against Trial Chamber I's Decision on Victims' Participation of 18 January 2008, 11 July 2008, ICC-01/04-01/06-1432, para 32; ICC, Trial Chamber I, *Prosecutor v Laurent Gbagbo*, 6 March 2015, ICC-02/11-01/11, para 33; ICC 2010.

[109] See, for instance, ICC, Pre-Trial Chamber I, *Situation in the Democratic Republic of Congo*, Decision on the Applications for Participation in the Proceedings of VPRS1, VPRS2, VPRS3, VPRS4, VPRS5, VPRS 6, para 82; ICC, Pre-Trial Chamber II, *Prosecutor v Bosco Ntaganda*, Decision on Victims' Participation at the Confirmation of Charges Hearing and in the Related Proceedings, 15 January 2014, ICC-01/04-02/06, para 33.

[110] De La Fayette 2002, p. 181.

[111] See Stop Ecocide Foundation 2021's comments regarding severe damage.

[112] French 2003, p. 266.

[113] See Pope et al. 2021, p. 2. The reference to traditional knowledge is also relevant if the hierarchy within Anthropos is introduced in the debates related to human victims of environmental harm.

[114] Mazzocchi 2006.

instance, suggests that biotic components do not pose further challenges to the notion of physical harm. Physical harm to abiotic components can be articulated in light of the notion of environmental integrity.[115] The determination of mental injury and emotional suffering, in his view, requires a careful analysis of the social embedding, psychological complexity, and emotional capacities of biotic components in the cognitive realm.[116]

Even though the differentiation between the concepts of direct and indirect victims relies on a mechanical understanding of causation, which might not be the most appropriate approach to the analysis of the interactions among abiotic and biotic environmental factors, they can also contribute to the thematisation of environmental harm before the ICC. Direct victims were defined by the Appeals Chamber in the *Lubanga Dyilo* case as "those whose harm is the result of the commission of a crime within the jurisdiction of the Court".[117] In the same decision, the Appeals Chamber defined indirect victims as "those who suffer harm as a result of the harm suffered by direct victims".[118] Within this differentiation, one could say that large-scale illegal fires cause direct harm to plants and animals (biotic component) as well as to the soil (abiotic element).[119] It is also possible, in principle, to conceive the moral or physical harm of a biological organism (including a human being) because of the disruption of the physical integrity of a non-biological system, such as in cases related to illegal mining.[120] Similarly, abiotic components can be considered indirect victims, as in cases related to illegal logging. Whilst trees are directly harmed by illegal logging, deforestation can indirectly harm the soil as it leads, among others, to soil erosion.[121]

Regarding the assessment of the nature, severity and persistency of the harm caused to the environment, Cymie brings to our attention the relevance of a multidisciplinary approach.[122] An example of such approach is provided by the United Nations Compensation Commission review of environmental damage claims arising from the 1990–1991 Gulf War, which has relied on experts from various fields including

---

[115] According to Wildman, "the best case for injury in nonbiological systems of nature turns on showing that there is a kind of physical integrity to some nonbiological systems that can be disturbed in a way that is loosely similar to the way injury disrupts the integrity of a biological organism". Wildman 2007, p. 58.

[116] Ibid., p. 66. For the challenges that such analysis might put forward, see Lostal 2021, p. 595.

[117] ICC, Appeals Chamber, *Prosecutor v Thomas Lubanga Dyilo*, Judgment on the appeals of The Prosecutor and The Defence against Trial Chamber I's Decision on Victims' Participation of 18 January 2008, 11 July 2008, ICC-01/04-01/06-1432, para 31.

[118] Ibid.

[119] See, for instance, Certini 2005, p. 1.

[120] See, for instance, Collins 2023. For the consideration of the victimisation of humans and nonhumans, the discussions regarding the link between cultural and biological diversity can be particularly relevant as it allows us to consider the potential impact of cultural losses on biological diversity and vice-versa.

[121] See, for instance, Anyanwu et al. 2015, p. 64.

[122] Paynes 2024.

desert ecology, botany, biology, agriculture, forestry, and many others.[123] The interaction between disciplines that adopt different relevant timeframes can certainly better contribute to the understanding of the long-term, diffuse consequences of environmental crimes. Similarly, such an interaction might contribute to a better identification and understanding of damage that might not be geographically contained.[124] A denser understanding of environmental damage might also be facilitated by the incorporation of Indigenous Traditional Knowledge, due to, among others, long periods of observation, interaction and experimentation with species, ecosystems and ecosystems processes as well as its relational understandings of ecosystem components, including humans.[125] A comprehensive analysis of the interactions among biotic and abiotic components within an ecosystem avoids the undue characterisation of environmental crimes as victimless crimes. Within the ICC, the notions of physical and moral harm as well as direct and indirect victims can contribute to this process.

10.3.3 The Nexus Between the Harm Suffered and the Crimes Under the Jurisdiction of the Court

The assessment of this criterion in the ICC jurisprudence involves, firstly, the discussion of how the phrase 'crimes under the jurisdiction of the Court' should be interpreted. Trial Chamber I, in the *Lubanga Dyilo case*, did not impose any limitations to the phrase: a crime under the jurisdiction of the Court would be relevant to the determination of victim's status regardless of when and where it had allegedly been committed.[126] Victim's status, in this perspective, did not imply victims' right to participate in the proceedings. A second analysis of the applications was necessary to assess the criteria established in Article 68(3) of the Rome Statute. Pre-Trial Chamber I interpreted the phrase differently. To Pre-Trial Chamber I, the phrase 'crime under the jurisdiction of the Court' needed to be interpreted in accordance with the different stages of ICC proceedings.[127] This approach differentiated between situation victims and case victims. The phrase crimes under the jurisdiction of the Court during the situation stage of the proceedings meant "a crime within the subject-matter jurisdiction of the Court allegedly committed within the temporal, territorial

---

[123] Ibid.

[124] Sknnider 2011, p. 2.

[125] Jessen et al. 2022. The contribution of indigenous knowledge can be also considered from a broader ethical and epistemological perspective, see Natarajan 2022.

[126] ICC, Trial Chamber I, *Prosecutor v Thomas Lubanga Dyilo*, Decision on Victims' Participation, 18 January 2018, ICC-01/04-01/06-1119, para 93.

[127] ICC, Pre-Trial Chamber I, *Situation in the Democratic Republic of the Congo*, Decision on the Applications for Participation in the Proceedings of VPRS 1, VPRS 2, VPRS 3, VPRS 4, VPRS 5 and VPRS 6, 17 January 2006, ICC-01/04-101-tEN-Corr, para 65.

and personal parameters that define the relevant situation".[128] During the case stage of the proceedings, the phrase meant "a crime within the subject-matter jurisdiction of the Court allegedly committed in the context of the specific incidents included in the relevant arrest warrant or summons to appear (and subsequently charging document)".[129] The Appeals Chamber, in the *Lubanga Dyilo case*, has rejected the approach followed by Trial Chamber I, stating that:

> whilst the ordinary meaning of Rule 85 does not per se limit the notion of victims to the victims of the crimes charged, the effect of Article 68(3) of the Statute is that participation of victims in trial proceedings, pursuant to the procedure set out in Rule 89(1) of the Rules, is limited to those victims who are linked to the charges.[130]

This approach clearly illustrates the impact that Article 68(3) of the Rome Statute can have on the interpretation of RPE Rule 85(a). As explained by Kendall and Nouwen, this process results "in a narrowing, like a pyramid, of the victims that are considered legally relevant".[131] Differences between situation victims and case victims of ecocide might lead to the creation of hierarchies not only between human and nonhuman victims, but also among nonhuman victims within the proceedings.

When causation is being assessed to grant victims status to participate in the proceedings it has been broadly interpreted. In the *Gbagbo* case, for instance, Trial Chamber I determined that it was sufficient to demonstrate "that the alleged crimes could have objectively contributed to the harm suffered" and that the "crimes charged do not have to be the only cause of the harm suffered by the applicant."[132] Similarly, in the *Bemba* case, the Single Judge of Pre-Trial Chamber III followed a broad approach, noting that, in that case, "the circumstances surrounding the crime(s) [...] must be appropriate to bring about the harm alleged and [were] not entirely outside the range of expectation or probability, as viewed ex post by an objective observer".[133] A more restrictive approach to causation has been adopted when victim status has been related to the right to have the harm suffered repaired. Within this context, Trial Chamber II, in the *Katanga* case, dismissed the claims related to transgenerational

---

128 See Pre-Trial Chamber I, *Situation in Darfur, Sudan*, Corrigendum to Decision on the Applications for Participation in the Proceedings of Applicants a/0011/06 to a/0015/06, a/0021/07, a/0023/07 to a/0033/07 and a/0035/07 to a/0038/07, 14 December 2007, ICC-02/05-111-Corr, para 49.

129 See ICC, Pre-Trial Chamber I, *Prosecutor v Germain Katanga and Mathieu Ngudjolo Chui*, Decision on the Applications for Participation in the Proceedings of Applicants a/0327/07 to a/0337/07 and a/0001/08, 31 March 2008, ICC-01/-4-01/07-357, Pre-Trial Chamber II, *Prosecutor v Bosco Ntaganda*, Decision on Victims' Participation at the Confirmation of Charges Hearing and in the Related Proceedings, 15 January 2014, ICC-01/04-02/06, para 18.

130 Appeals Chamber, *Prosecutor v Thomas Lubanga Dyilo*, Judgment on the appeals of The Prosecutor and The Defence against Trial Chamber I's Decision on Victims' Participation of 18 January 2008, 11 July 2008, ICC-01/04-01/06-1432, para 58. See also ICC, Trial Chamber V, *Prosecutor v William Samoei Ruto and Joshua Arap Sang*, 03 October 2012, ICC-01/09-01/11, para 47.

131 Kendall and Nouwen 2013, p. 241.

132 ICC, Trial Chamber I, *Prosecutor v Laurent Gbagbo*, Decision on victim participation, Prosecutor v Gbagbo, ICC-02/11-01/11, 06 March 2015, para 36.

133 ICC, Pre-Trial Chamber III, *Prosecutor v Jean-Pierre Bemba Gombo*, Fourth Decision on Victims' Participation with Confidential Annex, ICC-01/05-01/08, 12 December 2008, paras 76–77.

harm, because it understood that it could have been caused by events unrelated to the attack on Bogoro.[134]

The approach followed to understand the link between harm and ecocide can have a significant impact on the recognition of the environment as a victim. As an unlawful or wanton act can damage a global ecosystem, its impact on human and nonhuman life might take place without a linear causal relationship. If, in addition to that, the limits to our understanding of the dynamism, instability, and unpredictability of the interactions between the different elements of the environment are taken into account, Trial Chamber II's understanding of causation might end up reproducing the perception of "environmental crimes as victimless crimes".[135]

10.4 Conclusion

The IEP proposal to criminalise ecocide can be situated among the efforts to shift from an exclusively anthropocentric protection approach of the environment to a perspective that is at least partly ecocentric. Within the legal framework of the ICC, the recognition of the victimisation of the environment can be expected to contribute to this process, rejecting not only the view that crimes against the environment are victimless crimes, but also the incorrect understanding that such crimes harm only humans.[136] Nonetheless, the ICC legal framework has not been developed with an ecocentric approach in mind. In this context, any potential amendments to the Rome Statute to incorporate a definition of ecocide would also benefit from the introduction of specific provisions related to environmental victimisation.[137]

This chapter acknowledges that the environment can be indirectly considered within the framework of RPE Rule 85(b). However, RPE Rule 85(b) does not enable the recognition of the environment as a victim on its own right. Within a broader context of paradigmatic shift, this chapter argues that definition of victim put forward in RPE Rule 85(a) can inform such recognition, once communications, representations or observations submitted on behalf of the environment as a victim are considered by the prosecutor or the relevant ICC Chamber. It can also take place within the procedures related to victims' participation in the proceedings within Article 68(3) of the Rome Statute or through common legal representation.

It is, nonetheless, important to note that the recognition of the environment as a natural person requires rethinking the intuitive and exclusive association between

[134] ICC, Trial Chamber II, *Prosecutor v Germain Katanga*, Decision on the Matter of the Transgenerational Harm Alleged by Some Applicants for Reparations Remanded by the Appeals Chamber in its Judgment of 8 March 2018, ICC-01/04-01/07-3804-Red-tENG, 19 July 2018, para 134.

[135] Sknnider 2011, p. 2.

[136] On the overall relevance of law to the shape human behaviour in the Anthropocene, see Pope et al. 2021.

[137] The IEP proposal did not suggest any amendments to the provisions related to victims. It, nonetheless, acknowledged that consequential amendments may also be required for other provisions of the Rome Statute and the RPE.

humans and natural persons. This might be one of the most challenging aspects of the application of RPE 85(a) to the environment. Despite that, it has been argued that, if this discussion is considered as part of a broader paradigmatic shift towards a less anthropocentric understanding of the law, the materiality that characterises both humans and nonhumans might enable the construction of a new understanding of a natural person. Similarly, whilst the types of harm already identified by the ICC provide an initial framework for the assessment of the harm suffered by nonhumans, the discussion of environmental harm through the lens of indigenous traditional knowledge or in light of a better understanding of the interactions among biotic and abiotic facts might indicate the need for the articulation of other types of harm.[138] The existing ambiguity in the interpretation of the causal nexus between the harm suffered and the crimes under the jurisdiction of the ICC opens a space for the consideration of the complex, non-linear relations that characterise the environment. Nonetheless, this same ambiguity enables the adoption of a restrictive approach. Therefore, even though RPE Rule 85(a) can support the recognition of the environment as a victim, it can also lead to the denial of such recognition.

As there is no system of binding precedent in the ICC, the extent to which RPE Rule 85(a) will indeed enable the recognition of environmental victims rests on the convincing force of the arguments put forward by the parties and participants in the legal process and on the ability of each Chamber to consider such arguments in a context of paradigmatic change. This is particularly important if one considers that the non-recognition of the status of victims to nonhumans might be interpreted as the denial that a specific act constitutes ecocide if it does not harm humans, contradicting the paradigmatic shift that underlies the efforts to criminalise ecocide. In this context, it is important to note that the interpretation of the criteria established by RPE Rule 85(a) has the potential to influence our understanding of ecocide and, more broadly, of the environment.

In developing its reasoning, each Chamber will need to be critical of the overall potential of international criminal law as a means of promoting the full consideration of the intrinsic value of the environment. In this regard, it is important to note that the discussion of whether the environment can be considered a victim within the ICC has followed a mechanistic approach in this chapter. Not only were the criteria of the definition of victim analysed individually, but also the ambiguity in the jurisprudence of the ICC was gradually discussed. The complexity of the victimisation process was reduced to compartmentalized discussions, which followed a linear approach. This same mechanistic approach has been considered unable to fully address the current planetary socio-ecological crisis.[139] In fact, it has been considered an essential element of the crisis, as it supports the view that nature is the object of humanity's control, domain, and property.[140] In this context, the potential recognition of the environment as a victim also needs to take into account the limits that such an analytical approach presents to our understanding of the interaction between humans

[138] See Mazzocchi 2006.

[139] Ibid. Pope et al. 2021.

[140] Pope et al. 2021.

and the environment, including the challenges related to the representation of the environment.

Acknowledgements I would like to thank Dr Christophe Paulussen, Professor Elizabeth Kirk, Professor Kevin Jon Heller, Professor Louis Kotze, Dr Stavros Pantazopoulos, Dr Laura Burgers and Merle Kooijman for all their thoughtful comments and suggestions. As always, any remaining errors are my own. This chapter draws on a Brief prepared for the International Crimes Database.

References

Articles, Books and Other Documents

Anyanwu JC, Egbuche CT, Amaku GE, Duruora JO, Onwuagba SM (2015) The Impact of Deforestation on Soil Conditions in Anambra State of Nigeria. Agriculture, Forestry and Fisheries. https://doi.org/10.11648/j.aff.s.2015040301.21. Accessed 10 November 2025

Baumgartner E (2008) Aspects of Victim Participation in the Proceedings of the International Criminal Court. International Review of the Red Cross 90:409–440

Bertenthal A (2019) Standing up for Trees: Rethinking Representation in a Multispecies Context. Law and Literature 32(3):355–373

Blanco E, Grear A (2019) Personhood, jurisdiction and injustice: law, colonialities and the global order. Journal of Human Rights and the Environment 10(1):86–117

Boyd DR (2015) Constitutions, human rights and the environment: national approaches. In: Grear A, Kotze LJ (eds) Research Handbook on Human Rights and the Environment. Edward Elgar Publishing, Cheltenham, pp 170–199

Brisman A, South N (2018) Green Criminology and Environmental Crimes and Harms. Sociology Compass. https://doi.org/10.1111/soc4.12650. Accessed 10 November 2025

Castellos MA (2024) ICC Submission: Towards a new policy initiative to advance accountability for environmental crimes under the Rome Statute (RS). https://www.iucn.org/our-union/commissions/group/iucn-wcel-environmental-security-and-conflict-law-specialist-group-0-0. Accessed 20 July 2025

Certini G (2005) Effects of fire on properties of forest soils: a review. Oecologia 143:1–10

Collins D (2023) Illegal gold mining exposing Peru's indigenous tribes to mercury poisoning. https://www.theguardian.com/environment/2013/sep/09/peru-amazon-indigenous-tribe-gold-mining. Accessed 20 July 2025

Clark C, Emmanouil N, Page J, Pelizzon A (2018) Can you hear the rivers sing? Legal personhood, ontology and the nitty gritty of governance. Ecology Law Quarterly 45(4):787–843

Darpö J (2021) Can nature get it right? A study on the rights of nature in the European context. https://www.europarl.europa.eu/thinktank/en/document/IPOL_STU(2021)689328. Accessed 20 July 2025

De La Fayette L (2002) The concept of environmental damage in international liability regimes. In: Bowman M, Boyle A (eds) Environmental Damage in International and Comparative Law: Problems of Definition and Valuation. Oxford University Press, Oxford, pp 149–189

De Vido S (2021) A Quest for an Eco-centric Approach to International Law: the COVID-19 Pandemic as Game Changer. Jus Cogens 3: 105–117

Doran P, Killean R, McDermott MC, McErlean K, Millar L, Rodgers S (2021) Criminalising Ecocide at the International Criminal Court. https://pure.qub.ac.uk/en/publications/criminalising-ecocide-at-the-international-criminal-court. Accessed 20 July 2025

Falk R (1973) Environmental Warfare and Ecocide – Facts, Appraisal and Proposal. Bulletin of Peace Proposals 4(1): 80–96

Fischer-Lescano A (2020) Nature as Legal Person: Proxy Constellations in Law. Law and Literature 32(2):237–262

Fredengren C (2015) Nature: Cultures - Heritage, Sustainability and Feminist Posthumanism. Current Swedish Archaeology 23:109–130

French DA (2003) Review: Environmental Damage in International and Comparative Law: Problems of Definition and Valuation. Journal of Environmental Law 15(2): 266–268

Gaujer A, Rabatel-Fernel MP, Kulbicki L, Short D, Higgins P (2012) Ecocide is the missing 5th Crime Against Peace. https://sas-space.sas.ac.uk/4830/1/Ecocide_research_report_19_July_13.pdf. Accessed 20 July 2025

Gellers JC (2020) Earth system law and the legal status of non-humans in the Anthropocene Earth System Governance. https://doi.org/10.1016/j.esg.2020.100083. Accessed 10 November 2025

Gieseken HO, Murphy V (2023) The protection of the natural environment under international humanitarian law: The ICRC's 2020 Guidelines. International Review of the Red Cross. https://doi.org/10.1017/S1816383123000401. Accessed 10 November 2025

Gillett M (2017) Eco-Struggles: Using International Criminal Law to Protect the Environment During and After Non-International Armed Conflict. In: Stahn C, Iverson J, Easterday JS (eds) Environmental Protection and Transitions from Conflict to Peace: Clarifying Norms, Principles and Practices. Oxford University Press, Oxford, pp 220–254

Gillett M (2024) Comment on OTP Environmental Crimes Policy 'Taking an environmentally-protective approach'. https://www.iucn.org/sites/default/files/2024-04/icc_submission_matthew_gillett1.pdf. Accessed 20 July 2025

Gordon GJ (2018) Environmental Personhood. Columbia Journal of Environmental Law 43:49–88

Gray AM (1996) The International Crime of Ecocide. California Western International Law Journal 26(2):215–271

Grear A (2015) The closures of legal subjectivity: why examining law's person is critical to an understanding of injustice in an age of climate crisis. In: Grear A, Kotze LJ (eds) Research Handbook on Human Rights and the Environment. Edward Elgar Publishing, Cheltenham, pp 79–101

Hall M (2013) Victims of Environmental Harm: Rights, Recognition and Redress under National and International Law. Routledge, Oxon

Heller KJ (2021) Skeptical Thoughts on the Proposed Crime of "Ecocide" (That Isn't). https://opiniojuris.org/2021/06/23/skeptical-thoughts-on-the-proposed-crime-of-ecocide-that-isnt. Accessed 20 July 2025

Higgins P (2012) Seed-Idea: Seeding Intrinsic Values: How a Law of Ecocide will Shift our Consciousness. Cadmus 5(4):9–10

Higgins P, Short D, South N (2013) Protecting the Planet: A Proposal for a Law of Ecocide. Crime, Law and Social Change 59(3):251–266

Houge AB (2019) Narrative expressivism: A criminological approach to the expressive function of international criminal justice. Criminology & Criminal Justice 19(3):277–293

Human Rights Advocacy Collective (CADHu) and the ARNS Commission São Paulo (2019) Informative Note to the Prosecutor: International Criminal Court pursuant to Article 15 of the Rome Statute requesting a preliminary examination into incitement to genocide and widespread and systematic attacks against indigenous peoples by President Jair Messias Bolsonaro in Brazil. https://apublica.org/wp-content/uploads/2019/11/e-muito-triste-levar-um-brasileiro-para-o-tribunal-penal-internacional-diz-co-autora-da-peticao.pdf. Accessed 20 July 2025

ICC (2010) The Booklet Victims before the ICC: A Guide for the Participation of Victims in the Proceedings of the Court. https://www.icc-cpi.int/sites/default/files/NR/rdonlyres/8FF91A2C-5274-4DCB-9CCE-37273C5E9AB4/282477/160910VPRSBookletEnglish.pdf. Accessed 20 July 2025

ICC Assembly of States Parties (2009) Report of the Court on the Strategy in Relation to Victims, ICC-ASP/8/45, https://asp.icc-cpi.int/sites/asp/files/asp_docs/ASP8/ICC-ASP-8-45-ENG.pdf. Accessed 20 July 2025

Jessen TD, Ban NC, Claxton NX, Darimont CT (2022) Contributions of Indigenous Knowledge to Ecological and Evolutionary Understanding. Frontiers in Ecology and the Environment 20(2):93–101

Jonhson ST (2010) Neither Victims nor Executioners: The Dilemma of Victim Participation and the Defendant's Right to a Fair Trial at the International Criminal Court. ILSA Journal of International & Comparative Law 16(2):489–496

Kendall S, Nouwen S (2013) Representational practices at the international criminal court: the gap between juridified and abstract victimhood. Law and Contemporary Problems 76(3):235–262

Killean R, Dempster L (2022) Greening' transitional justice. In: Evans M (ed) Beyond transitional justice: transformative justice and the state of the field (or non-field). Routledge, London, pp 54–64

Kooijman M (2022) From Anthropos to Oikos in International Criminal Law: A Critical-Theoretical Exploration of Ecocide as an 'Ecocentric' Amendment to the Rome Statute. Netherlands Yearbook of International Law 52:101–131

Kotzé LJ, French D (2018) The Anthropocentric Ontology of International Environmental Law and the Sustainable Development Goals: Towards an Ecocentric Rule of Law in the Anthropocene. Global Journal of Comparative Law 7(1):5–36

Kurki VAJ (2019) A Theory of Legal Personhood. Oxford University Press, Oxford.

Larsen PB, Wijesuriya G (2017) Nature–Culture Interlinkages in World Heritage: Bridging the Gap. The George Wright Forum 34(2):142–153

Leebaw B (2014) Scorched Earth: Environmental War Crimes and International Justice. Perspectives on Politics 12(4):770–788

Lostal M (2021) De-objectifying animals: could they qualify as victims before the International Criminal Court? Journal of International Criminal Justice 19(3):583–610

Lostal M (2024) Comment on OTP Environmental Crimes Policy submitted on 16 March 2024 — The Environment and the ICC Legal Framework concerning Victims. https://www.iucn.org/sites/default/files/2024-04/icc_submission_marina_lostal1.pdf. Accessed 20 July 2025

Mandi S, Panitzer J (2022) Who is a victim? The Concept of Victim in the Victims' Rights Directive: A human rights analysis of the concept of victim from a gender-specific perspective. Journal for Police Science and Practice 12:49–63

Mazzocchi F (2006) Western science and traditional knowledge: despite their variations, different forms of knowledge can learn from each other. EMBO Reports. https://doi.org/10.1038/sj.embor.7400693. Accessed 10 November 2025

McDermott Y (2009) Some are more equal than others: victim participation at the ICC. Eyes on the ICC 5(1):583–610

Mistura A (2018) Is there space for environmental crimes? Columbia Journal of Environmental Law 43(1):182–225

Natarajan U (2022) Who Do We Think We Are? Human Rights in a Time of Ecological Change. In: Natarajan U, Dehm J (eds) Locating Nature: Making and Unmaking International Law. Cambridge University Press, Cambridge, pp 200–228

Natarajan U, Khoday K (2014) Locating nature: making and unmaking international law. Leiden Journal of International Law 27(3):576–593

O'Donnell E (2018) At the Intersection of the Sacred and the Legal: Rights for Nature in Uttarakhand, India. Journal of Environmental Law 30(1):135–144

Office of the Prosecutor of the ICC (2016) Policy Paper on Case Selection and Prioritisation. https://www.icc-cpi.int/sites/default/files/itemsDocuments/20160915_OTP-Policy_Case-Selection_Eng.pdf. Accessed 20 July 2025

Office of the Prosecutor of the ICC (2024) The Office of the Prosecutor launches public consultation on a new policy initiative to advance accountability for environmental crimes under the Rome Statute. https://www.icc-cpi.int/news/office-prosecutor-launches-public-consultation-new-policy-initiative-advance-accountability-0. Accessed 20 July 2025

Olásolo H, Kiss A (2010) The role of victims in criminal proceedings before the International Criminal Court. Revue Internationale de Droit Penal 81:125–163

Paynes CR (2024) Comment on OTP Environmental Crimes Policy. https://www.iucn.org/sites/default/files/2024-04/icc_submission_cymie_payne1.pdf. Accessed 20 July 2025
Pereira R (2020) After the ICC Office of the Prosecutor's 2016 Policy Paper on Case Selection and Prioritisation: Towards an International Crime of Ecocide? Criminal Law Forum 31:179–224
Pietrzykowski T (2017) Towards modest naturalization of personhood in law. Revus 32:59–71
Pope K, Bonatti M, Sieber S (2021) The what, who and how of socio-ecological justice: tailoring a new justice model for earth system law. Earth System Governance. https://doi.org/10.1016/j.esg.2021.100124. Accessed 10 November 2025
Porto-Gonçalves CW, Leff E (2015) Political Ecology in Latin America: the Social Re-Appropriation of Nature, the Reinvention of Territories and the Construction of an Environmental Rationality. Desenvolvimento e Meio Ambiente 35:65–88
Sands PJ (1989) The Environment, Community and International Law. Harvard International Law Journal 30: 393–420
Schilz KA (2017) Decolonizing political ecology: ontology, technology and "critical" enchantment. Journal of Political Ecology 24:125–143
Shelton D (2015) Nature as a Legal Person. VertigO: La revue électronique en sciences de l'environnement. https://doi.org/10.4000/vertigo.16188. Accessed 10 November 2025
Simma B, Paulus AL (1998) The 'International Community': Facing the Challenge of Globalization. European Journal of International Law 9(2):266–277
Sknnider E (2011) Victims of Environmental Crime – Mapping the Issues. https://globalinitiative.net/wp-content/uploads/2017/12/ICCLR-Victims-of-Environmental-Crime.pdf. Accessed 20 July 2025
Stahn C, Olásolo H, Gibson K (2006) Participation of Victims in Pre-Trial Proceedings of the ICC. Journal of International Criminal Justice 4(2):219–238
Sterling C (2020) Critical heritage and the posthumanities: problems and prospects. International Journal of Heritage Studies 26:1029–1046
Stop Ecocide Foundation (2021) Independent Expert Panel for the Legal Definition of Ecocide: Commentary and Core Text. https://www.stopecocide.earth/legal-definition. Accessed 20 July 2025
Tănăsescu M (2020) Rights of Nature, Legal Personality and Indigenous Philosophies. Transnational Environmental Law 9(3):429–453
Timm B (2001) The Legal Position of Victims in the Rules of Procedure and Evidence. In: Fischer H, Kress C, Lüder SR (eds) International and National Prosecution of Crimes under International Law: Current Developments. Arno Spitz GmbH, Berlin, pp 306–308
Trumbull CP IV (2008) The Victims of Victim Participation in International Criminal Proceedings. Michigan Law Review 29:780–825
UN Preparatory Committee on the Establishment of an International Criminal Court (1998a) Draft Statute for the International Criminal Court, UN Doc A/CONF.183/2/Add.1
UN Preparatory Committee on the Establishment of an International Criminal Court (1998b) Report of the Inter-Sessional Meeting from 1 to 30 January 1998 in Zutphen, the Netherlands, UN Doc A/AC.249/1998/WG.4/DP 19
Valverde M (2017) From persons and their acts to webs of relationships: some theoretical resources for environmental justice. Crime, Law and Social Change 68:547–562
Villalpando S (2010) The Legal Dimension of the International Community: How Community Interests are Protected in International Law. European Journal of International Law 21(2):387–419
War Crimes Research Office (2013) Obtaining victim status for purposes of participating in proceedings at the International Criminal Court. https://www.american.edu/wcl/impact/initiatives-programs/warcrimes/our-projects/icc-legal-analysis-and-education-project/upload/18_wcro-report-18-obtaining-victim-status.pdf. Accessed 20 July 2025
Wesche T (2022) Who owns nature? About the rights of nature. Estudios de Filosofia. https://doi.org/10.17533/udea.ef.347573. Accessed 10 November 2025

White R (2017) The Four Ways of Eco-global Criminology. International Journal for Crime Justice and Social Democracy 6(1):8–22

White R (2018) Green Victimology and non-human victims. International Review of Victimology. https://doi.org/10.1177/0269758017745615. Accessed 10 November 2025

Wienhues A (2017) Sharing the Earth: A Biocentric Account of Ecological Justice. Journal of Agriculture and Environmental Ethics 30:367–385

Wildman WJ (2007) The Use and Meaning of the Word "Suffering" in Relation to Nature. In: Murphy N, Russell RJ, Stoeger WR (eds) Physics and Cosmology: Scientific Perspectives on the Problem of Natural Evil. Vatican Observatory Foundation, Vatican, pp 53–66

Youatt R (2014) Interspecies Relations, International Relations: Rethinking Anthropocentric Politics. Millennium. https://doi.org/10.1177/0305829814536946. Accessed 10 November 2025

Giovanna Maria Frisso is a Senior Lecturer in Law at the University of Lincoln, United Kingdom. She holds a PhD from the University of Nottingham, where her research focused on victims' rights at the International Criminal Court (ICC). Dr. Frisso was a Visiting Professional at the ICC's Victims Participation and Reparation Section and volunteered as a legal assistant at the Tribunal Internacional de Justicia Restaurativa in El Salvador. Her scholarly work explores international criminal law, victims' rights, transitional justice, and environmental harm.

GPSR Compliance

The European Union's (EU) General Product Safety Regulation (GPSR) is a set of rules that requires consumer products to be safe and our obligations to ensure this.

If you have any concerns about our products, you can contact us on ProductSafety@springernature.com

In case Publisher is established outside the EU, the EU authorized representative is:

Springer Nature Customer Service Center GmbH
Europaplatz 3
69115 Heidelberg, Germany

Batch number: 10053913

Printed by Printforce, the Netherlands